🌲 **sappi**

NEWMAN'S
Birds
OF SOUTHERN AFRICA
THE GREEN EDITION

Kenneth Newman

ILLUSTRATED BY THE AUTHOR

SOUTHERN
BOOK PUBLISHERS

To Ursula, Vanessa, Nicholas and Pamela

ISBN 1 86812 623 4 (Hard cover)
ISBN 1 86812 611 0 (Soft cover)

First edition, first impression 1988
Second edition, first impression 1989
Second edition, second impression 1990
Third edition, first impression 1991
Fourth edition, first impression 1992
Fourth edition, second impression 1993
Fourth edition, third impression 1993
Fourth edition, fourth impression 1994
Fifth edition, first impression 1996
Fifth edition, second impression 1996

Southern Book Publishers (Pty) Ltd
PO Box 3103, Halfway House 1685

Cover design by Alix Gracie
Illustrations by Ken Newman
Set in 8 on 9 pt Univers by Unifoto (Pty) Ltd, Cape
Printed and bound by National Book Printers,
Drukkery Street, Goodwood, Western Cape

NEWMAN'S
Birds
OF SOUTHERN AFRICA

A FEW WORDS FROM THE AUTHOR

In this age of worldwide indigenous forest depletion by an ever-hungry consumer market, I am proud to announce that this Green Edition of my book has been printed on paper made with a content of 60 per cent post-industrial sugar cane waste, and the balance made from wood grown in sustainable man-made plantations, thanks to SAPPI, makers of Dukuza Fine Art paper. SAPPI has perfected the process whereby sugar cane pith can be utilised in the local manufacture of these fine quality papers.

I am further proud to say that this entire book can claim to be a 100 per cent local production, from the original paintings for the colour plates to the printing and binding in Cape Town and its publication by Southern Book Publishers, a wholly-owned local company.

Users of this Green Edition will not fail to notice that the long established use of bird numbers (or Roberts numbers, as they are often called) has regrettably come to an end. This has been brought about by the comparatively recent reclassification of birds worldwide, based on DNA analysis. The relationships of species as the world has long known them have been radically revised, from the order level all the way down to the species level. Some 50 or 60 birds on the southern African list, both passerines and non-passerines, are affected by this. A few examples: batises are no longer flycatchers; crows, orioles and drongoes are no longer the close relatives we once thought them to be; the flamingoes, pelicans and shoebill have been placed in different groupings. Already it has become clear that, with the inevitable reshuffle of species in the not too distant future, bird numbers as they now stand – consecutively according to taxonomic order – will no longer make any sense. It has already proved impossible to maintain a proper numbering sequence because of the ever-increasing list of new species that are being sighted in our subregion. Any numbers allocated to such new species are meaningless in a system that is supposed to reflect taxonomic order.

In fact South Africa has always been one of very few countries that have a numbering system for their birds. In the USA a numbering system has been created for the world's birds, but if we were to adopt that system, each of our birds would be allocated any number between 1 and 9 000, according to the world's systematic list.

For all these reasons the decision has been taken to drop the numbering of southern African birds altogether.

Readers will also notice that we have retained the names of former South African provinces in this edition. This is a temporary measure until finality on the names and boundaries of the new provinces has been reached. In both the map on page 19 and the text, reference is therefore still made to the old province names and boundaries.

Kenneth Newman

CONTENTS

SPONSOR'S FOREWORD

In southern Africa we are fortunate in having an extremely rich diversity of bird life. We are also fortunate in having Ken Newman, who has a well-deserved reputation as one of the country's leading ornithologists.

Ken's knowledge and understanding of his subject is clearly evident on every page of this meticulously researched, beautifully illustrated fieldguide. *Newman's Birds of Southern Africa* makes it easy for everyone – even for people with limited experience – to identify and learn more about birds.

Knowledge is the key not only to integrated environmental management, but also to promoting an awareness of the world around us. Through his work, Ken has played a key role in heightening awareness of the environment and the need for conservation. We are proud to sponsor this new edition of *Newman's Birds of Southern Africa*.

I hope you enjoy it as much as I do.

Eugene van As
Executive Chairman
SAPPI Limited

ACKNOWLEDGEMENTS

I wish to express my sincere thanks to those colleagues who, in one way or another, helped me in the preparation of this fieldguide. I am grateful to the late Charles Clinning, to Digby Cyrus, Ian Sinclair, Rob Martin, Warwick Tarboton, Carl Vernon and the late Jack Winterbottom, who kindly reviewed my draft manuscripts and helped in numerous other ways. In subsequent revisions I received further valuable help with the improvement of distribution maps for Namibia from Chris Brown.

Warwick Tarboton from the start showed great enthusiasm for the project and, in addition to the help already described, he not only checked all my illustrations as they were painted, providing much critical guidance, but also went to great lengths to obtain and describe unknown bird calls and bird behaviour. In this regard I am also indebted to Alex Masterson for his succinct descriptions of certain cisticola calls. Their assistance has been most valuable.

Gordon Maclean also very kindly checked the distribution maps. I am grateful to him for this and also for completing the task of revising, in conjunction with others, the vernacular names of southern African birds.

The reference specimens used for illustrating were mostly obtained on loan from the Transvaal Museum and I am obliged to Alan Kemp, Curator of Birds, for making them available to me in such enormous numbers, and to Tamar Cassidy for tirelessly selecting and assembling them. Certain specimens were obtained from the Durban Museum through the kindness of P.A. Clancey (then Director of the Museum) and John Mendelsohn, while others came from the Bulawayo Museum in Zimbabwe with the kind help of the late Bryan Donnelly, then Curator of Ornithology.

A great many of the bird calls described in this fieldguide were taken from the bird call tapes made by the late Len Gillard and Guy Gibbon and by AudioThree of the Natal Bird Club, to whom I am thankful. Further help with bird calls was generously given by Geoff Nicholls, and also by Tony Harris of the FitzPatrick Bird Communications Library.

Thank you, all those friends in the Southern African Ornithological Society who supplied certain items of information about birds, who gave me copies of their regional bird lists or who lent me photographs of lesser-known species; in this regard I should like to mention especially Gordon Bennett, Norman Elwell and Dorothy Hall. Rosemary Hilton kindly produced my final manuscripts.

Finally, a big thank you to my wife for her help with the typing of the numerous draft manuscripts, her ever-ready counsel whenever problems arose, and for her understanding and patience during countless late hours when I was still bent over the desk. Such is the way this fieldguide was produced.

COLOUR CODING GUIDE

Ocean birds

Inland water birds

Ducks & wading birds

Large terrestrial birds

Raptors

Sandgrouse, doves, parrots, louries,
    cuckoos & coucals

Owls & nightjars

Aerial feeders, mousebirds,
    hole nesters & honeyguides

Insect eaters (1) — larks to robins

Insect eaters (2) — warblers to starlings

Oxpeckers & nectar feeders

Seedeaters

Ocean birds

Inland water birds

Ducks and wading birds

Large terrestrial birds

Raptors

Sandgrouse, doves, parrots, louries, cuckoos and coucals

Owls and nightjars

Aerial feeders, mousebirds, hole nesters and honeyguides

Insect eaters (1) – larks to robins

Insect eaters (2) – warblers to starlings

Oxpeckers and nectar feeders

Seedeaters

INTRODUCTION

This fieldguide covers the whole of the Southern African subregion as well as the Subantarctic region adjacent to the continent.

Southern Africa is generally accepted as being that part of Africa lying south of the Zambezi-Okavango-Cunene Rivers, or approximately 17°S. Embracing as it does many national states and a diversity of geophysical regions, ranging from tropical coasts to the most arid desert, its bird fauna is correspondingly diverse. As might be expected, it shows strong affinities with the avifauna of the rest of Africa south of the Sahara Desert (the Afrotropical region) so that the great majority of birds found in the subregion also occur north of its limits. Of special interest, however, are the endemics, those species found in Southern Africa and nowhere else. These number 113 species and include such striking birds as the Blue Crane, Cape Vulture, Bald Ibis, Black Oystercatcher, Black Harrier, South African Shelduck, the unique Ground Woodpecker and the two sugarbirds, as well as five korhaans and no less than fifteen larks. Many birds have been introduced into Southern Africa in past years, but only seven species survive today. They are the Indian Mynah, European Starling, European House Sparrow, Chaffinch (now becoming very scarce), Mute Swan, Feral Pigeon and, most recently, the Indian House Crow, which seems to have introduced itself into Natal from passing ships whose crew members keep them as pets.

In addition to the wide variety of landbirds, the Southern African coasts are visited by numerous pelagic seabirds, many of which breed on islands in the southern oceans. These seabirds, ranging in size from the diminutive storm petrels to the enormous albatrosses, are often very difficult to identify. Not only are many identified only by small details of plumage or flight pattern, but, in addition, they are normally glimpsed from the pitching deck of a ship or from wind- and rain-lashed shores as they mount upwards briefly from a wave trough before descending again out of sight. Such are the difficulties of getting to grips with seabird identities that for many years little interest was shown in them by the average land-based birdwatcher. Even so, the birds of the northern seas have always been better known than those of the southern oceans through their more frequent contact with land. In recent years, more especially since the 1960s, a gradual change has come about as the result of a new interest by leading nations of the world in the southern islands and in Antarctica itself. Permanent stations have been established for, among other things, weather-monitoring. Teams of scientists are permanently or temporarily stationed in these inhospitable regions for the purpose of studying the ocean and its resources. As an example, the Percy FitzPatrick Institute of African Ornithology in Cape Town has for many years been studying seabird life in the seas adjacent to Southern Africa. A succession of its researchers has been based on Marion Island, from where periodic visits are made to other islands as far afield as the Tristan da Cunha group, and much has been learned about the population dynamics, feeding ecologies and the breeding biologies of some ocean birds. Stemming from this new interest in the southern seabirds, and the increased need for a specific guide to those found in Southern African seas, the entire region south to the pack-ice has been included in this fieldguide. Not only does it embrace all seabirds known to reach the shores of Southern Africa, but also those that will be seen on or in the vicinity of the Tristan group (Tristan, Nightingale and Inaccessible Islands), Gough, Bouvet, Marion and Prince Edward islands — a total of 19 additional species including some landbirds.

Fieldguides and handbooks

The fieldguide concept itself was spawned in the late 1930s in response to the need for portability coupled with ease of reference. First was the now famous series by Roger Tory Peterson, covering the birds of the United States of America. Later the idea caught on in Britain, Europe and elsewhere. For the serious birdwatcher a fieldguide is only a supplement to a more comprehensive and informative bird handbook, the latter usually being too bulky and cumbersome for normal fieldwork. Its main purpose is to help the observer identify a species speedily from an illustration and a brief description of plumage and song. More comprehensive information about the bird may then be sought at leisure from the appropriate handbook. Leading handbooks of the birds of the Southern African subregion are the multi-volume *Birds of Africa* by the late Leslie Brown *et al.* and *Birds of South Africa* by the late Austin Roberts, in its revised edition.

Bird habitats

All birds have a preferred habitat with usually a specialised niche within that habitat, and many will disappear entirely if their habitat is destroyed or degraded, because they are unable to adapt to different living conditions. Thus, in order to see many bird species it is necessary to know and seek their preferred habitat, often a very restricted area or one difficult of access. In Southern Africa, as in many other parts of the world, one of the most vulnerable habitat types is that generally known as wetlands — estuaries, marshes and floodlands — these being all too frequently drained or filled for industrial development or agriculture. Throughout Africa indigenous forests are being increasingly cut back for fringe agriculture, or the trees felled for charcoal production. These animal-rich regions have taken millions of years to reach their present-day climax, and are irreplaceable. As they disappear the birds that depend on them, and much other animal life besides, disappear too.

Probably the richest bird habitats in Southern Africa are those known as bushveld and woodland. Bushveld is a somewhat loose term applied to the woody veld found over much of the northern and eastern Transvaal. It is comprised of various types of deciduous, small tree woodland and mixed bush varieties and may include such diverse vegetation as scrub mopane, mixed thorn and broadleafed bushes and even small patches of pure thornbush. The presence of all these bush types is dictated by variations in soil types so that one sees frequent changes, each type intergrading with another. Woodland is made up of broadleafed trees, usually deciduous, with wider spacing than is found in bushveld, so that their canopies do not touch. Together mixed bushveld and woodland cover a great part of the Afrotropical Region and approximately three-quarters of Southern Africa.

Vying with bushveld and woodland for total bird numbers is fynbos, a mixed scrub occurring around the southern littoral and similar to that known as Macchia in the Mediterranean Region. Fynbos is home to many small bird species including several endemics.

In apparent contrast to the woody habitats outlined above the vast grasslands, and the great Namib Desert with its fringing semi-desert zone, may at first appear impoverished, whereas in reality they support a varied and highly interesting avifauna with many specialised endemic species. These and the others illustrated and described on the following eight pages make up the mosaic of habitats used by the birds of Southern Africa. Familiarity with them will provide a key to the birds likely to be found in them.

PAN. A natural depression that is filled seasonally by rain or seepage. Often the only surface water within a region, pans attract many water-associated birds in addition to others. According to its size a pan may harbour ducks, coots, moorhens, herons, spoonbills, ibises, plovers, snipes and other waders while Cape Turtle Doves, Grey Louries, Redbilled Queleas and many others will visit to drink or bathe. Saline pans attract flamingoes. *Photo: K. Newman.*

RIVER ESTUARY. Tidal estuaries, with their numerous sandbanks, mudflats, lagoons and adjacent coastal bush are usually rich in birds. Most evident are the gulls, terns, herons and migrant waders that normally feed in the shallows, and these are sometimes joined by pelicans, oystercatchers and even flamingoes. Less evident are the birds of the adjacent coastal bush, which may be home to the Tambourine Dove, Green Coucal, Goldenrumped Tinker Barbet, Yellowbellied Bulbul, Natal Robin, Rudd's Apalis and Green Twinspot. *Photo: Peter Newman.*

MANGROVES. Low-growing trees adapted to the mud and silt of tidal estuaries. Mangroves were once relatively common on the Natal coast but have been much reduced or destroyed by development; they occur more extensively in Mozambique. The only bird endemic to mangroves is the Mangrove Kingfisher, but extensive mangrove forests on lagoons are frequently used for large-scale breeding by colonies of freshwater birds. At low tide they are frequented by numerous wading birds. *Photo: Peter Newman.*

DUNE FORESTS AND LAGOONS. Dune forests occur in coastal regions of high rainfall and humidity. Their bird fauna divides roughly into canopy and undergrowth dwellers. Those in the higher stratum include Knysna Louries, Narina Trogons, Emerald Cuckoos, Squaretailed Drongos, Barthroated Apalises and Bluemantled Flycatchers. In the lower stratum are Cinnamon Doves, Natal, Chorister, Starred and Brown Robins, Sombre Bulbuls and Spotted Thrushes. Coastal lagoons, particularly numerous in the Knysna region, are usually tidal and are frequented by gulls, the Osprey, cormorants, kingfishers and herons. *Photo: K. Newman.*

4

RIPARIAN FOREST. Riparian or riverine forests frequently form evergreen swaths in areas of otherwise dry, deciduous bush. A striking example is the course of the Kuiseb River in Namibia, which is marked by large *Acacia* trees and provides birds with a favourable habitat in an otherwise hostile desert. Riparian forests serve a similar purpose elsewhere, attracting a greater variety of insectivorous and frugivorous birds than are found away from the rivers. *Photo: K. Newman.*

FLOODLANDS. Grasslands or woodlands temporarily inundated by the overflow of rivers, deltas or man-made water impoundments. These seasonal occurrences provide havens for small fish seeking refuge from the main water flow and they, in turn, attract many waterbirds such as ducks, herons, ibises and water-associated storks. Flooded woodlands often induce nesting by Greenbacked and Rufousbellied Herons, Reed Cormorants, Darters, egrets and Openbilled Storks. *Photo: K. Newman.*

EVERGREEN FOREST. Indigenous evergreen forests are tree communities in which the canopies interlock; within the subdued light of the interior the trees are festooned with mosses, ferns and orchids. Birds of the forest canopy include the Knysna Lourie, Grey Cuckooshrike, Squaretailed Drongo and Blackfronted Bush Shrike. The mid-stratum supports Yellowstreaked Bulbuls, Cape Batises, Yellow-throated Warblers, Bluemantled Flycatchers and Olive Bush Shrikes. In the lower stratum are robins such as the Chorister, Starred, Swynnerton's and Brown plus Buffspotted Flufftails, Cinnamon Doves and Orange Thrushes. *Photo: K. Newman.*

PLANTATION. A stand of exotic trees, commonly gums, pines and wattles, planted for timber. The trees are closely planted, allowing for little light penetration, and the ground is therefore devoid of cover. Plantations are unattractive to most birds although Rameron Pigeons, Redeyed Doves and both Forest and Steppe Buzzards enter the fringes; Narina Trogons may frequent the edges of pine plantations adjacent to evergreen forests. *Photo: K. Newman.*

MIOMBO. A broadleafed, deciduous woodland in which trees of the genus *Brachystegia* predominate. The tree canopies do not interlock and there is good ground cover of grasses and shrubs. Brachystegia woodland occurs widely in Zimbabwe and Malawi. Most birds occur in mixed feeding parties and some, including the Woodland Pipit and Miombo Doublecollared Sunbird, are endemic to this habitat. *Photo: Gordon Holtshausen.*

BUSHVELD. A term loosely applied to small-tree woodland found mostly below 1 500 metres. In the main it is comprised of mixed trees and bushes 5-10 metres high and often touching each other below canopy height. The plant species present are related to soil type but usually include both broadleafed and thorn bushes, the latter sometimes forming small thickets, while the substrate is well grassed. Bushveld is normally rich in birdlife including both arboreal and terrestrial species. *Photo: K. Newman.*

THORNVELD. Thornveld is a community of small *Acacia, Albizia* or *Dichrostachys* trees seldom growing higher than 5 metres, often on sandy soils with sparse grass cover. The thorny canopies are highly attractive to small birds such as Whitebrowed and Kalahari Robins, Titbabblers, Burntnecked Eremomelas, Crimson Boubous and various waxbills and firefinches. *Photo: K. Newman.*

THICKET. Dense, tangled bush and associated rank grass, often found on termite mounds and frequently with larger trees dominating, as seen here. These thickets are the preferred habitat of many small birds including the Whitebrowed Robin, Crimson Boubou, Blackcrowned Tchagra, Blue Waxbill, Melba Finch and Greybacked Bleating Warbler. *Photo: K. Newman.*

FYNBOS. Endemic scrubland found in the rocky, mountainous regions of the Cape Province and composed of proteaceous species, small-leaved heaths and reed-like restios. Here tall *Mimetes* and yellow *Leucadendrons* are seen in the Red Hill region of the Cape Peninsula. Fynbos is home to a number of endemic bird species including Victorin's Warbler, Cape Sugarbird, Orangebreasted Sunbird and Protea Canary. *Photo: M.W. Fraser.*

MONTANE GRASSLAND. High altitude grasslands are mostly found in the mistbelt of the Drakensberg escarpment and extending northwards into the north-eastern Transvaal and Zimbabwe. The slopes are usually strewn with rocks and protea trees while pockets of evergreen forest grow in the kloofs. The grasslands are inhabited by Ground Woodpeckers, Sicklewinged Chats, Gurney's Sugarbirds, Malachite Sunbirds and francolins while, in isolated locations, the Blue Swallow is a summer breeder. In many regions montane grasslands have become much reduced in recent years through the planting of exotic pines and gums. *Photo: Gordon Holtshausen.*

9

KAROO. Stony plains, either flat or undulating and dotted with succulent plants, scrubs and small trees. Rocky hills with scrub may also be present. Annual rainfall is 150-300 mm except in the more arid regions where it may be as little as 50-200 mm and where desert grasses predominate. Birdlife is mostly comprised of korhaans, larks, warblers and canaries plus raptors including Black and Martial Eagles and kestrels. *Photo: K. Newman.*

SEMI-DESERT. Semi-desert, as typified by the semi-arid tree and bush savanna of the central Kalahari in Botswana, is home to a surprisingly wide variety of birds both resident and seasonal. Residents most in evidence are the Whitequilled Korhaan, Pale Chanting Goshawk, Greater Kestrel, Doublebanded Courser, Black Crow, Redeyed Bulbul, Capped Wheatear and Marico Flycatcher. During summer Redbacked and Lesser Grey Shrikes, Caspian Plovers and various migrant warblers arrive. *Photo: Gordon Holtshausen.*

Simplified map of natural habitats in Southern Africa

Descriptions of these habitats and explanations of terminology used in conjunction with them are given in the Glossary of Terms on pages 446-50.

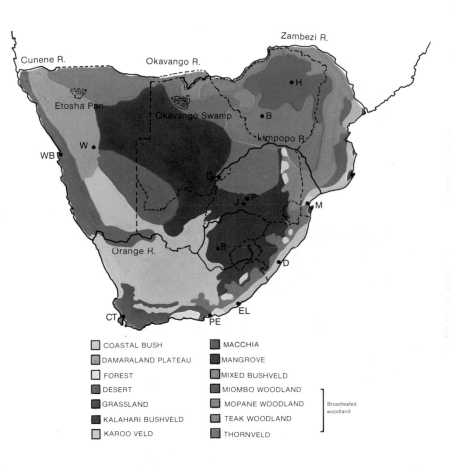

COASTAL BUSH

DAMARALAND PLATEAU

FOREST

DESERT

GRASSLAND

KALAHARI BUSHVELD

KAROO VELD

MACCHIA

MANGROVE

MIXED BUSHVELD

MIOMBO WOODLAND

MOPANE WOODLAND   } Broadleafed woodland

TEAK WOODLAND

THORNVELD

Habitats and their descriptions are based on *Veld Types of South Africa* by J.P.H. Acocks, Memoirs of the Botanical Survey of South Africa No. 40 (1975); *A Preliminary Vegetation Map of South West Africa* by W. Giess, *Dinteria:* 4 (1971); and *A Preliminary Checklist of the Birds of South West Africa* by J.M. Winterbottom (1971).

11

Bird populations

A question frequently asked is, 'How many bird species are there in Southern Africa?'. The answer is difficult to give with certain accuracy because the known total is constantly changing as new species (usually visitors) are often recorded, because various authorities disagree on the specific status of some birds and because some of the older records are now in doubt. However, a recently compiled list, checked by a substantial number of interested persons, gives a total of over 900, all doubtful species having been omitted. These are the birds, plus the Subantarctic species, that are illustrated and described in this fieldguide.

Total bird numbers within Southern Africa fluctuate within a year and also from year to year. Annual fluctuations are brought about primarily by the arrival each spring of large numbers of birds from elsewhere in Africa (intra-Africa migrants) and from the northern hemisphere (Palaearctic migrants). These annual visitors, which number countless millions, depart again in late summer, and return to their breeding grounds or their non-breeding ranges. Some, such as the European Swallow, spend as much as seven months in Africa without breeding, while many of the small warblers seem scarcely to arrive before they again depart. On the other hand, many resident species, those that regularly breed in Southern Africa, are intra-Africa migrants and spend as much time away from their breeding grounds as in them. In this category are some of the kingfishers, cuckoos, rollers and the Wahlberg's Eagle among others.

On a more local scale, many bird species undergo regular migrations or irregular movements within Southern Africa itself, often from one altitude to another (altitudinal migrants). In this group are some swallows and robins and the diminutive Fairy Flycatcher. These movements may be dictated by rainfall, temperatures, food, breeding requirements, or a combination of these and other factors not fully understood. Certainly, rain and drought have a marked influence on birds, on the one hand triggering large-scale breeding by waterbirds especially, on the other inhibiting breeding by all but the hardiest of arid-land species.

Looking at birds

Binoculars are an essential part of the birdwatcher's equipment; many of the smaller birds cannot be properly studied without them. Many good makes are available and 7 x 30, 8 x 35, or 10 x 40 are recommended; the first figure relates to magnification and the second to the field of view. Generally speaking, the greater the diameter of the front, or objective, lens in proportion to the rear, or eyepiece, the more light is gathered and transmitted, and so the brighter the image. Many people also use a telescope to study distant, difficult-to-identify species.

Left: Barrel type binoculars. Right: Typical roof type binoculars.

Species' descriptions

In the descriptive text for each species, opposite the illustration of that species, the bird's vernacular name is given first in **bold** capital letters. This is the name recommended by the Southern African Ornithological Society. In some cases a bird will have a second vernacular name which is also in wide use, and this appears in brackets after the first name. Immediately following the vernacular name is the scientific name of the species, known throughout the world regardless of language. This appears in *italic* type and refers to the bird's genus and species in that order. These scientific names call for some explanation for the benefit of those unaccustomed to them. Birds, in common with all other forms of animal life, have all been placed in distinct groups for clarity of expression. It is all very well for the layman to refer to a 'Willie Wagtail' — his friends may understand to what he is referring, but in other countries, even in other parts of the same country, these popular names may in fact refer to totally different species. In Australia the Willie Wagtail is a very different bird to that found in Africa. Even the accepted vernacular names tend to vary from country to country. Thus, based on the international system of scientific nomenclature originated in the eighteenth century by the Swedish naturalist, Carl Linnaeus, all animals (and this includes birds) have been placed in clear groups or taxa, using names based on Latin or, in some cases, ancient Greek, which obviates any risk of confusion. No two birds can have the same scientific name. First, all animal life is placed in classes, and birds belong to the class Aves, mammals to the class Mammalia, insects to Insecta, and so on. These classes are then divided into major groups known as orders. The orders are subdivided into families, the families into genera (genus in the singular), and the genera into one or more species. A species can further be divided into races or subspecies.

When the above system of scientific nomenclature is applied to the common House Sparrow, its credentials look like this:

Class:	Aves
Order:	Passeriformes
Family:	Ploceidae
Genus:	*Passer*
Species:	*domesticus*

Thus, within the bird family PLOCEIDAE there is a genus known as *Passer*, and within that genus a specific bird known as *domesticus*. The name *Passer domesticus* can be regarded, in human terms, as first and second names, although the sequence is reversed. The use of an animal's scientific name ensures that serious students throughout the world will at once know, without any possibility of confusion, which species is being referred to. Within the genus *Passer* there are several other species all closely related to *P. domesticus: P. diffusus*, the Greyheaded Sparrow; *P. motitensis*, the Great Sparrow; and *P. melanurus*, the Cape Sparrow, to name a few. The present form of the local Southern African House Sparrow is descended from a species introduced into Natal from India earlier this century. The Indian race differs in minor respects from the nominate European race and is given the subspecific name of *Passer domesticus indicus* or, again in human terms, a second personal name. In fact the nominate race of the House Sparrow, *Passer domesticus domesticus* (identical specific and subspecific names denote that the bird is of the nominate race), was also introduced from Europe to various places in the old Cape Colony and elsewhere at about the same time. It interbred with the Indian race and seems to have been subjugated, very little trace of its specific plumage pattern being now discernible in the Southern African bird. The third or trinomial name is used in this fieldguide only in rare instances where it has been felt necessary to draw attention to the subspecific status of a bird.

When writing scientific names it is customary to write them in italic characters, to use an initial capital letter for the generic name, and small or lower-case letters only for the specific and subspecific names. It is also normal practice when writing for the more formal scientific journals, to follow a species name with the name of the person who first described it, together with the date and location or type-locality, e.g. *Passer domesticus indicus* Jardine & Selby, 1831: *India*, but this convention need not concern the user of this fieldguide.

Following the bird's names in the descriptive text is a brief statement of its known status. This is an attempt to give the reader an idea of the bird's relative abundance, whether it is rare, common, etc., and whether it is a seasonal visitor, a resident or a vagrant. These terms are set out and explained on page 18. It should be understood that the term 'common' for instance relates to the bird's frequency *within* its preferred or normal habitat, and not to the entire region.

Next follows a brief description of the bird, enlarging on what is shown in the illustration and, where possible, comparing it with other species with similar plumage. After this description is given the bird's call or song, written as closely as possible to the sound heard or, where it cannot be written, a general description of the type of song uttered. The transcription of birdsongs into words is no easy matter, and no two people hear it or describe it in quite the same way. These descriptions should, therefore, be regarded as approximations only, and reference to one of the popular bird-call tapes is recommended.

The bird's usual habitat and behaviour is then briefly described. The first provides a clue to its usual haunts and the second is a further guide to its identity. Many species which closely resemble another can be accurately identified by small traits of behaviour, such as wing-flicking, tail-wagging, or display procedure.

Finally, the bird's measurement is given. It is not practicable to measure a bird while it is standing, perched or swimming because various species hold themselves in different ways at different times. A long-necked bird may hold its head and neck outstretched or tucked in, some birds have a hunched posture while others of similar size may habitually stand erect. The measurements given therefore represent those of a dead bird lying flat on a table, neither stretched nor compressed. If the bird has long legs which project beyond the tail, these are included in the total measurement. In a few cases only, where a species has seasonally long tail-plumes, the measurements with and without tail are given.

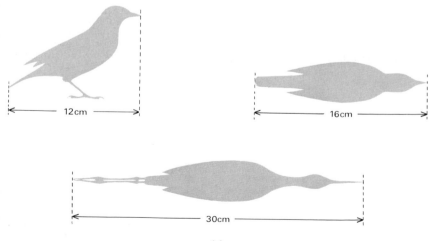

Terms used to describe a bird's anatomy

In relation to the written description of the birds, it is important that the reader be familiar with certain terms used to describe avian anatomy. These are clearly indicated in the 'Topography of a Bird' drawing overleaf.

Distribution maps

Each bird description is accompanied by a small distribution map showing the areas in which it is likely to be found. Only very rare species do not have a map, and in these cases the localities where they have been seen are given when known. These species ranges are rough guides only, based on present-day knowledge of the bird's occurrence. Solid areas are the normal range, solid spots are known local ranges of isolated populations, and open circles indicate where a species has been recorded but is not regular. In certain cases, notably among the waterbirds, shaded areas have been added to indicate temporary range extensions that occur under favourable weather conditions. Because birds are highly mobile creatures, they frequently appear in the most unlikely places and one should be ever watchful for species occurring beyond the range shown on the maps. Comparison with the Master Maps (page 19) will provide an accurate key to the locations shown on the distribution maps or in the text.

The colour plates

The birds depicted in this fieldguide have been drawn, so far as is possible, in such a way as to reveal their characteristic shapes, colours, markings and stance, or 'jizz' as it is known in ornithological parlance. Where several species on a plate closely resemble each other, they are all drawn, at risk of monotony, in a similar stance to facilitate direct comparison. All the main figures on a plate are in approximate proportion to each other and, wherever possible, all birds in a family are drawn to the same proportions whether on the same plate or not. In a few cases it has been necessary to depict larger birds of a family to a smaller scale than the others on the same plate, and in such cases they are clearly separated by a solid line. Secondary figures showing birds in flight or performing some other characteristic action are not drawn to the same proportions as the main figures.

It is customary in bird books to present species in strict taxonomic order, that is to say, in the order used by the national checklist. This usually means that one starts with the ostrich and the grebes, continues with seabirds, herons, ducks, etc., and finishes with canaries and buntings. In this fieldguide this order of presentation has been applied with elasticity. Because its basic purpose is to help with bird identification, and in the knowledge that many users may not be familiar with the various bird families and their characteristics, some species that have a visual resemblance to birds of another family have been illustrated with those they most closely resemble.

TOPOGRAPHY OF A BIRD

CREST

SUPERCILIARY
CROWN
LATERAL
CROWN STRIPE

EYE-
STRIPE

LORES
CERE
CULMEN

NAIL

MALAR
STRIPE
EAR
COVERTS
MOUSTACIAL
STRIPE
GULAR STRIPE

GAPE

FOREHEAD
FRONT
UPPER
MANDIBLE

LOWER MANDIBLE
CHIN
THROAT

ORBITAL RING
NAPE

BREAST
MANTLE

WATTLES
HIND NECK

SCAPULARS

LESSER COVERTS

GREATER WING
COVERTS
SECONDARIES

CARPAL
JOINT

MEDIAN
WING COVERTS
BELLY

TERTIALS

LESSER
COVERTS

THIGH

BACK

ALULA
GREATER
COVERTS

TERTIALS
RUMP

TIBIA

TIBIO-TARSAL JOINT

UPPER
TAIL COVERTS

TARSUS

SECONDARIES

VENT

UNDER
TAIL COVERTS
PRIMARIES

HIND TOE

UPPER WING PLAN

ALULA
GREATER WING COVERTS
MEDIAN COVERTS
MARGINAL COVERTS

MEDIAN PRIMARY COVERTS
GREATER PRIMARY COVERTS

SCAPULARS

TERTIALS

SECONDARIES
PRIMARIES

SPECULUM
(DUCKS ONLY)

16

Six simple rules for quick bird identification

Memorise the following six rules. With practice they will come to mind automatically when you look at a new bird and will help you to remember its important features. If possible write what you have seen in a notebook at the time of sighting.

1. What is the bird's relative size?

Compare the bird with common ones that are well known to you.
Is it larger or smaller than a SPARROW?
If larger, is it larger or smaller than a CITY PIGEON?
If larger, is it larger or smaller than a GUINEAFOWL?

2. What is the bird's beak shape and colour?

The shape of its beak is a guide to what it eats and therefore to the kind of bird it is. Is its beak short, stout and conical like that of a sparrow, or is it small and slender, long and slender, long and curved, powerful and hooked, etc.?
What colour is its beak? Many birds have blackish beaks but some beaks are brightly coloured.

3. What length and colour are its legs?

Does the bird have unusually long legs, such as are found in many that wade in water or walk in long grass, or short legs as seen in swallows and swifts? Are its legs a distinctive colour?

4. What plumage colours or markings strike you?

If the bird has bold markings on its head, wings, body or tail these should be noted, as should any bright colours. Many birds have white wing-bars or tail-bars, others have distinct eyebrows, breast-bands, etc.

5. In what habitat do you see the bird?

Is it in the garden, in water, in grassland, bushveld or forest? The habitat in which the bird is seen is another important clue to the kind of bird it is.

6. What is the bird doing?

Is it walking, hopping, wading or swimming? Does it peck at the ground, probe in mud or feed in a tree? Try to detail its behaviour as closely as possible.

Often the details of a bird's structure, plumage or behaviour are soon forgotten and the observer may spend much time trying to recall them. If these six points are remembered or noted at the time of the observation an analysis can be made later at leisure.

Terms used to indicate bird status and abundance

Vagrant:	a species not normally seen in Southern Africa
Rare:	a species recorded 10 times or less in any year in suitable habitat
Very rare:	a species recorded five times or less in any five year period
Uncommon:	a species recorded 30 or less times a month in suitable habitat
Fairly common:	a species recorded 1-10 times a day in suitable habitat
Common:	a species recorded 10-50 times a day in suitable habitat
Very common:	a species recorded 50-100 times a day in suitable habitat
Abundant:	a species recorded 100 or more times a day in suitable habitat
Seasonal:	a species seen at certain times of the year only
Winter:	April-August
Summer:	September-March
Localised:	a species seen only in restricted areas of suitable habitat
Resident:	a species which breeds in Southern Africa
Visitor:	a non-breeding species (Palaearctic or intra-Africa migrant)

Symbols used on the colour illustrations

♂ denotes MALE
♀ denotes FEMALE
J denotes an immature bird
Br denotes breeding plumage
N-Br denotes non-breeding plumage

Key location maps of Southern Africa and the Subantarctic Region (opposite)

These key maps give the location of place names and areas mentioned in the text and are intended for use in conjunction with individual distribution maps, which are a reduction of the maps opposite. On species' distribution maps, solid red areas indicate the normal range and solid red spots the known ranges of isolated populations, while open circles show where a species has been recorded by occasional or even single sightings but is not regular.

SOUTHERN AFRICAN REGION

SUBANTARCTIC REGION

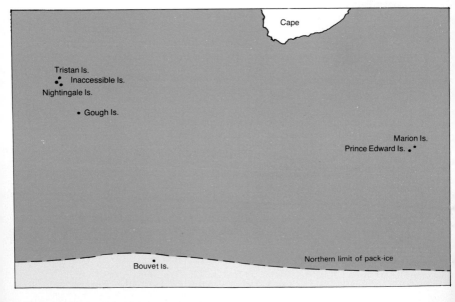

EXTRALIMITAL SUBANTARCTIC BIRDS

(This section does not include vagrant birds to the region)

Cormorants. Family PHALACROCORACIDAE. See also page 64.

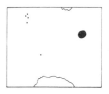

1 IMPERIAL CORMORANT *Phalacrocorax atriceps.* Common resident on Marion Island. The only cormorant in that region. Gregarious, breeds in small colonies on rocky headlands and low cliffs. 61 cm.

Penguins. Family SPHENISCIDAE. See also page 28.

2 GENTOO PENGUIN *Pygoscelis papua.* Common. Bright orange bill and feet and triangular, white ear-patches diagnostic. Immatures resemble adults but have duller bill and grey-mottled throat. Occurs in small breeding colonies on Marion and Prince Edward Islands. Unlike other penguins shows fear of man, and runs away when approached. 76 cm.

3 CHINSTRAP PENGUIN *Pygoscelis antarctica.* Common. Thin black line across throat diagnostic for adults and immatures. Found with Adelie Penguins (next species) in pack-ice in small groups. Very common breeder on Bouvet Island; vagrant to Marion Island. 76 cm.

4 ADELIE PENGUIN *Pygoscelis adeliae.* Common. Identified by short stubby bill, black head with white eye-rings. At long range immatures resemble previous species but have the black of the face extending below the eyes. Most often seen in small groups in the pack-ice, resting out of water or 'porpoising' at speed through the water. 71 cm.

5 EMPEROR PENGUIN *Aptenodytes forsteri.* Uncommon. Largest penguin in the world. Distinguished from smaller King Penguin (page 28) by pale yellow, not orange, patches on sides of head and shorter, more decurved bill. Confined to the ice-shelf and pack-ice within the Antarctic; rarely seen at sea. Mostly found singly or in small groups. 112 cm.

22

Storm Petrels. Family OCEANITIDAE. See also page 46.

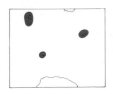

1 GREYBACKED STORM PETREL *Garrodia nereis*. Uncommon in offshore waters at Gough, Marion and Prince Edward Islands. Dark head and flight-feathers contrast with ash-grey back and rump; the only storm petrel in the region with *uniform grey back and rump*; cf. next species. Usually solitary at sea. Flight swallow-like, hovering buoyantly when feeding and skipping from side to side low over the water. 17 cm.

2 WHITEFACED STORM PETREL *Pelagodroma marina*. Common offshore at Tristan group. The only storm petrel in the region with white throat and breast and distinctive head markings. Rump pale grey (not white as in most other storm petrels) and contrasting with dark back; legs very long and projecting beyond end of tail. Occurs in small groups of 2-4 which fly in ships' bow-waves, and has peculiar, fast swinging action as it skips and trails its long legs through the waves. 21 cm.

Diving petrels. Family PELECANOIDIDAE. Very small, short-necked, short-winged and short-tailed seabirds of the southern hemisphere. They fly close to the water's surface with rapid wing-beats, bouncing off the waves like flying fish or plunging through them with no perceptible change of wing-beat or speed. When settled on the water, they float high like grebes (page 96) and take off after a short run across the surface.

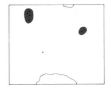

3 COMMON DIVING PETREL *Pelecanoides urinatrix*. Common resident on the Tristan group, Marion and Prince Edward Islands. At sea indistinguishable from the next species, differing mainly in bill shape and size; see illustrations. Otherwise seen as small, black and white birds with fast direct flight on short, whirring wings. Singly or in small groups around islands. 20 cm.

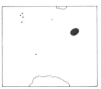

4 SOUTH GEORGIAN DIVING PETREL *Pelecanoides georgicus*. Common resident on Marion and Prince Edward Islands; cf. previous species and bill illustrations. At sea behaviour identical to previous species. On land breeds at higher elevations on islands, usually on non-vegetated cinder cones, where their small rat-like tunnels bury deep into the scoria. 19 cm.

23

Terns. Family LARIDAE. See also pages 54-60.

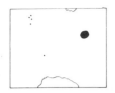

1 KERGUELEN TERN *Sterna virgata.* Resident on Marion and Prince Edward Islands. Differs from Arctic Tern (page 58) in darker grey colour, grey tail, grey underwings and shorter, thinner bill. Immatures much darker and more heavily barred than immature Antarctic terns. Flight buoyant, reminiscent of a marsch tern (page 60). Regularly feeds on insects taken from the ground on open grassy plains. 31 cm.

Petrels. Family PROCELLARIIDAE. See also pages 34-40.

2 SNOW PETREL *Pagodroma nivea.* Common on pack-ice and adjacent seas, breeds on Bouvet Island. Unmistakable, all-white bird. Flight rapid over sea and ice; more agile on land than other petrels, it sometimes runs over pack-ice in the manner of a wader. 34 cm

Sheathbills. Family CHIONIDIDAE. White, pigeon-like, scavenging birds of the southern islands and ice-floes. Fly laboriously and reluctantly but can swim.

3 LESSER SHEATHBILL *Chionis minor.* Common resident on Marion and Prince Edward Islands. Unmistakable, plump white bird with black bill and facial skin and pink legs. Usually in pairs or small groups which frequent penguin rookeries and grassy coastal plains feeding on corpses, penguin eggs and regurgitated food from adult penguins which they obtain by disturbing penguins feeding their young. 38 cm.

AMERICAN SHEATHBILL see page 444.

Rails. Family RALLIDAE. See also pages 96-104.

4 GOUGH MOORHEN *Gallinula nesiotes.* Common on Gough Island; introduced to Tristan Island in recent years following past extirpation. Very similar to Moorhen (page 98) but has red (not yellow) legs. Most frequent on coastal plateau but more often heard than seen as it is very secretive, and keeps within thick, tangles of tree fern and bracken to avoid predation by skuas (page 50). Wings very small but can flap for a short dfistance when disturbed. 27 cm.

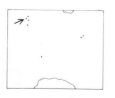

5 INACCESSIBLE ISLAND RAIL *Atlantisia rogersi.* Inaccessible Island only, where common. Unmistakable, the only small rail on the island. Very vocal, the call 'pseep' heard all over the island. Individuals frequently glimpsed as they race, rodent-like, between tussock clumps. Inquisitive, coming into open areas to inspect unusual objects. 17 cm.

Br

1

N-Br

2

3

4

5

Buntings. Family FRINGILLIDAE. The so-called buntings of the Tristan group and Gough Island differ from mainland buntings (page 442) in several ways, being more closely allied to the Fringillidae of South America.

1 TRISTAN BUNTING *Nesospiza acunhae*. Common resident; confined to Inaccessible and Nightingale Islands. Distinguished from Wilkins' Bunting (3) by smaller, thinner bill. The song is a melodious twittering or chirping 'chickory-chikky', followed by a wheezy 'tweeyer'. Birds on Inaccessible Island are larger billed, more buffy on the breast and have a greater variety of higher-pitched calls than those on Nightingale Island. Pairs or small flocks forage on the ground or clamber over *Phylica* bushes in search of insects. 16 cm.

2 GOUGH BUNTING *Rowettia goughensis*. Common resident on Gough Island. Sexes markedly different but the only bunting on the island. Immatures resemble females but are more richly coloured (orange-buff). Has a penetrating 'tissik' call note and a soft 'pseeping' while feeding. Pairs and small groups are found throughout the island foraging on the ground or clambering over tussock and *Phylica* bushes. Inquisitive and unafraid of man but dives for cover when a skua passes overhead. 16 cm.

3 WILKINS' BUNTING *Nesospiza wilkinsi*. Common resident on Inaccessible and Nightingale Islands. Occurs alongside Tristan Bunting (1) but is more heavily built and has massive thick bill used for cracking open hard *Phylica* nuts. The call of Nightingale Island birds is a clear 'tweet-twee-yeer, tweet-tweeyer'. Inaccessible Island birds have a similar but harsher call. Occurs mostly in the *Phylica* bush and tree-fern zone, less often in open grassy and tussock areas. 18 cm.

Thrushes. Family TURDIDAE. See also page 312.

4 TRISTAN THRUSH *Nesocichla eremita*. Common resident on Tristan, Inaccessible and Nightingale Islands. Unmistakable, orange-brown thrush with heavy overlay of dark brown blotches, the wings showing much orange at rest and in flight. Immatures have more orange spotting and streaking on the upperparts, smaller, more clearly defined spots on the underparts. In Nightingale birds the breast is more streaky. The song is 'chissik, chissik, trrtkk, swee, swee, swee' or 'pseeooee, pseeooee, pseeooee, pseeptee', sung from inside of canopy of *Phylica* bush. Found in clearings in undergrowth where it hops about with typical thrush-like stance, turning over moss and leaf-litter in search of food. Birds on Tristan Island more secretive than those on Inaccessible and Nightingale Islands. 22 cm.

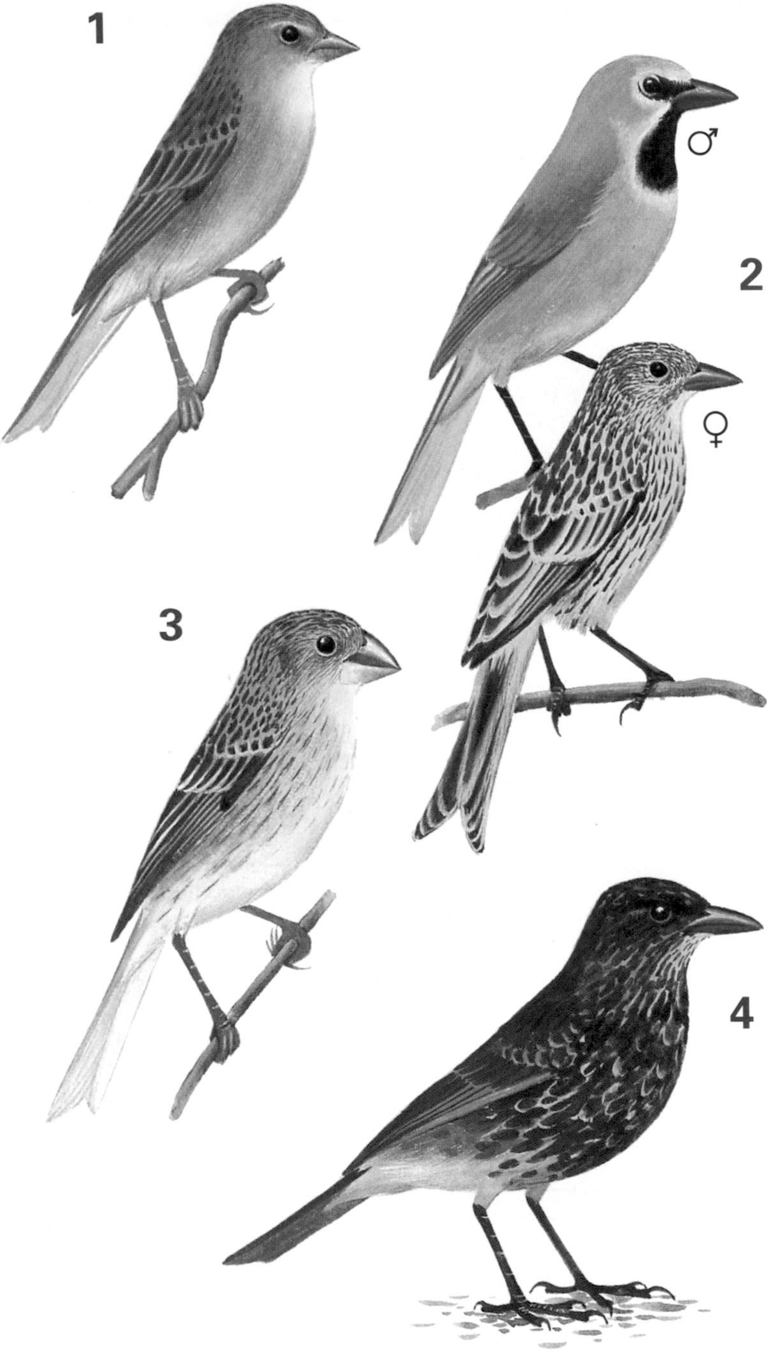
1
♂
2
♀
3
4

BIRDS OF SOUTHERN AFRICA

Penguins. Family SPHENISCIDAE. Flightless marine birds of the southern oceans. Characterised by stocky build, flipper-like wings, short legs and, on land, an erect stance. Walk with a shuffling gait or, on rough terrain, a series of hops and slides in which the bill and stiff tail may be used as props. On snow and ice may lie prone, propelling themselves with their feet and flippers. In water the flippers are used in an oar-like action, and the feet as an aid to steering; they dive to considerable depths in pursuit of fish. On the surface they swim with most of the body submerged, head held high. Colours basically black and white, sexes alike.

1 ROCKHOPPER PENGUIN *Eudyptes chrysocome.* Vagrant. Distinguished by short, stubby red bill and pale yellow stripe from in front of the eye to the nape where it ends in a shaggy plume. Differs from the next species in *black forehead* and fairly stiff lateral head-plumes. Individuals, usually moulting birds, occasionally ashore on Cape coast; otherwise not normally at sea in South African waters. A summer breeder on Tristan group, Marion and Prince Edward Islands. 61 cm.

2 MACARONI PENGUIN *Eudyptes chrysolophus.* Rare vagrant. Distinguished from previous species by more robust bill plus orange-yellow eyebrows *which meet on the forehead*, the plumes loose and floppy. At sea distinguished from Rockhopper with difficulty, but pale, fleshy sides of gape and white rump-spot diagnostic. Immatures differ from immature Rockhoppers by yellow stripe starting *above eye* (not before eye). At sea makes a harsh, nasal bark. A few individuals ashore on Cape coast; not known at sea in South African waters. Summer breeder on Bouvet, Marion and Prince Edward Islands. 71 cm.

3 JACKASS PENGUIN *Spheniscus demersus.* Very common to abundant endemic resident. Black-and-white facial pattern and white underparts with encircling black bar diagnostic; individuals sometimes with double bar as (a). Chicks (b) and immatures (c) as illustrated. The call is a donkey-like braying, heard mostly at night. Singly or in groups in coastal waters or large numbers on offshore islands; individuals occasionally on mainland beaches. 63 cm.

4 KING PENGUIN *Aptenodytes patagonicus.* Rare vagrant. Large size, long, pointed bill and bright orange ear-patches distinguish this from all other penguins in Southern African waters; in Antarctic waters distinguished from larger Emperor Penguin (page 20) by orange, not pale yellow, ear-patches. At sea makes a monosyllabic 'aark'. Rarely ashore on Cape coast. Breeds on Marion and Prince Edward Islands. 94-100 cm.

ALBATROSSES

Albatrosses. Family DIOMEDEIDAE. Huge, narrow-winged pelagic seabirds, occurring most frequently in Southern African waters during the winter months. They glide close to the water's surface on motionless wings and are best identified by underwing patterns and bill colouring, immatures being different from adults. Many breed on southern ocean islands during summer.

1 ROYAL ALBATROSS *Diomedea epomophora.* Uncommon visitor. Race (a) distinguished by combination of dark upperwings (*not* extending across the back) and *no markings on head or tail.* Race (b) closely similar to next species but differs in thick black leading edge to wing from carpal joint to wing-tip; at close range black eyelids and black cutting-edge to bill diagnostic. Immatures start with dark upperwing and *white leading edge*, which progressively extends *backwards* until upperwing is almost entirely white as next species. Recorded occasionally in Cape waters. 120 cm.

2 WANDERING ALBATROSS *Diomedea exulans.* Uncommon visitor. Mature birds of white form (a) almost indistinguishable from adults of race (b) of previous species, except at close range. Young of all races initially with all-dark upperwings and body except for white face; belly then whitens as (c), becoming progressively paler, while upperwings whiten from *centre outwards* as (b); (cf. previous species which whitens from leading edge); stage (b) most commonly encountered. All waters, but sparse. Breeds Prince Edward, Gough, Marion and Inaccessible Islands. 120 cm.

3 SHY or WHITECAPPED ALBATROSS *Diomedea cauta.* Common winter, uncommon summer visitor. Largest black-backed albatross, approaching size of (1) and (2), but upperwings paler than other dark-winged species, underwings with *very narrow black borders* at all ages. Adults with greyish cheeks, white crown. Immatures with varying amounts of grey on head, neck and breast, plus grey bill with black tip; cf. smaller immature Blackbrowed Albatross (overleaf) which has similar bill but dark underwing. All waters. 95 cm.

4 GREYHEADED ALBATROSS *Diomedea chrysostoma.* Rare winter visitor. Grey head plus black bill with yellow ridges to upper and lower mandibles diagnostic. Immatures with *all-dark underwings* and darker grey head but, through wear, head sometimes appears as pale as immature Blackbrowed Albatross (overleaf), then all-dark bill is diagnostic; cf. also Yellownosed Albatross (overleaf). Sparse in all waters. Breeds on Prince Edward and Marion Islands. 80-90 cm.

1 BLACKBROWED ALBATROSS *Diomedea melanophris.*
Common summer visitor; all year in the Cape. All-yellow, pink-
tipped bill diagnostic of adults. Immatures have grey bill with dark
tip and varying amounts of grey on head and sides of neck which
sometimes form a collar; underwing initially all-dark becomes paler
centrally with age; cf. immature Greyheaded Albatross (previous
page), which also has dark underwing but all-dark bill and smoky-
grey head; also immatures of next species plus Shy Albatross
(previous page), which have predominantly white underwings
with black borders. Most common albatross in Cape waters.
80-95 cm.

2 YELLOWNOSED ALBATROSS *Diomedea chlororhynchos.*
Common winter visitor to east coast, uncommon on west coast.
Smallest, most slender albatross, race (a) with all-white head, race
(b) (Tristan birds) with grey heads; bill in both races black with
yellow upper ridge. Race (b) distinguished from Greyheaded
Albatross (previous page) by narrower black borders to
underwings and the yellow on the bill confined to the upper
mandible. Immatures have same underwing pattern as adults but
have *all-white head* and *black bill.* Summer breeder on Tristan
group and Prince Edward island. 75-81 cm.

LAYSAN ALBATROSS see page 444.

3 SOOTY ALBATROSS (DARKMANTLED SOOTY ALBA-
TROSS) *Phoebetria fusca.* Rare visitor. All-dark, slender albatross
with narrow wings and long, wedge-shaped tail. Differs from the
next species in *uniformly dark back,* rarely showing contrast with
upperwings except in very worn plumage but never as pale as
Lightmantled Sooty Albatross; at close range pale yellow stripe on
bill diagnostic. Immatures of this and next species difficult to
identify at sea, but this species shows a *pale buffy collar* with grey
not extending to lower back. Summer breeder on Tristan group,
Marion and Prince Edward Islands. Rare in Cape waters. 86 cm.

4 LIGHTMANTLED SOOTY ALBATROSS *Phoebetria palpe-
brata.* Rare vagrant. Adults differ from previous species in having
ash-grey mantle and body contrasting sharply with dark head,
wings and tail; at close range pale blue stripe on bill diagnostic.
Immatures have all-pale back, slightly mottled, and pale
underbody. Summer breeder on Bouvet, Marion and Prince
Edward Islands. Very rare in Cape waters. 86 cm.

33

Petrels, fulmars, shearwaters and prions. Family PROCEL-LARIIDAE. A large and varied group of long-winged pelagic birds, ranging in size from the small (14-20 cm) prions to the giant petrels, which approach the size of a small albatross. They are characterised by a single nasal tube (enclosing both nostrils which open obliquely or vertically) surmounting the upper mandible, drab plumage colours and a typically stiff-winged mode of flight. All breed beyond our limits on islands in the Subantarctic and visit Southern African coasts mainly during the winter months, when they may be seen around fishing-boats foraging for offal.

1 NORTHERN GIANT PETREL *Macronectes halli*. Common all-year visitor. This and the next species distinguished from the sooty albatrosses (previous page) by massive pale bill, thinner wings, bulkier bodies and a hump-backed appearance in flight. This species difficult to tell from the next species unless bill colour seen: *fleshy-yellow with a dark tip*. Adults have some white around the face but never as extensive as in (2). Immatures identifiable only at close range by bill colour. Congregates around seal islands on the west coast. Breeds on Marion and Prince Edward Islands. 75-90 cm.

2 SOUTHERN GIANT PETREL *Macronectes giganteus*. Common all-year visitor. Two morphs, (a) normal with extensive area of white or speckled-white on head extending to upper breast (more extensive than in previous species), (b) entirely white except for a few scattered black feathers; bill pale flesh with greenish tip. Immatures cf. (1). Singly or in small numbers, especially around trawlers in Cape waters. Breeds on Gough, Bouvet (?), Marion and Prince Edward Islands. 75-90 cm.

3 WHITECHINNED PETREL (CAPE HEN) *Procellaria aequinoctialis*. Common all-year visitor. Differs from all other dark petrels, except (1) and (2) by much larger size and very pale greenish bill; white chin variable (absent in immatures) but usually small (a), whereas in birds from Tristan group (b) white extends onto throat and over eyes. At long range distinguished from Wedgetailed and Fleshfooted Shearwaters (page 44) by larger size, darker colour and pale bill. Gregarious in large numbers around trawlers. Summer breeder on Inaccessible, Nightingale and Marion Islands. 51 cm.

4 GREATWINGED PETREL *Pterodroma macroptera*. Uncommon all-year visitor. Characterised by long, thin wings held at sharp angle at the carpal joint. Differs from similar-sized Sooty Shearwater (page 44) in *dark underwings*, from the previous species by smaller size and *short black bill*. Singly at sea, moving with dashing, twisting flight, often towering high above the water. Winter breeder on Tristan group, Marion and Prince Edward Islands. 42 cm.

1 ANTARCTIC FULMAR (SILVERGREY PETREL) *Fulmarus glacialoides*. Rare winter visitor. Identified by pale grey upperparts with white patches at the base of the primaries; underparts white except for grey trailing edge to wings (cf. Snow Petrel (page 24) which is entirely white). Occurs singly, most often at trawlers in Cape seas. Breeds on Bouvet Island. 46 cm.

2 ANTARCTIC PETREL *Thalassoica antarctica*. Rare vagrant. Resembles Pintado Petrel (overleaf) but is larger, lacks white patches and checkering on the upper wings, has instead broad white area on trailing edge of upper wings; from below is white with brown head, bold brown leading edge to wings and tail narrowly tipped b.own; general appearance browner than Pintado Petrel. Common in the pack-ice, gathering in large flocks and resting on icebergs and ice-floes, often in company with Snow Petrels (page 24). Vagrant to Marion Island and Cape waters. 43 cm.

3 ATLANTIC PETREL (SCHLEGEL'S PETREL) *Pterodroma incerta*. Rare winter visitor. Essentially an all-dark-brown petrel with white lower breast and belly (in worn plumage throat and breast can appear mottled), upperparts uniformly dark brown. Superficially resembles Softplumaged Petrel (overleaf) but is larger and lacks the white throat and breast-band of that species; also the Grey Petrel (page 42) but is much darker above and has a short black bill (not slender pale bill). Solitary at sea but gathers in rafts off islands of the Tristan group where it breeds in summer. 43 cm.

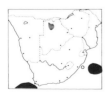

4 WHITEHEADED PETREL *Pterodroma lessonii*. Rare winter visitor. Snowy-white head with dark eye-patches; entirely white underbody and tail and dark underwings render this species unmistakable. The upperparts are grey-brown with a conspicuous open M across the back and wings. Solitary at sea and *avoids* foraging at trawlers. 45 cm.

38

1 SOFTPLUMAGED PETREL *Pterodroma mollis*. Uncommon winter visitor. Resembles Atlantic Petrel (previous page) but is smaller, has *dusky breast-band* on entirely white underparts from *throat to tail*; faint shadow of open M pattern across upper-wings and back. Rare dark phase (b) differs from larger Greatwinged Petrel (page 34) in less uniform, slightly mottled underparts, and from the next species by these features plus less grey appearance. At sea occurs singly or in pairs; does *not* scavenge, around trawlers. Summer breeder on Gough, Marion and Prince Edward Islands. 32 cm.

2 KERGUELEN PETREL *Pterodroma brevirostris*. Rare offshore visitor occasionally 'wrecked' in large numbers on Eastern Cape coast. Very similar in shape and outline to Greatwinged Petrel (page 34) but is *much smaller* and is grey, not dark brown. The head appears unusually large, the underwings have a thin, pale leading edge from body to carpal joint which is noticeable at close range. Differs from the dark phase of the Softplumaged Petrel (1) by greyer colouration and more uniform underparts. Flight very fast with rapid wing-beats interspersed with long glides over the waves, then towers high above the sea, *much higher than any other petrel*. Summer breeder on the Tristan group, Marion and Prince Edward Islands. 36 cm.

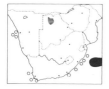

3 PINTADO PETREL (CAPE PIGEON) *Daption capense*. Abundant winter visitor. An unmistakable pied petrel with two white patches on each upperwing and a checkered pattern on back and rump; underparts white with dark brown borders to wings (bolder on the leading edge) and tail-tip; cf. Antarctic Petrel (previous page). Occurs singly or in vast flocks which attend trawlers in Cape waters; regularly seen from shore in stormy weather. Breeds on Bouvet Island. 36 cm.

4 BULWER'S PETREL *Bulweria bulwerii*. Rare vagrant. Prion-sized, all-dark-brown petrel with long wings and long, wedge-shaped tail which appears pointed; pale diagonal wing-bar on upperwings seen only at close range. No similar-sized, all-dark petrel occurs in the Southern African region; cf. prions (overleaf). Flight action prion-like but much more erratic, staying closer to wave-surface. Seen rarely in S.W. Cape waters. 26-8 cm.

5 DOVE PRION *Pachyptila vittata desolata*. Included for size comparison. See overleaf.

40

1 BLUE PETREL *Halobaena caerulea.* Offshore winter visitor. Occasionally blown ashore in large numbers. A small blue-grey petrel resembling a prion (see below) but larger and with dark markings on the crown, nape, sides of breast and a square-cut, *white-tipped tail.* Open M pattern across upper wings and back fainter than in prions. Often seen in company with flocks of prions. Breeds on Marion and Prince Edward Islands. 30 cm.

Prions. Small blue-grey petrels with such closely similar plumage patterns as to be specifically indistinguishable at sea. All have a dark open M mark across the upper wings and mantle, their tails *wedge-shaped and dark-tipped;* cf. previous species. Their underparts are white. Prions fly fast and erratically, twisting from side to side and alternately revealing their white underparts and dark upperparts. They are frequently blown ashore in 'wrecks', large numbers of corpses then littering the beaches. In the hand, specific identification is possible by examination of bill shape and size; see illustrations. The two species and four subspecies all have separate vernacular names.

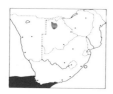

2 BROADBILLED PRION *Pachyptila vittata.* Uncommon visitor. Identified with difficulty at sea from the Dove Prion (next subspecies) and Slenderbilled Prion (4) unless seen at close range when the extremely broad and flattened bill is diagnostic. Larger, bulkier in body and darker about the head than Fairy Prion (6), the tail only *slightly tipped black;* cf. that species. Summer breeder on the Tristan group. 30 cm.

3 DOVE PRION *Pachyptila v. desolata.* Common winter visitor. A race of the previous species. Illustrated as (5) on previous page. Most abundant prion in offshore waters, occurring in large numbers and usually the dominant species in 'wrecks'; cf. previous species and bill illustrations. 29 cm.

4 SLENDERBILLED PRION *Pachyptila v. belcheri.* Rare winter visitor. A race of the Broadbilled Prion (2); cf. that species and bill illustrations. 29 cm.

5 MEDIUMBILLED PRION (SALVIN'S PRION) *Pachyptila v. salvini.* Rare visitor. A race of the Broadbilled Prion (2); cf. that species and bill illustrations. 28-30 cm.

6 FAIRY PRION *Pachyptila turtur.* Rare winter visitor. Slightly smaller than all other prions, appearing bluer and pale-headed. The tail is *broadly tipped black*, this feature separating it from other prions. Summer breeder on Marion and Prince Edward Islands. 23 cm.

7 FULMAR PRION *Pachyptila t. crassirostris.* Rare vagrant. A race of the previous species, only distinguishable from that species by bill characters. 24 cm.

41

Shearwaters differ from other petrels in having long thin bills and, with a few notable exceptions, short, rounded tails. The smaller species fly with short bursts of rapid wing-flapping alternating with long, stiff-winged banking glides low over the water.

1 GREY PETREL (GREY SHEARWATER) *Procellaria cinerea*. Rare visitor to western Cape waters. A large grey and white petrel which resembles Cory's Shearwater (3), but differs in having a conspicuous dark underwing and undertail. Flight action stiff with shallow wing-beats on straight, ridged wings. Solitary at sea and rarely scavenges around ships. Winter breeder on the Tristan group, Marion and Prince Edward Islands. 48 cm.

2 GREAT SHEARWATER *Puffinus gravis*. Common visitor. Similar in size to the next species from which it differs in having darker upperparts, distinctive black cap, white collar and dark smudges on belly. At close range white on rump and dark bill may be seen. Usually in small flocks, but large rafts gather on feeding grounds in western Cape waters. Summer breeder on the Tristan group. 45-50 cm.

3 CORY'S SHEARWATER *Calonectris diomedea*. Common summer visitor. Ashy-brown upperparts, lack of any capped appearance and yellow bill distinguish this from the previous species. The flight is also slower and more laboured. In worn plumage can show a white rump. Gregarious in small numbers and regularly seen from the shore. 46 cm.

4 MANX SHEARWATER *Puffinus puffinus*. Rare summer visitor. The second smallest shearwater of the region. All blackish above, underbody and underwings white extending almost to the wing-tips. Distinguished from Little and Audubon's Shearwaters (overleaf) by larger size, more extensive black on the head extending below the eyes and white undertail coverts. Flight action less fluttering than either Little or Audubon's Shearwaters, with longer glides between wing-beats. Occurs singly in flocks of Sooty Shearwaters (overleaf). 35-7 cm.

43

1

2

3

4

44

1 SOOTY SHEARWATER *Puffinus griseus*. Abundant all-year visitor. A sooty-brown shearwater with *conspicuous pale areas on the underwings*, this separating it from all other dark petrels in the region. Feeds in mixed flocks of Cape Gannets (page 48) and Cape Cormorants (page 64), sometimes in thousands. Often seen close inshore in Cape waters. Less commonly forages around deep-sea trawlers. 46-53 cm.

2 WEDGETAILED SHEARWATER *Puffinus pacificus*. Vagrant to east coast. Closely resembles next species, but differs in being smaller and having a *dark bill*. Tail wedge-shaped (not rounded) and appears pointed when not spread. Wings broad at the base and held slightly bowed, not straight and stiff as in previous species. Rare pale morph not recorded in our region. Singly or in small groups. 42 cm.

3 FLESHFOOTED SHEARWATER *Puffinus carneipes*. Rare winter visitor to east coast. Larger than Sooty Shearwater (1) and differs in having dark underwings. Smaller than Whitechinned Petrel (page 34), the bill pink with a dark tip (not pale green). Differs from the previous species by larger size, narrower, longer wings and rounded (not pointed) tail. Flesh-coloured legs and feet when extended appear as a pale vent at long range. Accompanies foraging flocks of Cape Gannets (page 48) in Agulhas current. 45 cm.

4 LITTLE SHEARWATER *Puffinus assimilis*. Rare visitor, chiefly to Cape coast in summer. A very small, black and white shearwater which flies with rapid wing-beats interspersed with short glides. Much smaller size, white face (a) and flight action separates it from Manx Shearwater (previous page). Race (b) has dark grey upperparts; cf. next species. Occurs singly with Sooty Shearwater (1) and occasionally at trawlers. 28 cm.

5 AUDUBON'S SHEARWATER (BAILLON'S SHEAR-WATER) *Puffinus lherminieri*. Rare vagrant to east coast. Similar in size to previous species and with similar flight action, but differs in having upperparts dark brown (not black) and a dark undertail; race (b) of the previous species has dark grey upperparts which can appear brown, dark undertail is therefore best character for identifying Audubon's Shearwater. 30 cm.

6 Storm Petrel included for comparison of size with shearwaters. See overleaf.

46

Storm Petrels. Family OCEANITIDAE. Swallow-size petrels of generally dark appearance, some with white rumps, underbodies or underwings, all with long, delicate legs. Fly with fluttering bat-like action, erratic bounding action or with more direct, swallow-like flight. Many feed from the water's surface with feet pattering in the sea, and appear to walk on the water while remaining airborne with raised wings. Specific identification difficult except at close range. See previous page for size comparison with shearwaters. See also page 22 for Subantarctic Storm Petrels.

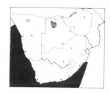

1 EUROPEAN STORM PETREL *Hydrobates pelagicus*. Common summer visitor. The smallest seabird in the region. Identified from Wilson's Storm Petrel (3) by more pointed wings, white stripe on underwing, and legs that do not project beyond the tail in flight. Flight bat-like, direct, occasionally pattering water with feet. Occurs in large flocks and is frequently beach-wrecked. 14-18 cm.

2 LEACH'S STORM PETREL *Oceanodroma leucorhoa*. Uncommon summer visitor. Differs from Wilson's and European Storm Petrel in slightly larger size, longer wings, more slender appearance and, at close range, forked tail. Flight erratic, bounding over the waves and sometimes flying like a small shearwater. Unlike other storm petrels *does not patter feet on water*. Occasionally seen in small flocks, but usually solitary at sea. 22 cm.

3 WILSON'S STORM PETREL *Oceanites oceanicus*. Common all-year visitor. Best identified by rounded wings, uniformly dark underwing pattern and long, spindly legs projecting well beyond a square tail; has yellow-webbed feet but almost impossible to see at sea. Flight action more swallow-like as opposed to bat-like action of European Storm Petrel (1). 16-19 cm.

4 BLACKBELLIED STORM PETREL *Fregetta tropica*. Uncommon winter visitor. Larger than previous species, differing in white underwings and *white belly with black stripe down the centre* which broadens on the vent and encompasses entire undertail coverts. Differs from Greybacked Storm Petrel (page 22) by larger size and white rump. Habitually flies in front of and alongside ships and has a bounding flight action, occasionally bouncing off waves on their breasts; cf. next species. Solitary at sea. Summer breeder on Bouvet (?), Marion (?) and Prince Edward Islands. 20 cm.

5 WHITEBELLIED STORM PETREL *Fregetta grallaria*. Uncommon winter visitor. Difficult to tell from the previous species unless seen at close range but has *entirely white belly which extends onto the undertail coverts;* mantle and wing-coverts tipped grey, giving paler-backed appearance (darker in Blackbellied Storm Petrel). Habitually flies in front of and alongside ships with bounding flight, occasionally bouncing off waves on their breasts; cf. previous species. Solitary at sea. Summer breeder on the Tristan group of islands. 20 cm.

MATSUDAIRA'S STORM PETREL see page 444.

Tropicbirds. Family PHAETHONTIDAE. Tern-like seabirds with the two central tail-feathers elongated into streamers; lacking in immatures. Usually seen singly, the flight is fluttering interspersed with long glides. They catch fish by plunge-diving from a height of 12-16 m above the sea. Their normal distribution is pan-tropical.

1 WHITETAILED TROPICBIRD *Phaethon lepturus*. Uncommon visitor. Distinguished from the next species by yellow bill, white tail-streamers and black marks on the upper wings. Immatures with blacker wingtips than immatures of the Redtailed Tropicbird. Indian Ocean waters, occasional on the eastern Cape coast; infrequent on the west coast. 40 cm (excluding tail-streamers).

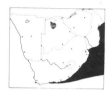

2 REDTAILED TROPICBIRD *Phaethon rubricauda*. Uncommon visitor. Distinguished by red bill and red tail-streamers. Plumage almost entirely white or flushed pink when in breeding condition. Immatures have a distinctive black bar through the eye; the bill initially black, later becoming yellow, then orange. Indian Ocean waters, occasional on the eastern Cape coast. 46 cm (excluding tail-streamers).

REDBILLED TROPICBIRD see page 444.

Boobies and gannets. Family SULIDAE. Large, robust seabirds with long, thick necks and straight, conical bills. The smaller boobies with a tropical distribution, gannets with a temperate one. All catch fish by mostly plunge-diving from *c.* 20 m above the sea. Flight stiff-winged with powerful, fairly rapid wing-beats, head and neck stretched forward.

MASKED BOOBY *Sula dactylatra*. Occurrence in southern African waters not proven. Like a Cape Gannet (4) but head white not yellow.

3 BROWN BOOBY *Sula leucogaster*. Very rare vagrant. All-brown with pale bill, white underbody separated from brown neck by sharp demarcation on upper-breast and clear white central underwing; cf. immature of next species. Occurs rarely in east coast waters. 78 cm.

4 CAPE GANNET *Sula capensis*. Common or locally abundant endemic resident. Unmistakable, large black-and-white seabird with yellow head and hind neck, at close range with distinctive black lines on the bill and face plus a *long black line* down the centre of the throat. The tail is normally black, but rare individuals have white outer tail-feathers. Immatures all-dark initially, heavily spotted and freckled all over, the body, head and neck becoming white in that sequence, finally wings (*c.* two years). Singly or in straggling flocks offshore with large aggregations over fish shoals, individuals plunge-diving repeatedly. Roosts at night colonially on offshore islands or at sea. 84-94 cm.

5 AUSTRALIAN GANNET *Sula serrator*. Rare vagrant to the Cape. Identical to the Cape Gannet but has *much shorter central throat stripe* (see illustration) and white outer tail-feathers. 84-92 cm.

Skuas, gulls and terns. Family LARIDAE. Skuas are robust, predominantly brown, predatory seabirds with characteristic white flashes at the base of their primary feathers, wedge-shaped tails with the two central feathers elongated, plus dark bills and feet. Immatures all very similar with heavily barred bodies. Gulls and terns described on following pages.

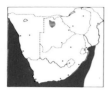

1 ARCTIC SKUA *Stercorarius parasiticus*. Common summer visitor. Larger than Hartlaub's Gull (overleaf); plumage sequences very variable between pale (a) and dark (b) morph birds. Differ from Pomarine Skua (3) in smaller size, narrower-based wings and more agile flight. In adults of both colour morphs pointed central tail-feathers project 3-4 cm beyond tail-tip. A falcon-like species which chases small gulls and terns. Occurs close inshore singly or in small groups. 46 cm.

2 LONGTAILED SKUA *Stercorarius longicaudus*. Uncommon summer visitor. Adults in summer unmistakable, with greyish backs and very long, pointed tail-projections. Adults in winter and immatures more difficult to distinguish from previous species, the tail-projections being absent, but are smaller, more tern-like in flight, have *heavily barred flanks and vent*, longer, thinner wings and proportionately longer tail. Less parasitic than other skuas and regularly scavenge at trawlers with Sabine's Gulls (overleaf) in western Cape waters. 55 cm (including central tail-feathers).

3 POMARINE SKUA *Stercorarius pomarinus*. Uncommon summer visitor. Larger than Arctic Skua (1), approaching size of Kelp Gull (page 54). Broader wings, bulkier body and longer tailed appearance also help to distinguish it from Arctic Skua. In breeding plumage central tail-feathers project 4-8 cm and are blunt and twisted; pale (a) and dark (b) morphs occur. Usually in pairs or small groups which chase gulls and terns. 50 cm.

4 SOUTH POLAR SKUA *Catharacta maccormicki*. Rare vagrant. Pale morph unmistakable with creamy-grey head and body contrasting with dark brown upper-wings and back; less common dark morph and immatures difficult to distinguish from next species but are generally smaller, more compact, with smaller bills and heads. At close range feathering at base of bill paler than rest of head. Occurs singly at sea and chases Cape Gannets (previous page) at trawlers. Common in pack-ice and on ice-shelf. 52 cm.

5 SUBANTARCTIC SKUA *Catharacta antarctica*. Common all-year visitor. Superficially like a juvenile Kelp Gull (page 54) but larger, darker, with conspicuous white flashes at base of primaries. Distinguished from all small skuas by bulky, broad-winged appearance and short, wedge-shaped tail; cf. previous species. Usually singly at sea but gathers in flocks at trawlers. Summer breeder on the Tristan group, Marion and Prince Edward Islands. 58 cm.

52

Gulls. A well-known group of scavenging sea and shore birds, most with white underparts and grey or black upperparts. Their tails are rounded or shallowly forked, their bills and feet yellowish or reddish. Gulls do not dive into the water, but pluck offal or refuse from the surface or from land. Flocks make loud screaming sounds when feeding.

1 HARTLAUB'S GULL *Larus hartlaubii*. Common to abundant resident. Slightly smaller than Greyheaded Gull (5). In breeding plumage differs in having only traces of a grey hood, *dark eyes* and deeper red bill and legs; at other times head entirely white. Immatures also have all-white head plus dark brown bill and legs and show only a few spots on tail-tip. Individuals and flocks scavenge in coastal regions. The common small gull in the Cape, sometimes breeding on beachfront rooftops. 38 cm.

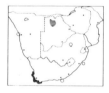

2 FRANKLIN'S GULL *Larus pipixcan*. Rare summer vagrant. Breeding adults have all-black heads with white eyelids, rosy flush on breast and diagnostic grey wings, with a white bar across the wing separating grey from black tip. In non-breeding adults head is grizzled black and white. Immatures have dark mantle and wings, white underparts and rump, broad black tip to tail and dark smudges on nape. Solitary or in company with other gulls. 33 cm.

3 SABINE'S GULL *Larus sabini*. Common summer visitor. The only small gull in our region with *all-black forewings and forked tail*. Smaller than Hartlaub's Gull (1) and very tern-like in flight. In breeding plumage with all-dark grey head and, at close range, black bill with yellow tip. Non-breeding adults and immatures lack dark grey heads, but have a dark patch on napes and hind necks. Singly or in very large flocks at sea, rarely onshore. 33 cm.

4 BLACKHEADED GULL *Larus ridibundus*. Rare vagrant. Dark chocolate-brown head of breeding adult unmistakable. Differs from next species and Hartlaub's Gull (1) also in smaller size, shorter, thinner bill, much greater expanse of white on forewing and white underwing. In non-breeding plumage head is all-white with black spot behind eye. Singly in company with next species. 35-8 cm.

5 GREYHEADED GULL *Larus cirrocephalus*. Common to abundant resident. Breeding adults have all-grey hood, pale yellow eyes and bright red bills and legs; non-breeding adults have a grey smudge on the ear-coverts only, cf. Hartlaub's Gull (1). Immatures have the frontal half of the head pale grey with a darker ear-patch which extends over the crown, plus a dark bill; see illustration. A gull of our inland waters (where they breed) and coasts. 42 cm.

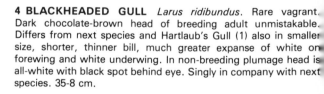

6 BLACKLEGGED KITTIWAKE *Rissa tridactyla*. Rare vagrant. *Yellow bill*, grey upper-wings with small black tip diagnostic of adults. Immatures very similar to Sabine's Gull (3) but larger, lack the forked tail and have a dark bar across hind neck, plus conspicuous open M pattern across upper-wings. Solitary at sea or in company with Sabine's Gulls. 41 cm.

1 KELP GULL (SOUTHERN BLACKBACKED GULL) *Larus dominicanus.* Very common resident. Adults have dark eyes and whitish-yellow feet; cf. next species. Immatures initially mottled dark brown all over with paler barred rump (could be mistaken for a skua (page 51) but *lacking white patches at primary bases*); with age become paler, going through mottled brown and white stages with dark brown legs. Singly or in small groups scavenging along coasts, especially harbours; rarely inland. 60 cm

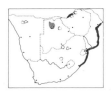

2 LESSER BLACKBACKED GULL *Larus fuscus.* Uncommon visitor. Very similar to previous species but smaller and more slender, with wings projecting well beyond end of tail, bill less robust, thinner and more slender, *eyes pale straw colour* (not dark), legs and feet bright chrome-yellow. Immatures with similar plumage sequence to previous species but generally paler, with same slender shape as adults and flesh-coloured (not dark brown) legs and feet. Singly or in small groups at river estuaries and inland waters. 53-6 cm.

HERRING GULL see page 444.

Skimmers. Family RYNCHOPIDAE.

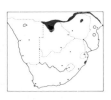

3 AFRICAN SKIMMER *Rynchops flavirostris.* Fairly common localised resident. Brown and white tern-like birds with distinctive bill structure, this and feeding action diagnostic. Immatures have streaked foreheads, buff-edged feathers on upperparts and blackish bill with yellow base. Feed by flying low over the water's surface with the long lower mandible immersed in skimming action. Rest on sandbanks. Small flocks on large, permanent rivers, lakes and lagoons. 38 cm.

Terns differ from gulls in more agile flight, more slender proportions and, in most species, deeply forked tails. The majority feed at sea, plunge-diving for fish, a few (the marsh terns) feed mainly on insects caught in dipping flight or plucked from the surface of inland ponds, lakes and inland rivers. Bills and feet red, yellow or black.

4 ROYAL TERN *Sterna maxima.* Rare vagrant. Differs from very similar Swift Tern (overleaf) in black cap extending to bill in breeding plumage and orange (not yellow) bill; in non-breeding plumage by almost white head, orange bill and paler grey back colour. Solitary on coasts, sometimes in company with Swift Terns. 48-50 cm.

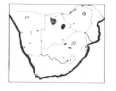

5 CASPIAN TERN *Hydroprogne caspia.* Common resident. Largest tern in our region. Massive red bill and overall size render this tern unmistakable. In pairs or small parties at coastal lagoons and large inland waters. 52 cm.

1 Ja

Jb

1

1

2

3 J

4 N-Br Br

5 N-Br Br

56

1 LITTLE TERN *Sterna albifrons*. This and the Damara Tern (overleaf) are the smallest terns in our region. In breeding plumage distinguished from the Damara Tern by well-defined white forehead, yellow legs and black-tipped yellow bill; in non-breeding and immature plumage by shorter black bill, darker grey back and, in flight, by dark leading edge to wings which contrasts with pale secondaries. Has very fast wing-beats and frequently hovers when feeding. Small flocks at coast. 24 cm.

2 BLACKNAPED TERN *Sterna sumatrana*. Rare vagrant. Intermediate in size between the previous species and Common Tern (overleaf). A small, very pale tern with diagnostic black line running from eyes which broadens to form black patch on nape. In flight, first primary feather noticeably black. Immatures resemble previous species but are larger, have longer, slightly decurved bill and pink flush on breast if seen at close range. Associates with Little and Common Terns on coast. 33 cm.

3 GULLBILLED TERN *Gelochelidon nilotica*. Rare vagrant. Similar in size to next species, but differs in having a thick, stubby, black bill unlike that of any other tern. At rest reveals unusually long legs and stands higher than other terns. Occurs mostly over inland waters and feeds like the marsh terns (page 60), often pursuing insects. 38 cm.

4 SANDWICH TERN *Sterna sandvicensis*. Common summer visitor. Much larger than Common Tern (overleaf), its back paler than other similar-sized terns. Differs from previous species in a much slimmer appearance and long thin bill, *black with a yellow tip*. Coastal, occurs in small groups, feeds just offshore and rests on beaches. 40 cm.

5 LESSER CRESTED TERN *Sterna bengalensis*. Common summer visitor. Similar in size to previous species, but with darker back and *orange bill*. Differs from next species in its smaller size and orange bill, from much larger Royal Tern (previous page) in size and darker grey back. Feeds over estuaries and open sea in small numbers. 40 cm.

6 SWIFT TERN (GREATER CRESTED TERN) *Sterna bergii*. Common resident. Intermediate in size between Caspian Tern (previous page) and Sandwich Tern (4). Bill colour *yellow*, not orange as in previous species and Royal Tern (previous page). Immatures have heavily barred back and tail, pale yellow bill and sometimes yellow legs. Occurs in small groups in coastal waters, roosts on beaches and estuaries. 50 cm.

58

1 DAMARA TERN *Sterna balaenarum.* Uncommon resident. Small size and all-black cap diagnostic of breeding plumage; at other times differs from Little Tern (previous page) in longer, slightly downturned bill and paler grey back, the body shape dumpier; at long range appears almost white, cf. Little Tern. Small groups on Atlantic coast, feeding offshore and in bays and estuaries. 23 cm.

2 WHITECHEEKED TERN *Sterna repressa.* Rare vagrant. In breeding plumage almost identical to Antarctic Tern (5), differing in back, rump and tail being uniform dark grey, otherwise difficult to tell from next species, but is slightly smaller, a much darker uniform grey above and retains much grey on underparts. Flies like a marsh tern (overleaf). Occurs singly in roosts of Common Terns. 33 cm.

3 COMMON TERN *Sterna hirundo.* Abundant summer visitor. Differs from next two species in longer bill and noticeably longer legs when at rest; in flight in non-breeding plumage by grey rump and tail (not white as in Antarctic and Arctic Terns) and by inner primaries *only* being translucent. Note black tip to red bill in breeding plumage. Occurs in thousands offshore, roosting in estuaries and on beaches. 35 cm.

4 ARCTIC TERN *Sterna paradisaea.* Common summer visitor. Differs from Common Tern (3) in having very short legs and shorter, thinner bill. In flight in non-breeding plumage grey back contrasts with white rump and tail while *all primaries appear translucent*, and differs from previous species in much whiter appearance, thinner bill and more buoyant flight. Frequents roosts of Common Terns on beaches and estuaries. 35 cm.

5 ANTARCTIC TERN *Sterna vittata.* Common winter visitor. Breeding plumage unmistakable: all-dark grey with long, white cheek-stripe and black cap. Differs from rare Whitecheeked Tern (2) by white (not grey) rump and tail and from next species by darker grey colour, plumper body and thicker, more robust bill. Non-breeding plumage retains much of the grey underparts, bill remains dark red with black at tip and along ridges. Immatures heavily barred buff on mantle. Roosts on rocky shorelines and sandy beaches, feeds far out to sea. Breeds on Tristan group, Marion and Prince Edward Islands. 38 cm.

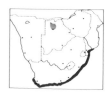

6 ROSEATE TERN *Sterna dougallii.* Uncommon resident. Differs from all other small terns in much paler back and red bill with dark tip. In breeding plumage breast is suffused with pink but looks white at distance. Tail-streamers very long in this species. Singly or in small groups at coast and found in Common Tern roosts. 38 cm.

7 FAIRY TERN (WHITE TERN) *Gygis alba.* Status uncertain. A small, all-white tern, sedentary on equatorial islands. Not recorded on the African mainland and its occurrence in Southern Africa is considered unlikely; past records suspect. 30 cm.

59

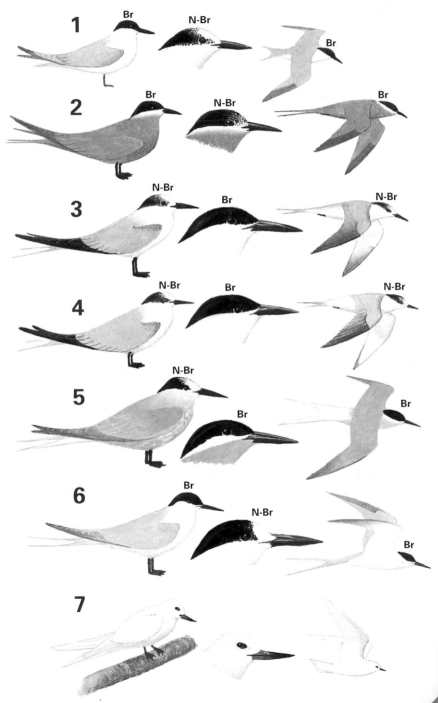

1 Br N-Br Br

2 Br N-Br Br

3 N-Br Br N-Br

4 N-Br Br N-Br

5 N-Br Br Br

6 Br N-Br Br

7

1 SOOTY TERN *Sterna fuscata*. Uncommon visitor. Very like next species but has dark brown (not grey-brown) back and small triangular white forehead patch with no white stripe over the eyes. Immatures are sooty-brown above and below with buff speckling on back, pale vent and white outer tail-feathers. The call is a harsh 'wekawek'. Normally seen only in small numbers after cyclonic weather in the Indian Ocean. 42 cm.

2 BRIDLED TERN *Sterna anaethetus*. Rare vagrant. Slightly smaller than previous species, differing in grey-brown back and white on forehead narrower, extending as white eyebrow stripe above and behind eyes. Immatures are white below, upperparts barred buff (not speckled). Occurs on east coast with Sooty Terns following cyclones. 38 cm.

3 COMMON NODDY *Anous stolidus*. Rare vagrant. Cf. next species; main differences between these two terns lies in size, bill length and extent of white on crown; see head illustrations. Occurs singly and is normally mobbed by Hartlaub's Gulls, which mistake it for a skua. Summer breeder on the Tristan group. 41 cm.

4 LESSER NODDY *Anous tenuirostris*. Rare vagrant. Differs from the previous species in size, bill and white of crown; see head illustrations. Immatures very like adults but have whiter foreheads. Occurs on east coast in Common Tern roosts after cyclones. 36 cm.

Marsh terns. Small terns of mainly inland waters. Fly with buoyant action, feed on insects taken from the water's surface, and make floating nests on inland ponds.

5 BLACK TERN *Chlidonias niger*. Uncommon summer visitor. In non-breeding plumage differs from other marsh terns in slightly smaller size, generally much darker appearance, the rump and tail being uniform with back, more extensive black on head and diagnostic black smudges on sides of breast. Rarely seen inland over fresh water; occurs on coasts alongside Common Terns (previous page) and feeds at sea. 23 cm.

6 WHISKERED TERN *Chlidonias hybridus*. Uncommon resident. Unmistakable in breeding plumage, differing from Whitecheeked Tern (previous page) in short tail and white vent and from Antarctic Tern (previous page) by short grey (not white) tail. In non-breeding plumage differs from other marsh terns in less extensive black on head, thicker, heavier bill and less buoyant flight. Occurs in small numbers over fresh water. 23 cm.

7 WHITEWINGED TERN (WHITEWINGED BLACK TERN) *Chlidonias leucopterus*. Common summer visitor. Unmistakable in breeding plumage. In non-breeding plumage differs from Black Tern (5) in paler head, grey rump, tail paler than back and lack of dark smudges on sides of breast. Occurs over fresh waters, sometimes in large numbers. 23 cm.

PELICANS

Frigatebirds see page 452.

Pelicans. Family PELECANIDAE. Huge, white waterbirds with large bodies, short legs with webbed feet, long necks, long bills and a naked distensible pouch beneath the lower mandible. They catch fish by gathering in flocks and driving the shoals into shallow waters where they are scooped up in their bill-pouches. Walk awkwardly but soar effortlessly, sometimes to great heights.

1 PINKBACKED PELICAN *Pelecanus rufescens.* Uncommon, localised resident. Adults in non-breeding plumage have grey upperparts and greyish-white heads and underparts, the bill pale yellow with a pink tip, legs buffy-yellow; in flight told from the next species by greyish underwing and dark grey (not black) flight feathers. Adults in breeding condition have the bill pouch rich yellow surmounted by a pink edge to the upper mandible, the legs and feet rich orange-yellow; at close range pinkish feathers can be seen on the back. Immatures have rust-brown head, neck and upperparts, white underparts, pale yellow bill and pouch; see illustrations. Breeding populations occur from Zululand northwards and in the Okavango Delta of northern Botswana; a vagrant elsewhere. 135 cm.

2 WHITE PELICAN *Pelecanus onocrotalus.* Common, localised resident. Adults in non-breeding plumage told from the previous species by larger size and all-white appearance; the upper mandible is pink and grey, the pouch yellow, legs yellow. In flight the underwings are white contrasting with *black* flight feathers. Adults in breeding condition have a pink flush to the body and a yellow patch on the upper breast; the upper mandible remains pink and grey and the pouch yellow, the legs and feet pink. Immatures have heads and necks dusky in various degrees (darkest when young), dark brown wings and tail, the underparts yellowish as illustrated. Occurs in flocks on coastal islands (including man-made guano islands), estuaries, bays, lagoons and occasionally on large dams; locally common in the western Cape, Walvis Bay and Swakopmund in Namibia and in the Okavango Delta of northern Botswana. 180 cm.

1

J

N-Br

Br

Br

2

N-Br

J

64

Cormorants. Family PHALACROCORACIDAE. Webbed-footed, long-necked, hook-billed, fish- and frog-eating waterbirds, which hunt their prey under water and surface to swallow it. Swim with body partially submerged and habitually stand out of water with wings outspread to dry. (1-3) marine, (4-6) mainly fresh water. Silent birds.

1 CAPE CORMORANT *Phalacrocorax capensis.* Common or abundant resident. Breeding adults told by entirely glossy green-black plumage, head *without* crest, orange-yellow bill-base; non-breeding adults and immatures dusky brown, paler on belly. Single birds and flocks (sometimes thousands) in coastal waters, roosting on offshore islands. Habitually fly in long lines over the sea and fish in flocks. Winter visitor to Natal coast. 64 cm.

2 BANK CORMORANT *Phalacrocorax neglectus.* Common resident. Told by heavy-bodied appearance, crested head and usually (not always) a white rump; wings dark brown, rest black with bronze sheen. Immatures duller black. Single birds or small groups in coastal waters, especially standing on small islands and offshore rocks. 75 cm.

3 CROWNED CORMORANT *Phalacrocorax coronatus.* Fairly common resident. A marine version of the next species and recognised by its overall *blacker appearance*, permanent crest all year and shorter tail. Immatures are brown. Singly and in small groups on rocky coastlines and coastal islands, occasionally lagoons. 54 cm.

4 REED CORMORANT *Phalacrocorax africanus.* Common resident. Longer-tailed than the previous species. Males, with small crest on forehead, all black except for brown-speckled wings, females browner with the underparts off-white, blotched brown; both sexes have the bill and facial skin yellow or red, eyes red. Immatures are brownish with *off-white* (never white) underparts. Singly or in groups on any inland water, especially dams and sewage-farm pans. 60 cm.

5 WHITEBREASTED CORMORANT *Phalacrocorax carbo.* Common or localised resident. Identified by large size and white throat to breast or, in immatures, entirely white underparts, *much whiter* than the immature Reed Cormorant (4). In adults the eyes are green, the bill pale grey with a darker culmen and the facial skin yellow. Singly or in groups on coastal rocks, islands and estuaries, plus large inland waters where they often perch or nest in dead trees. 90 cm.

Darters. Family ANHINGIDAE.

6 DARTER *Anhinga melanogaster.* Common resident. Distinguished from cormorants by longer, thinner neck with a characteristic 'kink', straight (not hooked) bill, more rufous colouring and generally slender appearance. Males are blacker than females and have long beige plumes on their mantles when breeding, the bill grey. Females generally browner, their bills creamy-white; immatures similar to females as illustrated, head and neck markings indistinct. Swims with only the head and neck above water and perches with outstretched wings after swimming. Singly or in small groups on large inland waters. 79 cm.

Herons. Family ARDEIDAE. Water-associated birds with long bills and necks and long legs, the white ones known as egrets. When breeding, many species have long, filamentous plumes on their backs or lower breast, or on both, while others have more or less permanent long plumes on their napes. In flight their heads are tucked into their shoulders, thus differing from storks, ibises and cranes. They seldom soar. Many herons are solitary in habit and secretive, others are gregarious and much in evidence. Most perch in trees and nest in reeds or even on the ground. All have voices of a harsh, squawking nature heard usually when flushed. The four comparative silhouettes on the page opposite represent A: Dwarf Bittern (1); B: Squacco Heron (page 68); C: Little Egret (page 72); D: Grey Heron (page 74).

1 DWARF BITTERN (RAIL HERON) *Ixobrychus sturmii*. Uncommon summer resident and visitor. Adults unmistakable with slate-grey upperparts and heavily streaked underparts but look all-dark at a distance; orange-yellow legs and feet hang down in flight. Immatures with rufous underparts and rufous-tipped feathers to the upperparts, differing from other immature small herons in this and orange-yellow legs. The flight is direct and pigeon-like. Usually solitary (sometimes breeds in loose colonies) and largely crepuscular or nocturnal. Frequents well-wooded rivers and bushes or thickets, standing in floodwaters. When disturbed may adopt a 'sky-pointing' posture; see illustration. Perches in a tree when flushed. Nomadic. 25 cm.

2 LITTLE BITTERN *Ixobrychus minutus*. Uncommon resident and visitor. Bold markings of males unmistakable; females recognised by buffy neck and black cap. Immatures differ from those of previous species mainly in paler, less rufous underparts and olive (not orange-yellow) legs; from immatures of the next species by tawny (not dark) folded wings. Solitary or scattered birds in reed-beds or sedges. A diurnal species. Difficult to flush, 'sky-pointing' to avoid detection. Nomadic. 26 cm.

3 GREENBACKED HERON *Butorides striatus*. Common resident. In the field upperparts appear grey-green, the feathers all clearly edged creamy, sides of neck plus flanks grey, cap black; when taking off yellow feet prominent. Immatures identified by dark upperparts with *whitish spots on folded wings*; cf. immatures of (1) and (2). A common small heron, usually singly on well-wooded rivers, large dams, pans and estuaries or lagoons with mangroves. Active by day, hunting from a low-hanging branch, or dead tree in water or on shoreline. Perches in a tree when flushed. 41 cm.

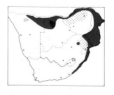

4 RUFOUSBELLIED HERON *Butorides rufiventris*. Uncommon summer resident and visitor. A robust, all-dark heron, adults with pale yellow bill (upper mandible grey), facial skin and legs when not breeding. When breeding the bill, facial skin and legs become coral-pink as illustrated. Immatures have the upperparts with buff-edged feathers. Nomadic, solitary and secretive on secluded waters with ample fringing and surface vegetation. When flushed perches in a tree or drops into dense vegetation. 58 cm.

67

A

B

C

D

J

1

♀

J

♂

2

J

3

Br

4

N-Br

68

1 MADAGASCAR SQUACCO HERON *Ardeola idae*. Very rare winter vagrant. Occurs only in non-breeding plumage differing from next species in much darker brown upperparts, neck-streaks broader and bolder; in flight these contrast strongly with white wings. Bill greenish with black tip and culmen. Recorded once in eastern Zimbabwe, possibly more frequent in Mozambique; regular in East Africa. 47 cm.

2 SQUACCO HERON *Ardeola ralloides*. Fairly common resident. In non-breeding plumage differs from previous species by paler, less contrasting upperparts, the bill yellowish with blackish culmen, legs normally pale yellow but pinkish-red for a few days when breeding. In flight looks like a white egret unless upperparts visible. Solitary at lakes, lagoons, sewage ponds and streams. 43 cm.

3 BLACK EGRET *Egretta ardesiaca*. Uncommon to locally common resident. Differs from the next species in more robust proportions, uniform overall colouring and dark legs with *bright yellow feet*. Has unique habit of forming a canopy with its wings when fishing. Single birds or groups, sometimes large flocks, at the fringes of lakes, lagoons, flood-pans and dams, less often on rivers. Nomadic. 66 cm.

4 SLATY EGRET *Egretta vinaceigula.* Uncommon, localised resident. In proportions like a slate-grey Little Egret (page 72). Distinguished from the previous species by yellow *lower legs* and feet and, at close range, by buff foreneck plus yellow eyes and facial skin. Plumes on the nape sometimes absent. Seen mostly singly in shallow, well-vegetated flood-pans and river backwaters of the Okavango Delta and Chobe River regions of northern Botswana; a vagrant elsewhere. 60 cm.

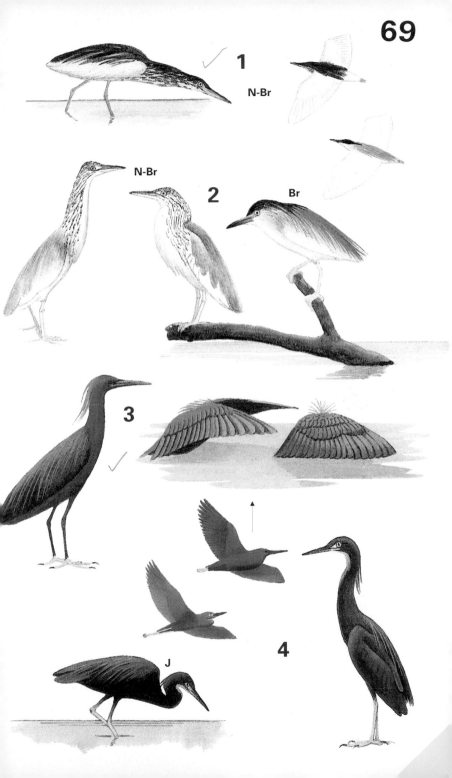

1 N-Br

2 N-Br Br

3

4 J

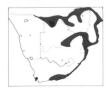

1 WHITEBACKED NIGHT HERON *Gorsachius leuconotus.* Uncommon resident. Black hood, yellow facial markings and legs plus rufous plumage diagnostic. White back plumes are present at all ages. When alarmed into flight makes a toad-like 'kraak'. Singly or in pairs, sparsely distributed on quiet rivers and dams where secretive, hiding by day in dense waterside vegetation and emerging only at night. 53 cm.

2 BLACKCROWNED NIGHT HERON *Nycticorax nycticorax.* Common resident and visitor. Adults have characteristic black cap and back contrasting with white and grey wings and underparts; nape plumes may be absent. Immatures differ from adults of the next species in being smaller, with orange eyes and white spots to the tips of the feathers of the upperparts. Single birds, pairs or groups occur on river backwaters, dams and lagoons, roosting by day in trees or waterside vegetation, emerging late afternoon in preparation for nocturnal hunting. Nomadic when not breeding. 56 cm.

BITTERN *Botaurus stellaris.* Rare resident and visitor. Similar to the immature of the previous species but larger with a more thickset appearance, more heavily streaked overall, with black cap and yellow or red-brown eyes. In flight has a much greater wingspan than the Blackcrowned Night Heron and the entire foot protrudes beyond the tail. Normal take-off call is 'squark', otherwise makes a booming call day or night during the breeding season (summer). Solitary in seasonal vleis, permanent marshes and streams in grassland; highly secretive. When alarmed adopts an upright, 'sky-pointing' stance. Is not easily flushed. 64 cm.

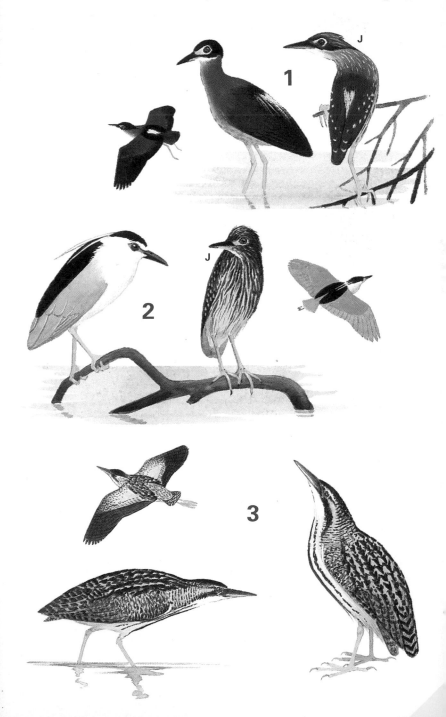

EGRETS

1 CATTLE EGRET *Bubulcus ibis*. Very common resident. Buff feathers present on breeding adults October–March only. Bill short, yellow or coral, legs the same, feet dusky. Immatures differ from next species in smaller size, shorter, thicker neck and *black feet*. Small flocks attendant on grazing cattle or wild animals in reserves, or flying to and from roosts. In large numbers when breeding in reeds or trees over water. Most common in summer. 54 cm.

2 LITTLE EGRET *Egretta garzetta*. Fairly common resident. Larger, longer-necked, more slenderly proportioned than previous species, bill and legs longer and black, *feet yellow*; head plumes constant, breast and back plumes only when breeding. Immatures lack head plumes. Solitary on quiet inland waters, estuaries and coastal pools, always near water. Stands quietly in shallows or walks forward slowly, stealthily hunting. 64 cm.

3 YELLOWBILLED EGRET *Egretta intermedia*. Uncommon resident. Larger than the previous two species, more heavily built, but smaller than the next. Plumes usually absent or reduced when not breeding. Bill normally yellow (orange-red briefly when breeding), *upper legs yellow* (reddish briefly when breeding), lower legs and feet blackish-green. The neck has the characteristic 'kink' of the larger herons and, in profile, the long lower neck-feathers tend to stick out; cf. next species. Often confused with the next species but can be told by the short gape which finishes below the eye (not behind it). Usually solitary on quiet, well-vegetated pans and floodlands. 68 cm.

4 GREAT WHITE EGRET *Casmerodius albus*. Fairly common resident. Large, long-necked, long-legged egret with normally orange-yellow bill, thus frequently misidentified as the previous species but is much larger with *entirely black legs* and feet. The line of the gape extends behind the eye; cf. (3). For a few weeks when breeding the bill is black, often with yellow base, and filamentous plumes are present on the back. Single birds are usually seen standing motionless in shallows of large rivers, dams, estuaries and flood-pans. 95 cm.

73

Br N-Br J 1

N-Br Br 2

Br N-Br 3 4

30 cm

1 GREY HERON *Ardea cinerea.* Common resident. At rest adults differ from the Blackheaded Heron (4) in having a white crown above a broad black band that extends from forehead to nape; head and neck otherwise white; bill and legs yellow (reddish briefly when breeding). In flight shows *entirely grey underwings.* Immatures are much paler than adults and immatures of (4), also differing in the yellow (not grey) bill and legs. Solitary, feeding in the shallows of quiet dams, pans, rivers, lagoons and estuaries; may sometimes forage in coastal rock pools. Stands motionless for long periods or creeps forward stealthily in crouched attitude. 100 cm.

2 PURPLE HERON *Ardea purpurea.* Fairly common resident. Often confused with the next species but much smaller, more slender, the neck thin and snake-like with a thin bill. Immatures less brightly coloured about the neck, markings less clearly defined. Solitary and secretive, preferring the shelter of reeds and other emergent vegetation fringing quiet dams, pans and marsh pools. Nomadic. 89 cm.

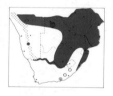

3 GOLIATH HERON *Ardea goliath.* Uncommon resident. Larger than all other herons, more robustly proportioned, with slate-grey upperparts and rich rufous underparts. Flies with very slow wing-beats. Immatures browner above, whitish streaked brown below. Singly or in pairs on large stretches of water, rivers, lakes, pans and estuaries. Hunts in deeper waters than most other herons, standing motionless for long periods or walking slowly. 140 cm.

4 BLACKHEADED HERON *Ardea melanocephala.* Common resident. Differs from the superficially similar Grey Heron (1) in entirely black (or dark blue-grey) top to the head and back of the neck, plus slate-grey bill and legs; in flight told by *black and grey underwings.* Immatures greyer than immatures of (1), bill and legs pale grey (not yellow). Solitary or in scattered groups in grasslands (especially pastures), grassy road verges, farmlands and marshes. *Seldom feeds in water* but roosts and breeds in trees or in reeds over water. 97 cm.

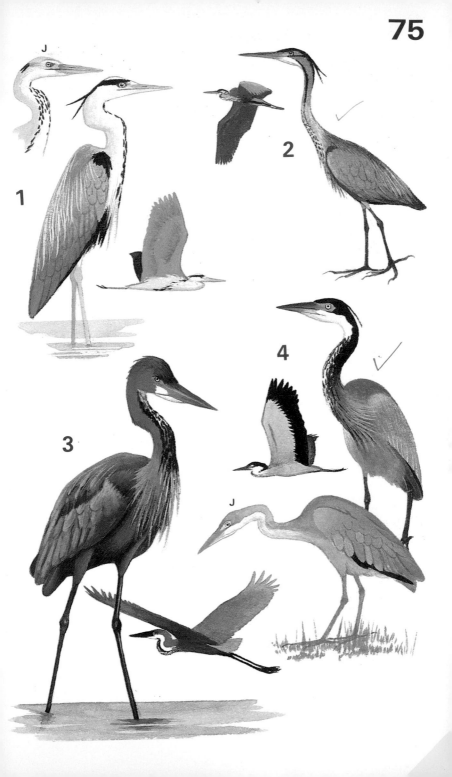

Storks. Family CICONIIDAE. Large to very large long-legged and long-necked birds with straight, stout bills. Colouring mostly black and white or blackish. Storks walk with stately gait and frequently rest on the ground with the lower part of their legs stretched forward; see illustration of immature Marabou. In flight the neck is stretched out (unlike herons, which fly with the neck retracted) and the legs usually trail down at a slight angle to the body. Most members of this family sometimes soar to great heights during the heat of the day, many are communal in habits and most frequent water or damp places to some extent. Food ranges from large insects, reptiles, frogs and other waterlife to carrion in one species. They have no voice except guttural sounds and hisses made at the nest, but bill-clapping is used as a greeting between pairs. The nests are large stick structures placed in trees, on rocks and cliffs or on the ground, according to species.

1 SADDLEBILLED STORK (SADDLEBILL) *Ephippiorhynchus senegalensis*. Uncommon resident. A large, strikingly coloured stork unlikely to be confused with any other. Immatures with grey instead of black markings, the white areas mottled with black, bill dull, blackish. Singly or in pairs in the shallows of large rivers, lakes, dams and floodplains or in marshes. 145 cm.

2 MARABOU STORK *Leptoptilos crumeniferus*. Uncommon or locally common visitor and resident. Huge, bare-headed, bare-necked stork with a distensible fleshy pouch on the lower foreneck. Unlike other storks, they fly with their necks tucked in. Immatures, as illustrated, with a woolly covering to the heads. Generally in groups of a few birds, sometimes larger flocks, frequently associating with vultures at animal carcasses and refuse dumps. Mostly found in wildlife sanctuaries where they congregate at kills or around camps. Also gather on river sandbanks to bathe and rest. Sometimes soar to great heights. Otherwise spend much time standing inactive or perched. 152 cm.

♀

♂

1

2

J

STORKS

1 WHITE STORK *Ciconia ciconia*. Common summer visitor and resident. Unmistakable, large black and white stork with red bill and legs. Seen singly or in small groups. In summer large flocks feed in grasslands, farmlands and bushveld, often mixing with Abdim's Storks (3). Flocks often soar and travel at great heights on hot days. May suddenly appear in a district and remain a few days to feed, then depart, this behaviour especially linked to infestations of agricultural pests. Summer influxes vary from year to year. 117 cm.

2 BLACK STORK *Ciconia nigra*. Uncommon resident. Similar to the next species but differing from it in larger size, red bill and longer, red legs. Immatures have the bill and legs yellowish-green, the plumage duller black. Occurs *singly or in pairs* but groups sometimes gather to roost in trees at night. Frequents cliffs and gorges when breeding, otherwise feeds on rivers, dams and estuaries. 122 cm.

3 ABDIM'S STORK (WHITEBELLIED STORK) *Ciconia abdimii*. Common summer visitor. Smaller, shorter-legged than the previous species, the bill tawny, face blue, legs pink with red joints and feet. In flight this and the previous species difficult to identify one from the other unless seen at close range, but this species usually in flocks, sometimes in hundreds. Feeds in grassland, agricultural lands and bushveld, often mixing with White Storks (1). Flocks soar to great heights when moving and, like the White Stork, move about in response to insect outbreaks. 76 cm.

1

2

3

1 YELLOWBILLED STORK *Mycteria ibis.* Fairly common to locally common resident and visitor. Told by white plumage, yellow bill and red face, forehead and legs; the white plumage has a pink tinge when breeding. Immatures have greyish plumage, the bill grey with a yellow base while the red on the head is lacking; see inset. Small groups or large flocks occur on flood-pans, large rivers, lakes and estuaries, usually near woodlands. Feeds by wading and probing with the bill partly opened beneath the water while constantly moving. 97 cm.

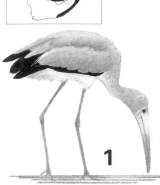

J

1

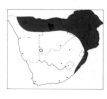

2 WOOLLYNECKED STORK *Ciconia episcopus.* Fairly common to very common resident and visitor. Identified by woolly white neck and head with black face; undertail-coverts *project beyond the tail.* Immatures similar but duller, the bill horn-coloured. Usually singly but large influxes during summer at lakes, flood-pans and estuaries in well-wooded regions. 86 cm.

3 OPENBILLED STORK *Anastomus lamelligerus.* Uncommon to locally common resident and visitor. A small stork appearing all-black with a tawny bill; at close range the gap between the mandibles is visible; this is lacking in the young. Singly or in flocks at large rivers, floodlands and pans in wooded regions. Feeds on water snails caught while wading. Rests at the waterside or perches in trees. Nomadic; flocks on the move soar to great heights. 94 cm.

Hamerkop. Family SCOPIDAE.

4 HAMERKOP *Scopus umbretta.* Common resident. Small, dull-brown waterbird with a large, backward-projecting crest and heavy, conical black bill; sexes alike, immatures similar. In flight sometimes utters a nasal 'wek . . . wek . . . wek . . .'; at rest may make a wavering, high-pitched 'wek-wek-warrrrk' repeatedly. Singly, sometimes in groups when feeding, at almost any freshwater locality plus estuaries. Feeds in the shallows, shuffling its feet to disturb frogs and fish. At deeper waters of large lakes may hover briefly before swooping down to seize fish near the surface. Builds huge, domed nests in waterside trees (see illustration) or on cliffs. 56 cm.

81

Flamingoes. Family PHOENICOPTERIDAE. Occur in flocks of many thousands or singly, and the two species may be found together if the one outnumbers the other. They prefer shallow saline pans, dams and estuaries, as well as sheltered coastal bays, but are nomadic and remain in one place only for as long as conditions are suitable. Over most of the region they are infrequently seen. Both species have a honking call which, in flocks, sounds like a babbling. Immatures are grey-brown with a bill-pattern similar to adults.

1 LESSER FLAMINGO *Phoenicopterus minor*. Locally abundant resident and visitor. Its regular haunts are indicated on the map in solid red but it may occur temporarily anywhere within the shaded area. Distinguished by evenly coloured *dark maroon bill* which looks black at a distance; pinker, more evenly coloured than the Greater Flamingo. In flight the wing-coverts are mottled with dark red. 102 cm.

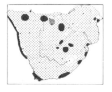

2 GREATER FLAMINGO *Phoenicopterus ruber*. Locally abundant resident and visitor. Its regular haunts are indicated on the map in solid red but it may occur temporarily anywhere within the shaded area. Distinguished by *pink bill with black tip;* in company with Lesser Flamingo appears taller and whiter. In flight the wing-coverts are an even scarlet. 140 cm.

Ibises and spoonbills. Family PLATALEIDAE. Fairly large waterbirds with longish legs, ibises with decurved bills, spoonbills with spatulate bills. All but the Hadeda Ibis are silent.

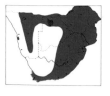

3 AFRICAN SPOONBILL *Platalea alba*. Fairly common resident. Distinguished from other white waterbirds by pink legs and pink, spoon-shaped bill. Immatures with wings and head streaked brown. Single birds or in groups on seasonal pans, floodplains, dams, lagoons and rivers. Nomadic when not breeding. 91 cm.

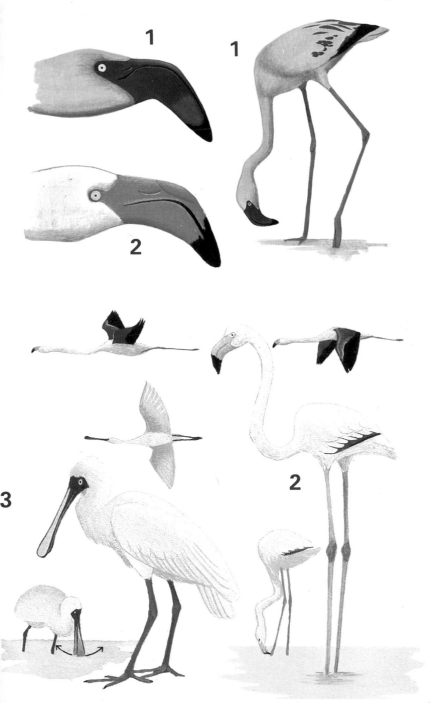

1

1

2

3

2

84

1 SACRED IBIS *Threskiornis aethiopicus.* Common resident. The curved black bill, black head, neck and legs contrast with otherwise white plumage; in immatures the black head and neck are speckled white, front of the neck white; see inset. Groups or flocks forage in marshy ground, dams, on shorelines, agricultural lands, rubbish dumps and in breeding colonies of other large birds. Migratory to some degree within Africa; most common in summer. 89 cm.

2 HADEDA IBIS *Bostrychia hagedash.* Common resident. Identified by heavy body with fairly short legs, decurved bill and iridescent pink shoulder plus white cheek-stripes; in flight shows heavy, broad wings. Immatures are dull, fluffy-headed. Very noisy, when perched or in flight make a raucous 'HA! ha-a-a . . . ha-ha-a-a . . .' or 'ha, ha, haadedaa', often several calling in unison; mostly early morning and evening. Usually two to six or more birds on damp ground, often near water or in vleis, plantations, agricultural lands, playing-fields and suburban gardens. Roost in tall trees and fly to and from feeding grounds early and late in the day. 76 cm.

3 BALD IBIS *Geronticus calvus.* Uncommon to locally common resident. Distinguished by bright red, bald head and bill, and pink legs, iridescent plumage appearing black at a distance. Immatures are duller, the head and neck covered in greyish feathers. Sometimes makes a high-pitched 'keeauw-klaup-klaup'. Small flocks frequent montane grasslands, breeding and roosting on cliffs. Also disperse to feed in grasslands, agricultural lands and burnt veld. 79 cm.

4 GLOSSY IBIS *Plegadis falcinellus.* Locally common resident and visitor. Slender, lighter-bodied than other ibises, bronze-brown with iridescent green wings when breeding; at other times the head and neck are flecked with white; see illustrations. Immatures are a paler brown, the throat whitish. Single birds or small flocks frequent flooded lands, farmlands, vleis, pans, sewage-disposal grounds and lake shores. 71 cm.

Finfoots. Family HELIORNITHIDAE.

5 AFRICAN FINFOOT *Podica senegalensis.* Uncommon resident. Differs from ducks and cormorants in bright orange-red bill and legs. Has no characteristic call. Solitary or in pairs on quiet, tree-fringed rivers where they swim quietly beneath the overhanging branches. Swim with much of the body submerged, head and neck stretched forward with each foot-stroke. Shy and retiring. If disturbed, fly low across the water paddling with their feet, which makes a distinctive splashing sound. Seldom fly. Roost at night on a low, overhanging branch. 63 cm.

85

86

Swans, geese and ducks. Family ANATIDAE. Most of our ducks are either migratory to some extent or locally nomadic, their movements being dictated by food, rainfall and breeding requirements. Many have marked sexual-plumage differences (sexual dimorphism) and all undergo a flightless period each year when they moult their wing-feathers entirely.

1 MUTE SWAN *Cygnus olor*. Rare. An exotic species of which a feral population lived for many years in the eastern Cape, but which appears to no longer exist as a viable breeding community. Birds seen now are probably from parks and private estates. A large, unmistakable white water bird with orange bill and black facial skin. Swims with neck arched, often with partially raised wings. Normally silent but will hiss in anger. 145-60 cm.

2 WHITEFACED DUCK *Dendrocygna viduata*. Common resident. Distinguished from female South African Shelduck (overleaf) by black head and neck, darker plumage and erect stance. Immatures have the face smudged brown. The call is a loud, shrill 'swee-swee-sweeoo', often by many birds in a flying flock. Flocks, often large, on large rivers, lakes, dams, estuaries, floodplains, sewage-disposal dams, especially those with surface and emergent vegetation. Spends much of the day on shorelines or sandbanks. 48 cm.

3 FULVOUS DUCK *Dendrocygna bicolor*. Fairly common resident. Cream-coloured flank feathers diagnostic. Immatures resemble adults. Less vocal than the previous species, two resonant notes repeated 'tsoo-ee'. Occurs in pairs or in small flocks on a variety of quiet waters, often shared with the previous species. Spends much time swimming during the day. 46 cm.

4 WHITEBACKED DUCK *Thalassornis leuconotus*. Uncommon resident. White back visible only in flight. Best told by pale spot at base of bill, sharply tapering bill with deep base and a humped back sloping down to submerged tail. Immatures resemble adults. Makes a soft whistle 'cur-wee'. In pairs or small groups on secluded pans, lagoons and dams with ample surface and emergent vegetation. Seldom seen out of water; dives readily. 43 cm.

2

3

4

88

1 PYGMY GOOSE *Nettapus auritus*. Locally common resident. Identified by small size, dark green upperparts and short, yellow bill. Immatures resemble females. Males make a soft twittering whistle 'choo-choo' or 'pee-wee' and a repeated, subdued 'tsu-tswi...tsu-tswi...'; females a weak quack and a twittering whistle. Pairs or groups on quiet, sheltered pans, dams and pools with clear water and waterlilies. When alert, remains motionless among the surface vegetation and is difficult to detect. Dives readily and perches in trees. 33 cm.

2 SOUTH AFRICAN SHELDUCK *Tadorna cana*. Common resident. A long-bodied duck with horizontal stance. Females differ from Whitefaced Duck (previous page) in grey (not black) head and neck; in flight both sexes differ from the next species in richer rufous body colouring and grey heads plus white face in female. Immatures are duller than adults. Females initially with white circles around the eyes, these extending over the face with maturity. Males utter a deep 'hoogh', 'how' or 'honk', the female alternating with a harsher 'hark'; while accompanying young, females hiss. Courting pairs are noisy and aggressive. Pairs or flocks frequent brackish pans, dams and lakes, large deep waters especially when in wing-moult, then diving if pursued. May also be seen away from water when breeding. Nomadic when not breeding. 64 cm.

3 EGYPTIAN GOOSE *Alopochen aegyptiacus*. Common resident. Distinguished from previous species by long neck, long pink legs and pink bill plus rufous eye-patches. Immatures are duller. Very noisy in social interactions, males making a husky wheezing sound, females a harsh, nasal, high-pitched 'hur-hur-hur-hur'. Both sexes extend their heads and necks when calling. Pairs occupy small waters or sections of rivers, but large numbers may gather on deep waters to moult wing-feathers or on sandbanks when large rivers are in spate. Often fly in evenings to communal grazing grounds. 71 cm.

4 SPURWINGED GOOSE *Plectropterus gambensis*. Common resident. Very large size and glossy black plumage diagnostic. Mature males have a fleshy caruncle on the forehead and a variable amount of white on the face and underparts, least in southern populations. In flight the prominent white forewings separate this species from the Knobbilled Duck (page 94). Immatures are brown, showing little or no white. Not very vocal; males utter a soft, high-pitched 'cherwit' in flight, either sex a four-syllable 'chi-chi-chi-chi'. Occurs in flocks in a variety of wetlands, especially favouring floodplains. They fly in V-formations or staggered lines and readily perch in dead trees. Very large numbers may gather on deep waters during the winter wing-moult, diving if pursued. 102 cm.

1 HOTTENTOT TEAL *Anas hottentota*. Common resident. Differs from the next species in very small size, grey-blue (not red) bill and absence of any speckling on the rear part of the body. When swimming the flank feathers usually overlap the wing to form a zigzag dividing line. Normally silent. Pairs and groups frequent shallow freshwater marshes, pans and dams, especially sewage-disposal waters. Spends much of day resting out of water. 35 cm.

2 REDBILLED TEAL *Anas erythrorhyncha*. Very common resident. Larger than the previous species, differing in pinkish-red bill and completely spotted body. In flight shows a creamy speculum. The few sounds made by this species are soft, audible only at close range. Frequently in large flocks on lakes, flood-plains, dams and sewage pans; smaller numbers or pairs during the rainy season. 48 cm.

3 SOUTHERN POCHARD *Netta erythrophthalma*. Common resident. Males differ from males of the next species in darker colouring, the head and back uniform, longer neck and more elegant proportions. Females recognised from female Maccoas by *whitish crescentic mark on sides of head* plus white throat and bill-base. In flight the white specula extend the full width of the wings. Has no distinctive calls. Pairs or flocks occur on deep fresh waters. 51 cm.

4 MACCOA DUCK *Oxyura maccoa*. Fairly common, localised resident. A small, squat species with a thick-based bill. Breeding males unmistakable. Females and males in non-breeding plumage differ from females of the previous species in *horizontal facial stripes* and squat appearance. Generally silent. Occurs on dams and lakes with extensive, fringing reed-beds, usually more females than males. Seldom seen out of the water. Swims low in the water with tail trailing, the tip submerged, or with tail stiffly erect. Males often swim with head and neck stretched forward, the neck inflated and the bill in the water making bubbles, tail erect. Both sexes dive frequently. 46 cm.

DUCKS

1 CAPE SHOVELLER *Anas smithii*. Common resident. Dull, brownish ducks identified by large, black, spatulate bill and yellow-orange legs; cf. next species. In flight shows a pale blue speculum. Immatures duller. Normally silent ducks but males sometimes utter an explosive 'rrar' or a series of quiet, hoarse 'cawick' sounds with rising inflection, sometimes interspersed with a fast, rattling 'rararara'; females may give a series of notes with downward inflection, a rippling chatter 'chachachachacha' or a persistent quacking. Pairs or flocks in shallows of tidal estuaries, lagoons, floodlands and sewage-disposal pans; indifferent to large, open waters. 53 cm.

2 EUROPEAN SHOVELLER *Anas clypeata.* Very rare visitor. Males most likely to occur in non-breeding plumage as illustrated; then differs from the previous species in larger, pale buff (not black) bill and paler overall appearance. Single birds and pairs occur occasionally in widely separated localities, mostly July-December. Males in breeding plumage are probably escapees from private wildfowl collections. 51 cm.

3 GARGANEY *Anas querquedula*. Very rare visitor. Males most likely to occur in eclipse plumage which resembles that of the female. A small, brownish duck with distinct streaks *above and below* the eyes; differs from female Maccoa Duck (previous page) by this and a more slender bill. Sits low in the water when swimming. Occurs occasionally in Zimbabwe, Botswana and Transvaal in December–March. 38 cm.

4 CAPE TEAL *Anas capensis*. Common resident. A small, pale-coloured duck with a pink, upturned bill; looks almost white at a distance. In flight shows a predominantly white speculum with a dark green central patch. Immatures resemble adults. Usually silent. In flocks—large flocks when in wing-moult—on shallow vleis, lagoons, salt-pans, sewage-disposal pans and tidal mud-flats with a preference for brackish waters and soda lakes. 46 cm.

DUCKS

1 PINTAIL *Anas acuta.* Very rare visitor. Males most likely to occur in eclipse plumage, resembling females. Told by slender proportions, dull grey bill and pale, grey-brown plumage; long tail may not be present. In flight appears pointed-winged, underbody, wing linings and trailing edge of secondaries white, upper-wings with green specula. May occur singly or in small groups on any inland waters. Recorded Zimbabwe and S.W. Transvaal in November–February. 51-66 cm.

2 AFRICAN BLACK DUCK *Anas sparsa.* Common resident. Characterised by dark grey-brown plumage with bold white spotting on wings and back, speculum green with white border. Immatures browner, spots buffy, belly barred white. When swimming appears short-necked, long-bodied. Most calls heard when pairs flying; females make persistent, loud quacking, males an almost imperceptible 'weep . . . weep . . . weep . . .'. During the daytime pairs inhabit streams and small rivers with stony bottoms (often in well-wooded valleys), moving to large, open waters at sunset to roost. 51-4 cm.

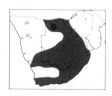

3 YELLOWBILLED DUCK *Anas undulata.* Very common resident. Bright yellow bill with black central patch diagnostic; feathers brown edged with white, broadly on flanks and underparts, giving ashy appearance; head and neck dusky. In flight shows bright green speculum. Immatures with feathers edged buffy, underparts more heavily spotted. No distinctive calls but on taking off females make loud, evenly spaced 'quacks'. Pairs and flocks on various open waters: estuaries, lakes, dams, flooded lands, pans and slow-running rivers with pools. In the dry season large numbers often congregate. 53-8 cm.

4 KNOBBILLED DUCK *Sarkidiornis melanotos.* Uncommon to locally common resident. Male (much larger than female) distinguished by glossy dark blue upperparts, white underparts, the head and neck well speckled black (washed yellow when breeding) and a large fleshy caruncle on forehead and bill. Female duller and lacking caruncle. Young birds quite different from adults: see below. In first year (a) has dark brown upperparts and pale buff underparts plus distinct eye-stripe; sub-adult (b) more like female but underparts orange-buff, heavier spotting on head and neck. A mostly silent species. Flocks, often large in the dry season, frequent marshes, temporary bushveld pans, floodplains and estuaries. Often perches in dead trees. 64-79 cm.

Grebes. Family PODICIPEDIDAE. Small to fairly large, almost tailless waterbirds. Feed beneath the surface by diving, remaining submerged 20-50 seconds. Seldom seen on land but fly long distances at night to new waters. Breeding and non-breeding plumages differ. Small chicks are striped on the upperparts, the head stripes remaining until nearly full-grown. Ride on parents' backs when small.

1 DABCHICK (LITTLE GREBE) *Tachybaptus ruficollis*. Common resident. Smaller than any duck. Rufous neck and creamy spot at base of bill diagnostic of breeding birds, at other times differ from the next species in dull (not white) underparts and dark eyes. The call is a descending, laughing trill. Single birds or loose groups occur on inland waters, seldom large rivers. Dives frequently and skitters across the water when chasing rivals. 20 cm.

2 BLACKNECKED GREBE *Podiceps nigricollis.* Locally common resident. Larger than the previous species, the black plumage and golden ear-coverts of adults in breeding plumage unmistakable; when not breeding differs from non-breeding Dabchick (1) in having a white throat and foreneck. The eyes are red at all times. Makes a quiet 'poo-eep' or a rapid chattering. Small groups on quiet saline waters or densely packed flocks in sheltered bays on the Atlantic coast. When preening habitually exposes white underparts by rolling to one side on the water. Highly nomadic. 28 cm.

3 GREAT CRESTED GREBE *Podiceps cristatus*. Uncommon resident. In non-breeding plumage differs from the previous species in white head with cap only black, darker ruby-red eyes, larger bill and larger overall size. Normally silent. Pairs occur on large inland waters bordered by low, emergent vegetation. On water, when preening, habitually exposes its white underparts as previous species. 50 cm.

Coot, gallinules, moorhens, crakes and rails. Family RALLIDAE. Small to fairly large, long-legged, large-footed, mainly freshwater-associated birds. A few species inhabit grasslands, vleis or lush forest undergrowth. Most water-associated species habitually flick their tails to reveal white undertail-coverts. Coots and moorhens blackish with brightly coloured forehead shields and beaks; gallinules with blue-green plumages; crakes and rails with mostly cryptic colouring; the minute flufftails or pygmy crakes with marked sexual dimorphism. Make various clucks, croaks, grunts and hoots.

4 REDKNOBBED COOT *Fulica cristata*. Very common resident. The only all-black waterbird with white frontal shield and beak; legs and lobed feet grey. Immatures are ashy-brown, no white shield. Normal call 'clukuk' or 'crornk'. Singly or many on open inland waters with reed-beds. Swim, occasionally dive, or walk at edges of reed-beds or on shoreline, occasionally further afield in marshlands. Habitually stand on floating nest-mounds. Frequently pursue other coots and other species in noisy, overwater chases. 43 cm.

1 Br   N-Br

2 N-Br   Br

3 Br   N-Br

4

98

1 AMERICAN PURPLE GALLINULE *Porphyrula martinica.* Vagrant. Adults differ from the next species in small size, *pale blue* frontal shield, yellow-tipped bill and *pale yellow* legs. Most arrivals are immatures as illustrated, mainly dull khaki-brown with a greenish flush on the back and wings, belly dull blue. At least twelve records for the western Cape coast. 33 cm.

2 PURPLE GALLINULE *Porphyrio porphyrio.* Common resident. Larger than the previous species, differing in *red* frontal shield and bill plus *pink legs.* Immatures are duller, brownish with red-brown legs. Has a deep, explosive bubbling call plus various shrieks and groans. Singly or in pairs in marshes and the vegetation surrounding inland waters, especially sewage-disposal pans. Walks about on mud-flats and reed-bed fringes, sometimes clambering about tangled reeds. Can swim and is not secretive. 46 cm.

3 LESSER GALLINULE *Porphyrula alleni.* Uncommon and irregular resident. Small, large-footed waterbird with green upperparts, dark blue body, neck and head, red bill and legs. The frontal shield is variable in colour; dull apple-green to bluish. Immature as illustrated; cf. immature of next species. The call is a series of rapidly delivered clicks 'dik-dik-dik-dik . . .' or a melodious, rolling 'purrrrr-pur-pur-pur' during courtship. A shy bird; occurs singly or in pairs on secluded ponds with dense fringing vegetation where it climbs about tangled reeds, walks on water lilies or swims. 25 cm.

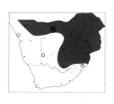

4 LESSER MOORHEN *Gallinula angulata.* Uncommon summer resident. Small, blackish waterbird differing from (5) in smaller size and yellow bill (only culmen and frontal shield red as illustrated). The legs are greenish or red-brown. Immatures much duller; see inset. The call is three to five rapid hoots 'tu-tu-tu- . . .'. Singly or in pairs on shallow ponds with surface and fringing vegetation, vleis and flooded grasslands, but erratic and secretive. 23 cm.

5 MOORHEN *Gallinula chloropus.* Common resident. Larger than the previous species, with bright red bill and frontal shield, tip of bill and legs yellow, flank feathers white. Immatures are browner. The call is a high-pitched descending 'kr-rrrrk'. Frequents dams, pans and quiet rivers with fringing reed-beds, singly or in pairs. Swims more in open water than the previous species but also feeds out of water in vleis and marshlands. 30-6 cm.

1

J

2

4

♂ Br

3

5

J

Flufftails. Smallest of the crakes, Family RALLIDAE. Highly secretive and difficult to flush, but once airborne fly a short distance with legs dangling before dropping back into cover; can seldom be flushed a second time. Calls are usually the only indication of a species' presence.

1 WHITEWINGED FLUFFTAIL *Sarothrura ayresi.* Uncommon, localised resident. Identified by white wing-patches when flushed. The call is a soft, deep 'woop, woop, woop, woop, woop...', often several birds calling simultaneously. Occurs in upland marshes but known from only a few scattered localities. 14 cm.

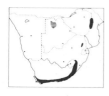

2 STRIPED FLUFFTAIL *Sarothrura affinis.* Rare and localised. Males with combination of chestnut head *and* tail; females probably indistinguishable from females of Buffspotted Flufftail (overleaf). The call is loud and distinctive, a drawn-out 'huuuuuuuuuuuuuuuu'. Frequents rank vegetation bordering forests and woodland as well as montane grassland. 15 cm.

3 STREAKYBREASTED FLUFFTAIL *Sarothrura boehmi.* Rare summer resident. Best identified by call, a deep and rapid 'booooo' at about two-second intervals and repeated about twelve times; also a high-pitched 'bee' about twelve times with no appreciable pause. Occurs in vleis, grasslands and grass bordering lakes and swamps. 15 cm.

4 SPOTTED CRAKE *Porzana porzana.* Rare summer visitor. Differs from the African Crake (overleaf) by generally paler colouring, less boldly barred flanks and a yellow bill with red base, and from the next species by more spotted, less streaked appearance plus yellow bill. The call is a series of whip-like notes 'hwitt-hwitt-hwitt', seldom heard in Southern Africa. Occurs in dense vegetation in shallow water, occasionally that fringing pans in drier regions. 24 cm.

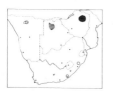

5 STRIPED CRAKE *Aenigmatolimnas marginalis.* Very rare summer resident. Differs from the previous species in more streaky, less spotted upperparts, paler underparts and thicker, darker bill. The call (heard at night) is a constant ticking like a wristwatch 'tak-tak-tak-tak-tak...'. Found in flooded grassland and small pools. Secretive and shy. 24 cm.

102

1 REDCHESTED FLUFFTAIL *Sarothrura rufa*. Uncommon resident. Very similar to the next species, but reddish colouring of males extends onto mantle and lower breast. Females are much darker but paler on chest and throat. The normal call is a much-repeated 'ooo-ooo-ooo-ooo-dueh-dueh-dueh...' but also makes a quail-like 'ick-kick-kick-kick...' and a loud rapid squeaking 'dui-dui-dui...' up to 40 or more times, fading off at the end. Calls mainly at night and on dull days. A secretive bird of marshes, damp valleys and vleis where it remains concealed in dense vegetation. 15-17 cm.

2 BUFFSPOTTED FLUFFTAIL *Sarothrura elegans*. Uncommon resident. Males told from previous species by less extensive reddish colouring and spotted, not streaked, plumage. Females are paler and uniform. The call is long, drawn-out and mournful, 'wooooooooooo-eeeeeeeee', like the sound of a tuning-fork and rising at the end. Frequents the moister areas of evergreen forests, overgrown wastelands and long grass, occasionally in well-wooded suburban gardens, but very secretive. 17 cm.

3 BAILLON'S CRAKE *Porzana pusilla*. Rare resident and visitor. Male illustrated. Female has whitish throat and central breast. Makes a low, piping 'quick-quick'. Highly secretive, inhabiting marshes, lush waterside herbage and flooded grassland. Sometimes emerges into the open but dives into cover again at the least disturbance. 18 cm.

4 CORNCRAKE *Crex crex*. Uncommon summer visitor. A short-billed tawny crake with blackish upperparts, barred flanks and chestnut wing-coverts. Silent in Southern Africa. Found in lucerne, rank grass, fallow fields and airfields, sometimes near streams. When flushed flies off with legs dangling, the chestnut wings conspicuous. 37 cm.

5 AFRICAN CRAKE *Crex egregia*. Uncommon summer visitor. Heavily mottled upperparts and boldly barred underparts distinctive. Has a high-pitched chittering trill of 8 or 9 notes. Found in grassland, vleis and thickets. Secretive but will emerge to visit rain puddles on roads. 20-3 cm.

6 BLACK CRAKE *Amaurornis flavirostris*. Common resident. The call is an explosive, harsh 'rr-rr-rr' ending in a resonant croak; also various clucking sounds. Single birds or scattered individuals are seen at the waterside on quiet rivers, lakes, dams and flood-pans, or walking on floating vegetation. 20-3 cm.

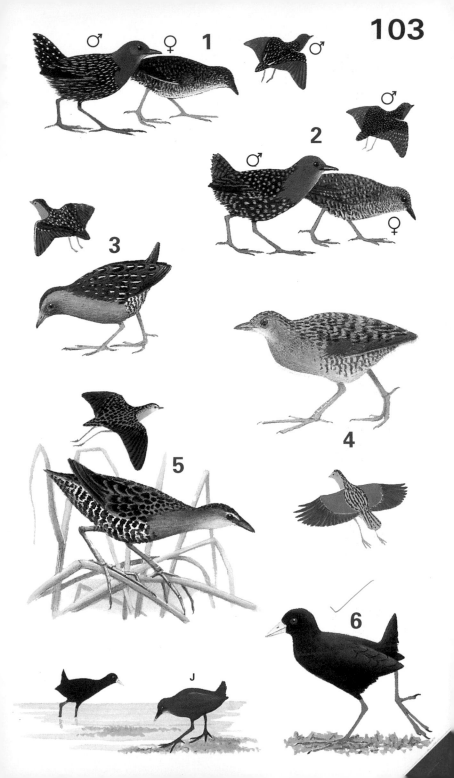

104

1 AFRICAN RAIL *Rallus caerulescens*. Fairly common resident. Identified by long red bill and legs, brown upperparts and striped underparts. Immatures are sooty-brown, white of throat extending to central breast, flanks barred rufous. The call is a shrill, trilling rattle 'creeea-crak-crak-crak . . .'. A shy, skulking bird of reed-beds and thick swamp vegetation, only occasionally emerging at pool fringes. Moves with stealth and speed, flicking its tail continuously. 36 cm.

Painted snipes. Family ROSTRATULIDAE. Not related to true snipes. More colourful.

2 PAINTED SNIPE *Rostratula benghalensis*. Uncommon, nomadic resident. Immatures resemble males. Not a vocal species. Pairs and groups are found on muddy shorelines of dams, pans and swamp pools, usually where reeds or other waterside herbage offer immediate refuge. When walking frequently bob their hindquarters up and down. Shy and retiring. 28-32 cm.

Families CHARADRIIDAE **(plovers and turnstones)** and SCOLOPACIDAE **(sandpipers, snipes and allies)**. Terrestrial and waterside birds, large plovers are long-legged, erect-standing, small plovers have bodies held horizontally, postures hunched. Sandpipers, often called waders, are plover-like migrants breeding in the northern hemisphere (when males assume richly coloured plumage) and migrating south in drab, non-breeding plumage. On their arrival or prior to their departure, many have partial or even full breeding plumage. Illustrations show waders in non-breeding plumage unless otherwise indicated.

3 GREAT SNIPE *Gallinago media*. Rare summer visitor. Differs from the next species in spotted upper wing-coverts and more heavily streaked underparts plus flight behaviour. Silent in Africa. Flushes with reluctance but when doing so rises silently and *flies straight* before dropping down again. Singly in marshy localities; sparsely distributed, few recent records south of range shown. 35 cm.

4 AFRICAN SNIPE (ETHIOPIAN SNIPE) *Gallinago nigripennis*. Common resident. Differs from previous species in having whiter underparts, no white in tail. When flushed takes off with a 'chuck' call and *zigzags at low level* before resettling. In breeding season flies high then zooms down steeply with fanned tail-feathers vibrating to make a soft 'whinnying' sound known as 'drumming'. Singly or in pairs in marshes, vleis and estuaries. 32 cm.

5 CASPIAN PLOVER *Charadrius asiaticus*. Fairly common summer visitor. The male illustrated is in breeding plumage (often seen Feb/March). Females may have rufous breast-band incomplete, the dark lower edge always absent. Non-breeding adults resemble immatures as illustrated, the grey of the breast confined to a patch on either side; then differing from Sand Plover (overleaf) by whiter underparts and *quite different habitat*. The call is a shrill 'ku-wit', loudest at night, softer and more piping by day. Flocks on plains with short grass and burnt areas, often in arid regions, not necessarily near water. Habitually run rather than fly; most active at night. 21- 3 cm.

106

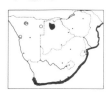

1 MONGOLIAN PLOVER *Charadrius mongolus*. Rare summer visitor. Differs from the next species in having a less heavy bill and lack of any clear mark between bill and eye (lores), and from Whitefronted Plover (overleaf) in heavier bill and unmarked lores plus lack of a white collar. Makes a 'chitic, chitic' call on take-off and, occasionally, a short soft trill. Singly or in small groups on east coast tidal flats. 20 cm.

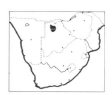

2 SAND PLOVER *Charadrius leschenaultii*. Rare summer visitor. Differs from the previous species in much heavier bill, longer legs and larger size; cf. also immature Kittlitz's Plover (6) which is smaller and has a white collar. Flight call a short 'drrit'; also makes a trill 'chirrirrip', longer than in (1). Singly or in small groups on tidal mud-flats, especially east coast estuaries and lagoons. 22 cm.

3 CHESTNUTBANDED PLOVER *Charadrius pallidus*. Common resident. Females lack the black forecrown and lores. Makes a soft 'chuck' on take-off. Singly, in pairs and flocks on salt-pans, coastal lagoons and sand-flats, less frequently singly or in pairs inland at pans, gravel pits, dams and banks of large rivers. Inland records widespread but irregular. 15 cm.

4 RINGED PLOVER *Charadrius hiaticula*. Uncommon summer visitor. Single bold black breast-band extending around neck diagnostic; cf. Threebanded Plover (5). In flight differs from that species in distinct white wing-bar. The call is 'coo-eep' or 'too-li'. Singly or in small parties, often with (6), on shorelines of coastal lagoons, estuaries and inland waters. 18 cm.

5 THREEBANDED PLOVER *Charadrius tricollaris*. Common resident. Identified by double black breast-bands either side of white band encircling neck; cf. Ringed Plover (4). Immatures have the upper band brown, incomplete, the lower band flecked white, the head uniformly brown. The call is 'wick-wick' or 'tiuu-it, tiuu-it'. Singly, in pairs or small parties on shores and shallows of almost any inland water. 18 cm.

6 KITTLITZ'S PLOVER *Charadrius pecuarius*. Common and widespread resident. Distinguished by black mask and forecrown, white *band encircling back of neck* and yellow-buff breast. Immatures have the mask and forecrown *dusky brown* not black, and lack the yellow breast; distinguished from the similar Mongolian Plover (1) mainly by white collar, darker upperparts and habitat. In-flight call of adult 'tip-peep'; also has a trilling 'trit-tritritritritrit'. Usually found in small parties at the edges of inland waters, coastal estuaries, open ground and airfields. 16 cm.

6 J

KENTISH PLOVER   see page 446.

1

N-Br

2

N-Br

♂

3

J

J

4

5

6

108

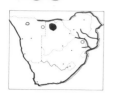

1 WHITEFRONTED PLOVER *Charadrius marginatus*. Common resident. Differs from rare Mongolian Plover (previous page) in much smaller size, dark line between bill and eye, plus more slender bill and white collar. Immatures resemble female. Makes a soft 'wit' or 'twirit' in flight. Singly or in pairs on sandy seashores; also on some inland lakes and large rivers with sandbanks, e.g. Zambezi, Limpopo and Olifants. Feeds on wet sand close to receding waves, running rapidly or flying away low as next wave advances. 18 cm.

2 MARSH SANDPIPER *Tringa stagnatilis*. Common summer visitor. Clear white underparts diagnostic. Differs from the next species in smaller size, straight, slender bill and yellowish legs. In flight shows white back and rump as (3) but feet protrude further. When put to flight calls 'tchick' frequently. Singly or in small groups on coastal lagoons and estuaries or inland waters. Feeds by probing in shallows. 23 cm.

3 GREENSHANK *Tringa nebularia*. Common summer visitor, a few all year. Clear white underparts as previous species but larger, with more robust, slightly upturned bill and green-grey legs. In flight shows extensive white back and rump, feet slightly protruding. On take-off calls a *triple* 'tew-tew-tew'. Usually singly on coastal or inland waters. Shy and difficult to approach. When flushed *towers up and makes its triple call* before flying off some distance. 32 cm.

4 RUFF *Philomachus pugnax*. Abundant summer visitor. Males much larger than females. Characterised by short, straight bill with slightly bulbous tip, featureless face and *boldly scaled or mottled upperparts* caused by pale edges to dark feathers, plus *white oval patches on sides of dark tail*; legs orange in adults, grey-green in immatures. Male breeding plumage variable, may be seen spring or autumn with black, white or rufous neck. Birds in a flock may call 'chit' in a twittering chorus. Singly, in groups or large flocks in shallows of coastal and inland waters, flooded fields and farmlands. Take flight in dense flocks. 24-30 cm.

1 ♂ ♀ ♂

2 N-Br

3

4 N-Br

♂ J
Br
Br
Br

4 ♀

N-Br

110

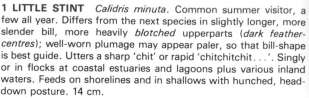

1 LITTLE STINT *Calidris minuta*. Common summer visitor, a few all year. Differs from the next species in slightly longer, more slender bill, more heavily *blotched* upperparts (*dark feather-centres*); well-worn plumage may appear paler, so that bill-shape is best guide. Utters a sharp 'chit' or rapid 'chitchitchit...'. Singly or in flocks at coastal estuaries and lagoons plus various inland waters. Feeds on shorelines and in shallows with hunched, head-down posture. 14 cm.

2 REDNECKED STINT *Calidris ruficollis*. Rare summer visitor. Identified from previous species only with care; bill slightly shorter, more robust and less tapered; upperparts paler, more grey feathers with *dark central shafts* not blotches; general appearance longer, shorter-legged than Little Stint. Breeding plumage diagnostic with rufous head, neck and breast. Voice a weak, short trill 'tirriw' or 'tirriw-chit-chit'. Coastal estuaries and lagoons, especially east coast; singly or few mixing with previous species. 15 cm.

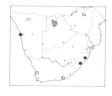

3 BROADBILLED SANDPIPER *Limicola falcinellus*. Rare summer visitor. Identified by fairly long bill with *downcurved tip*, streaked head and short legs; cf. larger, longer-legged Curlew Sandpiper (overleaf). In breeding plumage shows additional stripes on mantle, these and head-stripes giving snipe-like flight pattern. Calls 'chrreet, chetter-chetter-chetter-chit-chit' plus a soft trill. Single birds on coastal estuaries, quiet bays, lagoons and pans, rarely inland. 17 cm.

Phalaropes. Long-legged oceanic 'waders'. Swim buoyantly like small gulls and (with the exception of No. 6) feed from the surface with pirouetting action. Occasionally on inland waters, otherwise well offshore in Atlantic waters. Female breeding plumages brighter than males, non-breeding plumages identical. Normally silent.

4 REDNECKED PHALAROPE *Phalaropus lobatus*. Rare summer visitor. In non-breeding plumage identified by thin bill (about same length as head) and *dark grey* upperparts; may have dark cap. In breeding plumage by rufous band from ear-coverts to upper breast. Flocks at sea or small groups on lagoons and shallow ponds. 17 cm.

5 GREY PHALAROPE *Phalaropus fulicarius*. Rare summer visitor. In non-breeding plumage identified by short, fairly robust bill with (usually) yellow base; pale *uniform* upperparts. In breeding plumage by *rufous underparts*. Flocks at sea or singly on deep inland waters. 20 cm.

6 WILSON'S PHALAROPE *Phalaropus tricolor*. Summer vagrant. Identified in non-breeding plumage by long, needle-like bill, *lack* of eye-patch, *straw-coloured* legs, no wing-bar. In breeding plumage has *black* legs, black eye-patch extending to upper neck, rufous patch from lateral neck to mantle and white underparts. Single birds on shallow inshore waters. May feed by *wading in shallows*, running about on partially flexed legs while lunging rapidly from side to side with bill or with sideways sweeping action. If swimming stabs rapidly at surface, occasionally spinning. 22-24 cm.

All migrant waders in non-breeding plumage unless otherwise indicated.

111

Br 1

Br 2

3 **Br**

♀ **Br** 4

5 ♀ **Br**

♀ **Br**

6

112

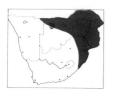

1 GREEN SANDPIPER *Tringa ochropus*. Rare summer visitor. Differs from Wood Sandpiper (4) in having darker, less obviously spotted upperparts and longer bill. In flight larger white rump, barred tail and *dark underwing-coverts.* When flushed towers up, uttering a loud, shrill 'weet-a-weet', then makes off with erratic, snipe-like flight. Solitary on quiet streams and small grassy ponds. 23 cm.

2 COMMON SANDPIPER *Actitis hypoleucos*. Common summer visitor, a few all year. Has diagnostic white pectoral region showing above the folded wing, medium-short, robust bill and habit of frequently bobbing its hindquarters. In flight shows no white rump but faint wing-bar and white outer tail-feathers. When flushed makes off, uttering a shrill 'twee-wee-wee'; flies low with stiff, downward-bowed wings, flapping with sporadic flicking action below the horizontal. Singly on shores of rivers, lakes, dams, estuaries and rocky coasts. 20 cm.

3 CURLEW SANDPIPER *Calidris ferruginea*. Abundant summer visitor. The most common small, curved-billed wader. Differs from very similar but *rare* Dunlin (page 116) by gently tapering bill and, in flight, *broad white rump*; from *rare* Broadbilled Sandpiper (previous page) by evenly curved bill (not curved at the tip only), longer legs, less contrasting upperparts and broad white rump. Calls 'chiet-chiet' in flight and 'tchirrrr' when standing; often very vocal when chasing each other. Occurs in small flocks on inland pans and dams (especially sewage-farms) and in very large flocks at coastal lagoons, estuaries and west coast bays. 19 cm.

4 WOOD SANDPIPER *Tringa glareola*. Common summer visitor, some all year. Has well-spotted upperparts, broad, distinct eyebrow, short, straight bill and fairly long legs. In flight shows white underwing-coverts, differing mainly in this and bill length from Green Sandpiper (1); feet protrude beyond tail. When flushed towers up and calls a flat, triple 'chiff-iff-iff'; also has a high-pitched alarm call 'tchi-tchi-tchi-tchi-tchi'. Solitary or in small groups on most shallow inland waters, flooded grasslands and coastal estuaries. 20 cm.

All migrant waders in non-breeding plumage unless otherwise indicated.

113

114

1 PECTORAL SANDPIPER *Calidris melanotos*. Rare summer visitor. Differs from Ruff (page 108) by smaller size, shorter yellow legs and well-streaked breast terminating in a sharp line and contrasting with pure white underparts; full breeding plumage is slightly more rufous. In flight no clear wing-bars but snipe-like streaks on back. Usual call 'kreek' or 'prritt' one or more times. Takes off with erratic snipe-like action, then flies straight. Single birds on coastal estuaries and inland on sewage-farms, moist grasslands, often mixing with other waders. 20-3 cm.

2 SANDERLING *Calidris alba*. Common summer visitor. A small shorebird of very white appearance with dark shoulder-patch and short, thick bill; larger and paler than any stints (page 110). When flushed calls a liquid 'blt-blt'. Flocks, large or small, mostly on open seashores, characteristically running along the water's edge at speed and feeding where the waves have receded. Feeds in a hunched, head-down posture, probing wet sand hurriedly, continuously. Flight low and direct, white wing-bars conspicuous. 19 cm.

3 TEREK SANDPIPER *Xenus cinereus*. Common summer visitor. Distinguished by long upcurved bill, short, orange-yellow legs and pale grey-brown upperparts with a dark shoulder. In flight the white secondaries and grey rump are diagnostic. Breeding plumage similar. Calls 'tur-lip' or 'turr-loo-tew'. Single birds or flocks occur in coastal estuaries and lagoons, occasionally on inland waters. Bobs its rear end up and down like a Common Sandpiper (previous page). When feeding moves about rapidly, sometimes running at speed between bouts of deep probing with its bill. 23-5 cm.

4 KNOT *Calidris canutus*. Common summer visitor. Differs from other short-billed waders by plump-bodied appearance; frequently assumes semi-breeding plumage before departure in autumn. In flight the wings appear long, pointed, the white wing-bars conspicuous. Calls 'knut', sometimes in a series; a flock may call a more liquid 'whit-wit'. Flocks at coastal lagoons, estuaries and rocky shores, especially west coast; individuals rarely inland. Feeds with a slow forward movement while probing mud several times between steps. Flocks fly in dense packs, twisting and turning at speed. 25 cm.

5 TURNSTONE *Arenaria interpres*. Common summer visitor. Characterised by long-shaped body, hunched, head-in-shoulders appearance and horizontal stance plus striking plumage pattern; all stages between full breeding and non-breeding plumages occur. Flight or contact call 'kuiti-kuiti-kuiti' or 'tuck-a-tuck' in mild alarm given about five times, then tails off to 'ti-tititi'. Flocks of 5 to 20 frequent coastal mud-flats and shorelines, especially rocky shores; occasionally on inland waters. Feed by turning over small stones, shells, caked mud and debris. If flushed fly off low, revealing extensive white back and wing-bars. 22 cm.

All migrant waders in non-breeding plumage unless otherwise indicated.

115

1

2

Br

3

4

Br

5

Br

N-Br

VERY RARE VAGRANT WADERS

The species on this plate have, at best, been seen a few times only in southern Africa.

1 LONGTOED STINT *Calidris subminuta*. Fractionally smaller than Little Stint (page 110) from which it is best distinguished by greenish-yellow (not black) legs and richer, darker brown upperparts streaked with pale buff. Differs from the next species in having richly marked (not uniform) upperparts. Adopts characteristic stance when it stretches its neck and stands very upright.

2 TEMMINCK'S STINT *Calidris temminckii*. Very similar to Little Stint (page 110) but has yellowish (not black) legs and feet and fairly uniform, unmarked grey upperparts. In flight the outer tail-feathers are white, not grey as in Little Stint.

3 BAIRD'S SANDPIPER *Calidris bairdii*. Larger than Little Stint (page 110) but smaller than Curlew Sandpiper (page 112). Has characteristic upperparts, appearing very scaled and similar to the Ruff (page 108). Overall body shape slender, streamlined, wing-tips projecting well beyond tail. Head shape diagnostic, appearing squarish like a wader of the *Tringa* genus rather than a stint.

4 WHITERUMPED SANDPIPER *Calidris fuscicollis*. Similar in shape and size to previous species but has longer, very slightly decurved bill, and lacks the scaled upperparts. Differs from the Curlew Sandpiper (page 112) which also has a white rump by much smaller size and shorter bill.

5 DUNLIN *Calidris alpina*. Can be confused with Curlew Sandpiper (page 112) but is smaller and has a dark (not white) rump, shorter, less decurved bill and browner, more marked upperparts.

6 BUFFBREASTED SANDPIPER *Tryngites subruficollis*. Appears like a richly coloured, diminutive Ruff (page 108). The short, straight bill and small, rounded head, combined with an absence of wing-bars or white oval patches on the sides of the tail, should rule out confusion with Ruff.

7 LESSER YELLOWLEGS *Tringa flavipes*. Could be confused only with the Wood Sandpiper (page 112) from which it differs in always having bright, lemon-yellow legs. Larger, longer-legged and much more slender than Wood Sandpiper.

GREATER YELLOWLEGS   see page 446.

117

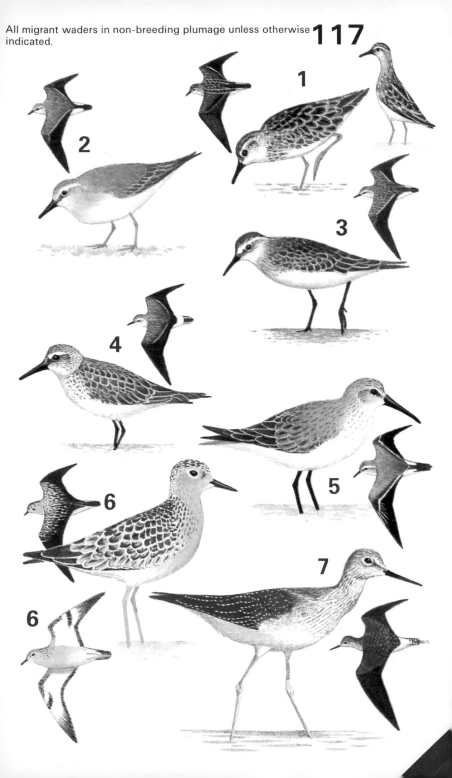

1

2

3

4

6

6

5

7

118

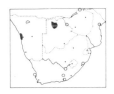

1 REDSHANK *Tringa totanus.* Rare summer visitor. Differs from the next species in less lanky, browner appearance; from most other waders by red or orange legs and reddish base to moderately long, straight bill; from orange-legged Ruff (page 108) in plain upperparts and bill shape. In flight the only wader with white triangular patches on the wings, plus white back, rump and tail, the latter faintly barred. Calls 'teu-he-he' on take-off. Flight erratic with jerky, deliberate wing-beats, feet slightly protruding beyond the tail. Usually singly, often with other waders, on coastal mud-flats, estuaries and lagoons; occasionally on inland waters. 25 cm.

2 SPOTTED REDSHANK *Tringa erythropus.* Rare summer vagrant. Lankier and more gracefully proportioned than the previous species, bill and legs longer, of overall greyish appearance with usually some spotting on the upperparts; whitish underparts. Posture fairly erect. In flight shows no wing-bar and has white oval patch on back; feet protrude more than in Redshank. The call is a deep 'cheewit'. May occur at either inland or coastal waters. 30 cm.

3 BLACKTAILED GODWIT *Limosa limosa.* Rare summer visitor. Despite *straight bill* and *longer legs* is not easily distinguished from the next species when at rest, but head, neck and breast are of uniform tone, *not* streaked. In flight the broad, black tail-band and prominent white upper wing-bars are distinctive. When flying may call a loud 'wicka-wicka-wicka'. Usually singly, mostly at inland waters but a few coastal records. 40-50 cm.

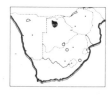

4 BARTAILED GODWIT *Limosa lapponica.* Fairly common summer visitor. Of stockier appearance, shorter-legged than the previous species; bill long (longest in females) and gently *upcurved* (not straight); head, neck and breast more obviously streaked. In flight the tail shows numerous light bars at close range, the wings without bars. The call is a deep 'god-whit'. Singly or in flocks (sometimes several hundreds) on tidal mud-flats, especially on the west coast; occasionally on inland waters. See page 446 for Hudsonian Godwit. 36-9 cm.

5 AFRICAN JACANA *Actophilornis africanus.* Common resident. Immatures have *black* stripe through eye and *black* crown; cf. next species. The call, uttered while standing or flying, is 'kyowrrr'. Individuals or scattered groups walk on floating vegetation on lily-covered pans, dams and river backwaters. Frequently chase one another in short dashes or in low flight while calling loudly. 40 cm.

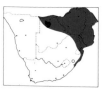

6 LESSER JACANA *Microparra capensis.* Uncommon, localised resident. Very much smaller than the previous species (sparrow-size minus feet). Differs from the young of that species by pale feather-edges to brown upperparts giving 'scaled' effect; central mantle and back deep bronze-brown, *crown and eye-stripe chestnut*, darkening only towards the front, underparts white. Immatures have a dark crown, the nape golden-chestnut. Silent except for an occasional 'kruk'. Occurs on lily-covered ponds, dams and river backwaters. 20 cm.

1 PACIFIC and GOLDEN PLOVERS (previously treated as Lesser Golden Plover, races a and b). These rare vagrants reach our shores in non-breeding plumage when their specific identity can be problematical. Both differ from (2a) in dull grey (not black) 'armpits', fairly long upper legs and a golden wash to the upper plumage (note, however, that the immature of (2) can also have golden spots on the upperparts). May occur on tidal mudflats, inland pans, moist grasslands or roadside verges.

1a PACIFIC GOLDEN PLOVER *Pluvialis fulva*. Slimmer than (1b), eyebrow and most of head with yellow wash, rest of upperparts grey-brown spotted golden-yellow, the breast greyish with yellow wash. In flight the legs protrude beyond tail. Probably even less frequent than (1b). 23-6 cm.

1b AMERICAN GOLDEN PLOVER *Pluvialis dominica*. Of more bulky appearance than (1a), differing also in clear white eyebrow and less yellow head, upperparts grey-brown spotted off-white and yellow, the breast dull greyish mottled off-white. Few records for both coastal and inland localities. 24-28 cm.

2 GREY PLOVER *Pluvialis squatarola*. Common summer visitor, a few all year. Non-breeding plumage (a) resembles previous species but is a more chunky bird with *greyish* overall appearance. Larger size, short, stout bill and fairly long legs distinguish this from other smaller waders. In flight shows *black* 'armpits'. Both partial breeding plumage (b) and full breeding plumage occur in spring and autumn. Has a far-carrying whistle 'tlui-tlui' or 'pee-u-wee'. Singly or in flocks on tidal flats, secluded seashores; occasionally inland. 28-30 cm.

3 LESSER BLACKWINGED PLOVER *Vanellus lugubris*. Uncommon resident. Closely resembles the next species but upperparts *olive brown* (not warm brown), the white forehead *forward* of the eye, the dark lower breast-band usually narrow, legs dark brown. See illustrations for upper and underwing flight patterns. The call is a piping 'thi-wit'. Small parties in dry grassland and open woodland. 23 cm.

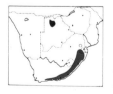

4 BLACKWINGED PLOVER *Vanellus melanopterus*. Fairly common visitor and resident. Differs from the previous species in white forehead extending to *above* the eye, a bright red eye-ring, a broad dark band on the lower breast and dark red legs. See illustrations for upper and underwing flight patterns. The normal call is a harsh 'tlu-wit', the alarm call a shrill 'che-che-che-cherek', rising to a scream when highly agitated. Usually in flocks in hilly grasslands, on golf courses and playing fields where grass is short. 29 cm.

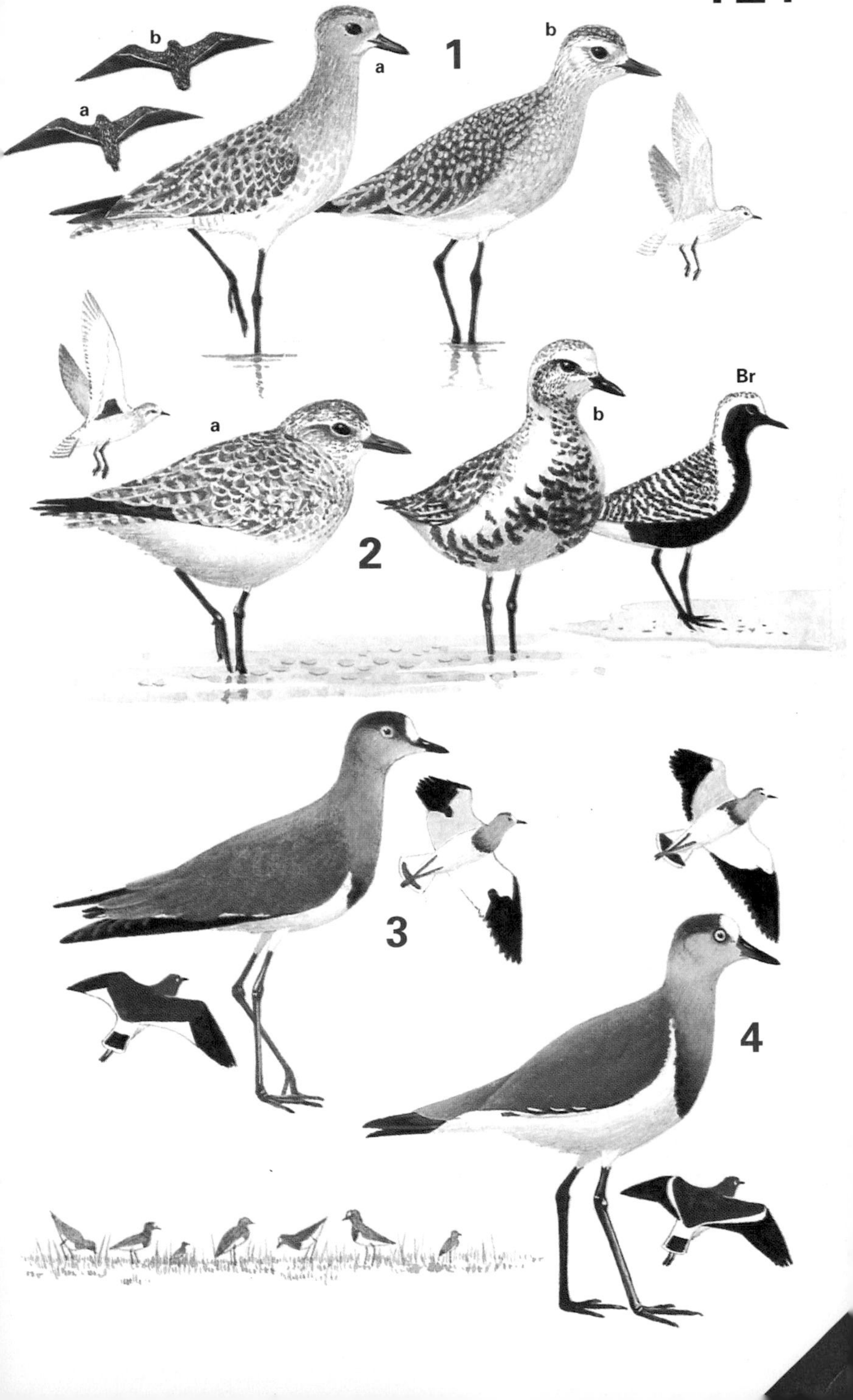
b
a
a
1
b
a
b
Br
2
3
4

122

1 LONGTOED PLOVER (WHITEWINGED PLOVER) *Vanellus crassirostris*. Uncommon, localised resident. Distinguished by white frontal half of head, neck and upper breast contrasting with black nape, rear neck and breast-band, plus very long toes. In flight reveals predominantly white wings; cf. Whitecrowned Plover (5). The call is 'wheet' and, in flight, a clicking 'kick-k-k-kick-k-k-k'. Pairs or groups occur on quiet sections of large rivers (especially the Zambezi) and their backwaters, lakes, flood-pans and flood-plains where they feed by walking on floating vegetation. 30 cm.

2 BLACKSMITH PLOVER *Vanellus armatus*. Very common resident. A pied plover with *grey wings and mantle*. Immatures, as illustrated, with basic plumage pattern of adults but in tones of speckled brown. The call is a metallic 'klink, klink, klink...' repeated loudly and continuously when the birds are disturbed. Pairs and scattered individuals frequent the shores of a wide variety of inland waters and in marshy ground, flooded fields and other moist places. 30 cm.

3 CROWNED PLOVER *Vanellus coronatus*. Very common resident. Distinguished by a white circle surrounding a black cap, plus mainly red bill and red legs; eyes usually pale yellow, sometimes dark brown. At times very noisy, calling 'kie-weeet' on the ground or a repeated 'kree-kree-kreeip-kreeip...' in flight, day or night. Pairs and groups are found on dry open ground where the grass is short or burnt, especially on airfields; also in lightly wooded country. Often fly about in small groups at some height calling repeatedly. 30 cm.

4 WATTLED PLOVER *Vanellus senegallus*. Common resident. Bright yellow bill, wattles and legs distinguish this plover from all but the next species, from which it differs in shorter wattles, white patch *only* on forecrown, a streaked neck, lack of a white bar on the folded wing and *brown breast and underparts* excepting the belly. The call is a shrill 'kwep-kwep-kwep-kwep-kwe-kwe-kwe-kwe-kwekwekwekwekwek', speeding up with increased agitation. Pairs and small groups frequent grassy waterside localities: riverbanks, dam walls, fringes of sewage-disposal pans and vleis. 35 cm.

5 WHITECROWNED PLOVER *Vanellus albiceps*. Uncommon, localised resident. Distinguished from the previous species by longer wattles (longer than the bill), a broad white band (dark-edged in males) extending from the bill over the crown, *entirely* white underparts and a black wing bordered with white above. In flight the wings appear mainly white; cf. Longtoed Plover (1). A noisy species, the call a sharp 'peep, peep-peep, peep...' uttered at rapid speed if the birds are flushed. Pairs and groups frequent the shores and sandbanks of the larger perennial rivers. 30 cm.

123

1

J 2

2

3

4

5

124

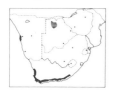

1 EUROPEAN OYSTERCATCHER *Haematopus ostralegus*. Rare visitor. Fairly large, pied shorebird with orange bill, pink legs. Usually occur as non-breeding or immature birds, latter with dark bill-tips. In breeding plumage lacks white throat. The call is a shrill 'kleeep' and a shorter 'pic, pic'. Solitary or in small groups on sandy coastlines. 43 cm.

2 AFRICAN BLACK OYSTERCATCHER *Haematopus moquini*. Common resident. The only black shorebird with reddish bill, eye and legs. Immatures are browner. Normal call 'klee-weep, klee-weep', alarm call a sharp 'ki-kik-kiks'. Singly or in small groups on rocky coastlines, estuaries and coastal lagoons. 51 cm.

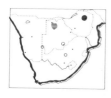

3 WHIMBREL *Numenius phaeopus*. Common summer visitor, a few all year. Differs from the next species in markedly smaller size, shorter curved bill (about two and a half times length of head) and dark cap with pale central line (see illustration). In flight shows extensive white back and rump. Call a twittering 'peep-eep-eep-eep-ee'. Singly or in small groups on coastal lagoons, rocky shorelines, estuary and harbour mudbanks, less frequently on inland waters. 43 cm.

4 CURLEW *Numenius arquata*. Uncommon summer visitor. Much larger than the previous species, with enormously long, curved bill. Shows no distinctive pattern on crown. In flight shows similar large white area on back and rump to (3) and generally paler all-over appearance. Calls various, include 'cur-lew' or 'coorwe-coorwe' and 'quee-quee-quee'. Groups, up to about 50 to 60, on coastal shorelines (especially southern and western coasts), estuaries, coastal lagoons, tidal rivers, harbours. A vagrant to inland waters. 59 cm.

Br

1   N-Br

2

3

4

Crab Plover. Family DROMADIDAE.

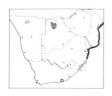

1 CRAB PLOVER *Dromas ardeola*. Rare visitor. Long-legged, mainly white shorebird; immatures browner as illustrated. Differs from other similar black and white birds in *heavy thick bill*. Has a stiff-winged flight, the legs protruding well beyond the tail. Makes a harsh 'crook' or 'cheeruk' when flushed. Occurs in small flocks (up to about 30) on east coast shoreline, coastal lagoons and estuaries, often in association with mangroves. Most frequent in Mozambique where it may breed. 38 cm.

Avocets and stilts. Family RECURVIROSTRIDAE. Elegant, long-legged, long-billed, black and white wading birds, avocets with up-turned bills, stilts with straight bills.

2 AVOCET *Recurvirostra avosetta*. Common resident and visitor. Thin, up-turned bill diagnostic. Immatures dark brown where adults black. Calls a liquid 'kluut', several birds sometimes calling together. Flocks, varying from few individuals to hundreds, occur in shallow waters of inland lakes, dams and pans (especially sewage-farms) and at coastal lagoons and estuaries. Feeds by wading, the immersed bill being swept from side to side while the bird walks slowly forward, or while swimming. Nomadic when not breeding and irregular in many regions. 43 cm.

3 BLACKWINGED STILT *Himantopus himantopus*. Common resident. Black and white plumage and long red legs conspicuous both at rest and in flight. Adults may have a dusky crown to the head, while immatures are even duskier about the head as illustrated. The call, often given in flight, is a loud 'kik-kik-kik-kik-kik' or 'kyik'. Individuals, pairs or flocks at inland pans, dams and vleis, especially at sewage farms, plus coastal lagoons and estuaries. Wades in the shallows with the legs well immersed while feeding on the surface. 38 cm.

1 J

2

3 J

128

Dikkops. Family BURHINIDAE. Plover-like birds with large heads and eyes, long legs, feet without a hind claw and tawny colouring. Normally walk with short, mincing steps. Nocturnal and crepuscular, spending the daytime resting in some concealed position. Sexes alike, young resemble adults.

1 SPOTTED DIKKOP *Burhinus capensis*. Common resident. Distinguished from the next species by heavily spotted upperparts, no wing-bar and by habitat preference. Most vocal on moonlit nights, flying about restlessly and calling a shrill, eerie 'chwee-chwee, chwee-chwee, chwee, chwee, chwee, tiu-tiu-tiu . . .', trailing off at the end. Pairs frequent dry rocky ground with short grass, open fields and open areas within woodland; frequently in little-developed urban areas. Rests by day under bushes or among rocks, running off with lowered head if disturbed. 44 cm.

2 WATER DIKKOP *Burhinus vermiculatus*. Common resident. Distinguished from previous species by distinct *grey wing-bar*, edged black, plus habitat. Calls at night and at dusk, a piping, melancholy 'whee-wheeoo-wheeoo'. Single birds and small groups on the banks of large rivers or lakes where there is fringing vegetation. Lies up during the day in reeds or beneath overhanging bushes, becoming active at dusk. 40 cm.

Pratincoles and coursers. Family GLAREOLIDAE. Pratincoles are migratory and nomadic birds, with very short legs in relation to body-length. At rest or in their elegant, often erratic, flight resemble terns. Feed mostly in the air in flocks. Their calls are of a 'kip-kip-kip . . .' nature. The related coursers are more plover-like with erect stance, but unlike plovers lack a hind toe; they are terrestrial feeders. Sexes alike in both groups.

3 REDWINGED PRATINCOLE *Glareola pratincola*. Uncommon summer resident. Differs from the next species in *rufous underwing-coverts and white-tipped secondaries;* see flight illustration. Flocks occur on floodlands, estuaries and lakesides, occasionally on farmlands. At times flocks rise in great, wheeling columns and perform remarkable aerial manoeuvres. When settling, habitually stands briefly with wings raised. 25 cm.

4 BLACKWINGED PRATINCOLE *Glareola nordmanni*. Uncommon summer visitor. Differs from the previous species in entirely blackish underwings, less red on the gape and slightly more extensive yellow-buff colouring on the lower breast. Flocks on floodlands, estuaries, lakesides and farmlands. Behaviour as for previous species. 25 cm.

5 ROCK PRATINCOLE *Glareola nuchalis*. Common, localised resident. Smaller that (3) and (4), has no throat-patch and outer tail-feathers only slightly elongated; narrow white collar and *red legs* diagnostic. Found in flocks on large rivers and lakes, especially near boulder-strewn rapids. Perches on rocks protruding from the water and feeds by hawking over the water. 18 cm.

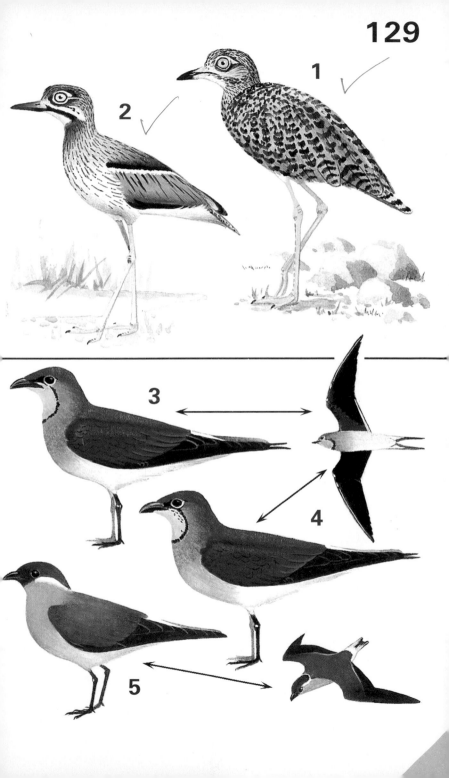

COURSERS

1 BRONZEWINGED COURSER *Rhinoptilus chalcopterus*. Fairly common visitor and resident. Larger than other coursers with *red legs* and distinctive head markings, these less clearly defined in immatures. At night calls a shrill 'ji-ku-it' or a plaintive 'groraag'. A nocturnal species of well-wooded regions, roosting by day beneath a bush and feeding at night in open areas and on roads. 25 cm.

2 TEMMINCK'S COURSER *Cursorius temminckii*. Fairly common resident. A small white-legged, *rufous-capped* courser; cf. next species. Immatures are speckled buff on upperparts and crown. May call a sharp 'err-err-err' in flight. Pairs and small groups are found in freshly burnt or well-grazed grasslands and airfields. Stands with erect stance then runs rapidly forward before stooping briefly to feed; occasionally bobs its head and tail. Nomadic. 20 cm.

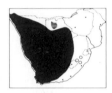

3 BURCHELL'S COURSER *Cursorius rufus*. Fairly common resident. Differs from the previous species mainly in having a grey back to the crown. Immatures are mottled on upperparts. A quiet species, may call 'kok-kok-kwich'. Habitat and habits very similar to the previous species; small groups in short grasslands. Also bobs its head and hindquarters and jerks its body backwards and forwards or sideways. Nomadic. 23 cm.

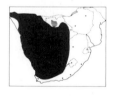

4 DOUBLEBANDED COURSER *Smutsornis africanus*. Common resident. A distinctive, pale-coloured courser with two black bands encircling the lower neck and upper breast. Immatures are similar. Normally silent but may call 'pee-wee' if put to flight; also calls 'chik-kee, chik-kee, chik-kee-kee-kee-kee' while flying at night. In pairs or scattered groups in arid grasslands or semi-desert, fringes of dry pans and barren, stony flats. Active day and night and seemingly indifferent to hot conditions. Runs rather than flies. 22 cm.

5 THREEBANDED COURSER *Rhinoptilus cinctus*. Uncommon visitor and resident. Darker than the previous species with bold head markings and bands spanning the upper breast (not encircling the neck). Immatures with lower band poorly defined. Calls mainly at night, 'chick-a-chuck-a-chuck-a-chuck'. Singly or in pairs in well-grassed woodland and thornveld of the drier regions. When approached they freeze, usually with their backs to the observer. 28 cm.

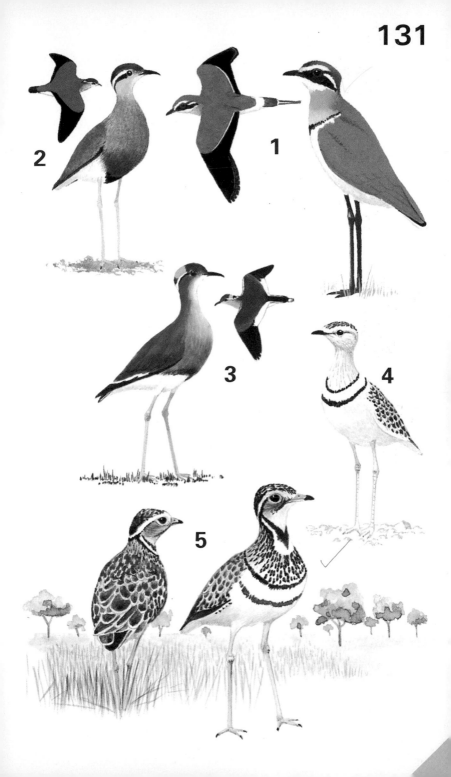

Bustards and korhaans. Family OTIDIDAE. Large, long-legged, long-necked terrestrial birds, cryptically coloured, tails short, feet with three forward-facing toes. Most have elaborate displays involving plumage transformations, flight or unusual calls.

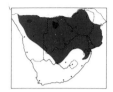

1 REDCRESTED KORHAAN *Eupodotis ruficrista.* Common resident. Told from other small korhaans by creamy-white V-marks on the upperparts; shorter legged and shorter necked than Blackbellied Korhaan (page 136). Female has a broad white band across the lower breast, reduced in the male to a small patch on either side of breast. Red crest of courting male, when crown, breast and neck feathers are also raised, is seldom seen and is *not* a field feature. Territorial call of male starts with a series of clicks increasing in speed and changing to a series of shrill, piercing whistles 'phee-phee-phee-phee . . .' repeated 5-10 or more times. Courting pairs perform a duet, a rapid 'wuk-wuk-wuk-wuk . . .' rising in volume and frequency to 'wuka-wuka-wuka-wuka . . .' before the male switches to the whistling call. In aerial display male flies up steeply to c.20 metres and then tumbles as though shot. Singly or in pairs in bushveld. 53 cm.

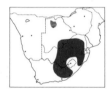

2 WHITEBELLIED KORHAAN *Eupodotis cafra.* Fairly common resident. A small, distinctive korhaan, males with dark cap and throat plus blue-grey neck-front. The call, heard morning and evening, is 'takwarat' repeated several times in decreasing volume; this is sometimes preceded by several 'throat-clearing' sounds thus: 'aaa-aaa-aaa-takwarat-takwarat-takwarat . . .'. If flushed calls 'kuk-pa-wow' as it flies off. Pairs and small parties are found in grassland, farmlands and occasionally in thornveld. 53 cm.

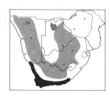

3 BLACK KORHAAN *Eupodotis afra* and **WHITEQUILLED KORHAAN** *Eupodotis afraoides.* Common residents. These two closely related species appear identical unless flying, at which time (3b) displays white markings on the primary feathers, lacking in (3a); see illustrations. Males distinctive; females best told from other korhaans by pink bill with pale tip. Males call a raucous 'krra-a-a-a-ak-wet-de-wet-de-wet-de . . .' in flight or from a slightly elevated position on the ground. Found in pairs or small groups. The Black Korhaan, with the more southerly range (see map) frequents Karoo scrub and coastal dunes, the Whitequilled Korhaan dry open grassveld, arid scrublands and Kalahari sandveld. 53 cm.

4 BLUE KORHAAN *Eupodotis caerulescens.* Common resident. The only korhaan with entirely blue-grey neck and underparts. Males call mostly early morning 'kakow, kakow, kakow . . .', and several birds may call in unison; the flight call is a deep-throated 'knock-me-down . . .'. Pairs and small groups frequent highveld grassland and irrigated lands. 50-8 cm.

1

♀

♂

♀

♀

♂

2

a

♂

♀

3

b

♂

♀

4

♂

134

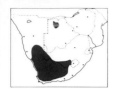

1 KAROO KORHAAN *Eupodotis vigorsii*. Common resident. Lacks the extensive head and neck markings of the next species, the black throat-patch and plain crown distinguishing it from all other small korhaans. Sexes are alike. Calls in duet, loud frog-like sounds 'graag-uurg-og-og, graak-squark-kok-kok...'. Pairs or small parties in dry grassland, semi-desert and thornveld, preferring stony ground with sparse vegetation. The extent to which this species penetrates northwards into SWA/Namibia is not currently known. 56-60 cm.

2 RÜPPELL'S KORHAAN *Eupodotis rueppellii*. Common resident. Similar to the previous species, but with more elaborate head and neck markings. Sexes are alike. Calls in duet, a deep, resonant 'waaa-a-re-e, waaa-a-re-e,...' first sound by the male, next three by the female, repeated in long sequences. Individuals also draw the head back and then thrust it forward, calling a deep 'augh'. Flight call a rapid 'quark-quark-quark...'. Pairs frequent very arid regions, stony desert plains of north-west Namibia. The extent to which this species penetrates southwards is not currently known. 56-60 cm.

3 LUDWIG'S BUSTARD *Neotis ludwigii*. Fairly common resident. Differs from the next species in brown (not black) cap and absence of large black and white areas on the folded wings. The call, heard during courtship, is a deep-voiced 'klop...klop... klop'. At this time (October–November) males fluff out their plumage and inflate their necks, revealing white under-feathers while calling at about ten-second intervals. 75-90 cm.

4 STANLEY'S BUSTARD (DENHAM'S BUSTARD) *Neotis denhami*. Common resident. Larger than the previous species, but differing mainly in *black cap* with white central parting plus black and white wing-coverts and secondaries, which are visible as a large black patch on the folded wing; see illustrations. Breeding males have no grey on their necks. Normally silent. In courtship males fluff their plumage, erect their fanned tails, revealing white under tail-coverts, and inflate their necks. Pairs and small groups occur in hilly grassland, Karoo and Kalahari veld. 86-110 cm.

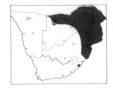

1 BLACKBELLIED KORHAAN (LONGLEGGED KORHAAN) *Eupodotis melanogaster*. Common resident. Characterised by long legs (proportionately longer than any other korhaan), males in flight by *white upper-wings*. Males have entire underparts black, extending in a line up the front of the neck to the chin, females have *white underparts.* Males call while posturing as illustrated; (1) head and neck withdrawn, wings drooped; (2) head and neck fully stretched upwards while a dull 'waak' or 'phwoe' is uttered; (3) head is lowered about half way to the body and it utters a throaty grunt followed by a five-second pause; then (4) it makes a sharp, whip-like sound 'ooor-whip'. Found singly or in pairs in rank, moist grassland. During courtship males perform an aerial display in which the white upper-wings are strikingly presented; after taking off and flying some distance they coast in silently, with their wings held rigidly aloft in a V-shaped position with head and neck arched up and black breast puffed out like a balloon. On settling, the wings are folded abruptly and the normal cryptic colouring is assumed; see flight illustration below. 58-65 cm.

2 KORI BUSTARD *Ardeotis kori*. Common resident. Identified by huge size and crested head. Sexes are alike but males *c*. 20 per cent larger than females. In courtship males call a deep 'wum, wum, wum, wum, wummmmm'. Singly, in pairs or groups in woodland, bushveld and grassland. Walks slowly with measured strides and flies reluctantly. Males have an elaborate courtship display. The throat-pouch is inflated and the frontal neck feathers splayed outwards revealing their white bases, the head with raised crest is drawn back, the wings are drooped and the tail deflected upwards and forwards to the neck with the white under tail-coverts splayed outwards conspicuously. The small illustration shows a male in partial display. 135 cm.

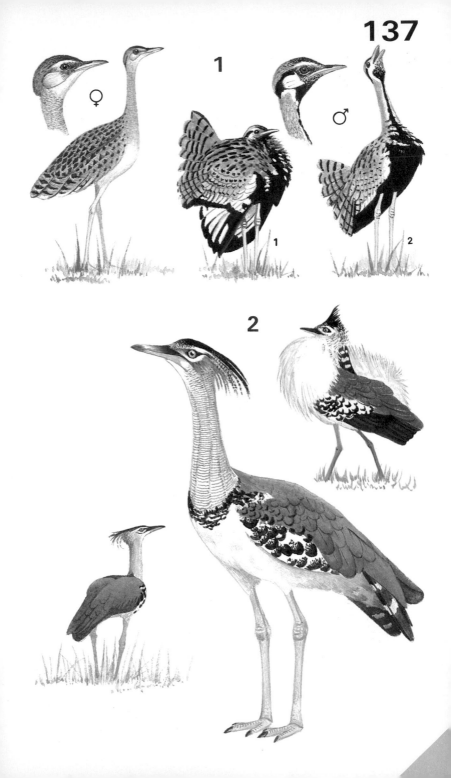

1

♀ ♂

1

2

2

Cranes. Family GRUIDAE. Large, long-legged, terrestrial birds, differing from storks in having short bills and being quite vocal. Like storks, they fly with heads and necks outstretched. They indulge in elaborate dancing displays with wings outstretched when courting, sometimes involving more than two birds.

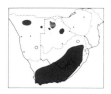

1 BLUE CRANE *Anthropoides paradiseus*. Common resident. Distinctive blue-grey, long-legged bird with bulbous head and long wing-plumes appearing like a trailing tail. Immature birds lack these plumes. The call is a loud, rattling, nasal 'kraaaarrk'. Occurs in pairs and flocks, sometimes in flocks of 50 to 500, in Karoo, hilly grasslands, moist valleys, farmlands and lakesides. Prefers higher altitudes and is nomadic when not breeding. 105 cm.

2 CROWNED CRANE *Balearica regulorum*. Common resident. Immatures with crest and wattles less developed, of browner appearance. The call is a two-syllabled trumpeting, sounding like 'ma-hem'. Usually in flocks in grasslands, farmlands, near vleis and other marshy regions, both in highlands and at the coast. Roosts on offshore islands, reed-beds in river estuaries and in trees. Nomadic when not breeding. 105 cm.

3 WATTLED CRANE *Grus carunculata*. Uncommon resident. A very large crane with distinctive wattles hanging either side of the chin, these being absent in immatures. Seldom vocal but can make a loud, drawn-out, bell-like 'horuk'. Pairs and small groups are sparsely distributed in vleis, swamplands, fringes of large lakes and high-altitude grasslands. Often wades in shallow water while feeding. Wary and difficult to approach. 120 cm.

Note: Whereas these cranes may be fairly common in some parts of southern Africa their numbers have become very reduced in the Republic of South Africa and the species should be regarded as endangered in that country.

3

1

2

3

Quails and francolins. Family PHASIANIDAE. Terrestrial birds of mostly gregarious habits (quails excepted). Male francolins have leg-spurs (lacking in females) and crowing, ringing or cackling call-notes which are useful identification features. Immatures resemble adults but are duller. Quails are nomadic and irruptive, whereas francolins are more sedentary.

1 BLUE QUAIL *Coturnix adansonii*. Rare summer resident. Males told by dark overall colouring and large white throat-patch, females from other female quails by smaller size and *lack* of white eyebrow or throat-patch. The call is a piping, three-note, descending whistle, the first note much louder than the others. Pairs or small parties in moist grasslands and vleis. Sparsely distributed at all times, its occurrence infrequent. 15 cm.

2 COMMON QUAIL *Coturnix coturnix*. Common resident and visitor. Told by pale underparts in both sexes, cf. (1) and (3); in flight difficult to tell from the next species. The call is a penetrating 'whit-*whi*ttit, whit-*whi*ttit . . .' uttered day or night when breeding; if flushed calls 'pree-pree-pree'. Pairs in bushveld, grassland, pastures and cultivated fields. Usually flush with reluctance. 18 cm.

3 HARLEQUIN QUAIL *Coturnix delegorguei*. Uncommon to common summer resident, a few all year. Males told by bold black markings on white throat and chestnut underparts, females distinguished from females of previous species by dark 'necklace' across throat to ear-coverts. The call is a loud 'wit, wit-wit, wit, wit-wit-it', similar-sounding to the previous species but more metallic. Pairs in rank grass, especially in damp regions, grasslands and bushveld. Habits as the previous species. Nomadic, sometimes irrupting in great numbers locally, then suddenly disappearing again. 18 cm.

142

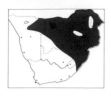

1 COQUI FRANCOLIN *Francolinus coqui*. Common resident. A small species, the males with tawny heads and necks plus barred underparts; females with white throats bordered black plus black eyebrow extending to the upper neck. The call is a piping 'ko-kwee, ko-kwee...' or 'be-quick, be-quick...' repeated continually; males also make a loud, high-pitched crowing 'kek, KEKekekekekekekekekekekek', the second note loudest and all others diminishing in volume. Pairs or small groups frequent well grassed bushveld and woodland. Habitually walks in a slow, stooped manner as the female illustrated, especially when crossing roads and other open spaces, and crouches motionless when alarmed. 28 cm.

2 CRESTED FRANCOLIN *Francolinus sephaena*. Common resident. Identified by dark cap (the feathers are raised in alarm) over a prominent white eyebrow, red legs and the habit of holding the *tail raised like a Bantam chicken*; in flight black tail conspicuous. Race (a) is widespread; race (b) (previously known as Kirk's Francolin) differs in having no dark blotching on the upper breast, by streaked underparts and orange-yellow legs; this race restricted to north of the Beira district and beyond the Zambezi. Call a shrill 'kwerri-kwetchi, kwerri-kwetchi', sounds like 'beer and cognac, beer and cognac'. Pairs or small groups in bushveld, broadleafed woodland, thickets near rivers and forest edges, mostly keeping within cover. 32 cm.

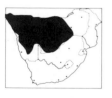

3 REDBILLED FRANCOLIN *Francolinus adspersus*. Common resident. Identified by red bill, yellow skin surrounding the eyes and *finely barred* underparts; cf. Natal Francolin (page 146). Has a very loud, harsh crowing call which increases to a frenzied cackling. Occurs in pairs and groups in Kalahari thornveld, frequents low scrub and thickets, especially along rivers, but feeds on open ground. 30-8 cm.

4 CAPE FRANCOLIN *Francolinus capensis*. Common resident. A large, dark francolin, only the underparts prominently streaked white. Shows a blackish tail in flight. The call is a loud, high-pitched cackling 'kwek, kwek, kwek, kwekek-kwekek-kwekek-kwekek-kwekek-kek-kek-kek...', the sound rising and then decreasing in volume and fading at the end. Singly or in small groups in Macchia, wooded kloofs and riverside scrub. 40-5 cm.

143

144

1 HARTLAUB'S FRANCOLIN *Francolinus hartlaubi*. Fairly common, localised resident. Differs from other francolins in small size, males with heavily streaked underparts and disproportionately large bills, females by general buff colouring. Has a squeaky alarm call; other calls unknown. Found in small parties on koppies. 25-30 cm.

2 GREYWING FRANCOLIN *Francolinus africanus*. Common resident. Predominantly grey, the *throat well spotted with black*, the underparts *closely barred black* thus differing from all white-throated species (overleaf). Immatures have more white about the throat and the barring of the underparts extends to the lower neck. The normal call is a squeaky 'kwe-kwe-kwe-kwe-skwekeeoo-skwekeeoo-skwekeeoo-keeoo-keeoo'. If flushed groups rise steeply into the air with much noise. Occur in groups of five to ten on grassy hillsides, montane grasslands and coastal flats. 31-3 cm.

3 REDNECKED FRANCOLIN *Francolinus afer*. Common resident. At least six different plumage forms but *in all* bill, facial mask, throat and legs are red: (a) Swaziland, eastern and northern Transvaal; (b) eastern Cape to Natal; (c) eastern Zimbabwe to Beira district; (d) (the smallest) Cunene River region, Namibia; other forms intermediate between these. The call is a harsh crowing 'choorr, choorr, choorr, chwirr' fading at the end or, when flushed, 'choor-choor'. Small groups occur in valley bush, forest fringes, coastal bush and fallow agricultural lands. If pursued takes refuge in trees. 32-44 cm.

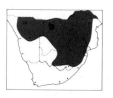

4 SWAINSON'S FRANCOLIN *Francolinus swainsonii*. Common resident. The *only red-necked francolin with black legs and black bill*, the basic plumage colour uniform overall; cf. previous species. Makes a harsh crowing 'krrraaak-krrraaak-krrraaak ...' fading at the end. Single birds or small groups are found in bushveld, woodland and fallow agricultural lands, usually not far from water. Males call from a low branch or anthill. 34-9 cm.

145

♂ 1 ♀

2

a

c

d

3

4

b

146

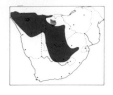

1 ORANGE RIVER FRANCOLIN *Francolinus levaillantoides*. Common resident. The palest forms (a) occur in central and northern Botswana and, with more deep red spotting on the underparts, also in Namibia; elsewhere is more rufous about the head and underparts, more liberally spotted deep red (b) and (c). Distinguished from the Redwing (3) by the red spotting of the underparts *extending up to the white throat* and lack of a black and white speckled patch on the upper breast. The call is 'pirrie-perrie, pirrie-perrie, pirrie-perrie...'. Groups of about twelve are found in dry regions with sparse vegetation, flat, hilly or montane. 33-5 cm.

2 SHELLEY'S FRANCOLIN *Francolinus shelleyi*. Uncommon to locally common resident. Differs from the Greywing Francolin (previous page) in *clear white throat with black surround*, clear white stripe over the eye and ear-coverts, plus a *large patch* of deep red blotches on the upper breast and extending to the flanks. The call is a shrill, musical crowing, sounding like 'I'll drink yer beer' repeated three or four times. Found in bushveld and grassland (montane grassland in eastern Zimbabwe) especially near koppies. Most common in the north of its range. 33 cm.

3 REDWING FRANCOLIN *Francolinus levaillantii*. Uncommon resident. Differs from the Orange River Francolin (1) in having an extensive ochre patch extending from the eye to the lower hind neck and a *large patch of black and white speckling on the upper breast*. The call is a high-pitched 'cherp-cherp-cherp-cherp-chirreechoo-chirreechoo-chirreechoo....'. Favours grasslands at all altitudes. Usually in small groups. 38-40 cm.

4 NATAL FRANCOLIN *Francolinus natalensis*. Common resident. Identified by entirely *black and white barred underparts* (bolder bars than those of the Redbilled Francolin, page 142), plus red legs and red bill with a yellow base. The call is a harsh 'kwali, KWALI, kwali'; when alarmed makes a raucous cackling. Favours granite koppies, riverine forests, wooded valleys and thornveld, generally in rocky situations and seldom far from water in parties of six to ten. 30-8 cm.

5 CHUKAR PARTRIDGE *Alectoris chukar*. An introduced species, feral on Robben Island. Has bold black barring on the flanks plus a black band encircling the foreparts from forehead to upper breast. Has a cackling call. 33 cm.

Buttonquails. Family TURNICIDAE. Very small terrestrial birds, superficially similar to true quails (page 140) but lacking a hind toe. Colour patterns similar in both sexes but females are more richly coloured than males. Immatures are like males but spotted all over their breasts. They flush reluctantly, usually at one's feet, then fly low for a short distance before settling again.

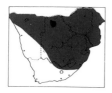

1 KURRICHANE BUTTONQUAIL *Turnix sylvatica*. Common resident. Told from the next species by whitish sides to the head, cream-coloured eye and heart-shaped spots on the sides of the neck and breast. The call is a deep, resonant 'hoo hoo' made at two second intervals by the female. Singly or in pairs in grassland with patches of tall grass, bushveld with good grass cover, cultivated and fallow farmlands. 14-15 cm.

2 BLACKRUMPED BUTTONQUAIL (HOTTENTOT BUTTON-QUAIL) *Turnix hottentotta*. Uncommon resident. Told from the previous species by chestnut sides to the head, brown eye; in flight by dark rump. The call resembles that of the previous species but is lower in pitch. Singly or in pairs in moist grassland and irrigated lands. Sparse and irregular. 14-15 cm.

Guineafowls. Family NUMIDIDAE. Differ from the related pheasants, partridges and francolins in having bare heads surmounted by casques or plumes, unfeathered necks in adults, predominantly grey plumages and lack of leg-spurs. Highly gregarious unless breeding.

3 HELMETED GUINEAFOWL *Numida meleagris*. Very common resident. Told by blue neck, red cap and horny casque on head. Chick (a) is buffy-brown, striped darker; juveniles (b) predominantly brown, darker on upperparts, head-stripes remaining until casque has started growing (cf. francolins, pages 142-46); immatures (c) resemble adults but have feathered necks, dark brown helmet and rudimentary casque. Normal adult call is a much-repeated 'ker-bek-ker-bek-ker-bek, krrrrrr...'; females also make a continual piping 't-phueet-t-phueet-t-phueet...'. Flocks when not breeding, sometimes very large, in grasslands, bushveld and farmlands. Go to water regularly in the evenings. 53-8 cm.

4 CRESTED GUINEAFOWL *Guttera pucherani*. Locally common resident. Blacker than the previous species, with characteristic black head-plumes. Immatures are barred on the upperparts with chestnut, buff and black. Has a rattling alarm call and, when breeding, 'tick-tack, ticktack-tirr-tirr-tirr'. Flocks occur in lowland and riverine forests, lowveld broadleafed woodland and thickets, coastal bush and dune forests. 50 cm.

150

1 OSTRICH (Family STRUTHIONIDAE) *Struthio camelus*. Common resident. Well-known, enormous, flightless bird. Immatures are like small scruffy females and are usually accompanied by adults. Males make a lion-like roar. Usually in pairs or groups, sometimes with many young birds present. In the wild state occurs in isolated pockets throughout Southern Africa and especially in the larger wildlife reserves. Is found in woodland and wooded grassland in the east and in thornveld or grassland in the more arid western regions. The tail colour of adult males varies, according to region, from whitish to grey or cinnamon-brown. *c.* 2 m.

2 SECRETARYBIRD (Family SAGITTARIIDAE) *Sagittarius serpentarius*. Common resident. Large, long-legged grey and black bird with long, loose black feathers projecting behind the head; adults with orange faces, immatures with yellow faces. Normally silent, but sometimes makes a frog-like croak. Usually in pairs walking through grassland, bushveld or thornveld at all altitudes. Sometimes runs a short distance with spread wings and may also soar to a great height. Roosts on top of thorn trees. 125-50 cm.

1

♂

♀

2

Vultures, kites, eagles, buzzards, hawks, harriers and Gymnogene. Family ACCIPITRIDAE. Diurnal birds of prey (raptors) characterised by hooked beaks suited to a mainly carnivorous diet. Each group hereafter described separately.

Vultures are typified by large size, heavy, hooked bills, necks wholly or partially devoid of feathers (the exception being the aberrant Bearded Vulture) and, for a bird of prey, relatively weak feet not suited to grasping prey. Vultures feed on carrion, soar with ease during much of the day, and bathe in ponds and rivers. Normally silent birds, but hiss and squeal when squabbling over food.

1 WHITEBACKED VULTURE *Gyps africanus.* Common resident. Adults difficult to distinguish from the next species unless the white back is seen, but at close range the eye is dark (not honey-coloured); old birds become very pale. Immature birds lack a white rump but differ from young of the next species in darker, less rufous plumage, black (not pink) skin on neck and no white collar-feathers. A bushveld vulture, it normally outnumbers all others in this habitat and gathers regularly in considerable numbers at carrion. Otherwise in good weather soars all day at a great height. Roosts and nests in trees; cf. next species. 90-8 cm.

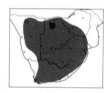

2 CAPE VULTURE *Gyps coprotheres.* Common resident. Similar to, but larger than, the previous species. Adults are very pale in colour and may have almost white backs; at close range eye is honey-coloured. Immatures more rufous, warmer brown than immature Whitebacked Vultures, the neck pink with white feathers at the base. Frequents high cliffs when breeding (May-October), colonies then comprise dozens or hundreds of birds, otherwise singly or in groups anywhere but rare in Zimbabwe and Mozambique. The common vulture of the central regions and ranging widely when not breeding. Often perches on electricity pylons. 105-15 cm.

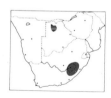

3 BEARDED VULTURE (LAMMERGEIER) *Gypaetus barbatus.* Uncommon, localised resident. Differs from all other vultures in loosely feathered head and legs, the 'beard' visible in both adults and immatures. Unlikely to be confused with any other bird of prey within its restricted range; in flight wedge-shaped tail diagnostic. Singly or in small numbers in the Drakensberg Mountains of Natal, eastern Orange Free State, Lesotho and north-eastern Cape, rarely further afield. Soars by day and roosts on inaccessible cliffs. 110 cm.

UNDERWING:
Cape Vulture

UNDERWING:
Whitebacked Vulture

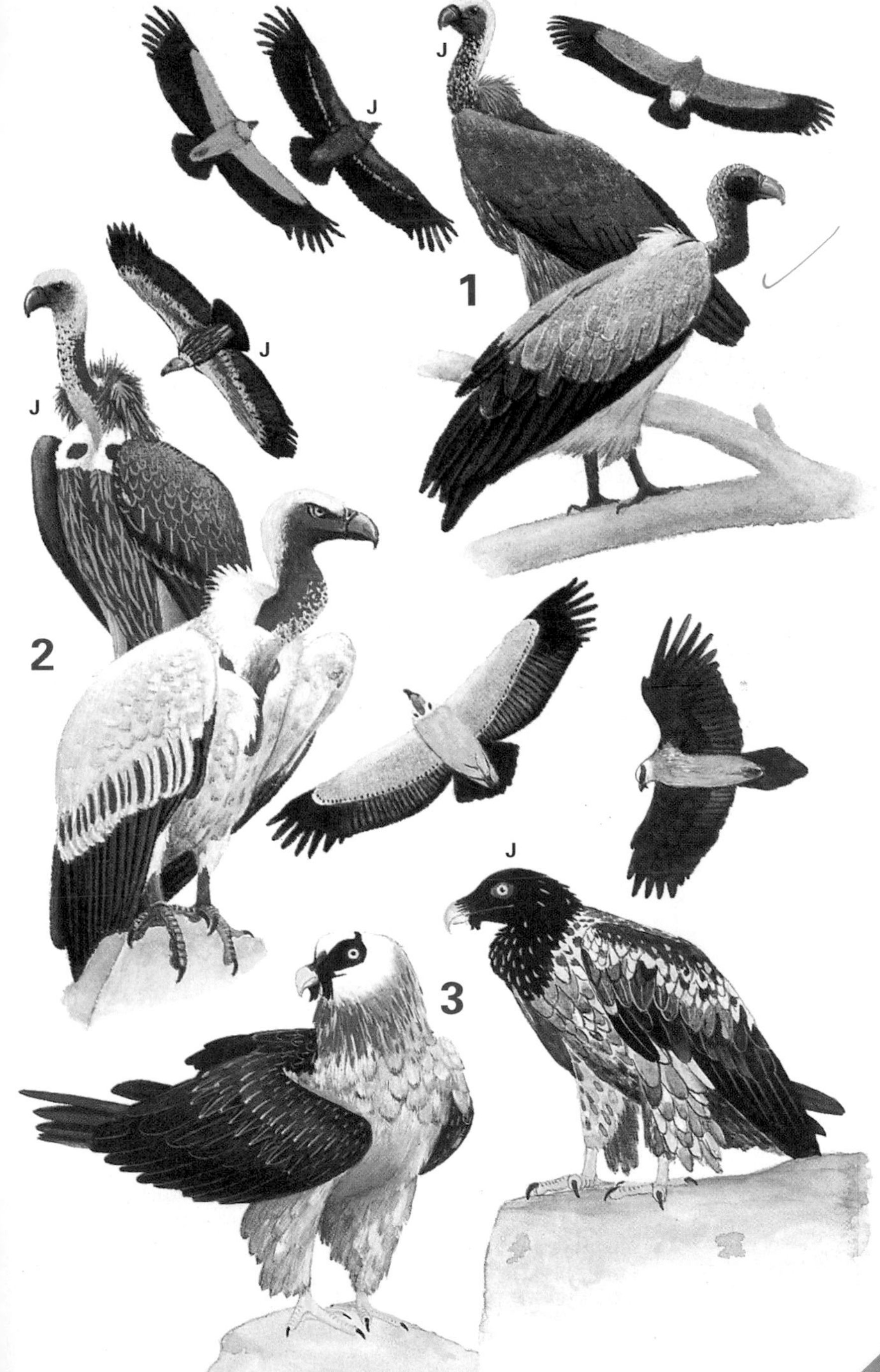
J
J
1
J
J
2
J
3

154

VULTURES

1 HOODED VULTURE *Necrosyrtes monachus*. Fairly common resident. A small, slender-billed vulture, adults with white downy feathers of the hind neck forming a hood over the head plus white ruff, 'pants' and legs; cf. others on this page which all have heavy bills. See underwing flight patterns below. Immatures are all-brown including downy head and neck, the face only pink; the rare Egyptian Vulture immature (overleaf) also has a slender bill but differs in having a well-feathered head. Occurs in bushveld regions in small numbers and joins other vultures at carrion. Most frequently seen in game reserves where mammalian predators occur. 70 cm.

HOODED VULTURES FROM BELOW

Adult   Immature

2 WHITEHEADED VULTURE *Trigonoceps occipitalis*. Uncommon resident. Distinguished by large size, adults with white heads, necks, underparts and heavy red and blue bill plus pink face and legs. Females differ from males in having white inner secondary wing-feathers visible both at rest and in flight; see below. Immatures much browner on underparts, head-feathers tawny. At carrion usually seen in pairs, greatly outnumbered by other vultures. 85 cm.

WHITEHEADED VULTURES FROM BELOW

Male   Female

3 LAPPETFACED VULTURE *Torgos tracheliotus*. Fairly common resident. A huge, massive-billed vulture, adults with crimson head and neck, plus streaked underparts with white 'pants' which contrast with dark body and underwings in flight; see below. The immature has dark 'pants' and various amounts of white mottling on the mantle. The long feathers of the ruff can be raised to frame the head, as illustrated. Usually in pairs in bushveld regions or, in the arid west, thornveld and desert. A powerfully built vulture which dominates all others at food sources. 115 cm.

LAPPETFACED VULTURES FROM BELOW

Adult   Immature

J

J

♀

J

1

2

J

3

J

1 EGYPTIAN VULTURE *Neophron percnopterus.* Rare visitor. Immatures can be confused with immatures of the Hooded Vulture (previous page), but the head is fully feathered not covered in woolly down. At all ages has a distinctly diamond-shaped tail when seen in flight; cf. next species. Singly, especially in wildlife reserves or scavenging in the more rural areas, but very infrequent. 64-71 cm.

2 PALMNUT VULTURE (VULTURINE FISH EAGLE) *Gypohierax angolensis.* Rare visitor and localised resident. Adults and immatures differ from the previous species in having no loose feathers on the head, heavier, more aquiline bills and, in flight, squarish (not diamond-shaped) tails. Adult distinguished by entirely white head, neck and body, black wing-feathers and tail; cf. African Fish Eagle (page 168). Occurs singly or in pairs most regularly in Mozambique, coastal Zululand, northern Botswana and northern Namibia, a vagrant to other scattered northerly points, particularly immature birds. At the coast frequents stands of oil palms (on which it feeds and in which it breeds) or forages on beaches and the shores of lagoons and pans. Spends long periods each day perched, but, unlike other vultures, flies at any time regardless of thermals. 60 cm.

J

1

J

J

2

J

Milvus kites. Large, long-winged raptors with V-shaped tails. Spend much of the day flying in leisurely fashion at low height while scanning the ground, their tails constantly twisting as they manoeuvre. Feed by scavenging and also catch various small animals.

1 YELLOWBILLED KITE *Milvus aegyptius.* Common summer resident. Distinguished from the Black Kite by yellow bill, brown head and more deeply forked tail. Immatures have a black bill (only the cere is yellow), but are distinguished from the Black Kite by brown head and more rufous colouring on underparts. While flying sometimes calls 'kleeeuw', ending with a trill. Occurs anywhere, sometimes in large flocks at a food source, and mixes with the Black Kite. 55 cm.

2 BLACK KITE *Milvus migrans migrans.* Common summer visitor. Distinguished from the Yellowbilled Kite by greyish head at all ages plus black bill (only the cere is yellow) and less deeply forked tail which appears square-cut when fanned. Immatures are paler below with brown blotches. More often seen in flocks than the Yellowbilled, especially large gatherings at emergences of flying termites; otherwise behaviour the same. 55 cm.

Snake eagles. Characterised by *unfeathered legs*, head with loose feathers which give a round-headed appearance, plus large yellow eyes. Still-hunt by watching the ground from a perch or hunt while flying.

3 WESTERN BANDED SNAKE EAGLE *Circaetus cinerascens.* Uncommon, localised resident. A small, robust, ash-brown eagle, distinguished from the next species at all ages by the single broad, dark tail-bar (a second bar is mostly obscured by the undertail-coverts) and by indistinct barring on belly only. Immature birds variable, at first mainly white about the head and underparts. Occurs in riverine forests and flood-plains, still-hunting from a leafless branch in a tall tree. 55 cm.

4 SOUTHERN BANDED SNAKE EAGLE *Circaetus fasciolatus.* Uncommon, localised resident. Distinguished from the previous species at all ages by longer tail with two bars, adults also by well-barred underparts from lower breast to vent. Young birds as young of previous species except for tail-bars. Occurs sparsely in coastal Zululand, Mozambique and eastern Zimbabwe. Frequents open areas near exotic plantations, riverine forests and lowland forests. Still-hunts from a tree. 60 cm.

SNAKE EAGLES

1 BATELEUR *Terathopius ecaudatus*. Common but localised resident. A distinctive, bulky-looking black eagle with red facial skin and legs and tawny wing-coverts, females with tawny secondaries; see (a). The back is normally chestnut-brown, less often creamy white as (b). In flight appears almost tailless, long wings tapered, males with widest black trailing edge; see below. Immatures have longer tails and progress from uniform dull brown with slaty face and legs (c) to brown mottling with purple face and legs (d). In flight may call a loud 'schaaaaaaaw', while perched often calls 'kau-kau-kau-ko-aaagh'. Sometimes makes wing-claps while flying. Normally flies at low altitude over bushveld and woodland with little wing-flapping; long, prolonged glides with a sideways rocking action as though balancing. 55-70 cm.

BATELEURS FROM BELOW

Adult male; Adult female

Sub-adult male; Immature female

2 BLACKBREASTED SNAKE EAGLE (SHORT-TOED EAGLE) *Circaetus gallicus*. Fairly common resident. Adults differ from the larger Martial Eagle (page 168) in having *bare legs*, unspotted underparts and, in flight, predominantly white (not dark) underwings. Immatures start as (a) then progress to stage (b), the head gradually darkening, underparts becoming clear. Usually singly in bushveld or grassland, occasionally perched, more often flying high and hovering; *the only eagle to hover regularly*. Snakes when caught are taken into the air, killed and eaten in flight. Nomadic. 63-8 cm.

BLACKBREASTED SNAKE EAGLES FROM BELOW

Adult

Immature

3 BROWN SNAKE EAGLE *Circaetus cinereus*. Common resident. Large brown eagle identified by whitish, unfeathered legs, large yellow eyes and erect stance when perched. In flight dark body and underwing-coverts contrast with silvery-white flight feathers, the tail with four clear, dark bands. Immatures start with similar plumage to adults, less dark (a), then progress to mottled stage (b). At all ages the downy under-feathers are white, therefore even adults appear speckled when moulting. Singly in any woodland or coastal grassland. Still-hunts from a bare branch or pylon, taking large snakes and killing them and eating them on the ground or in a tree. Occasionally hovers. Nomadic. 71-6 cm.

BROWN SNAKE EAGLES FROM BELOW

Adult

Immature

162

True eagles are distinguished from all other raptors by their *fully feathered legs*. Prey is killed either by impact or by crushing in powerful talons and the flesh is torn by the well-hooked bill. Most eagles hunt while flying, wheeling effortlessly in rising warm air, and are seldom seen perched during fair weather.

1 BOOTED EAGLE *Hieraaetus pennatus.* Fairly common resident and summer visitor. Occurs in two colour morphs, dark brown (a) and white or buffy (b), the latter most common. At rest buffy wing-coverts show as a broad bar on the folded wing, plus diagnostic white shoulder-patch. In flight (see below) a translucent wedge-shape is visible on the inner primaries. Upperwing pattern similar to *Milvus* kites (page 158) but tail not forked. Immatures similar to adults. Occurs mainly in the montane regions of the northern Cape and Namibia, ranging more widely in summer as shown by the shaded region of the distribution map. 48 - 52 cm.

Pale morph   BOOTED EAGLES FROM BELOW   Dark morph

2 LESSER SPOTTED EAGLE *Aquila pomarina.* Common summer visitor. Identified at rest by narrowly feathered 'stovepipe' legs, immature with white spots on the folded wings. In flight appears broad-winged, tail rounded; from above immatures show translucent patches at the base of the primaries, thin white edges to the coverts and a white crescent at the base of the tail; cf. larger Steppe Eagle (overleaf). Usually in well-wooded regions and often mixes with Steppe Eagle flocks at termite emergences. 65 cm.

Adult   LESSER SPOTTED EAGLES FROM BELOW   Immature

3 WAHLBERG'S EAGLE *Aquila wahlbergi.* Common summer resident. Occurs in several colour morphs shown as (a), (b) and (c); (a) probably most common. Dark-headed and white-headed individuals also occur; see (d) and (e). In flight shows fairly narrow, parallel wings and *square tail held mostly closed*; see below. Sometimes makes a whistling 'peeeeoo' in flight. A summer-breeding eagle in bushveld, broadleafed woodland and wooded valleys. 55 - 60 cm.

WAHLBERG'S EAGLES FROM BELOW

Brown morph   White morph

163

164

EAGLES

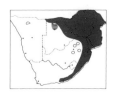

1 LONGCRESTED EAGLE *Lophaetus occipitalis*. Fairly common resident. Long-crested head and distinctive wing-pattern; the legs may be white or black and white. Sometimes calls in flight, a shrill 'weee-er' or 'peerr-wee' repeated. Usually singly in upland and coastal forest fringes, exotic plantations (especially *Eucalyptus*) and wooded valleys; prefers hilly, moist conditions. Soars mostly in the mornings, frequently perches prominently. 53-8 cm.

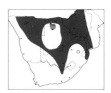

2 STEPPE EAGLE *Aquila nipalensis*. Fairly common summer visitor. Adults are darker and plainer than the darkest Tawny Eagle (3), and have prominent orange-yellow gapes extending back to a point *level with the back of the eyes;* a buffy patch is often present on the rear crown. Immatures at rest very like the next species but generally much paler and with the longer gape; in flight shows faint barring in the tail and much white in the wings (see illustrations below); cf. next species and Lesser Spotted Eagle (previous page). Eats termites and is often seen consuming them on the ground, especially in the Kalahari. Also raids breeding colonies of queleas (pages 402-4), feeding on eggs and nestlings. 75 cm.

STEPPE EAGLES FROM ABOVE

Adult

First-year immature

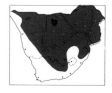

3 TAWNY EAGLE *Aquila rapax*. Fairly common resident. Adults either tawny with or without dark brown mottling on the wings (a and b), or red-brown with dark mottling (c). Immatures may be gingery-brown or pale as (d), then very similar to immatures of (2). At all ages the gape does not extend beyond the *centre of the eye.* In flight shows no barring in the tail, little white in the wings and none on the upper tail-coverts; see flight patterns below. Most frequent in wooded game areas where it perches conspicuously on the top of trees. 65-72 cm.

TAWNY EAGLES FROM BELOW

Adult (dark morph)

Immature (pale morph)

1 AYRES' EAGLE *Hieraaetus ayresii.* Uncommon resident. A small, rapacious eagle with white underparts either lightly spotted as (a) or dark and heavily spotted as (b). In adults forehead may be white or dark, then appears as a cap extending to below the eyes. Leading edge of the wing frequently unspotted, then shows as a white shoulder-patch on the folded wing, underwings heavily barred as illustrated; immatures much paler. Frequents well-wooded regions, wooded hillsides and *Eucalyptus* plantations, even in rural suburbia, but sparsely. 46-55 cm.

AYRES' EAGLE (IMMATURE)   AFRICAN HAWK EAGLE (IMMATURE)

FROM BELOW

2 AFRICAN HAWK EAGLE *Hieraaetus fasciatus.* Fairly common resident. Superficially resembles the previous species but is a medium-large eagle; females may be more heavily spotted than males. In flight underwing pattern diagnostic with characteristic white 'windows' at the base of the primaries and broad terminal tail-band. Immatures are rufous on the head and underparts with varying amounts of dark streaking on the breast as illustrated; cf. immature Black Sparrowhawk (page 180) which has *bare legs.* The call is a flute-like 'klu-klu-klukluee'. Usually in pairs in wooded savanna and well-wooded hillsides. Pairs soar conspicuously in the mornings, otherwise it perches within the canopies of well-foliaged trees for much of the day. 60-65 cm.

3 CROWNED EAGLE *Stephanoaetus coronatus.* Fairly common resident. Large and powerful, its comparatively short wings adapted to manoeuvring at speed through forest trees. Adults dark with crested head and heavily barred or blotched underparts; in flight barred underwings and tail plus rufous underwing-coverts are diagnostic. Young birds are initially white on the head and underparts (a), becoming progressively spotted and blotched with maturity (b). Pairs are very vocal within their territory, the male calling loudly during a daily undulating aerial display flight 'kewee-kewee-kewee . . .', repeated about 20 times as the bird dives and rises; female's voice lower-pitched: 'koi-koi-koi . . .'. Pairs have territories in evergreen forests, forested kloofs, dense riparian forests with large trees and well-wooded hillsides, often near water. 80-90 cm.

CROWNED EAGLE (IMMATURE) FROM BELOW

EAGLES

1 AFRICAN FISH EAGLE *Haliaeetus vocifer*. Fairly common resident. Well known and distinctive. Very young, free-flying birds (a) are easily mistaken for other brown eagles, but pale demarcation line of emergent white upper breast is usually detectable beneath the heavy brown markings; after one year the plumage pattern begins to resemble that of the adult although heavy brown streaks still remain on the white (b). The ringing, far-carrying call is 'weee-ah, hyo-hyo-hyo' or 'heee-ah, heeah-heeah', the male's voice more shrill than that of the female. Calls while perched or in the air. Usually in pairs at the larger rivers, lakes, dams, estuaries and seashores in remoter regions; immatures occasionally on small ponds. Conspicuous and noisy, perching on exposed waterside trees or flying over the water. 63-73 cm.

AFRICAN FISH EAGLE (IMMATURE) FROM BELOW

2 MARTIAL EAGLE *Polemaetus bellicosus*. Fairly common resident. Distinctive large, long-legged eagle, most similar to Blackbreasted Snake Eagle (page 160) but differing in spotted underparts and fully-feathered legs; in flight by dark (not whitish) underwings. Immatures as illustrated, differing from first-plumage Crowned Eagle (previous page) in brownish, not entirely white head. Calls a loud, ringing 'kloo-ee, kloo-ee...'. Singly in bushveld, woodland, thornveld, grassland and hill country. Hunts while flying or while perched in a leafy tree. 78-83 cm.

MARTIAL EAGLE (IMMATURE) FROM BELOW

3 BLACK EAGLE (VERREAUX'S EAGLE) *Aquila verreauxii*. Large black eagle with white 'V' mark on the back. In flight has characteristic narrow-based wings with white 'flashes' at the base of the primaries. Immatures mottled brown as illustrated, differing from Tawny Eagle (page 164) in rufous crown and nape, plus pale legs heavily marked with dark brown. Usually silent. Pairs are found in mountains, rocky hills and gorges, usually perched on rocks or flying at no great height. 84 cm.

BLACK EAGLE (IMMATURE) FROM BELOW

Jb

Ja

1

2

J

3

J

BUZZARDS

Buzzards are large, soaring hawks about the size of a small eagle, of robust build with fairly large, rounded heads, bills aquiline but small, ceres large, lower legs unfeathered, wings moderately long and rounded, tails rounded when spread.

1 STEPPE BUZZARD *Buteo buteo vulpinus*. Very common summer visitor. Adults variable, most commonly as (a) but dark form (b) and russet form (c) are frequently seen while other variations also occur. Diagnostic feature common to all except the very dark form is a distinct *pale zone across the breast*, which divides the streaked or smudged upper breast from the banded underparts. In flight the spread tail appears pale cinnamon with a dark terminal band. Immatures have the entire underparts streaked or blotched as illustrated, the eye paler. Much smaller than a Brown Snake Eagle (page 160) and lacks the large yellow eyes of that species. In flight sometimes calls 'kreeeeee', especially when two or more are flying together. This is the brown buzzard commonly seen on roadside telegraph poles in summer, or circling slowly overhead. Usually singly or two to three individuals in grassland and similar open situations, less often in wooded country, but flocks follow forested hills when migrating in October or early March. 45-50 cm.

2 FOREST BUZZARD *Buteo trizonatus*. Uncommon resident. Similar to the last species but smaller, at all ages the underparts with drop-shaped brown blotches (not horizontal bands), most densely in adults, with clear regions across the lower breast and under-belly. In flight from below wings appear whiter, tail with only indistinct terminal bar. Immatures have little spotting on underparts. The call, made in flight, is 'keeeo-oo'. Usually singly near montane plantations and forests or adjacent grassy plateaux, perching on the fringe of some open area. When disturbed flies easily through dense plantations. 45 cm.

LONGLEGGED BUZZARD *Buteo rufinus*. Very rare vagrant. Variable in colour but larger and more bulky-bodied than either (1) or (2) with pale head and longer legs. In flight (a) shows a dark under-belly and vent, broader, paler wings with dark carpal patches, white outer panels and a plain tail. A rare all-dark morph occurs; see (b). Seen rarely in southern Africa. 51-66 cm.

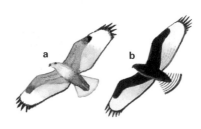

171

BUZZARDS

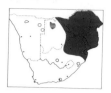

1 HONEY BUZZARD *Pernis apivorus.* Uncommon summer visitor. Slightly larger than the Steppe Buzzard (previous page) but could be mistaken for it. Plumage very variable; (a) probably most common, while a dark morph (b) and paler morphs occur (see below). Appears smaller-headed than a Steppe Buzzard with longer tail and with *yellow or orange* (not brown) eyes. In flight the head protrudes well forward of the long wings, underwings with dark carpal patches, tail with two dark central bands and one terminal band. Immatures lack distinct tail-bands have brown eyes. Prefers wooded country and may walk about the ground in search of wasps' and bees' nests. Sparsely distributed. 54 - 60 cm.

TWO PALE MORPH HONEY BUZZARDS FROM BELOW IN
FAST-GLIDE POSTURE

2 JACKAL BUZZARD *Buteo rufofuscus.* Common resident. In adults chestnut breast and tail distinctive; flight pattern shows rounded wings and wide, short tail. Occasionally occurs with breast blotchy-black, even all-white, then distinguished from the next species by dark (not white) underwing-coverts. Immatures are pale rufous, often much paler than illustrated, and show no tail-bands. The call is a jackal-like, high-pitched 'kweh' or a mewing 'kip-kweeeu, kweeeu, kweeeu' while flying. Occurs in hilly or montane regions and adjacent grasslands. Often perches on roadside telegraph poles. 44 - 53 cm.

3 AUGUR BUZZARD *Buteo augur.* Common resident. Adults distinctive with almost entirely white underparts and reddish tail. Female often has dark throat as illustrated, otherwise size and proportions same as previous species. In flight males are told from the Blackbreasted Snake Eagle (page 160) by reddish tail and more rounded wings. Immatures are similar to immatures of the previous species but lack the rufous tail; the underwing-coverts are slightly buffy, the secondaries and tail have light barring. Voice similar to that of the Jackal Buzzard (2). Prefers well-wooded hill country with rocky outcrops. 44 - 53 cm.

174

1 LIZARD BUZZARD *Kaupifalco monogrammicus.* Fairly common resident. A small, stocky grey hawk resembling an *Accipiter* (overleaf), but distinguished by diagnostic white throat with vertical black streak and two bold, white tail-bands (sometimes only one present). Immature more buffy above and below, throat-streak less clear. The call is a whistling 'klioo-klu-klu-klu' uttered regularly while perched. Occurs in broadleafed woodland, mixed bushveld and well-treed farmlands. Often perches partially concealed in a tree canopy. Nomadic. 35-7 cm.

2 BLACKSHOULDERED KITE *Elanus caeruleus.* Common resident. A distinctive small raptor with pure white underparts, grey upperparts, black carpal patches and ruby-red eyes. Graceful in flight, whitish with black wingtips; cf. the much larger summer-visiting Pallid Harrier (page 182). Immatures are similar but more buffy about the head and underparts as illustrated. Normally silent, but may utter a weak 'weeet-weeet-weeet' when agitated. Singly or in pairs in grasslands and lightly wooded country, including rural suburbia. Perches conspicuously on leafless trees, roadside poles and wires, often raising and lowering its tail while watching the ground. *In flight may hover* for periods of five to 20 seconds, and frequently hunts at dusk. Roosts communally in reed-beds or trees. 30 cm.

Goshawks and sparrowhawks. True hawks characterised by slender bodies, short, rounded wings, long tails, small sharp beaks and long bare, often slender, legs and toes. Secretive, catch their prey (usually small birds) in a low, rapid aerial pursuit from the cover of a leafy tree.

3 REDBREASTED SPARROWHAWK *Accipiter rufiventris.* Fairly common, localised resident. All-rufous, plain-bodied sparrowhawk, could be mistaken for immature Ovambo Sparrowhawk or smaller Gabar Goshawk (overleaf), but top of head and upperparts generally much darker. Singly in forests, dense woodland, exotic plantations and montane grassland with forest patches. Often hunts by flying through cover, surprising small birds; generally secretive. 33-40 cm.

1 LITTLE SPARROWHAWK *Accipiter minullus*. Fairly common resident. Adults identified by very small size, yellow eyes and slender yellow legs and, in flight, by two conspicuous white spots on the upper tail. Immatures recognised by heavy spotting on the underparts. Call a single-syllabled 'ki' rapidly repeated. Singly in densely wooded situations, forest fringes, riverine forests, woodland, wooded valleys and exotic plantations. Secretive. 23-5 cm

2 LITTLE BANDED GOSHAWK (SHIKRA) *Accipiter badius*. Fairly common resident. Adults identified by banded underparts extending to the throat, deep red eyes and, in flight, by *lack of any white on the rump* and upper tail; may sometimes show some white spots on the mantle. Immatures differ from immatures of the previous species in having more orange-yellow eyes and legs, and broad, reddish-brown streaks and banding on the underparts; from immatures of the next species in dark cap, plus eye and leg colour. Call a metallic, two-syllabled 'kli-vit' repeated, also a plaintive 'tee-uuu'. Singly in broadleafed woodland, thornveld, mixed bushveld and riverine bush. Less secretive than other small Accipiter hawks, frequently perching in the open, even on telephone poles. 30-4 cm.

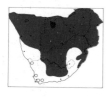

3 GABAR GOSHAWK *Micronisus gabar*. Fairly common resident. Normal adults (a) identified by grey throat and breast plus deep red eyes, red cere and legs and, in flight, by *broad, white rump-patch*. Melanistic form (b) has same colours of soft parts but lacks the white rump. Immatures as illustrated, boldly blotched rufous all over head, neck and breast, eyes yellow, cere and legs coral. In flight shows white rump; cf. immature of previous species. Call a high-pitched, rapid piping 'pi-pi-pi-pi-pi...'. Singly in thornveld and mixed bushveld. Hunts in low flight in more open country, otherwise from a perch within cover. 30-4 cm.

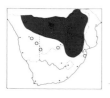

4 OVAMBO SPARROWHAWK *Accipiter ovampensis*. Fairly common resident. Adults identified by grey barring on underparts extending to throat, cere yellow, orange or red, legs yellow or red. In flight shows pale central tail feather-shafts, small white rump-patch variable, often absent. Immatures either pale (a) or rufous (b), the rufous form more common in Zimbabwe, lightly marked on underparts, cere and legs dull yellow or orange. A rare melanistic form occurs. Call a slowly repeated 'kiep, kiep, keip...' or 'wo-wo-wo-wo...' rising in scale. Sparsely distributed in thornveld and broadleafed woodland or, in the highveld, in stands of *Eucalyptus* or poplars (*Populus* spp.) where it is the most common small Accipiter. 33-40 cm.

1 AFRICAN GOSHAWK *Accipiter tachiro*. Fairly common resident. A medium-sized goshawk (females much larger than males), with slate-grey upperparts, the underparts finely barred rufous; eyes and legs yellow. Immatures browner above, the underparts well spotted with black drop-shaped blotches; cf. much smaller immature Little Sparrowhawk (previous page). Territorial males display in the mornings by flying high with bouts of fast wing-beats followed by glides while calling 'krit' at two- or three-second intervals; may also make the same call from cover while perched. Unobtrusive in montane and lowland forests, riparian forests and wooded valleys plus exotic plantations and suburban fringes. Partially crepuscular. 37-9 cm.

2 PALE CHANTING GOSHAWK *Melierax canorus*. Common resident. Large, pale grey goshawk with pink cere and legs. Difficult to tell from the next species when perched, except for slightly paler upperparts, but in flight shows much white on the upperwings plus a *white rump;* see below. Immatures of this and the next species very similar. In the breeding season adults call loudly and melodiously while perched, especially at dawn 'kleeeeuw, kleeeeuw, kleeeeuw, klu-klu-klu-klu'. Occurs in arid thornveld, Karoo and Kalahari sandveld. Perches conspicuously with upright stance on the top of a thornbush or on a roadside post. Also forages on the ground in search of small prey, peering under rocks and logs. Seldom flies high, usually moves with low swoops from perch to perch. South of the Limpopo River its distribution is mostly west of the next species. 53-63 cm.

3 DARK CHANTING GOSHAWK *Melierax metabates*. Fairly common resident. Very similar to the previous species but slightly darker grey. In flight the upperwings are more uniform grey, the rump finely barred (not pure white); see illustration. Immatures browner, the soft parts initially yellow, becoming orange or coral-red while still in immature plumage. In the breeding season adults call from a perch for long periods 'phaleeoo-phwe-phwe-phwe-phwe . . .', the last sound often repeated up to 30 times. Frequents broadleafed woodland and mixed bushveld; usually perches on the top of a tree for long periods. South of the Limpopo River its distribution is mostly east of the previous species. 50-56 cm.

1 BLACK SPARROWHAWK *Accipiter melanoleucus*. Fairl common resident. Large black and white hawk, normally wit white or partially white underparts (a), thighs and vent eithe speckled black and white or entirely black, eyes orange or re cere and legs dull yellow. Melanistic form (b) has only throat whit plus some white feathers on the flanks. Immatures buffy belo streaked with dark brown, may be more streaked than illustratio cf. immature African Hawk Eagle (page 167) which is larger and ha fully feathered legs. Usually silent but may call 'kew-kew-kew kew-kew' near its nest. Singly or in pairs in well-developed riverin forest, woodland or, more commonly, *Eucalyptus* plantations Though retiring and difficult to see, frequently breeds near huma habitations. 46-58 cm.

Harriers. Long-winged, long-tailed, long-legged hawks, whic inhabit grasslands or marshes. Usually fly low with leisurel buoyant flight, head bent downwards and legs hanging slightl bouts of flapping alternating with glides. Settle on the ground c perch on posts, seldom on trees. Silent birds.

2 BLACK HARRIER *Circus maurus*. Fairly common resider Adults appear entirely black when settled, but in flight sho striking white flight-feathers, white rump and banded tail. Sexe are alike. Immatures have pale buff underparts and heavily spotte upper breast, in flight show white wing flashes and white rum Singly or in pairs over Macchia, Karoo, grassland and cropland occasionally hovering briefly before dropping to the ground. 4 53 cm.

3 EUROPEAN MARSH HARRIER *Circus aeruginosus*. Ur common summer visitor. At rest males differ from African Mars Harrier (overleaf) in paler head; in flight by much paler unde wings plus grey upperwings and tail: see below. Females muc darker, almost black, with pale crown and wing leading edge Frequents marshlands and moist fields. 48-56 cm.

1 AFRICAN MARSH HARRIER *Circus ranivorus*. Common resident. Adults differ from the very rare European Marsh Harrier (previous page) in darker, more richly coloured underparts, although old birds may become whiter about the head; also more richly coloured on underparts than females of the next two species, tail not obviously barred from above. Immatures with diagnostic, pale breast-band. Usually singly, flying over marshlands and reed-beds, occasionally over cultivated fields. Rests on the ground, sometimes on a fence post. 44-9 cm.

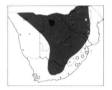

2 PALLID HARRIER *Circus macrourus*. Rare summer visitor. Males differ from males of the next species in appearing *much whiter* in the field, wing-tips with only narrow black sections, otherwise plain pale grey above, totally white below; cf. Black-shouldered Kite (page 174). Females indistinguishable from female Montagu's Harrier (3) unless white ruff-collar is visible behind the dark ear coverts; *white rump* and clearly banded tail separate these from African Marsh Harrier (1). Singly, flying low over lowland and montane grassland, often near the edges of woodland. Nomadic. 44-8 cm.

3 MONTAGU'S HARRIER *Circus pygargus*. Uncommon summer visitor. Males recognised by darker grey colouring than males of the previous species, this extending over the head, throat and breast, rest of underparts with brown streaks; in flight by *entirely* black wing-tips, the upper-wings with additional black bars along the centres, underwings with narrow black and rufous barring. Altogether less white than Pallid Harrier. Females hardly distinguishable from Pallid except for the lack of any white markings behind the ear coverts; white rump and well-barred tail preclude confusion with African Marsh Harrier (1). Single birds are usually seen flying low over grasslands, frequently in same areas as previous species. Nomadic. 40-7 cm.

184

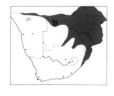

1 BAT HAWK *Macheiramphus alcinus*. Uncommon resident. A dark brown hawk with pale yellow eyes and white legs and feet. At close range diagnostic features are a dark centre line on a pale throat, two white spots on the back of the head and white eyelids. In flight appears sharp-winged, the flight rapid. The immature has white underparts with dark streaking on the lower breast plus a variable amount of white spotting on the underwings. When displaying adults may call a high-pitched 'kik-kik-kik-kik-keee'. By day roosts well concealed in a leafy tree, emerging to hunt bats and small birds only at dusk or, in dull weather, also in the early morning. Frequents riparian forests, evergreen forests and other heavily wooded regions, including the edges of exotic plantations. 45 cm.

2 OSPREY (Family PANDIONIDAE) *Pandion haliaetus*. Uncommon visitor. Slightly crested head, masked appearance and white underparts identify this species at rest, the breast-band often vestigial, strongest in immatures. In flight appears large-winged, small-headed, underwings with bold, dark carpal patches and dark central bar, tail well banded. Normally silent. Singly at coastal bays, estuaries and lagoons or large inland waters. Spends much of the day perched over or near water on a post, branch or rock. Hunts over water, flying slowly with shallow, loose wing-beats, occasionally hovering briefly; plunge-dives when catching fish. 55-63 cm.

3 GYMNOGENE *Polyboroides typus*. Common resident. A large grey hawk with black flight feathers and black tail with a *bold white central band,* bare yellow face (flushes red when excited) and legs. In flight appears broad-winged, white tail-bar diagnostic; sometimes has dark carpal patches on the upperwings. Young birds initially dark brown, later light brown and more mottled; see illustrations. In flight may make a high-pitched whistle 'su-eeee-oo', particularly near its nest, otherwise silent. Occurs in a wide range of habitats from montane forests and plantations to woodland, bushveld or thornveld at lower levels, especially riparian forests and wooded valleys. Clambers about trees and rocks, inserting its long legs into cavities in search of bats, lizards and other small creatures, and raids weaver, swift and woodpecker nests to eat the nestlings. 60-66 cm.

1 CUCKOO HAWK *Aviceda cuculoides*. Uncommon resident. Recognised by bulky appearance, high forehead and *crested head*. In flight shape is harrier-like with long wings and tail, but flight action buoyant and leisurely, wing-beats slow with spells of gliding, rufous 'armpits' diagnostic. Immatures with crested heads and wing pattern similar to adults. Calls 'ticki-to-you' repeated slowly. Usually singly, near edges of forests, riverine forests, mixed woodland and plantations. Spends much time perched at a conspicuous vantage-point but also makes occasional, high soaring flights. 40 cm.

Falcons. Small raptors characterised by pointed wings and, usually, prominent 'sideburns'. Females are larger than males. Aerial hunters, typically seizing smaller birds in a rapid dive from above. Characteristic calls are high-pitched 'kek-kek-kek-kek' sounds when agitated. Kestrels are small falcons which eat insects caught in the air with their feet or small mammals and reptiles caught on the ground. Their flight is more leisurely than that of true falcons.

2 PYGMY FALCON *Polihierax semitorquatus*. Common resident. Identified by very small size, entirely white underparts; in flight by speckled wings and white rump. A species of the dry west, less frequently in Mozambique. Pairs usually seen perched on thorn trees or baobabs, often close to the nests of the Sociable Weaver (page 406) or Redbilled Buffalo Weaver (page 404) with which it lives in close association. 19.5 cm.

3 TAITA FALCON *Falco fasciinucha*. Rare, localised resident. A stocky, short-tailed falcon identified by unmarked underparts; in flight by large *yellowish feet*. Haunts rocky gorges and cliffs, especially along the Zambezi River. Flies strongly and at speed. May be seen trying to catch swifts or bats in the evening. 28 cm.

4 SOOTY FALCON *Falco concolor*. Uncommon, localised summer visitor. Adults all-grey with blackish face and pale yellow cere and legs, differing from Grey Kestrel (page 190) in darker colour and long, pointed wings which extend beyond the tail when perched. Immatures also *greyer* than similar small falcons, with grey spots on creamy underparts, *white hind collar* and no rufous colouring. Occurs in coastal forests, bush and stands of exotic trees and is active mostly at dusk, otherwise perches most of day. 31 cm.

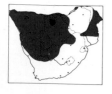

5 REDNECKED FALCON *Falco chicquera*. Uncommon resident. Identified at all ages by rusty head-top and nape plus well-barred appearance. Generally seen in association with *Hyphaene* palm trees in the north and east, with Camelthorn trees in the west. Mainly in arid areas, especially in dry riverbeds. Hunts other birds in sallies from a tree. 30-6 cm.

187

FALCONS

1 PEREGRINE FALCON *Falco peregrinus.* Uncommon resident and summer visitor. Resident birds (a) have closely barred underparts, visiting birds are whiter, lightly spotted (b); immatures lightly streaked. In flight appears sharper-winged than the next species, though less so than the Hobby Falcon (3). Usually near cliffs when breeding, otherwise anywhere, frequently in towns. Flies with rapid, shallow wing-beats followed by a brief glide, but spends much of the day perched. Sparsely distributed. 34-8 cm.

PEREGRINE FALCONS FROM BELOW

Adult

Immature

2 LANNER FALCON *Falco biarmicus.* Fairly common resident. The largest falcon in the region, identified at all ages by whitish underparts and *russet crown.* In flight appears broader-winged than the previous species, and the *tail is spread* much of the time. Immatures have heavily streaked underparts; the russet crown is paler than in adults. Occurs in almost any habitat, most often near cliffs or in lightly wooded country, but also frequents tall buildings in some towns and patches of *Eucalyptus* trees. More frequently seen in flight than the Peregrine, progressing with bouts of fast wing-flapping followed by circling glides. 40-45 cm.

LANNER FALCONS FROM BELOW

Adult female

Adult male

Immature female

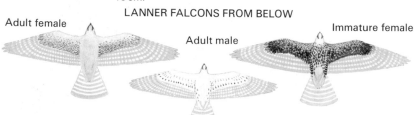

3 HOBBY FALCON *Falco subbuteo.* Uncommon summer visitor. A small falcon identified by heavily streaked body, adults with *rufous thighs and undertail-coverts;* in flight by long, pointed wings heavily marked on the undersides; see below. Singly or in small flocks in light woodland. Hunts mostly at dusk, flying rapidly and with agility in pursuit of swallows and bats, or more leisurely with much gliding when catching flying termites, which are seized with the feet. 30-35 cm.

HOBBY FALCONS FROM BELOW

Adult

Immature

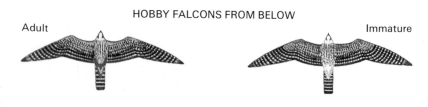

190

1 AFRICAN HOBBY FALCON *Falco cuvierii*. Rare summer resident and visitor. The most rufous falcon in the region, differing from any rufous kestrel (overleaf) in dark upperparts and behaviour. Likely to be seen singly in association with scattered palm trees in Kalahari sand, but sparsely distributed and irregular over much of its range. Flight shape and behaviour similar to the visiting Hobby Falcon (previous page). 28-30 cm.

2 GREATER KESTREL *Falco rupicoloides*. Common resident. At rest differs from Rock or Lesser Kestrels (overleaf) in entirely rufous plumage with blackish streaks, spots and bars all over, plus *whitish eyes*, and in flight by white underwings. Immatures are closely similar. Singly or in pairs in grassland or lightly wooded thornveld, especially in the more arid regions. Usually perches on top of a thorn tree or roadside post; sometimes hovers. 36 cm.

3 GREY KESTREL *Falco ardosiaceus*. Rare, localised resident. An all-grey kestrel with yellow soft parts, differing from the Sooty Falcon (page 186) mainly in shorter wings which *do not reach the end of the tail when perched*. Singly, in arid north-western, broadleafed woodland or thornveld, usually perched on tree or post from where it makes short, rapid, low flights to another perch or across open, grassy areas. Flight always fast and direct, *not* typically kestrel. Occurs sparsely. 30-3 cm.

4 DICKINSON'S KESTREL *Falco dickinsoni*. Fairly common, localised resident. Distinctive grey kestrel with almost white head and neck, very pale rump and yellow soft parts. Immatures are slightly browner on the underparts. Occurs singly or in pairs in broadleafed woodland, mixed bushveld and thornveld, especially in association with baobab trees and palms. Still-hunts from a tree perch, swooping to the ground to catch its prey. Capable of rapid flight but usually flies more leisurely. 28-30 cm.

191

192

1 ROCK KESTREL (COMMON KESTREL) *Falco tinnunculus*. Common resident. Females may or may not have grey heads, sometimes like immatures with head same colour at rest of plumage but heavily streaked dark brown (see margin illustration). Differs from next species mainly in lack of contrast between upper and lower parts, plus behaviour. Singly or in pairs in hilly country and grassland. Perches commonly on roadside telegraph poles or flies 5-20 m above ground, frequently turning into wind and *hovering*; cf. Blackshouldered Kite (page 174), the only other small raptor that regularly hovers. Roosts on cliffs or in trees. 30-3 cm.

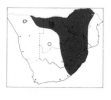

2 LESSER KESTREL *Falco naumanni*. Common summer visitor. Both sexes differ from previous species in paler underparts, (males with more grey in the wings), and different behaviour. Occurs in flocks, often hundreds in grassland and Karoo, perching on roadside posts, power pylons and lines, or bushes, or wheeling in leisurely flight. Flocks roost in tall trees (usually *Eucalyptus* trees) often in towns. 28-30 cm.

3 EASTERN REDFOOTED KESTREL (or FALCON) *Falco amurensis*. Common summer visitor. Small kestrels, both sexes distinctive. Immatures greyer, less rufous than immatures of next species. Occurs in flocks, often large, and frequently mixing with the previous or next species, in grassland and farmlands. Usually perches on power lines and roadside posts and fences, frequently taking flight for brief sorties before resettling. Roosts in tall trees. 28-30 cm.

4 WESTERN REDFOOTED KESTREL (or FALCON) *Falco vespertinus*. Uncommon summer visitor. Adults distinctive. Immatures more rufous than immatures of the previous species. Occurs in flocks and often mixes with that species. Habitat and behaviour identical but distribution usually more westerly. 28-30 cm.

193

Sandgrouse. Family PTEROCLIDIDAE. Pigeon-like birds with cryptic colouring, males more boldly patterned than females. Wings pointed, bills short, legs short with the front of the tarsus feathered to the toes. Walk in a shuffling manner but flight is swift and powerful, the birds often covering considerable distances daily to reach water where, at certain favoured pools, they gather in great flocks morning or evening. All inhabit arid western regions, the Doublebanded Sandgrouse ranging to the east.

1 DOUBLEBANDED SANDGROUSE *Pterocles bicinctus.* Common resident. Males distinguished by black and white bars on forehead, both sexes by fine black barring on belly. Calls 'chuck-chuck'; flocks come to drink after sunset calling 'Don't *weep* so Charlie'. Pairs or flocks in dry savanna and bushveld. 25 cm.

2 BURCHELL'S SANDGROUSE (SPOTTED SANDGROUSE) *Pterocles burchelli.* Common resident. Both sexes told from other sandgrouse by ochre colouring and all-over, heavy white spotting, male with grey about face, ear-coverts and throat, female with yellowish face and ochre barring on belly. If alarmed on the ground, utters a 'gug-gug-gug' sound but in flight calls 'chock-lit chock-lit, chock-lit'. Normally in pairs, but flocks at waterholes, in Kalahari sandveld. 25 cm.

3 NAMAQUA SANDGROUSE *Pterocles namaqua.* Common resident. Best told from other sandgrouse by long, pointed tails. Flight call 'kelkiewyn'. Pairs or flocks in sandy or stony deserts Kalahari, Karoo, thornveld and grassland. Frequently mixes with the previous species at waterholes, drinking mainly in the mornings. 28 cm.

4 YELLOWTHROATED SANDGROUSE *Pterocles gutturalis.* Locally common resident December–June. Larger than other sandgrouse, the male with bold black gorget, both sexes with clear, pale yellow throats and ear-coverts, blackish bellies and underwings. In flight calls a harsh 'tweet' or 'tweet-weet'; on arriving at a waterhole emits a hoarse 'golli, golli'. Pairs and flocks occur over much of Botswana, western Zimbabwe, northern Namibia and western Transvaal. 30 cm.

Pigeons and doves. Family COLUMBIDAE. A well-known group of birds. The distinction between pigeons and doves is ill defined: larger species tend to be called pigeons, smaller ones doves. Young are dull versions of the adults. All except the fruit eating pigeons feed on the ground.

1 MOURNING DOVE *Streptopelia decipiens*. Common resident. The only collared dove with a totally grey head plus *yellow eye* with red eye-ring. The call is distinctive, a soft 'kur-kurr' repeated once or twice; also a soft 'kur-r-r-r-r-r-r'. Occurs in thornveld and mixed bushveld adjacent to the larger rivers. Has a highly localised distribution, but is common where it occurs. Nomadic. 30 cm.

2 REDEYED DOVE *Streptopelia semitorquata*. Common resident. Differs from the previous species in having grey on top of the head only, *eye red* with a purple-pink eye-ring, the breast a deeper pink. The call is 'coo-coo, coo-*koo*-cuk-coo', the accent on the fourth syllable. Occurs in riverine forests, well-developed woodland, mixed bushveld, exotic plantations and suburbia. The largest of the ring-necked doves. 33-6 cm.

3 CAPE TURTLE DOVE *Streptopelia capicola*. Very common resident; locally abundant. The colouring varies locally from very pallid to quite sooty-grey, but in all the head is more or less uniform; has no eye-ring. In flight shows similar white outer tail feathers to (4), but mantle and wing-coverts greyish (no cinnamon). The call is a harsh 'work-*harder, work-harder* ..' much repeated; also a snarling 'kerrr' on landing. One of the commonest, most widespread birds in the region, occurring in a wide range of habitats, frequently with (4), but present also in more arid regions. 28 cm.

(EUROPEAN) TURTLE DOVE see page 446.

4 LAUGHING DOVE *Streptopelia senegalensis*. Very common, sometimes abundant resident. Has no black collar. Pinkish head and cinnamon breast with black spots plus rusty-coloured back diagnostic. In flight shows similar white outer tail-feathers to (3), but mantle is rusty or cinnamon coloured. The call is a soft 'coo-coo-CUK-coo-coo'. Widespread in a variety of habitats, often with (3), yet unaccountably absent from some regions. Frequently common in suburbia. 25 cm.

5 NAMAQUA DOVE *Oena capensis*. Common resident. At all ages identified by long tail, males with black patch from forehead to breast. In flight combination of brown flight-feathers and long tail diagnostic. The call is a seldom heard, explosive 'twoo-hoo'. Commonly seen in grassland, fallow fields, thornveld and eroded areas, particularly in drier regions. Perches on low bushes and fences, flies low at great speed. Nomadic and an irregular visitor to south and south-eastern coastal districts. 27 cm.

1

2

3

4

♂

5

♀

198

1 DELEGORGUE'S PIGEON (BRONZENAPED PIGEON) *Columba delegorguei*. Rare resident. A dark pigeon, males told by iridescent lower neck and mantle, showing purple-pink or green according to the fall of light, plus white feathering on mantle; female similar but head browner, no white on mantle. Call a quiet, rasping 'uh-hoo' followed by a softer, deeper 'cuck-koo, coo-coo-coo-coo-coo' descending the scale. Sparsely distributed in coastal and montane evergreen forests. Secretive, single birds or pairs remaining in the tree canopies, but highly mobile, flocks sometimes gathering to feed on ripe fruits. Most active early morning, late afternoon. 29 cm.

2 TAMBOURINE DOVE *Turtur tympanistria*. Fairly common resident. White underparts unique and conspicuous. Call 'coo, coo, cu-cu-du-du-du-du', very similar to Emeraldspotted Dove (overleaf) but speeding up, not tailing off, and terminates abruptly. Singly or in pairs in coastal bush, montane and riverine forests. Shy and elusive, perches in a low position or feeds on the ground. Makes off at great speed when disturbed. 23 cm.

3 GREEN PIGEON *Treron calva*. Common resident. Told by bright green colouring, yellow on wings and leg-feathers plus red base to bill and red legs. Call an explosive, high-pitched yet melodious bubbling, descending in pitch. Flocks frequent evergreen forest fringes, riverine forests and wooded hillsides where wild figs are fruiting. Difficult to locate from their habit of remaining still among the foliage, concealed by their cryptic colouring. When approached closely the flock 'explodes' from the tree and flies off rapidly. 30 cm.

4 CINNAMON DOVE *Aplopelia larvata*. Fairly common resident. Very shy and secretive, but its presence often revealed by its call, a soft, mournful and drawn-out 'hoo-oo'. Pairs inhabit the interiors of evergreen forests and plantations, feeding on the ground. Usually seen only when flushed, then flies off rapidly dodging through the trees. 25-30 cm.

5 ROCK PIGEON *Columba guinea*. Very common resident. Told by white-spotted upperparts and red facial mask. Call a loud cooing 'doo, doo, doo, doo...' rising to a crescendo, then falling. Flocks inhabit cliffs, mine-shafts, road bridges, caves and buildings, often making lengthy daily flights to water or to feed in grain-fields. 33 cm.

2 ♂ ♀

1

3

4

5

200

1 BLUESPOTTED DOVE *Turtur afer*. Rare localised resident. Very similar to the next species but upperparts browner, wing spots purple-blue and bill red with yellow tip. In flight both species show rufous wings and black back-bands, thus probably indistinguishable unless settled. Call like the next species and the Tambourine Dove (previous page) but more abruptly terminated. Singly or in pairs on edges of evergreen forest and woodland, in riverine forest and in dense thickets. 22 cm.

2 EMERALDSPOTTED DOVE *Turtur chalcospilos*. Very common resident. Apart from green wing-spots, differs from the previous species in all-dark, reddish bill and greyer upperparts. Typical wood dove flight pattern distinctive (see above) but not diagnostic. The well-known call is a soft, descending cooing 'du, du . . . du-du . . . du-du-dudu-du-du-du . . .' *tailing off at the end*. Occurs in woodland, bushveld, riparian forest and coastal bush. When flushed rises abruptly and makes off at speed. 20 cm.

3 FERAL PIGEON (Domestic or Town Pigeon) *Columba livia*. Common or abundant resident. Very well known and highly variable in colour. A wild-living domestic breed descended from the Rock Dove of North Africa and Europe. Main colour forms shown, but many combinations also occur including pure white, white with dark head and dark grey with white head. Calls 'coo-roo-coo'. Mainly in larger towns where very tame. Dependent on human habitation but flocks may frequent cliffs, mine-shafts and farmlands. 33 cm.

4 RAMERON PIGEON *Columba arquatrix*. Fairly common resident. Yellow bill and feet conspicuous, even in flight; otherwise appears as a large, dark pigeon with pale head. The call is a harsh 'crrooo'. Usually in small flocks where trees are fruiting, even entering suburban gardens. In montane regions they roost in evergreen forests or exotic plantations, flying considerable distances daily to their food source. Often go to roost early, sunning themselves conspicuously on tree-tops in late afternoon. 40 cm.

Parrots and lovebirds. Family PSITTACIDAE. A well-known group of gregarious birds with hooked bills. They use their feet and bills to clamber about trees. Parrots feed mainly in trees on fruits and kernels, the latter obtained by cracking the hard pericarps. Lovebirds feed on seeds, grain, berries and flowers, frequently foraging on the ground. All are highly social and make shrill shrieks. The various species are found in the dry west and the Caprivi-Zambezi regions.

1 ROSERINGED PARAKEET *Psittacula krameri.* Fairly common, localised resident. The only long-tailed, apple-green parrot in the region. Females lack the neck-ring. An introduced Asian species that has established itself just north of Durban, less frequently in Zululand. Small flocks of (presumably) aviary escapees also occur in the Gauteng region. 40 cm.

2 BROWNHEADED PARROT *Poicephalus cryptoxanthus.* Common resident. A green parrot with brown head and yellow eyes; in flight shows an apple-green back and yellow underwing-coverts. Immatures are duller than adults. Small flocks occur in broadleafed woodland, mixed bushveld and thornveld, feeding in the larger trees. 23 cm.

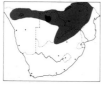

3 MEYER'S PARROT *Poicephalus meyeri.* Fairly common resident. Differs from the previous species in having entirely grey-brown upperparts, head and breast; has a yellow bar on the forehead, yellow shoulders and some yellow on the underwing-coverts. In flight shows *blue-green* back. Immatures lack yellow on the forehead and have very little on the shoulders. Pairs and small flocks in broadleafed and riverine woodland. In regions where their ranges overlap this and the previous species hybridise. 23 cm.

4 RÜPPELL'S PARROT *Poicephalus rueppellii.* Common, localised resident. Differs from the previous species in grey head and, in females, blue back, belly and vent plus yellow shoulders; *males lack the blue back and shoulder-patches.* Both sexes have yellow underwing-coverts. Immatures resemble females. Small flocks in arid woodland and thornveld. 23 cm.

5 CAPE PARROT *Poicephalus robustus.* Uncommon, localised resident. Large, mostly green parrot occurring in two distinct forms: (a) eastern Cape, Zululand-Natal and the Transvaal Woodbush Forest with yellow-brown head and neck, and (b) Kruger Park northwards with greyish head and neck. Both have orange leg-feathers and shoulders but orange forehead is variable; this colour absent or vestigial in young birds. In flight adults show pale green back and rump. Occurs in pairs and small flocks in evergreen forests and mature woodland. Small flocks often fly long distances to reach fruiting trees, returning nightly to favoured roosts. 35 cm.

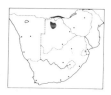

1 BLACKCHEEKED LOVEBIRD *Agapornis nigrigenis.* Rare and localised; enters southern Africa only in the Victoria Falls region of Zimbabwe. The dark face separates this species from other lovebirds. Flocks occur sparsely in thornveld and broadleafed woodland, especially in river valleys. 13 - 14 cm.

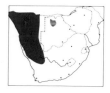

2 ROSYFACED LOVEBIRD *Agapornis roseicollis.* Locally common resident. Differs from the next species in having a pale-coloured bill and bright *blue back and rump* (not green), which is especially visible in flight. Occurs in flocks in dry woodland, tree-lined rocky gorges and along tree-lined watercourses in the arid west. 17 - 18 cm.

3 LILIAN'S LOVEBIRD *Agapornis lilianae.* Locally common resident. Differs from the previous species in having a reddish bill and *green* (not blue) back and rump. Flocks occur in thornveld and broadleafed woodland in the Zambezi River valley. 17 - 18 cm.

Trogons. Family TROGONIDAE.

4 NARINA TROGON *Apaloderma narina.* Fairly common resident. The only forest bird with bright red underparts and iridescent green upperparts. Immatures are like females but with breast and shoulders lightly barred. Difficult to locate in forests (since they often perch with their green backs towards the observer), but in the breeding season (October-December) draw attention to themselves by their call, a low 'hoot-hoot . . . hoot-hoot . . . hoot-hoot . . .', repeated regularly and slowly. Usually in pairs in evergreen forests (or adjacent plantations), coastal and valley bush. They move away from their high-altitude forest haunts in winter, and then may be seen at lower altitudes in riverine forests, plantations and gardens. 29 - 34 cm.

Louries. Family MUSOPHAGIDAE. Forest or bushveld, fruit-eating birds with crested heads, fairly long tails and an agile springing action when jumping along branches. Numbers (2), (3) and (4) are beautifully coloured and have crimson primary feathers which are strikingly revealed in flight. Immatures are dull versions of the adults.

1 GREY LOURIE *Corythaixoides concolor.* Common resident. All-grey with pronounced head-crest; sexes alike. The well-known call is 'kweh-h-h'or 'go-way-y-y', the latter giving rise to its popular name: Go-away Bird. Young birds call 'how, how, . . .'. Pairs and small parties in mixed bushveld, thornveld and well-wooded suburbia; usually in the upper stratum and invariably noisy. Flies with rather heavy wing movements, mostly below the tree-tops. 47-50 cm.

2 KNYSNA LOURIE *Tauraco corythaix* and **LIVINGSTONE'S LOURIE** *Tauraco livingstonii.* Two closely related species with mutually exclusive distributions. Knysna Lourie (a), with a short crest and green upperparts, ranges from the Knysna region northwards through coastal KwaZulu-Natal to the Drakensberg escarpment in the northern Transvaal. Livingstone's Lourie (b), with the longer crest and bluer upperparts, is found from northern Zululand and coastal Mozambique northwards. The sexes are alike in both species; immatures are duller. Both species make a hoarse breathing sound 'hurr . . . hurr . .' at intervals while feeding. Normal call a slow 'kerk-kerk-kerk-kawk-kawk-kawk-kawk'. Alarm call a high-pitched 'kek-kek-kek-kek . . .'. Usually in pairs or family groups in montane, mist-belt and coastal evergreen forests, sometimes in nearby plantations. Easily overlooked when feeding, but strikingly obvious in flight when the crimson wings are revealed. 47 cm.

3 PURPLECRESTED LOURIE *Tauraco porphyreolophus.* Common resident. Differs from the previous species in dark blue crest with a purple sheen, more blue on the folded wings and tail, ochre-washed breast and black bill. The call is a long sequence of notes, starting quietly and rising to a crescendo 'kerkerkerkerker-kok-kok-kok-kok-kok-kok . . .', the last sound repeated about 20 times, becoming more deliberate and spaced out. Also makes a jumbled series of 'kokokok . . .' sounds. Pairs occur in coastal forests, riverine forests in bushveld and in well-wooded valleys, usually preferring drier conditions to the previous species. Conspicuous only in flight. 47 cm.

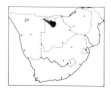

4 ROSS'S LOURIE *Musophaga rossae.* Very rare vagrant from Zambia. Recorded once in the Okavango Delta, northern Botswana. A pair, probably escapees, was known to breed in Gauteng in 1995. 50 cm.

Cuckoos and coucals. Family CUCULIDAE. Cuckoos are brood parasites, laying their eggs in the nests of other birds, and the majority leave southern Africa during the period March–September. The related coucals are larger, more robust and mainly sedentary birds which build their own nests and rear young in the conventional manner.

1 KLAAS'S CUCKOO *Chrysococcyx klaas.* Common summer resident, some present all year. Males differ from the next species in having a white mark *behind the eye only* and no white wing-markings; also *dark eyes, green bill* and white outer tail-feathers. Females differ from females of (3) in the *white mark behind the eye* and less barring below. The call is a mournful 'hueet-jie' repeated five or six times. Usually singly in a variety of wooded habitats including well-wooded suburbia. Parasitises a wide range of passerine birds. 17 cm.

2 DIEDERIK CUCKOO *Chrysococcyx caprius.* Common summer resident. Both sexes differ from the male of (1) in having white marks *before and behind* the eyes, a white central stripe over the crown and *multiple white marks on the wings;* also red eyes and a black bill. Females are more coppery on the upperparts. Immatures have coral-red bills, blue eyes and spotted underparts, young females mostly coppery above. Males call a plaintive 'dee-dee-dee-deederik'; females call 'deea-*deea*-DEEA'. Usually singly in a variety of wooded habitats including reed-beds and suburbia. Parasitises weavers, bishops and sparrows. 18,5 cm.

3 EMERALD CUCKOO *Chrysococcyx cupreus.* Fairly common summer resident. Males identified by yellow belly; females from females of (1) by the absence of a white mark behind the eye, much bronzier upperparts and heavily barred underparts, plus dark eyes and bluish bill and feet. The call is a clear 'teeu-tu-tui' or 'Pretty, Geor-gie'. Occurs in the upper stratum of forests and valley bush. Parasitises forest robins, warblers and flycatchers. 20 cm.

4 STRIPED CUCKOO *Clamator levaillantii.* Fairly common summer resident. Differs from the white morph of the next species in larger size and heavily streaked throat and breast. Sexes alike. The call is 'klew klew klew klew' followed by a long warbling 'chiriiriririri' and other shrill warbling sounds. Occurs in pairs in woodland, riparian woodland and bushveld. Parasitises babblers. 38-40 cm.

5 JACOBIN CUCKOO *Clamator jacobinus.* Common summer resident. Two colour morphs: (a) with clear white underparts (cf. previous species), and (b) totally black except for white wing-bar. Noisy and conspicuous, calling a shrill, flute-like 'kleeuw, pewp-pewp, kleeuw, pewp-pewp . . .'. Pairs occur in woodland, riparian forest, valley bush and bushveld. Parasitises bulbuls and other small birds. 33-4 cm.

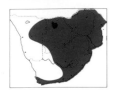

1 REDCHESTED CUCKOO *Cuculus solitarius.* Common summer resident. Told from others on this page by the *broad* russet upper breast; recently fledged birds have the entire head and upperparts dark charcoal-grey, all feathers edged white as illustrated. The well-known call of the male resembles the Afrikaans name 'Piet-my-vrou', loud and frequently repeated; the female calls 'pik-pik-pik-pik'. Occurs in a variety of wooded habitats including exotic plantations and suburbia. Males call from a high tree and often in flight when, in common with numbers (2)-(5), they appear hawk-like; see small illustration. Parasitises mostly robins. 28 cm.

2 EUROPEAN CUCKOO *Cuculus canorus.* Uncommon, non-breeding summer visitor. Females (illustrated) told from previous species by generally much fainter russet collar extending obscurely onto the nape and ear-coverts. Males lack russet colouring and are *almost indistinguishable from the next species;* the base of the bill *only* is normally greenish-yellow, but sometimes as (3); see bill illustrations. In males the undertail is barred white, but spotted in females, and in one race the upperparts, especially the head, are pale grey. Females also occur in a rare brown morph. Silent in Africa, occurring in any woodland. 30-33 cm.

3 AFRICAN CUCKOO *Cuculus gularis.* Fairly common summer resident. Scarcely differs from males of the previous species but the basal half of the bill is *yellow* and more conspicuous; see bill illustrations. Told from the next species by larger size and paler grey upperparts. Immatures well barred like those of (1) but with a paler head. Best identified by the male's call, a melancholy 'hoop-hoop' or 'coo-cuck', females a loud 'pikpikpikpik'; cf. (1). Occurs in woodland and mixed bushveld. A known host is the Forktailed Drongo. 32 cm.

4 LESSER CUCKOO *Cuculus poliocephalus* and **MADAGASCAR CUCKOO** *Cuculus rochii.* Rare, non-breeding visitors. Lesser Cuckoo visits January-April; Madagascar Cuckoo April-September. Small versions of the previous species and almost indistinguishable from (2) and (3) apart from size, darker upperparts and head. Lesser Cuckoo probably does not call in Africa; Madagascar Cuckoo calls like Redchested Cuckoo (1) but deeper, a four-syllabled 'Piet-my-vrou-vrou'. Both have been recorded in riparian forest and broadleafed woodland. 27 cm.

5 BARRED CUCKOO *Cercococcyx montanus.* Uncommon summer visitor and resident. Told by long tail plus brown and tawny colouring. Its calls are distinctive, a much repeated 'ree-reeoo . . .', rising to a crescendo and then fading. An elusive, localised species, recorded only in riparian and broadleafed forests in eastern Zimbabwe and the Zambezi River valley. A suspected host is the African Broadbill. 33 cm.

J

1

♀

2

♂

3

4

5

2

3

1 GREAT SPOTTED CUCKOO *Clamator glandarius.* Fairly common summer resident. A large cuckoo, distinguished by grey crested head, white-spotted upperparts and creamy-white underparts. Immatures similar but the cap is black, crest less pronounced and the primary feathers chestnut-brown. The common call is a rasping, rapid 'keeow keeow keeow keeow . . .' repeated in strophes of about eight. Occurs in woodland and savanna. Parasitises crows and starlings. 38 - 40 cm.

2 THICKBILLED CUCKOO *Pachycoccyx audeberti.* Uncommon summer resident. Adults told by plain grey upperparts and entirely white underparts, plus heavy bill. Immatures have a white head dappled grey on the crown plus broad white edges to the wing-feathers. Has a loud querulous call 'chee cher cher' and a rippling 'Oui yes yes'. Usually singly in any woodland; a restless, elusive species. Known to parasitise Redbilled Helmetshrikes. 34 cm.

3 BLACK CUCKOO *Cuculus clamosus.* Common summer resident. Entirely black; immatures more brown-black. Males have a much-repeated, monotonous call 'whoo whoo whee' rising on the last syllable; often expressed as 'I'm so sick'; females have an excitable-sounding 'wind-up' call 'yowyowyowyow-yowyow', reaching a crescendo and dying away. Usually singly in any well-wooded region, including suburbia. Perches in one place for long periods when calling. Parasitises boubou shrikes, including the Crimson Boubou. 30 cm.

4 BLACK COUCAL *Centropus bengalensis.* Uncommon summer resident. Breeding adults distinctive as illustrated; females noticeably larger than males. Non-breeding adults similar to the immature but darker above. The call, with the bird in a hunched, head-lowered stance, starts with a low 'ooom ooom ooom', then, with the head lifted, the bird makes a bubbling 'pop pop'. Also, when excited, calls 'kwik kwik kwik'. Occurs singly or in pairs in the long, rank grass and associated bush thickets of marshes and flooded grasslands. 32 - 7 cm.

5 GREEN COUCAL *Ceuthmochares aereus.* Fairly common resident. Large yellow bill and long green tail diagnostic. Immatures similar. Has several loud calls, 'tik tik tik tiktiktik ker ker ker kerkerkerker . . .', speeding up towards the end, plus long drawn-out sounds 'phooeeep, phooeeep, phooeeep . . .'. Occurs in thick vegetation in lowland and coastal forests; shy and secretive. 33 cm.

1

J

2

J

3

4

J

5

Note: The coucals on this page cannot be safely identified by their calls because they are nearly identical, a deep bubbling 'doo doo doo doo doo . . .' up to 20 times, descending then ascending, reminiscent of liquid pouring from a bottle. They also have harsh 'kurrr' alarm calls. Secretive, only occasionally perching conspicuously.

1 SENEGAL COUCAL *Centropus senegalensis.* Common resident. Distinguished from the next species with difficulty, but is smaller, has a less heavy bill and a shorter tail with a green iridescence. Differs from (3) in having *unbarred upper tail-coverts.* Immatures are duller, upperparts barred black, upper tail-coverts finely barred buff, thus very similar to immature of (3), but the ranges of these species are mutually exclusive. Occurs singly or in pairs in dense riparian vegetation, reed-beds and in thickets away from water. 41 cm.

2 COPPERYTAILED COUCAL *Centropus cupreicaudus.* Common resident. Larger than (1) and (3) with heavier bill, darker mantle, purple-black cap and longer tail *with a coppery sheen;* upper tail-coverts indistinctly barred buff. Immatures have the wing-feather tips barred dark brown, tail-feathers barred tawny. With experience can be told from other coucals by its deeper, richer call. Occurs in reed and papyrus beds plus riparian thickets in the Okavango Delta and Chobe River of northern Botswana, plus the western Zambezi River of Zimbabwe. 44-50 cm.

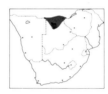

3 BURCHELL'S COUCAL *Centropus burchellii.* Common resident. Adults larger than (1) with finely barred upper tail-coverts, otherwise closely similar but ranges do not overlap. Fledglings have a small whitish eyebrow, fine whitish streaking on the head (see illustration) and dark barring on the upperparts; eyes blue-grey, not crimson. Singly or in pairs in reeds, dense riparian and bushveld thickets, tall rank grass and well-wooded suburbia. Mostly secretive but will sometimes perch conspicuously. 44 cm.

4 WHITEBROWED COUCAL *Centropus superciliosus.* Common resident. Adults differ from the previous species in having a white eyebrow and the head and nape well-streaked white, otherwise closely similar at all ages. Behaviour and habitat preferences as for Burchell's Coucal (3). 44 cm.

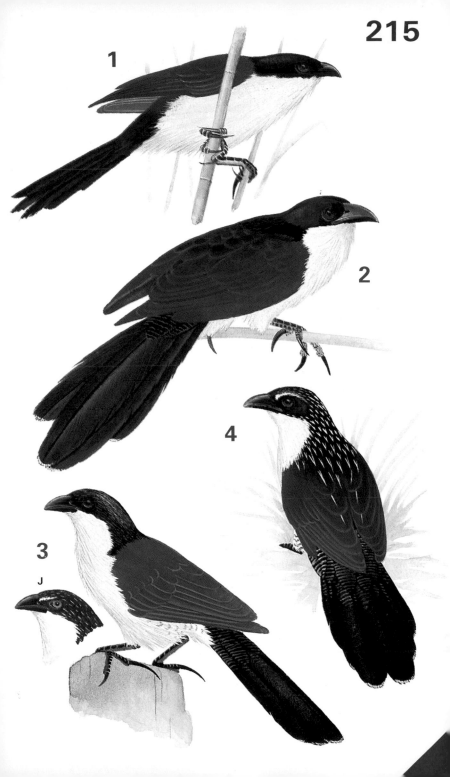

215

216

Owls. Families TYTONIDAE and STRIGIDAE. Nocturnal, erect-standing birds of prey, characterised by large, rounded heads, large forward-facing eyes set in a flattened face and feathered legs (except for Pel's Fishing Owl). Some have feather adornments on their heads which resemble ears. Immatures are usually darker, fluffier than adults.

1 MARSH OWL *Asio capensis*. Common to uncommon resident. Medium-sized, dark brown owl with small 'ear' tufts; shows russet wings in flight. Sometimes calls 'kraak' in flight. Singly or in pairs in long grass in marshy ground, vleis and near dams. Often active early mornings and late afternoons, flying low or perched on a fence pole. When flushed from the grass during daytime flies in circles over the intruder before resettling. 36 cm.

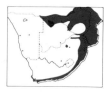

2 WOOD OWL *Strix woodfordii*. Fairly common, localised resident. Told by lack of 'ears', large pale, spectacle-like eye-orbits and barred underparts. Immatures with smaller eye-orbits and darker colouring. Males call a rapid 'HU-hu, hu-HU-hu-hu, hu-hu', females reply with a higher-pitched 'hoo'. Pairs and family groups in forests, well-developed riverine forests and exotic plantations. During the day roosts in large trees close to the trunks. 30-6 cm.

3 BARN OWL *Tyto alba*. Common resident. A pale, slimly built owl with heart-shaped facial disc and whitish underparts, told from the next species by paler upperparts. The call is an eerie, wavering screech. Singly or in pairs in a variety of habitats, roosting and breeding in large trees, caves, buildings and Hamerkop nests (page 81); common in suburbia. 30-3 cm.

4 GRASS OWL *Tyto capensis*. Uncommon resident. Closely similar to the previous species but distinguished by darker upperparts and different habitat. Hisses when disturbed; also makes a husky screech resembling the call of the Barn Owl. Singly or in pairs in moist grassland. When disturbed during the day flies directly away and resettles; cf. Marsh Owl (1). 34-7 cm.

218

OWLS

1 SCOPS OWL *Otus senegalensis*. Common resident. The plumage resembles tree-bark, the grey form (a) being commoner than the brown (b). The only very small owl with 'ear' tufts. Calls mostly at night, sometimes by day, a soft 'prrrrp' repeated at about ten-second intervals. Singly or in pairs in any woodland and mixed bushveld. By day perches close to a tree-trunk where its cryptic colouring makes detection difficult. This camouflage is further enhanced by its habit of depressing its feathers to appear long and thin, and of raising its 'ear' tufts and half closing its eyes, creating the illusion of a tree stump; see (a). 15-18 cm.

2 WHITEFACED OWL *Otus leucotis*. Common resident. Largest of the small owls. Predominantly grey with *orange* eyes, a distinct *black facial disc* and 'ear' tufts. The call, heard only at night, is an explosive, bubbling 'b-b-b-b-b-bhooo' repeated. Singly or in pairs in woodland, riverine forests, mixed bushveld and thornveld, preferring the larger trees. 25-8 cm.

3 PEARLSPOTTED OWL *Glaucidium perlatum*. Common resident. Very small 'earless' owl, upperparts brown with small white spots, underparts white streaked with brown with pearl-like spots. Has two black marks on its nape giving the appearance of eyes. The call, often heard by day, is a series of ascending notes 'tee-tee-tee-tee-tee-tee-tee-tee...' followed by a brief pause, then a series of descending notes 'teeew, teeew, tew, tew, tew, tew, tew...'. Occurs in any woodland, including Mopane, mixed bushveld and riverine forests. Is often seen by day and is frequently mobbed by other small birds. 15-18 cm.

4 BARRED OWL *Glaucidium capense*. Common resident. Slightly larger than the previous species, the upperparts finely barred, the wings with a row of bold white spots reaching the shoulder, underparts white with brown spots arranged in rows. The call is an urgent 'kerrooo-kerrooo-krrooo-krrooo-krrooo-krrooo-krrooo...' or 'krrooo-trrooo, krrooo-trrooo,...', either sequence repeated many times. Found mostly in well-developed riverine forests and large-tree woodland fringing lakes; also in mixed bushveld where it spends the day roosting in dense thickets. Less often seen by day than the previous species. 20 cm.

219

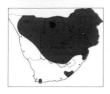

1 GIANT EAGLE OWL *Bubo lacteus*. Fairly common resident. Large grey owl. Young birds are browner. *Pink eyelids* and dark brown eyes at all ages. 'Ear'-tufts not always raised. Voice a series of deep grunts 'hu-hu-hu, hu-hu'; females and young make a long-drawn-out whistle which may be repeated all night. Singly in large trees in bushveld, especially along rivers and watercourses. 60·5 cm.

2 CAPE EAGLE OWL *Bubo capensis*. Uncommon resident. Large brownish owl of stocky proportions. Easily confused with the next species but differs in combination of larger size, orange-yellow eyes (orange in young birds) and heavily blotched underparts with *bold* barring; feet and talons larger. Birds in Zimbabwe and more northerly are larger than the southern race. Calls 'HU-hu-hu' or 'HU-hu', emphasis on the first syllable; alarm call 'wak-wak'. Pairs frequent valleys (bush or grassland) with cliffs or rocks at the higher end, or grassland with rock outcrops and trees. 48-55 cm.

3 SPOTTED EAGLE OWL *Bubo africanus*. Very common resident. Fairly large, grey-brown owl, easily confused with the previous species from which it differs in smaller size, pale yellow eyes, lightly blotched underparts with *fine barring*, smaller feet and talons. A rufous form (b) with orange-yellow eyes also occurs, though less commonly; this told from (2) by fine barring on underparts. Males call 'hu-hooo', females 'hu-hu-hooo', the sound rising on the second syllable. Usually in pairs in a wide range of habitats from bushveld to suburbia where it perches on buildings or feeds on lawns at night. Large exotic trees and rocky hillsides also much favoured. 43-50 cm.

1 PEL'S FISHING OWL *Scotopelia peli*. Uncommon, localised resident. A very large, distinctive owl, differing from others in cinnamon underparts and rufous-brown upperparts. In repose the head has a flattish appearance with the slightest suggestion of 'ear' tufts. When excited the head feathers are fluffed out, giving the head a rounded appearance. Normal call a deep, resonant 'oogh', the mate replying with a higher-pitched 'ooh'; also makes various other hoots, grunts and screeches. Pairs or single birds are found on the larger, well-forested rivers and lakes. Strictly nocturnal, spends the day perched in the dense foliage of a large tree or creeper. When flushed flies a short distance and resettles in another tree from where it watches the intruder. Fishes in quiet pools or slow-running waters from a low perch, dropping feet first onto its prey. 63-5 cm.

Nightjars. Family CAPRIMULGIDAE. Nocturnal, insectivorous birds with soft, cryptically coloured plumage, short beaks, wide gapes surrounded by stiff bristles, large eyes and short, weak legs. They hawk insects at night, lying up by day. If approached, may not flush until nearly trodden on; instead they close their eyes to narrow slits, thereby reducing the sun's reflection and so enhancing their camouflage. Habitually settle on country roads at night. All are so alike as to be nearly indistinguishable, but can be identified by characteristic calls; in the hand identified by wing and tail formulae, illustrated opposite and on pages 225-7.

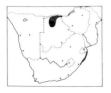

2 NATAL NIGHTJAR *Caprimulgus natalensis*. Rare, localised resident. Males have the entire outer web of the outermost tail-feathers white and half the outer web of the second tail-feather also white; wing-spots as illustrated. In females the wing and tail markings are buff-coloured. From the ground calls a continuous 'chookchookchookchook...' and a bubbling 'poipoipoipoipoi-poi....', both sequences less rapid than the call of the Mozambique Nightjar (overleaf). Occurs mainly in grassy, swampy and waterside locations of the eastern coastal belt and the Zambezi−Okavango regions. 23 cm.

1 PENNANTWINGED NIGHTJAR *Macrodipteryx vexillarius.* Fairly common summer resident. Males with long wing-pennants unmistakable, females lack any white in wings or tail. The call is a bat-like squeaking. Pairs occur in broadleafed woodland and mixed bushveld, especially on hillsides in stony or sandy terrain. May be seen flying before nightfall. 25-8 cm (excluding male's wing-streamers).

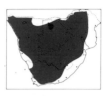

2 RUFOUSCHEEKED NIGHTJAR *Caprimulgus rufigena* Common summer resident. Identified by pale colouring and pale buff collar; see overleaf for full wing and tail formulae. Calls 'chwop, chwop, kewook-kwook' from ground or perch, and makes an even, sustained, purring sound like a small motor, with no variation. Occurs in woodland (especially *Protea* woodland), thornveld and sparsely vegetated Kalahari sandveld, often on stony or gravelly ground. Rests beneath trees during the day, but if flushed may settled in a tree temporarily. 23-4 cm.

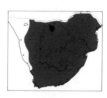

3 EUROPEAN NIGHTJAR *Caprimulgus europaeus.* Common summer visitor. Identified by large size and dark colouring; see overleaf for full wing and tail formulae. Mostly silent in Africa but sometimes calls 'coo-ic' in flight and 'quick-quick-quick' from the ground. Occurs singly in woodland, riverine forests and plantations, preferring large trees where it roosts by day *lengthwise on a horizontal branch*; perches on branches more often than any resident nightjar. 25-8 cm.

4 FIERYNECKED NIGHTJAR *Caprimulgus pectoralis.* Common resident. Has extensive rufous colouring about the neck, head and upper breast; see overleaf for full wing and tail formulae. Has a characteristic descending, quavering call, resembling the words 'Good Lord, deliver us'. Occurs in any wooded region, often in well-wooded suburbia, especially in stands of exotic trees. Roosts on the ground by day. 23-5 cm.

5 MOZAMBIQUE NIGHTJAR *Caprimulgus fossii.* Common resident. No distinctive colouring apart from wing and tail formulae; see overleaf. Makes a prolonged gurgling sound like an engine, which becomes louder or quieter with faster and slower frequency. Prefers open, sandy ground in woodland or near rivers and pans, plus coastal dunes. Roosts by day on the ground. 23-4 cm.

6 FRECKLED NIGHTJAR *Caprimulgus tristigma.* Common resident. Has *dark freckling* overall with few distinct markings, resembling weathered granite; see overleaf for full wing and tail formulae. The call is a high-pitched 'wheeoo-wheeoo' or 'cow-cow', at a distance like the yapping of a small dog. Associates with rocky koppies, escarpments and granite outcrops in woodland. By day roosts on shaded rocks, even on flat roofs in country districts. 27-8 cm.

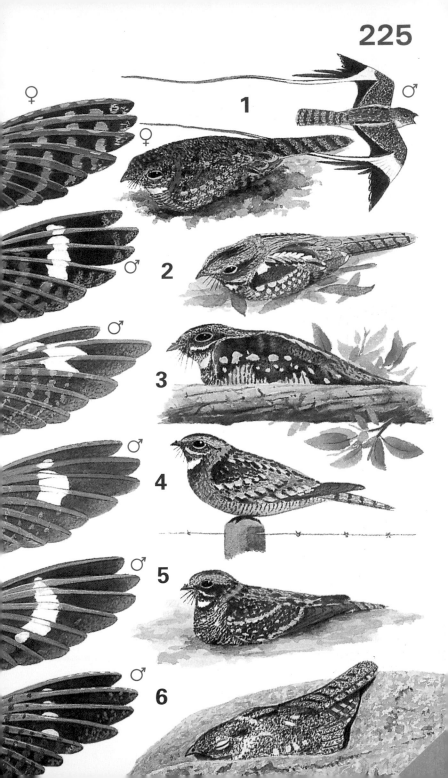

These illustrations show the major wing-feathers and outer tail-feathers with the outer webs of each blackened for clarity. The position of the wing emarginations or 'kinks' in relation to the wing-spots, the format and colouring of the wing-spots (if présent) plus the

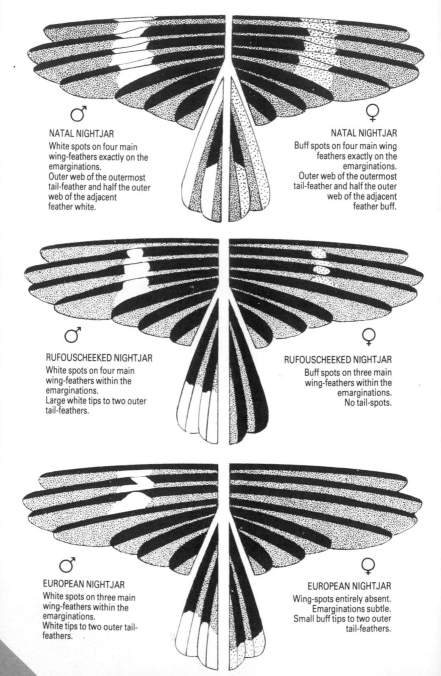

NATAL NIGHTJAR
White spots on four main wing-feathers exactly on the emarginations.
Outer web of the outermost tail-feather and half the outer web of the adjacent feather white.

NATAL NIGHTJAR
Buff spots on four main wing feathers exactly on the emarginations.
Outer web of the outermost tail-feather and half the outer web of the adjacent feather buff.

RUFOUSCHEEKED NIGHTJAR
White spots on four main wing-feathers within the emarginations.
Large white tips to two outer tail-feathers.

RUFOUSCHEEKED NIGHTJAR
Buff spots on three main wing-feathers within the emarginations.
No tail-spots.

EUROPEAN NIGHTJAR
White spots on three main wing-feathers within the emarginations.
White tips to two outer tail-feathers.

EUROPEAN NIGHTJAR
Wing-spots entirely absent.
Emarginations subtle.
Small buff tips to two outer tail-feathers.

presence or absence of bold tail markings are diagnostic for each species. The normal, irregular buff patterning present on nightjar feathers has been omitted. This diagram is intended to aid identification of nightjar road kills.

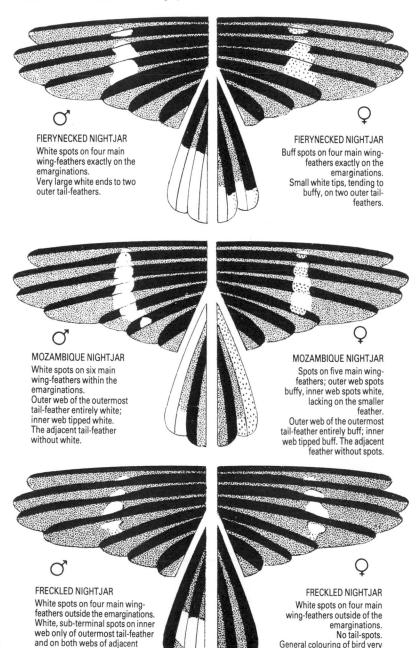

FIERYNECKED NIGHTJAR
White spots on four main wing-feathers exactly on the emarginations.
Very large white ends to two outer tail-feathers.

FIERYNECKED NIGHTJAR
Buff spots on four main wing-feathers exactly on the emarginations.
Small white tips, tending to buffy, on two outer tail-feathers.

MOZAMBIQUE NIGHTJAR
White spots on six main wing-feathers within the emarginations.
Outer web of the outermost tail-feather entirely white; inner web tipped white. The adjacent tail-feather without white.

MOZAMBIQUE NIGHTJAR
Spots on five main wing-feathers; outer web spots buffy, inner web spots white, lacking on the smaller feather.
Outer web of the outermost tail-feather entirely buff; inner web tipped buff. The adjacent feather without spots.

FRECKLED NIGHTJAR
White spots on four main wing-feathers outside the emarginations.
White, sub-terminal spots on inner web only of outermost tail-feather and on both webs of adjacent feather.

FRECKLED NIGHTJAR
White spots on four main wing-feathers outside of the emarginations.
No tail-spots.
General colouring of bird very dark speckling all over.

228

Swallows and martins. Family HIRUNDINIDAE. Small, long-winged, aerial-feeding birds, swallows with upperparts mostly glossy-blue (some with rufous caps), underparts whitish, rufous or streaked; an exception are the blackish saw-wing swallows (page 234), which have rough, saw-like leading edges to their primary feathers (not apparent in the field). The closely related martins are mostly brown above, white or brownish below and have square tails (most swallows have forked tails), except the House Martin which resembles a swallow. In all species immatures are duller than adults. They build nests with mud pellets or burrow tunnels in earth, drink and bathe in flight by skimming the surface of still water and perch to rest. See comparison between these and swifts on pages 238-9.

1 REDBREASTED SWALLOW *Hirundo semirufa*. Common summer resident; some all year. Identified by large size, blue cap extending to below the eyes and entirely orange-chestnut underparts. In flight differs from the next species by rufous (not white) underwing-coverts and longer tail-shafts. Immatures are duller above and much paler about the cheeks, chin and throat, the outer tail-feathers shorter, but differ from the next species in having the dark cap extending below the eyes and onto the ear-coverts. Adults make a soft warbling. Pairs occur in summer near their nest sites: road culverts, low causeways (not over water) and antbear holes. In winter in small flocks in coastal Zululand. Their flight is low and slow with much leisurely gliding. 24 cm.

2 MOSQUE SWALLOW *Hirundo senegalensis*. Fairly common, localised resident. Differs from the previous species in white throat and upper breast; in flight by *white* underwing-coverts and shorter tail-shafts. Makes a nasal, tin-trumpet-like 'harrrp', occasionally a guttural chuckling. Pairs and small flocks occur over large-treed woodland, usually near water. The flight is usually at some height, with bursts of fluttering flight followed by a glide. Frequently skims across dams and pans or perches in trees. 23 cm.

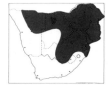

3 GREATER STRIPED SWALLOW *Hirundo cucullata*. Common summer resident. Identified by chestnut cap, pale chest-nut rump and *lightly streaked* underparts which appear almost white in flight; cf. the next species. The call, uttered in flight, is a soft 'chissik'. In pairs when breeding, otherwise small flocks over open terrain, montane grassland, near culverts, rocky koppies and human habitation. Flies with much gliding and perches frequently on trees and wires. 20 cm.

4 LESSER STRIPED SWALLOW *Hirundo abyssinica*. Common summer resident; some present all year. Differs from the previous species in more heavily streaked underparts, appearing very dark in the field, and orange cap extending *over the ear-coverts*. Flight call a characteristic descending series of four notes 'eh-eh-eh-eh'. Pairs and small flocks near bridges, road culverts and buildings. Flies more actively than the previous species, with less gliding. Perches frequently on trees or wires. 16 cm.

229

1

2

3

4

SWALLOWS

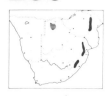

1 BLUE SWALLOW *Hirundo atrocaerulea.* Rare, localised summer resident. Told by entirely glossy-blue plumage and extended tail-streamers, longest in males; saw-wing swallows (page 234) are blacker and shorter-tailed. Has a wheezy, chittering call note and a short, soft warbling song. Singly or in small parties in the vicinity of forests and small streams in eastern montane grasslands. An endangered species. 20-25 cm.

2 SOUTH AFRICAN CLIFF SWALLOW *Hirundo spilodera.* Common summer resident. Square-tailed with mottled chin and throat; like European Swallow (overleaf) but with more robust appearance and pale throat. Immatures are browner and duller above. Has a three- or four-syllable call 'chor-chor-chor-choor'. Flocks frequent the vicinity of their colonial breeding sites: cliffs, bridges, water towers and other buildings in grassland regions. 15 cm.

3 WHITETHROATED SWALLOW *Hirundo albigularis.* Common summer resident; all year at low altitudes. Told from European Swallow (overleaf) by clear white underparts with black breast-band. Utters a soft twittering and has a warbling song. In pairs near nest site under rock overhang, bridge, culvert, outbuilding or other man-made structure, usually near or over water. 17 cm.

4 ANGOLA SWALLOW *Hirundo angolensis.* Rare vagrant to the extreme northern Caprivi region. Closely similar to European Swallow (overleaf) but chestnut chin colour extends to breast, the blackish band narrow, broken or indistinct, rest of underparts dull ash-brown, outer tail-feathers only slightly elongated. May give a warbling song in flight with wings depressed and quivering. Habits otherwise much the same as European Swallow. Occurs in a variety of habitats and in association with man. 15 cm.

REDRUMPED SWALLOW   see page 450.

SWALLOWS

1 EUROPEAN SWALLOW *Hirundo rustica*. Abundant summer visitor. Told by dark chin and throat; moulting birds often *without rufous chin or long tail-shafts* (November–January); young birds common October–December. Flocks make a soft twittering sound, especially when settled. Outnumbers all other swallows in summer, and mixes freely in flight with both other swallows and swifts. Large flocks perch on telephone wires or in roads and very large flocks gather to roost in reed-beds. 18 cm.

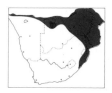

2 WIRETAILED SWALLOW *Hirundo smithii.* Fairly common resident. Told by *full* orange cap, entirely white underparts and *wire-like* tail-streamers. The call is a twittering 'chirrik-weet' repeated from a perch and 'chit-chit' while flying. Pairs, sometimes small groups, are found near river bridges, dam walls, river gorges and buildings, seldom far from water. Perches on dead trees in water and on bridge rails; settles on the *road surface* of bridges and causeways. 13 cm.

3 PEARLBREASTED SWALLOW *Hirundo dimidiata*. Uncommon to fairly common resident. Identified by entirely blue upperparts including the head, entirely white underparts and lack of tail-streamers. The call is a twittering 'chip-cheree-chip-chip'. Pairs in summer frequent woodland and human settlements; small flocks in winter often on vleis. Mostly in the drier regions but sparsely distributed throughout its range and present only in summer in many regions, especially the south. 14 cm.

4 GREYRUMPED SWALLOW *Pseudhirundo griseopyga.* Locally common resident. Grey-brown cap and pale grey rump are diagnostic, but cap not easily seen in flight and rump may appear almost white, then told from House Martin (page 236) by more deeply forked tail and slender appearance. Makes a grating 'chaa' in flight. Usually in flocks in grassland, vleis, coastal plains and grassy riverbanks. Nests in ground burrows and may be seen flying in and out of these. 14 cm.

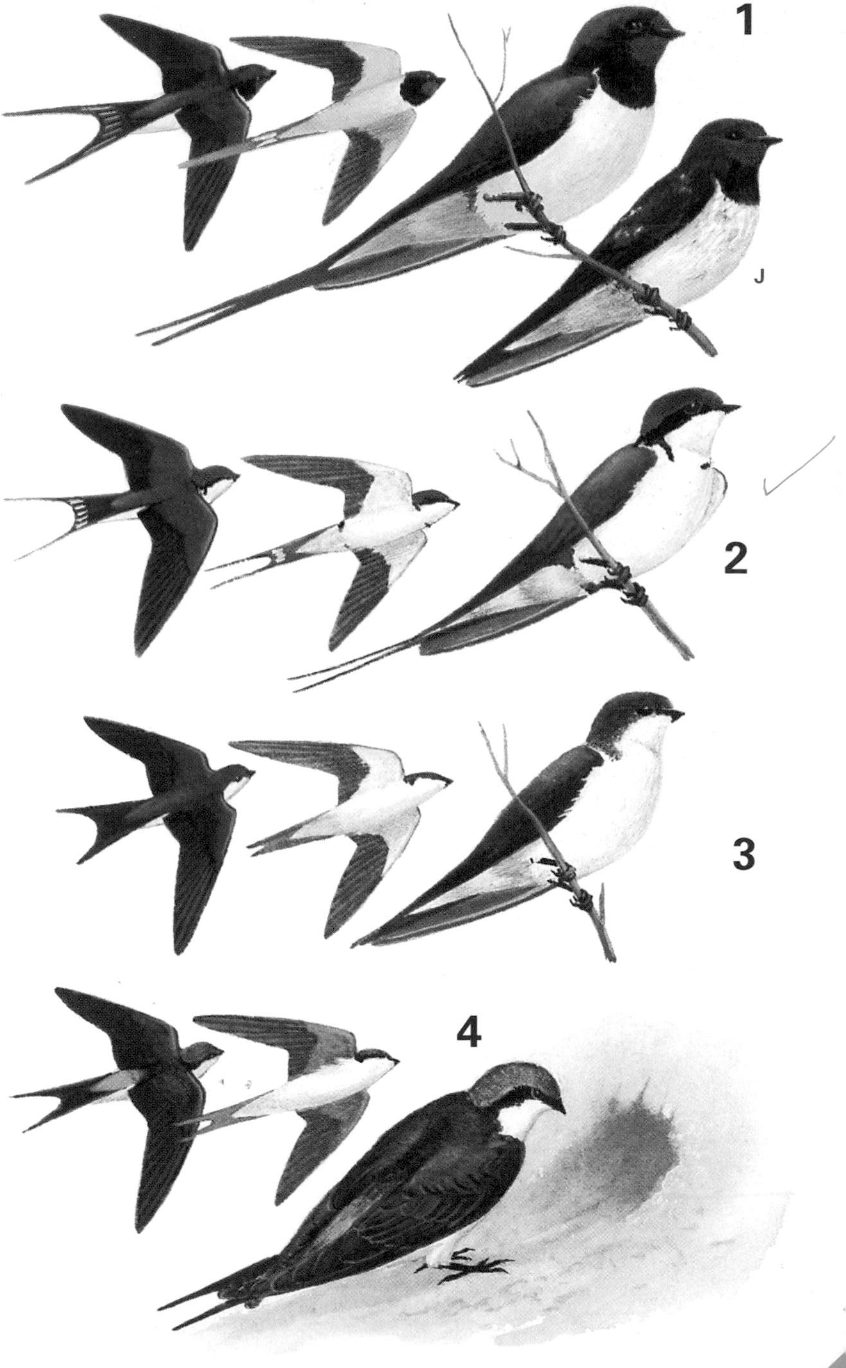
1
J
2
3
4

1 BLACK SAW-WING SWALLOW *Psalidoprocne holomelas*. Fairly common resident. All-black, fork-tailed swallow, differing from the next species only in colour of underwing-coverts. In flight differs from swifts in slower wing-beats and steadier flight with much gliding. Pairs and small parties occur near eastern coastal forests and in forested hills of the mistbelt region; also in northern Botswana, usually near wooded rivers. 15 cm.

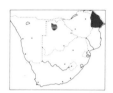

2 EASTERN SAW-WING SWALLOW *Psalidoprocne orientalis*. Uncommon resident. Identical to the previous species but for white or greyish underwing-coverts, this feature also identifying it from any swift. Habits and habitats similar to previous species. 15 cm.

WHITEHEADED SAW-WING SWALLOW   see page 450.

The name martin is loosely applied to certain species of swallows generally, but not exclusively, to those with brown plumage and square tails. Some martins build typical swallow-type mud nests, others breed in holes in banks.

3 (EUROPEAN) SAND MARTIN *Riparia riparia*. Uncommon to locally common visitor. A small martin differing from the Brownthroated Martin (overleaf) in white throat. Flocks usually occur near large inland waters or river estuaries and other eastern coastal localities, but may also occur anywhere with flocks of other swallows. 12 cm.

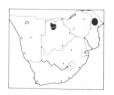

4 MASCARENE MARTIN *Phedina borbonica*. Uncommon winter visitor. In flight differs from other martins in having streaked underparts and very dark upperparts; cf. martins overleaf. Flocks occur over open woodland in Mozambique. 13 cm.

236

1 HOUSE MARTIN *Delichon urbica.* Common summer visitor. The only martin with blue upperparts, *white rump* and white underparts. Immatures (with off-white rumps) told from Grey-rumped Swallow (page 232) by *blue cap* (not grey-brown) and only slightly forked tail. The call is a single 'chirrup'. Flocks occur anywhere, often associating with European Swallows (page 232), from which it can be told in the air by smaller, more compact appearance, squarer tail and white rump. 14 cm.

2 BROWNTHROATED MARTIN *Riparia paludicola.* Locally common resident. A small, almost entirely brown martin except for white belly; see (a). Sometimes occurs with entirely brown underparts (b); then told from Rock Martin (4) by lack of 'windows' in the tail and by more slender appearance. The call is a soft twittering. Flocks forage over rivers with sandy banks (in which it breeds) and estuaries, roosting in reed-beds when not breeding. 13 cm.

3 BANDED MARTIN *Riparia cincta.* Uncommon to locally common summer resident; occurs all year in northern Botswana and the Zululand coastal plains. Differs from the Sand Martin (previous page) in broad breast band, white eyebrow and squarer tail. Makes a melodious twittering, perched or flying. Flocks forage over grasslands near water, breeding in riverbanks and termite mounds. The flight is slow and leisurely, the birds alighting frequently on a branch or fence to rest. 17 cm.

4 ROCK MARTIN *Hirundo fuligula.* Common resident. A stocky martin, told in flight by *broad wings and white 'windows'* in the fanned tail. Makes a melodious twitter. Pairs and small flocks frequent cliffs, bridges, dams walls and tall buildings, often associating with other swallows and swifts. The flight is slow, with much gliding, twisting and turning. 15 cm.

1

2

3

4

SWALLOWS AND MARTINS

Swallows and martins have wider, comparatively more rounded wings than swifts.

Swallows are blue on their upperparts, white or orange, sometimes spotted on their underparts.

Swallows may have orange caps, foreheads or throats, and buff or orange-coloured rumps.

Martins are brown, the underparts usually paler. The House Martin is the exception, since it has the appearance of a swallow.

Martins have squarish tails with white 'windows' in them, visible when the tail is fanned.

Swallows have forked tails, often with long streamers on the outer feathers, and frequently have 'windows' in the tail.

Swallows glide frequently between bouts of flapping flight.

Swallows and martins can perch.

COMPARED WITH SWIFTS

The wings of a swift are slender, scimitar-like and appear to sweep straight back from the body with little bend at the carpal joint.

Swifts are dark grey-brown, blackish or ash-brown, and mostly appear all dark in flight.

Swifts may have whitish throats and white rumps, but no bright colours.

Swifts may have square or forked tails; in our region only the Palm Swift has tail streamers.

Only the large Alpine Swift and the small Batlike Spinetail have white on the belly.

Swifts sometimes fly with their wings steeply angled upwards.

Most swifts fly very rapidly with only brief gliding spells.

Swifts cannot perch.

240

Swifts. Family APODIDAE. All-dark in appearance, some with white markings. No sexual differences, young as adults. Entirely aerial in habits, they feed on airborne insects, never intentionally settling on ground or perch, only clinging to vertical surfaces or scrambling into crevices. Their calls are high-pitched screams. See previous two pages for comparison with swallows.

1 PALM SWIFT *Cypsiurus parvus*. Common resident. The most slender, long-tailed swift; entirely grey-brown. Usually in flocks, flying rapidly around tall palm trees where they roost and nest, less commonly under bridges and eaves of buildings. May mix with other swifts when feeding, but slim build diagnostic. 17 cm.

2 BRADFIELD'S SWIFT *Apus bradfieldi.* Common, localised resident. Similar to Eurasian and Black Swifts (overleaf) but body and underwing-coverts paler, contrasting with the darker primaries and tail, these features apparent when seen flying in company with all-dark swifts. Flocks occur in the dry west, especially in the montane regions of Namibia in summer and in rocky gorges of the western Orange River; at other times singly or small groups away from mountains and gorges, then nomadic. 18 cm.

3 LITTLE SWIFT *Apus affinis*. Very common resident. Large white rump, which *curls around the sides of the body*, and square tail distinguishes this from all but the Mottled Spinetail (overleaf), from which it is told by *clear white throat*. Wings rather less pointed than other swifts. Often flies with wings held at right angles to body, tail fanned. A noisy species. During the day feed in flocks well away from their roosts and regularly mix with other swifts or swallows. Very common in towns where they roost and breed under eaves, under bridges, on silos and towers. 14 cm.

4 WHITERUMPED SWIFT *Apus caffer*. Very common summer resident. Most easily confused with the next species, but has slimmer build, more deeply forked tail and *thin white crescent shape on the rump* which does *not* extend over the sides of the body. Occurs in pairs anywhere except the most arid regions; common in suburbia, frequently occupying swallows' nests attached to buildings. 15 cm.

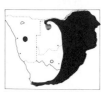

5 HORUS SWIFT *Apus horus*. Uncommon resident. Differs from the previous species in stouter appearance, less deeply forked tail and large white rump-patch which extends to the sides of the body. Small flocks occur near riverbanks, mine dumps, quarries and cuttings where they breed and roost in holes in the banks; on the Zululand coast in winter. 17 cm.

6 ALPINE SWIFT *Apus melba*. Common resident. Large size plus white throat and belly distinguish this from all other swifts. Seen mostly near high cliffs where they breed and roost, but also range far afield during the day. Fly with great power and speed, making an audible 'swishing' sound. 22 cm.

242

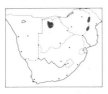

1 SCARCE SWIFT *Schoutedenapus myoptilus*. Fairly common, localised resident. Has no distinct markings. A light brown, fork-tailed swift, chin slightly paler than rest of underparts; looks like a robust Palm Swift (previous page). Groups and flocks occur near the rocky regions of mountains and hills of Zimbabwe above *c*. 1200 metres, breeding and roosting in fissures of inaccessible cliffs. 17 cm.

2 BLACK SWIFT *Apus barbatus*. Common resident. Fairly large, all-dark swift closely similar to the next species; identification very difficult but, from above, has marked contrast between paler inner secondaries and the back; cf. brown Asian race of (3). From below tail appears more deeply forked than in Eurasian Swift. Flocks are often seen flying in the vicinity of their roosts in mountain cliffs, especially in the late afternoon during the summer months. 19 cm.

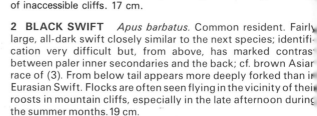

3 EURASIAN SWIFT (EUROPEAN SWIFT) *Apus apus*. Common summer visitor. European race all-blackish, differing from Black Swift (2) in *uniform upperparts* (no contrast between inner secondaries and body); from below closely similar but tail less deeply forked; darker than Bradfield's Swift (previous page). Asian race, particularly common in western regions, is *browner, from above pale inner secondaries contrast with dark wing-coverts and body;* cf. (2) which is generally blacker. Flocks November-February, always flying, often following thunderstorms; no known roosts. 18 cm.

4 PALLID SWIFT *Apus pallidus*. Very rare vagrant. One specimen from Kuruman in the northern Cape. A pale swift with white throat and forked tail. Probably flies with flocks of other swifts and could be more regular than records suggest. 18 cm.

5 MOTTLED SWIFT *Apus aequatorialis*. Uncommon, localised resident. A large swift with mottled body and pale throat; cf. Alpine Swift (previous page). Flocks occur near rocky cliffs in montane and hill regions of Zimbabwe, breeding and roosting there during summer, ranging more widely at other times. Fly with great power and speed. 20 cm.

6 MOTTLED SPINETAIL *Telecanthura ussheri*. Uncommon, localised resident. A square-tailed, white-rumped swift similar to the Little Swift (previous page), but with pale (not white) throat and upper breast and small white patches near the feet. Projecting tail-feather shafts not a field feature. Pairs and small parties frequent river valleys, broadleafed woodland and forest fringes of the north-east regions, normally in association with baobab trees, breeding and roosting in cavities. Sparsely distributed. 14 cm.

7 BÖHM'S SPINETAIL (BATLIKE SPINETAIL) *Neafrapus boehmi*. Uncommon, localised resident. A small, distinctive swift with white underparts, white rump and *tailless appearance*. Pairs and small parties are found in dry broadleafed woodland with baobab trees, often near rivers and lowland forests. Flight fluttering, bat-like and erratic. Breeds and roosts in hollow baobab trees and old mine-workings. c.9 cm.

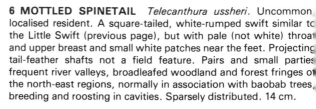

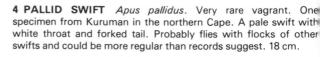

244

Mousebirds. Family COLIIDAE. Fruit-eating birds with creste
heads, soft, hair-like plumage and long stiff tails. Usually in partie
of up to a dozen birds which maintain contact by call. Whe
feeding they clamber, mouse-like, about bushes. Young bird
resemble adults, but are duller, shorter-tailed.

1 SPECKLED MOUSEBIRD *Colius striatus*. Commo
resident. Identified by dull brown colouring and bill; black uppe
mandible, white lower mandible. The call is a rasping 'zwit-wit
Flocks frequent dense bush, scrub, forest fringes and suburbia i
the moister regions. 30-5 cm.

2 WHITEBACKED MOUSEBIRD *Colius colius*. Commo
resident. Identified by pale grey upperparts, buff underparts, whi
back (visible in flight only) and *whitish bill with black tip* to uppe
mandible. The call is 'zwee, wewit'. In flocks in thornveld, riverir
bush and suburbia in the drier regions. 30-4 cm.

3 REDFACED MOUSEBIRD *Urocolius indicus.* Commo
resident. Identified by red facial mask. The call is a descendin
whistle 'tree-ree-ree', frequently repeated and uttered in flight a
well as at rest. Flocks, which fly in compact groups, occur i
thornveld, riverine forests and especially in suburbia, favourin
the drier regions. 32-4 cm.

Bee-eaters. Family MEROPIDAE. Highly coloured, aerial-feedin
birds with long curved bills, many with elongated tail-feather
(absent in young birds). Most occur in flocks, catching flyin
insects while twisting and turning in graceful aerial manoeuvres o
by hawking them from a perch in short aerial sallies, usuall
returning to the same branch or wire to eat their prey. Young bird
are dull versions of the adults.

4 BÖHM'S BEE-EATER *Merops boehmi*. Uncommon
localised resident. Distinguished from the much larger Olive Bee
eater (overleaf) by rich *russet* cap (not dull olive-brown) and riche
green colouring overall. The call is a chirping 'swee' plus a liqui
trill. Small flocks occur near riverine forests, on the edges of dens
thickets and in woodland clearings; sometimes hawk from a perc
within the forest-edge canopy. 21 cm.

5 SWALLOWTAILED BEE-EATER *Merops hirundineu*
Common resident. A small, fork-tailed bee-eater told from th
Little Bee-eater (overleaf) by bright blue collar and bluish unde
parts and tail. Immatures lack the yellow and blue throat, unde
parts pale apple-green as illustrated. The call is a soft 'kwit kwit
Flocks occur in a variety of bush habitats, being especially com
mon in the dry western regions. Hawks from a perch, often nea
pans and dry river beds. Nomadic when not breeding. 20-22 cm

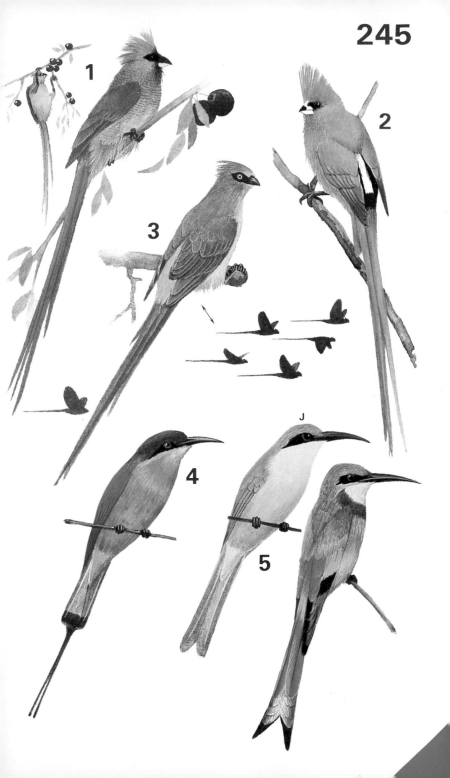

BEE-EATERS

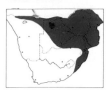

1 LITTLE BEE-EATER *Merops pusillus*. Common resident. Identified by small size, yellow throat, orange-buff underparts and squarish tail. Immatures lack the black collar and have pale green underparts. The call is a quiet 'chip, chip, trree-tree-tree'. In pairs or groups near rivers, open areas in any woodland or thornveld, usually perching on some low branch or fence-strand from where they hawk. 17 cm.

2 CARMINE BEE-EATER *Merops nubicoides*. Common summer resident and visitor. Immatures have brown upperparts, pale cinnamon underparts with traces of pink. Individuals call a deep 'terk, terk', flocks make a twittering sound. Flocks occur near rivers, marshes, in woodland and mixed bushveld where they hawk from trees and from the ground. 33-8 cm.

3 EUROPEAN BEE-EATER *Merops apiaster*. Common summer resident and visitor. Identified by golden-brown mantle, turquoise-blue forehead and underparts, plus yellow throat. The call in flight is diagnostic, a clear, liquid 'quilp' or 'kwirry'. Occurs in flocks anywhere, often mixing with other bee-eaters and frequently seen on roadside telephone wires. Frequently fly at a great height. 25-9 cm.

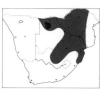

4 WHITEFRONTED BEE-EATER *Merops bullockoides*. Common resident. Identified by white forehead and upper-throat, plus red lower throat. The call is a querulous 'quirk' and other similar sounds. In flocks near rivers, often mixing with other bee-eaters. 22-4 cm.

5 BLUECHEEKED BEE-EATER *Merops persicus*. Uncommon to locally common summer visitor. Distinguished from the next species by *pale blue forehead, eyebrows and cheeks*, plus yellow and brown throat and upper breast; a large bee-eater of generally green appearance. The short liquid call is 'prruik' or 'prree-oo, prree-oo'. Usually in small flocks near large rivers, flood-pans, swamps and coastal grasslands where they often hawk from a dead tree standing in water. 27-33 cm.

6 OLIVE BEE-EATER *Merops superciliosus*. Uncommon summer resident and visitor. Distinguished from the previous species by *olive-brown* cap, all-brown throat and uniform pale green underparts; from Böhm's Bee-eater (previous page) by larger size, olive-brown (not russet) cap and paler green underparts. The call is probably similar to that of the previous species. Usually in small flocks near large rivers and swamps but far-ranging and may occur temporarily elsewhere. 29-33 cm.

WHITETHROATED BEE-EATER see page 450.

Kingfishers. Family HALCYONIDAE. Short-legged, dagger-billed fish- or insect-eating birds. The fish-eating species plunge-dive for their food from a perch or, in some cases, while hovering, the insectivorous species hunt from a low branch, watching for and seizing insects on the ground. Fish are taken to a perch or on the ground and beaten into immobility before being swallowed. They breed in holes in banks or trees. Young kingfishers resemble adults but are duller.

1 GIANT KINGFISHER *Ceryle maxima*. Common resident. Much larger than the next species, the sexes differing as illustrated. The call is a raucous 'kek-kek-kek-kek-kek'. Singly or in pairs near wooded rivers, wooded dams and coastal lagoons. Perches on a branch, bridge or wire from where it watches the water, sometimes hovers briefly. 43-6 cm.

2 PIED KINGFISHER *Ceryle rudis*. Common resident. Smaller than the previous species, entirely black and white, the sexes differing as illustrated. The call is a high-pitched twittering, often by two or more birds at the same time. In pairs or small parties inland on rivers or dams and at coastal lagoons, estuaries and shoreline rock pools. Habitually hover over water while fishing, then plunge-dive to seize their prey. 28-9 cm.

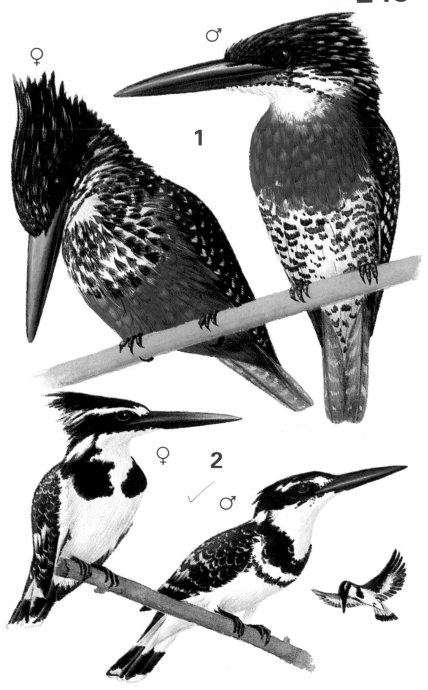

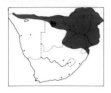

1 WOODLAND KINGFISHER *Halcyon senegalensis*. Common summer resident. Differs from the Mangrove Kingfisher (3) in having a red and black bill, whiter head and black patch from bill to ear-coverts. Immature bird usually has *all red bill*, sometimes with a black tip; then identified by eye-stripe and blue (not grey) crown. Males call continuously after arrival and until breeding is finished, a loud 'yimp-trrrrrrrrrrrrrrrrrrrrr', the last part drawn out and descending. Present October-April, occasionally later, in mixed bushveld and riverine woodland, usually in pairs. Catches insects on the ground by still-hunting from a perch. Pairs greet each other with spread wings. 23-4 cm.

2 GREYHOODED KINGFISHER (CHESTNUTBELLIED KINGFISHER) *Halcyon leucocephala*. Uncommon to locally common summer resident. Identified by grey head and mantle plus chestnut belly; cf. Brownhooded Kingfisher (overleaf). Not very vocal, the call a weak, descending 'chi-chi-chi-chi'. An insectivorous kingfisher, found singly or in pairs in woodland or mixed bushveld September–April. Occasionally catches fish. 20 cm.

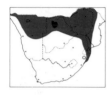

3 MANGROVE KINGFISHER *Halcyon senegaloides*. Uncommon resident. Differs from the similar Woodland Kingfisher (1) in having a completely red bill and greyish crown and mantle. At the coast the call is a raucous 'tchit-tchoo, tcha-tcha-tcha-tch-tch-tch', ending in a trill and performed with raised wings; inland the call is a quieter 'cling-cling-cling-cling...' with the bill pointed upwards. Singly or in pairs in mangroves at coastal estuaries, mainly during winter, or on major lowland rivers in bushveld and thornveld during summer. Very sparsely distributed on the coast in the south, commoner in the Beira region; inland records few. 23-4 cm.

1 BROWNHOODED KINGFISHER *Halcyon albiventris*. Common resident. Differs from the Greyhooded Kingfisher (previous page) in larger size and streaked brown head, streaked buffy breast and flanks, females with brown (not black) wings and shoulders; from the next species also by larger size, larger, heavier bill, less obvious black eye-stripes and buffy underparts; in flight by *bright blue back and rump*. The call is a loud 'kik-kik-kik-kik-kik . . . .'. Usually singly in mixed bushveld, woodland, riverine forests, suburban parks and gardens. Still-hunts for insects from a low branch away from water. 23-4 cm.

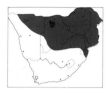

2 STRIPED KINGFISHER *Halcyon chelicuti*. Fairly common resident. A small, sombrely coloured kingfisher, distinguished from the previous species by smaller size, streaked head, two-coloured bill, bold black eye-stripe extending to the nape and white collar encircling the neck. In flight shows blue upper tail-coverts only, males with darker underwings than females. The call is 'tirrrrrr, deeeoo-deeeoo-deeeoo', frequently a pair calling in duet while performing a wing-opening display. Most often heard in the evening when several individuals may call from scattered points. Pairs in mixed bushveld and woodland, generally perched high on an outer branch far from water. 18-19 cm.

3 PYGMY KINGFISHER *Ispidina picta*. Fairly common summer resident. Very like the Malachite Kingfisher (5) but with mauve wash on ear-coverts, crown colour same blue as rest of upperparts (not turquoise) and does not reach the eyes. Has no territorial call but makes a 'chip' sound in flight. Singly in a wide variety of wooded habitats from sea-level to *c.* 1 350 metres, usually away from water. Still-hunts from a low perch, catching insects on the ground. Sparsely distributed. 13 cm.

4 HALFCOLLARED KINGFISHER *Alcedo semitorquata*. Uncommon resident. Identified by black bill, entirely bright blue upperparts and cinnamon-coloured lower breast and belly. Calls a shrill 'teep' or 'seek-seek'. Singly on small, heavily wooded inland waters and well-wooded estuaries. A fish-eater, perching low down over the water. Sparse. 20 cm.

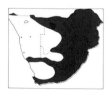

5 MALACHITE KINGFISHER *Alcedo cristata*. Common resident. Differs from Pygmy Kingfisher (3) in having a turquoise cap which *reaches the eyes* and no mauve on the ear-coverts. Young birds have black beaks, duller plumage: see margin illustration and cf. (4). When flushed utters a shrill 'peep-peep'. Singly on almost any waters with fringing vegetation, perching low down on a reed, branch or rock. 14 cm.

J 5

Rollers. Family CORACIIDAE. Colourful, heavy-billed birds with brilliant blue wing-feathers and harsh, croaking voices. Spend much of the day hunting from a convenient perch, flying down to catch and eat large insects and other small prey on the ground. They breed in holes in trees (sometimes holes in cliffs) and have active display flights, which involve violent aerial manoeuvres with much harsh calling.

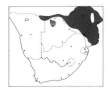

1 RACKET-TAILED ROLLER *Coracias spatulata*. Uncommon to locally common resident. Identified by plain blue underparts and spatulate tips to the tail-shafts; cf. (3) and (4). Immatures have no elongated tail-feathers, are more lilac on cheeks and sides of breast, but differ from immatures of (4) by deep blue primary wing-coverts (not greenish-blue) and generally browner upperparts. Has a high-pitched cackling call. Singly or in pairs in well-developed broadleafed woodland. Sparse and irregular south of the Limpopo River. 36 cm.

2 BROADBILLED ROLLER (CINNAMON ROLLER) *Eurystomus glaucurus*. Fairly common summer resident. Cinnamon colour and yellow bill diagnostic. Immatures have underparts greenish-blue, upperparts duller brown, streaked black. Makes a harsh croaking and various cackling sounds. Singly, in pairs or scattered groups in well-developed riverine forests, broadleafed woodland and the edges of lowland forests. 27 cm.

3 LILACBREASTED ROLLER *Coracias caudata*. Common resident. The only roller with lilac throat and breast and blue belly, vent and undertail; tail-shafts straight (not spatulate as in (1)), often absent when moulting. Immatures lack tail-shafts and are duller, browner. Makes various harsh rattling sounds when displaying. Singly or in pairs in mixed bushveld, broadleafed woodland and thornveld, preferring less densely wooded regions than the Racket-tailed Roller and frequently numerous in stunted Mopane woodland. A common roadside bird in some areas, perching on telephone wires. 36 cm.

4 EUROPEAN ROLLER *Coracias garrulus*. Common summer visitor. Differs from (1) and (3) in lacking tail-shafts. Pale blue over entire head and underparts, rest of upperparts brown, but shows electric-blue wings in flight. Mostly silent in Southern Africa but sometimes makes a harsh 'rack-kack, kacker'. Singly, often many birds within sight of each other, in woodland, bushveld and even grassland where it perches on power cables and telephone wires. 30-1 cm.

5 PURPLE ROLLER *Coracias naevia*. Fairly common resident. A large, heavily built roller with a square tail, upperparts olive-green, underparts deep reddish-brown heavily streaked white. Immatures are duller. Makes various harsh cackling and cawing sounds and, when displaying, a continuous 'ka-raa-ka-raa-ka-raa...' as it flies up. Usually singly in woodland or thornveld. Perches fairly low down and is normally less active than other rollers. Has a rocking display flight in which the wings appear to beat independently, calling as described above. Has seasonal movements in some regions. 36-40 cm.

256

Woodhoopoes and scimitarbill. Family PHOENICULIDAE. Glossy, dark blue-green birds with long graduated tails, long curved bills and short legs. They clamber about tree trunks and branches probing with their bills in search of insects. Also investigate the nests of weavers and sparrows in their search for insects and may throw out eggs or small chicks while so doing. They nest in tree cavities.

1 REDBILLED WOODHOOPOE *Phoeniculus purpureus*. Common resident. Larger than the Scimitarbilled Woodhoopoe (2) and with red (not black) bill and feet. Immatures do have a black bill, but less curved than that of the Scimitarbill. The call is a high-pitched cackling started by one and taken up by others to produce a cacophony of hysterical laughter similar to but more musical, less mechanical-sounding than the call of the Arrowmarked Babbler (page 310). Occurs in parties of three to eight in any woodland or well-wooded suburbia. Fly from tree to tree in straggling procession, settling low down and working their way to the top before flying off to the next tree. 30-6 cm.

VIOLET WOODHOOPOE *Phoeniculus damarensis*. Fairly common, localised resident. Larger than the previous species but less green, more violet-blue about the head and mantle; see illustration, left. Similar in all other respects to the Redbilled Woodhoopoe (1) and mixing with the western race of that species in northern Namibia. 40-2 cm.

2 SCIMITARBILLED WOODHOOPOE (SCIMITARBILL) *Phoeniculus cyanomelas*. Fairly common resident. Smaller than the previous two species, the bill more curved and black. Females and immatures have the throat and breast brownish. Calls during summer 'pwep-pwep-pwep-pwep . . .' repeated about ten times at half-second intervals. Singly or in pairs in well-developed broadleafed woodland and thornveld. Feeds in the larger trees, clambering about the outer branches and twigs. Quieter, less conspicuous than the Redbilled Woodhoopoe (1). 24-8 cm.

3 HOOPOE *Upupa epops*. Family UPUPIDAE. Common resident. The crest is normally held down, being raised when the bird is attentive or alarmed. Females and immatures are duller than males. Has an undulating, butterfly-like flight, black and white wings then conspicuous. The call is 'hoop-hoop, hoop-hoop-hoop' frequently repeated (cf. call of African Cuckoo, page 210); young birds being fed by adults call 'sweet, sweet'. Singly or in pairs in any woodland, bushveld, parks and gardens. Walks about probing the ground with its bill. Seasonal fluctuations occur in some regions. 27 cm.

258

Hornbills. Family BUCEROTIDAE. Insectivorous and frugivorous birds with heavy-looking, curved bills, sometimes with a horny casque on the upper mandible. Arboreal or terrestrial feeders, or both, they nest in holes in trees (among rocks in a few species) and, in most species, the female seals herself in during incubation. Their flight is heavy and undulating with periods of gliding.

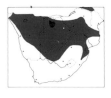

1 YELLOWBILLED HORNBILL *Tockus flavirostris*. Common resident. Large yellow bill (smaller in females) separates this from all other hornbills. Immatures have a duller yellow bill with a reddish base, the size of bill then serving to distinguish it from the next species. The call is 'wurk, wurk, wurk, wurk, wurk, wurk, wukwukak, wukwukak, wukak, wukak, wurk, wurk, wurk...', the sound working up to a crescendo then fading away. Often two birds call simultaneously with a wing-opening, head-bowing display. Pairs and small groups in dry bushveld, mixed woodland and thornveld. Feeds on the ground much of the time, also in fruiting trees. 48-60 cm.

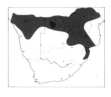

2 REDBILLED HORNBILL *Tockus erythrorhynchus*. Common resident. Identified by combination of red bill and black-and-white checkered upperparts; cf. next species which has plain brown upperparts. Immatures have shorter bills, the upperparts with buff spots. The call is similar to that of the previous species but is uttered more rapidly, 'wha, wha, wha, wha, wha, wha, kawacha, wacha, wacha, wacha, wacha, wacha...', also rising to a crescendo then fading. Pairs and small flocks frequent dry bushveld, broadleafed woodland (particularly Mopane) and thornveld, preferring drier conditions than the Yellowbilled, but often mixing with it. Forages mostly on open ground and probes actively with its bill. 42-50 cm.

3 CROWNED HORNBILL *Tockus alboterminatus*. Fairly common resident. Differs from the previous species in having a casque on the red bill and entirely dark brown upperparts. Immatures have the bill more orange, upperparts with feathers buff-tipped. The call is a series of melancholy, piping whistles. Singly or in pairs in riverine forests, the canopy and fringes of lowland and coastal forests and well-wooded valleys. Feeds in the trees and roosts conspicuously on high, slender branches. 50-7 cm.

4 GREY HORNBILL *Tockus nasutus*. Common resident. The rather small, dark bill of males is diagnostic; females have a smaller casque, that and the upper mandible creamy, the tip red; cf. Monteiro's and Bradfield's Hornbills (overleaf). Immatures have browner heads, eyebrows indistinct, bill of young females even more creamy. The call is a thin, piping, plaintive series of notes ascending and descending the scale, 'phe, phephee, pheephee, pheeoo, phew, pheeoo-pheeooo...'. Pairs and, in winter, flocks of up to about 30, in dry mixed bushveld, broadleafed woodland and thornveld. Mainly arboreal. 43-8 cm.

260

1 MONTEIRO'S HORNBILL *Tockus monteiri*. Fairly common, localised resident. Distinguished from the next species by having much white in the wings and tail. The call is 'tak-taack, tak-taack'. Singly or in pairs in rocky regions of northern Namibia, feeding mostly on the ground. 54-8 cm.

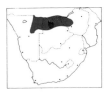

2 BRADFIELD'S HORNBILL *Tockus bradfieldi*. Fairly common resident. Distinguished from the previous species by brown wings and outer tail-feathers, only tail-tips white; from the Crowned Hornbill (previous page) by lack of a casque on the bill. The call is a series of piping whistles like the Crowned Hornbill. Seen in pairs in broadleafed woodland and mixed bushveld of the dry north-western regions. 50-7 cm.

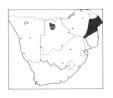

3 SILVERYCHEEKED HORNBILL *Bycanistes brevis*. Uncommon, localised resident. Identified by large size, pied colouring and heavy yellow bill with a large casque. A noisy species, the most common sound a loud braying or growling 'quark-quark-quark'. In pairs or flocks in forests and well-developed riverine forests where trees are fruiting, feeding in the canopy. Their wings make an audible soughing in flight. 75-80 cm.

4 TRUMPETER HORNBILL *Bycanistes bucinator*. Common resident. Distinguished from the previous species by smaller size, smaller casque on the bill and more white on the underparts. The characteristic call resembles the crying of a baby, a loud and far-carrying 'waaaa-aaa-aaa-aaa-aaaaaa' often uttered by several birds at once. Small flocks frequent well-developed riverine forests, lowland forests and moist woodland, feeding in the canopies of larger fruiting trees. 58-65 cm.

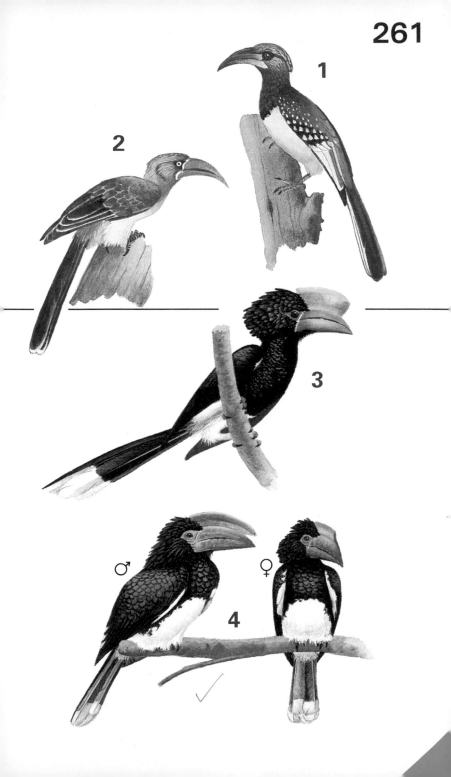

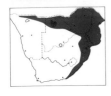

1 GROUND HORNBILL *Bucorvus leadbeateri*. Common resident. Turkey-sized, black birds with red faces and throat-pouches, females with a blue central patch on the pouch; in flight shows white wing-feathers. Immatures with yellow facial skin and throat-pouches. The call is a deep booming, mostly heard at dawn 'oomph, oomph-oomph' frequently repeated. Usually in groups of four to ten individuals in bushveld, woodland and montane grassland. Mainly terrestrial, walks slowly in loose array in search of food and takes off in low flight only if disturbed or when going to roost in a tree. 90 cm.

Barbets. Family CAPITONIDAE. Stout-billed, robust and often colourful relatives of the woodpeckers, with loud characteristic calls. They feed on fruits and insects and excavate nest-holes in trees. The smaller species are called tinker barbets from the likeness of their calls to the sound of a hammer on an anvil. Young birds are duller versions of the adults.

2 WOODWARDS' BARBET *Cryptolybia woodwardi*. Fairly common, very localised resident. Distinguished from Green Tinker Barbet (overleaf) by larger size plus black cap and yellow ear-patch, but the ranges of both are mutually exclusive. The call is a monotonous 'quop-quop-quop-quop...'. Found only in the Ngoye Forest, Zululand. 17 cm.

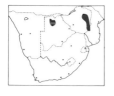

3 WHYTE'S BARBET (YELLOWFRONTED BARBET) *Stactolaema whytii*. Fairly common, localised resident. Identified by brownish appearance, yellow forecrown and white wing-feather edges. Makes a soft 'coo' at about one-second intervals. Small parties of about four birds are found in broadleafed woodland in the vicinity of fig trees, and in suburbia. 18 cm.

4 WHITE-EARED BARBET *Stactolaema leucotis*. Common resident. Identified by pied appearance and prominent white ear-stripe. The common call is a loud 'trreee, trrreetrreetrreetrree-trree', which may be uttered by several birds simultaneously. Usually in noisy, conspicuous groups of two to six birds in coastal and lowland forest canopies and fringes, riverine forests and moist woodland where fig trees are fruiting. 17 cm.

263

1 GOLDENRUMPED TINKER BARBET *Pogoniulus bilineatus*. Common resident. The only small barbet uniformly black from forehead to lower back. Immatures have yellow-tipped back feathers. The call is 'poop-poop-poop-poop-poop' usually in strophes of five or six; also a rapid, higher-pitched 'prrrr-prrrr-prrrr'. Occurs in coastal forest and montane forests (mostly below 1000 m) plus riverine forest. Frequents the canopy and midstratum singly or in pairs. An active, noisy species. 10 cm.

2 GREEN TINKER BARBET *Pogoniulus simplex*. Status unknown. A small, dull green bird with short heavy bill, pale yellow edges to wing-feathers and golden rump. Calls 'pop-op-op-op-op-op', sometimes ending with a trill. A forest canopy species recorded south of Beira. 10 cm.

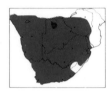

3 PIED BARBET *Tricholaema leucomelas*. Common resident. Differs from Redfronted Tinker Barbet (overleaf) in larger size and white underparts (eastern race has yellow wash on flanks, no black streaks) and black bib of varying extent. Immatures lack the red forehead. The call is a loud nasal 'peh-peh', less frequently a hoopoe-like 'poop-poop'. Occurs singly or in pairs in a wide range of dry woodland habitats. 17-18 cm.

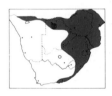

4 BLACKCOLLARED BARBET *Lybius torquatus*. Common resident. The only local bird with bright red forehead, face and foreneck and heavy black bill; the tone of red varies regionally. Rarely, yellow replaces the red. Immatures have red speckling on black. The call is a loud duet, starting with a whirring 'kerrr-kerrr-kerrr' and then becoming 'too-puddely-too-puddely-too-puddely-too-puddely...' about eight times, the calls usually accompanied by wing-quivering and swaying or bobbing. Also calls 'snaar'. Occurs in pairs or small groups in any woodland including well-wooded suburbia; in the drier regions is mostly restricted to riverine forests. 19-20 cm.

5 CRESTED BARBET *Trachyphonus vaillantii*. Common resident. The degree of red 'scaling' on the facial region is variable, and less profuse in females and immatures. The male call is a distinctive trilling like a muffled alarm clock 'trrrrrr...' which continues sometimes for long periods; louder, slower and of higher pitch when expressing agitation 'kekekekekek...'; females call 'puta-puta-puta-puta...'. Singly or in pairs in well-wooded regions, riverine forests and bushveld. Is attracted to fruit in suburban gardens. 23 cm.

1 YELLOWFRONTED TINKER BARBET *Pogoniulus chryso-conus*. Common resident. Forehead may be yellow *or orange*, underparts very pale yellow (cf. next species). Immatures have forehead black or with traces of yellow. The call is a monotonous 'phoo-phoo-phoo-phoo-phoo...', uttered for long periods on warm days. Also calls 'dit-dit-dit' in rapid morse-like strophes of three. Occurs in a variety of woodland habitats including riverine forests, mostly in the canopies of larger trees. Is greatly attracted to the mistletoe-type parasites of the genera *Viscum* and *Loranthus* and may be abundant when these are plentiful. 12 cm.

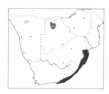

2 REDFRONTED TINKER BARBET *Pogoniulus pusillus*. Common resident. Differs from the previous species in *red* forehead, slightly yellower underparts. Immatures have black forehead or with traces of red. The call is a monotonous 'purp-purp-purp-purp-purp...', repeated for long periods; also a high-pitched, rapid 'kew-kew-kew-kew...'. Inhabits coastal and lowland forests, well-wooded rivers and valleys where it frequents the tree canopies. 10.5 cm.

Woodpeckers. Family PICIDAE. Small, robust birds with straight, pointed bills, stiff tails and zygodactylous feet in which the inner and outer toes are directed backward and the two central toes forward. They glean insects and their larvae from within crevices in trees and from beneath bark by tapping with their bills to loosen or chip the wood and by inserting their long sticky tongues. While feeding, their tail is used as a prop. They normally occur in pairs and excavate holes in trees for nesting, these frequently being used in turn by other hole-nesting species. Many woodpeckers are very similar in appearance and are best identified by head and breast markings plus call. The aberrant Ground Woodpecker is entirely terrestrial and nests in holes in banks.

3 OLIVE WOODPECKER *Mesopicos griseocephalus*. Common resident. The only olive-green woodpecker in Southern Africa. Calls a shrill 'chee-wit, chee-wit, chee-wit' or 'whir-it, whir-it, whir-it'. In pairs in both lowland and montane forests and adjacent forested streams. Feeds mostly in the mid and upper strata amidst moss- and lichen-encrusted branches. 18-20 cm.

4 GROUND WOODPECKER *Geocolaptes olivaceus*. Common resident. The only red-breasted woodpecker in Southern Africa, but red colouring often less bold, less extensive than illustrated, females without red moustachial streak. Immatures are duller than adults, underparts with little red. Has a loud, harsh call 'kee-urrr, kee-urrr, kee-urrr'. Found in hilly, rock-strewn grassland, mountain slopes and dry gullies. Feeds entirely on the ground among rocks, singly or in small parties, often perching on a prominent rock. 26 cm.

1 CARDINAL WOODPECKER *Dendropicos fuscescens*. Common resident. Identified by small size, *streaked* breast, black moustachial stripes and brown forehead in both sexes, males with crimson crowns, females with black crowns, The call is a high-pitched, chittering 'kekekekekekekek'. Pairs are found in any broadleafed woodland, thornveld or riverine bush, often in bird parties and frequently in quite small trees. Taps quietly. 14-16 cm.

2 GOLDENTAILED WOODPECKER *Campethera abingoni*. Common resident. Streaky-breasted but larger than the previous species, males with moustachial streak and entire crown red, spotted black; in females these are black and white, only the nape being red. The call is a single nasal 'waaa'. Pairs occur in broad-leafed woodland, thornveld and bush fringing dry riverbeds. 20-3 cm.

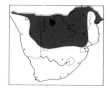

3 BENNETT'S WOODPECKER *Campethera bennettii*. Fairly common resident. Medium-sized woodpecker with *spotted* underparts (except in Namibia where unspotted), males identified by entirely red crowns and moustachial streaks, females by *brown facial- and throat-patches*. The call is an excitable, high-pitched chattering, sometimes by two or three birds together, 'whirrwhirrwhirrwhir-it-whir-it-whir-it-wrrrrrrrrr...', often accompanied by wing-flapping. Usually in pairs or groups in broadleafed woodland and thornveld, feeding mainly on the ground. 22-4 cm.

4 BEARDED WOODPECKER *Thripias namaquus*. Common resident. A large, long-billed species with *banded* underparts, bold black moustachial streaks and ear-patches, males with only top of crown red. The call is a loud 'wickwickwick-wick-wick'; the drumming particularly loud and far-carrying 'trrrrrr-tap-tap-tap-tap-tap'. Singly in any tall woodland and riverine forest. 23-5 cm.

1 LITTLE SPOTTED WOODPECKER *Campethera cailliautii*. Common, localised resident. Recognised by small size and lack of a moustachial-streak in both sexes; cf. Cardinal Woodpecker (previous page). The call is a shrill 'hee' repeated about four times. Pairs are found in thick woodland and on the fringes of forests. Taps with a rapid action. 16 cm.

2 SPECKLETHROATED WOODPECKER *Campethera scriptoricauda*. Uncommon, localised resident. A form of Bennett's Woodpecker (previous page). Males with *unspotted throat;* females differ from female Goldentailed Woodpecker (previous page) in spotted (not streaked) breast. Call as Bennett's Woodpecker. In Southern Africa recorded only in woodland between Beira and the Zambezi River in Mozambique. 19 cm.

3 KNYSNA WOODPECKER *Campethera notata*. Fairly common, localised resident. Both sexes have *well-spotted underparts* from chin to vent (except in southern Natal where less spotted), females with no distinct moustachial-streak, males with red moustachial-streak heavily spotted black, like the forecrown. The call is 'keeek'. Pairs occur in coastal and valley bush, woodland and forest fringes. 20 cm.

Wrynecks. Family JYNGIDAE.

4 REDTHROATED WRYNECK *Jynx ruficollis*. Common, localised resident. Identified by rust-brown patch on throat and upper breast, plus brown-speckled upperparts with blackish broken line from crown to mantle. The call, uttered frequently, is a high-pitched 'kek-kek-kek-kek'. Singly or in pairs in various types of woodland and in suburbia, often in wattle trees (Australian *Acacia* spp). Creeps about branches like a woodpecker, perches like a passerine or hops about the ground. 18 cm.

271

Honeyguides. Family INDICATORIDAE. Small, inconspicuous birds which show *white outer tail-feathers in flight*. Some species have distinctive calls and regular call-sites, others have weak, sibilant calls, which are seldom heard. Their food is mostly insects but a few species have developed the habit of leading man to wild bees' nests by continually chattering and fluttering conspicuously in the desired direction; when the bees' nest is broken open the honeyguides feed on the wax and grubs. Like cuckoos they build no nests but parasitise various other small birds. Young birds are dull versions of the adults.

1 EASTERN HONEYGUIDE *Indicator meliphilus.* Uncommon, localised resident. Resembles a small Lesser Honeyguide (2) but has a stubbier bill and greener upperparts, the underparts washed yellow with faint streaking, especially on the throat. Makes a high-pitched whistle plus chattering notes. Occurs sparsely on forest fringes and in woodland, with records from eastern Zimbabwe and Mozambique. Is known to parasitise at least the White-eared Barbet. 13 cm.

2 LESSER HONEYGUIDE *Indicator minor.* Common resident. Characterised by thick bill with a pale patch at the base and yellow edges to the wing-feathers; told from the Eastern Honeyguide (1) by larger size and lack of any streaking on the underparts. Uses a regular call-site from where it calls 'klew, klew, klew . . .' in series of 30-40 calls at a time. Occurs singly in various wooded habitats including suburbia. 15 cm.

3 SCALYTHROATED HONEYGUIDE *Indicator variegatus.* Fairly common resident. Told by streaky head and 'scaly' breast with yellow wash usually present. Makes a high-pitched 'foyt-foyt-foyt' or, from a call-site, a ventriloquial and purring 'trrrrrrrr', rising at the end. A bird of forest fringes, riverine forests and valley bush, usually singly. Has been known to 'guide' to bees' nests, otherwise hawks insects like a flycatcher. 19 cm.

4 GREATER HONEYGUIDE *Indicator indicator.* Common resident. In both sexes the yellow shoulder patch is frequently vestigial or absent, the dark throat of males is often incomplete, thus adults often appear as nondescript, bulbul-sized birds but *white outer tail-feathers* always present. Immatures are distinctive. as illustrated. From a regularly used call-site males call frequently in summer and for long periods 'vic-terrr, vic-terrr...', up to eleven times. Guides humans to bees' nests, the call then a high-pitched chattering sound while the bird flutters in an agitated manner. Occurs singly in woodland, bushveld and suburbia. Males perform a swooping display while making audible 'whirring' sounds with their wings. 19-20 cm.

1 SLENDERBILLED HONEYGUIDE *Prodotiscus zambesiae* Fairly common resident. Differs from the Sharpbilled Honeyguide (2) in *greener upperparts* with the flight feathers yellowedged; the throat is dark, finely streaked with white. The call is a harsh repetitive 'skee-aa' while in undulating display flight over the trees. Found singly in broadleafed woodland, usually in the canopy. Parasitises mostly white-eyes. 11,5 cm.

2 SHARPBILLED HONEYGUIDE *Prodotiscus regulus*. Uncommon resident. Told from (1) by *brown* (not greenish) upperparts, white rump and white throat. Has a thin, tinkling call-note resembling a weak version of the Crested Barbet's call 'tirrrrrrr . . .' lasting about four seconds; also a sharp 'tseet' in aerial display. Occurs singly in open bushveld, plantations and gardens. Usually perches high in a tree and *peers slowly from side to side while bobbing its head up and down* prior to calling. Catches insects on the ground or hawks them from a tree perch, then displaying the white rump and outer tail-feathers. 13 cm.

Creepers. Family SALPORNITHIDAE.

3 SPOTTED CREEPER *Salpornis spilonotus*. Uncommon, localised resident. Identified by curved bill, heavily spotted appearance and behaviour. The call is a series of rapid sibilant notes 'sweepy-swip-swip-swip-swip' or 'keck-keck-keck . . .', repeated five to six times. Singly or in pairs in broadleafed woodland; clambers about the trunks and branches of the trees like a woodpecker, working its way to the top before flying down at 45° to the base of the next tree. 15 cm.

Broadbills. Family EURYLAIMIDAE.

4 AFRICAN BROADBILL *Smithornis capensis*. Uncommon resident. Broad bill, dumpy appearance, black crown and heavily streaked underparts diagnostic. In display utters a frog-like 'purr-rupp'. Frequents forests, coastal bush and thickets where it perches low down and hawks insects like a flycatcher. When displaying makes a circular flight in the vertical plane over its perch and reveals white feathers on its back. 14 cm.

Pittas. Family PITTIDAE.

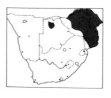

5 ANGOLA PITTA *Pitta angolensis*. Rare summer visitor and resident. Highly coloured and short-tailed, thrush-sized terrestrial bird. Sexes are alike. Normally occurs in swampy areas in forests and in riverine forests and thickets where it scratches about in ground debris, only flying into trees to hide when alarmed. Moves in quick hops. Individuals are occasionally found well south of their normal range. 23 cm.

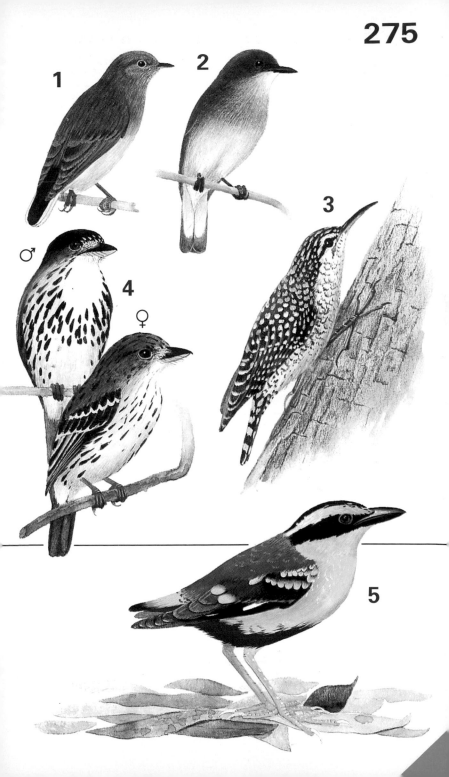

Larks. Family ALAUDIDAE. Small, sombrely-coloured terrestrial birds with confusingly similar, nondescript plumage patterns consisting of brownish or greyish speckled upperparts and pale underparts, usually with some speckling on the breast. Many species show regional plumage variations, palest or greyest in the north and west. Young resemble adults, but are generally more speckled. Best identified by the male's song or call as well as habitat and behaviour. Their flight is usually of a dipping nature and of short duration.

1 MELODIOUS LARK *Mirafra cheniana*. Fairly common endemic resident. Distinguished from the next species only with difficulty, but white eyebrow more distinct, upperparts darker and flanks more buffy than Monotonous Lark. Utters a lively song from a perch or in flight, the song continuing for long periods, and mimics the calls of other birds. Usually singly in grassveld or thornveld. 12 cm.

2 MONOTONOUS LARK *Mirafra passerina*. Common resident. Best told from the previous species by lack of distinct eyebrow, plus upperparts with less clearly defined markings. In many regions arrives in the summer rains and males immediately start calling, a monotonous and much-repeated 'corrr-weeoooo' throughout the day and on moonlit nights. Occurs in bushveld and woodland, with a preference for the more arid, stony regions. Calls from the ground, in the air or perched on a small tree. 14 cm.

3 SABOTA LARK *Mirafra sabota*. Common resident. Variable throughout its range, brownest in the east (a), palest in the north-west (b); bill shapes variable as illustrated, (c) being found in central Namibia. White eyebrow distinctive in all races, *no rufous wing-edges;* the outer tail feathers are white or pale buff. Has a melodious and variable song incorporating imitations of other birds, *usually uttered from a tree perch,* but occasionally in hovering flight. Singly in bushveld with sparse grass cover or stony ground. Perches in trees when disturbed. 15 cm.

4 FAWNCOLOURED LARK *Mirafra africanoides*. Common, localised resident. Best known by reddish-fawn (a) to distinctly fawn (b) colouring of upperparts (palest in the west) and white underparts. The song, given from the top of a small tree, is a rapid and urgent-sounding 'te-e-e-tee-ree-tee-ree-tee-ree-chee', with variations. Also has a display flight and song. Occurs in thornveld and the fringes of woodland in predominantly Kalahari sand, being most frequent in the dry west. Feeds in open ground but perches in trees when disturbed. 16 cm.

278

1 DUNE LARK *Mirafra erythrochlamys*. Common resident. Formerly treated as a race of the next species to which it is closely similar, differing mainly in much paler colouring, less heavy markings on upperparts and breast. In flight shows similar dark tail to the Karoo Lark while voice and behaviour are also much the same. A species of sandy regions, especially the dunes of the Namib Desert (not stony ground). 17 cm.

2 KAROO LARK *Mirafra albescens*. Common resident. Identified by rich colouring of the upperparts, pale lines above and below the eyes, dark streak through the eye, dusky or rufous ear-coverts and slender *bill shape*; cf. larger, thicker-billed Red Lark (page 282). The flight is heavy and the tail appears dark. Has an attractive song, frequently repeated clear notes 'chirrit-cheeoo-cherererere' with variations. Occurs in Karoo, especially areas of stony ground. Mostly terrestrial but occasionally makes short flights and may alight on bushes. Sings while perched or in flight. 17 cm.

3 FLAPPET LARK *Mirafra rufocinnamomea*. Common resident. Similar to the next species and best identified by territorial behaviour and mainly exclusive distribution. Pallid north-western race (a) has shorter, stouter bill than rufous eastern races (b). Has a soft 'tuee-tui' call; *does not sing in the air*. Singly in hilly grassland, grassland fringing woodland and bushveld with grassy areas. Unobtrusive in the non-breeding season. When breeding (early to late summer according to locality) males perform a high aerial cruise, making bursts of wing-claps, the sound a muffled 'purrit-purrit-purrit-purrit' with a pause before repeating; see illustration. Local variations occur in this flight pattern. May also ascend into wind to some height and then descend almost vertically before flying parallel to the ground prior to settling. 16 cm.

4 CLAPPER LARK *Mirafra apiata*. Common resident. A highly variable species, palest with most robust bill (a) in the north-west, most rufous (b) in the Orange Free State and Transvaal, the darkest with sharpest bill (c) in the south. Differs from previous species mainly in territorial behaviour, habitat and distribution. May sing from the ground but more strikingly while displaying; see opposite. Occurs singly or in pairs in grassland, low scrub and bushveld. Unobtrusive normally, but when breeding (October–February) males display by flying upwards, hovering briefly and clapping their wings, then dropping steeply while uttering a long, drawn-out 'fooeeeeeee'; see illustration. Also mimics the songs of other birds. 16-17 cm.

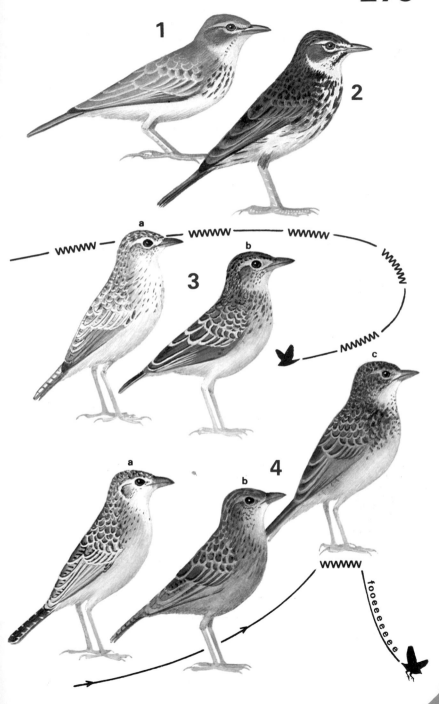

1 REDCAPPED LARK (SHORT-TOED LARK) *Calandrella cinerea*. Common resident. Orange-brown crown and pectoral-patches diagnostic. The crest is raised only when the bird is agitated or hot. Immatures are dark brown over entire upperparts, the breast well speckled blackish. The normal call is a brief 'cheep', 'chirrup' or 'cheeree'; also executes an aerial cruise early in the day while making a series of sibilant sounds terminating in a harsh 'tcheet, tcheet, tchrreet'. Usually in pairs or small flocks in short grass, especially dry pans, airstrips and dirt roads, walking rapidly or running, flying short distances then dropping down again. 15 cm.

2 RUFOUSNAPED LARK *Mirafra africana*. Common resident. Distinguished from other medium to large larks by rufous head-top and wing-feather edges, these showing as a rufous patch on the folded wing; typically with much rufous colouring above and below (a) or, in paler western birds (b), with white underparts faintly tinged buff and pale-edged feathers to upperparts. The call, a good recognition feature, is a melancholy 'tseep-tseeooo', repeated at about eight-second intervals. Also has an aerial-cruising song-flight, especially at dusk, when it imitates other birds. Usually seen singly in open grassland, males perching conspicuously on anthills, posts or bushes when calling, frequently shuffling the wing-feathers and raising the crest. 18-19 cm.

3 DUSKY LARK *Pinarocorys nigricans*. Locally common, non-breeding summer visitor. Dark colouring and bold markings of face and breast resemble Groundscraper Thrush (page 312), but upperparts darker, bill more robust. No distinctive call. Usually occurs in scattered flocks in bushveld and woodland, running about and occasionally perching in trees. Flies with sharply dipping flight. 19 cm.

4 SHORTCLAWED LARK *Mirafra chuana*. Uncommon resident. Shape and posture like Buffy Pipit (page 289) with longish, slender bill and tail, well streaked upperparts with no rufous on crown or wings, but rusty colour on rump. The call is a shrill 'phew-pheeoo-pheeoo, phew-pheeoo-pheeoo, pheeeeeoo, pheeeit . . .' with variations including several clear trills, usually uttered from the top of a bush. Also has a display flight in which it rises and then drops steeply calling a long, drawn-out 'foooeeee'; cf. Clapper Lark (page 278). Found in dry grassland with scattered bushes and *Acacia* savanna. 17-18 cm.

281

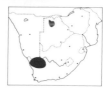

1 RED LARK   *Mirafra burra*. Fairly common, localised resident. In the Brandvlei region occurs with more boldly streaked upper-parts than the race illustrated; both races differ from the Karoo Lark (page 278) in larger size and *short, stout bill*. The tail appears dark in flight. Has a clear, canary-like song uttered from a bush or in flight. Found in vegetated red sand dunes and flats in the north-western Cape. 19 cm.

2 SPIKEHEELED LARK   *Chersomanes albofasciata*. Common resident. Many races, the two colour extremes illustrated: north-western (a) and south-eastern (b). Characterised by erect stance, long slender bill and short tail with white terminal bar; the hind claw is long and straight. Makes a rapid mellow trill in flight. Occurs singly or in small, loose parties in stony highveld grassland, Karoo and Kalahari dunes. Largely terrestrial in habits but flies a short distance if disturbed and perches briefly on low vegetation. 15-16 cm.

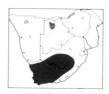

3 THICKBILLED LARK   *Galerida magnirostris*. Common resident. A robust, heavily marked lark with a fairly short tail; differs from Dusky Lark (previous page) in well-marked upperparts and lack of bold facial markings. The song is a short, musical 'chit-whitleooo-leooo', repeated at brief intervals from a low perch or while rising in a short flight. Occurs in pairs or small parties in grassland, montane grassland, Karoo and wheatlands, being especially common on grassy roadside verges. 18 cm.

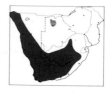

4 LONGBILLED LARK   *Mirafra curvirostris*. Common resident. A large, variable species, largest, darkest and longest-billed (a) in the south-west; more rufous and with bill shorter, less curved to the east and north-east, being darkest and dullest rufous in Natal (b) and with only faint markings in the Transvaal; smallest, most pallid, shortest-billed in the north-west (c). In early summer males display by rising steeply into the air and then plummeting down while calling a loud 'cheeeeeeeoo'; also calls 'phee-hee-hee' from the ground. Singly or in pairs on stony ridges in grassland and Karoo. Sometimes stands on elevated ground or large rocks with erect stance from where it may call. 20-2 cm.

1 RUDD'S LARK *Mirafra ruddi*. Uncommon, localised resident. Identified by long legs, almost tailless appearance, bulbous head with crown feathers projecting sideways like horns, pale eye-stripes and central head-stripe. In flight looks like a dumpy Spikeheeled Lark (previous page). In summer males cruise about at 15-35 m above ground alternately wing-flapping (noiselessly) and planing while calling 'whicha-ey' or 'whicha-ey-yo' or 'wree-jur', etc. Does not mimic like other aerial-singing larks. Singly or loose groups in high altitude grassland. 14-15 cm.

2 BOTHA'S LARK *Spizocorys fringillaris*. Uncommon, local-ised resident. Has a conspicuous eye-stripe and dark dappled upperparts, much darker than any other small lark. On take-off calls 'chuck', often repeatedly, otherwise calls 'tcheree' several times, in flight or while settled. In pairs or small parties in heavily grazed flats or upper slopes of high altitude grasslands and farmlands. Often associates with the next species, but is unde-monstrative and inconspicuous, with no aerial displays 12 cm.

3 PINKBILLED LARK *Spizocorys conirostris*. Common resi-dent. Palest race (a) in the west, most rufous race (b) in the south and east; short, conical pink bill in all races. The call is 'chi*zic*' or 'twee-twee-twee' on the ground or in flight. Usually in small parties in grassland, especially where grass is seeding; also burnt ground. 12 cm.

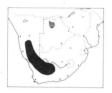

4 SCLATER'S LARK *Spizocorys sclateri*. Uncommon, local-ised resident. Differs from the next species in richer colouring, bolder markings, more slender bill and lack of crest; from the Larklike Bunting (page 442) by longer bill. Some races paler than illustrated. In flight calls 'turt-turt-turt'. Pairs, often flocks 6-20, in arid grassland. 13 cm.

5 STARK'S LARK *Eremalauda starki*. Common resident. A very pale lark with a small crest giving a peaked appearance to the head, this feature plus distinct markings on the upperparts distinguishing it from the next species. Has a melodious 'prrt-prrt'call. Occurs in arid grassland, sometimes in large flocks near pans in the dry season. When disturbed it takes off and flies in a wide arc before resettling. 13 cm.

6 GRAY'S LARK *Ammomanes grayi*. Common, localised resi-dent. Palest of the small larks, appearing *almost white* in the field. Differs from the previous species in plainer upperparts, no crest; from Tractrac Chat (page 320) in short conical bill *pale in colour*, pale legs and lack of white rump. The alarm call is 'cheep-cheep-cheep'. Occurs in small parties in desert, especially near rock outcrops. When first alarmed may remain motionless and unseen by the observer. If flushed, flies off low for a short distance; on settling may give a double, high-pitched whistle. 14 cm.

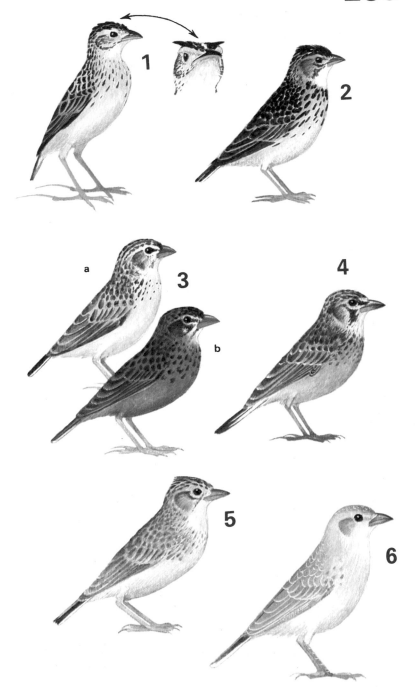

Finchlarks. Small, sparrow-like larks with marked sexual plumage differences, the males predominantly black. Occur in flocks, especially in drier regions, and are highly nomadic.

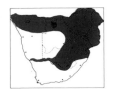

1 CHESTNUTBACKED FINCHLARK *Eremopterix leucotis*. Common to abundant resident. Both sexes differ from other finchlarks in having chestnut wing-coverts and grey underwings. Has a sharp, rattling call 'chip-chee-w' and a pretty song in fluttering flight. Flocks occur on open flats, airfields and cultivated lands, usually with low bushes nearby. Make off in low irregular flight when disturbed, then suddenly resettle. 12-13 cm.

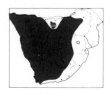

2 BLACKEARED FINCHLARK *Eremopterix australis*. Common resident. Male has no white plumage; upperparts of both sexes rufous, belly of female lacks black patch of other female finchlarks. Calls 'cht-cht-cht' in flight. Occurs in barren terrain, sometimes in very large flocks. 12-13 cm.

3 GREYBACKED FINCHLARK *Eremopterix verticalis*. Very common to abundant resident. Both sexes distinguished by grey upperparts. A shrill chirp is uttered while the birds are feeding. Flocks, often very large, occur in much the same habitat as (1), though less dependent on bushes. 12-13 cm.

Pipits, longclaws and wagtails. Family MOTACILLIDAE. Small, insectivorous terrestrial birds, water-associated in wagtails. Sexes alike or closely similar, all with white or buff outer tail-feathers. Pipits are lark-like in appearance and behaviour, many so similar as to make field identification difficult. Most pipits utter a 'chissik' call on take-off, their flight low and dipping. Longclaws are large, colourful pipits while wagtails, also colourful or striking, are mostly well known because of their confiding and friendly behaviour. They have the habit of continually bobbing their tails up and down.

4 SHORT-TAILED PIPIT *Anthus brachyurus*. Uncommon resident. Small size, short tail, dark upperparts and well-streaked chest diagnostic. Call a nasal, buzzy 'bzzht'. Singly or in pairs, sparsely distributed in grassland or woodland. Entirely terrestrial, never perching on bushes though may utter a short song (undescribed) while perched on a small earth clump or mound. When disturbed rises at one's feet and flits about in strong, erratic flight before resettling a short distance away. 12 cm.

287

288

1 GRASSVELD PIPIT *Anthus cinnamomeus.* Common resident. *Yellow* base to the bill, bold facial markings, boldly marked breast and *white* (not buff) outer tail-feathers distinguish this from other, similar pipits. When disturbed takes off with a 'chissik' call and characteristic dipping flight; may call in flight 'chree-chree-chree-chree' during each dip. Usually singly in grasslands. 16 cm.

2 ROCK PIPIT *Anthus crenatus.* Locally common, endemic resident. Drab, indistinctly marked, appearing almost plain-backed; cf. Plainbacked Pipit (4). At close range yellowish shoulder patch and feather edges visible, plus faint streaking on breast. Has a characteristic erect stance while calling 'treee-terroooo, treee-terroooo', the last syllable descending, from a low perch or while hovering. Secretive among rocks on grassy hillsides. 16 cm.

3 LONGBILLED PIPIT *Anthus similis.* Common resident. Differs from (1) in less distinct breast-streaking and *buff* (not white) outer tail-feather margins. The base of the bill is *yellow*, but the bill length is not a field feature. May call for long periods from a rock, bush or fence, a clear metallic 'kilink', or 'chip, chreep, chroop, chreep, chip . . .'. Occurs on hillsides, especially stony regions with sparse vegetation, and in burnt areas. 18 cm.

WOOD PIPIT *Anthus nyassae.* (Not illustrated.) Common resident. About identical to (3) in all respects but differs in that it occurs in Miombo woodland where it readily *perches in trees.* 18 cm.

4 PLAINBACKED PIPIT *Anthus leucophrys.* Fairly common resident. Told by *lack of distinct markings* on the upperparts and indistinct breast-markings; the edges of the outer tail-feathers are *buff,* the base of the bill is *yellow.* From the ground calls a sparrow-like 'jhreet-jhroot'. Singly or in small flocks in grassland with short or burnt grass, especially hilly regions. 17 cm.

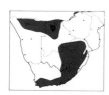

5 BUFFY PIPIT *Anthus vaalensis.* Uncommon resident. Moustacial streaks not pronounced, breast-streaking variable, often indistinct, edges of outer tail-feathers *pale buff,* the base of the bill *pink.* In flight makes an occasional 'chissik' call. *Bobs its tail more frequently than most pipits,* and has the habit of running a short distance then standing erect with breast thrown out. Occurs in short grasslands and hillsides with small bushes or rock outcrops. 19 cm.

6 MOUNTAIN PIPIT *Anthus hoeschi.* Localised, fairly common summer resident. Resembles a large Grassveld Pipit (1) but upperparts darker, breast more boldly streaked, base of bill *pink* (not yellow), outer tail-feathers *buff.* Call similar to that of (1) but deeper, slower. Occurs in montane grassland above 2 000 m in Lesotho and north-eastern Cape during summer and migrates through Botswana to overwinter in Angola. 18 cm.

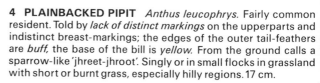

289

1 ORANGETHROATED LONGCLAW *Macronyx capensis*. Common resident. Orange throat with black surround diagnostic of adults; young birds may have throat same colour as underparts, then distinguished from Yellowthroated Longclaw (overleaf) by deeper yellow colouring and buff (not yellow) edges to wing-feathers. Normal call a mewing 'me-yew'; also a far-reaching whistle. Solitary or pairs in grassland. Often stands momentarily with upright stance on grass tuft, stone or anthill. If disturbed, flies a short distance uttering its characteristic call. 20 cm.

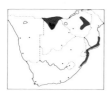

2 PINKTHROATED LONGCLAW *Macronyx ameliae*. Uncommon resident. Immature less pink, throat more buffy, black gorget vestigial. The call is a squeaky 'teee-yoo tyip-tyip-tyip-TEE YOOOO'. Singly or in pairs in marshy grasslands. Behaviour less conspicuous than other longclaws; lies low when approached, then makes off in erratic flight for a short distance (when white wing-bars and dark back markings can be seen) before settling and hiding again. 20 cm.

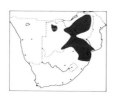

3 TREE PIPIT *Anthus trivialis*. Uncommon summer visitor. Short bill, white throat and breast with tear-shaped spots useful characteristics but best identified by behaviour. Flight call 'teez', or from the ground 'seea'. Singly or pairs but flocks when migrating, in woodland, parks and gardens, mostly in Zimbabwe. 16 cm.

REDTHROATED PIPIT see page 446.

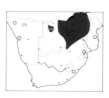

4 BUSHVELD PIPIT *Anthus caffer*. Fairly common resident. Differs from previous species in smaller size, off-white throat, breast markings less distinct but forming stripes, and more rufous colouring. From a treetop perch calls 'skeer-trurp, skeer-trurp, skeer-trurp-skee-skee . . .'; from the ground calls 'tshweep'. Usually singly in thornveld or dry bushveld. If disturbed on the ground, makes off with erratic flight, then settles on a tree from where it may call. 13.5 cm.

5 STRIPED PIPIT *Anthus lineiventris*. Common resident. Distinguished by clearly yellow-edged wing-feathers, these more obvious than in Rock Pipit (previous page) from which it also differs in well-streaked underparts. Has a loud, whistling, thrush-like song. Solitary or in pairs on stony slopes, ridges, road-cuttings and rocky banks of small rivers. When disturbed flies to a tree where it may perch lengthwise along a branch. 18 cm.

292

1 YELLOWBREASTED PIPIT *Hemimacronyx chloris.* Rare, localised resident. Winter plumage lacks yellow. Buffy-white below with light streaking on breast; immature has buffy flanks and breast. Males call from grass tufts and in hovering flight, a rapid chipping like a Longtailed Widow (page 418) 'chip chip chip chip . . .'. Occurs singly or in pairs in the dense grass of high-altitude montane grasslands where it breeds in summer, moving to lower-altitude grasslands in winter. Inconspicuous and secretive; lies close in the grass and flushes reluctantly, but finally flies far. 16-18 cm.

2 YELLOWTHROATED LONGCLAW *Macronyx croceus.* Common resident. Differs from Bokmakierie (page 380) in brown upperparts and pink-brown legs; cf. that species. Utters a monotonous mewing from the top of a bush 'triooo, triooo, trroo-chit-chit, trroo-chit-chit-trroo-chit' and sings in flight or from a perch. A terrestrial species, singly or in pairs in moist grassland with scattered trees. 20 cm.

FÜLLEBORN'S LONGCLAW *Macronyx fuellebornii.* Rare, possibly resident. Very similar to previous species, but yellow underparts suffused with buff, no black streaks on breast (see margin illustration). Makes a sparrow-like chirping 'weee', a whistling 'jee-o-wee' and, when breeding, a two-noted trill 'chree-er'. Calls from the tops of bushes. Tame and conspicuous, occurring in the arid thornveld of northern Ovamboland and beyond. 21 cm.

3 GOLDEN PIPIT *Tmetothylacus tenellus.* Very rare vagrant. Much smaller than (2), male's breast-band less extensive. Male appears rich yellow at all times, the female buffy and lacking a breast-band. In both sexes the visible upper leg (tibia) is un-feathered. A terrestrial species which, in its normal range, frequents dry bushveld, occasionally perching on bushes. 15 cm.

4 YELLOW WAGTAIL *Motacilla flava.* Fairly common summer visitor. Many races with varying head patterns, (a) and (c) most common in this region but (b) and (d) also known. Race (d) has the white eyebrow bolder than the Grey Wagtail (over-leaf); otherwise told by its shorter tail, green (not grey) upperparts including rump and entirely yellow underparts. Immature in first winter plumage can also be confused with Grey Wagtail; cf. that species. The call is 'tsee-ip'. Singly in wetlands and moist grasslands. 18 cm.

WAGTAILS

1 GREY WAGTAIL *Motacilla cinerea*. Rare visitor. Distinguished from Yellow Wagtail (previous page) by grey upperparts (not green), dark shoulder-patch and white throat. Tail long, yellow at base above and below. Underparts yellow and white with faint brownish smudges (cf. Yellow Wagtail). Call a short, metallic 'tit' or 'tidit'. Walks about bobbing its long tail constantly, unusally near fast-flowing water. 18 cm.

2 LONGTAILED WAGTAIL *Motacilla clara*. Fairly common resident. Told by very long tail and predominantly grey and white colouring, much paler than other wagtails. Calls 'chirrup' on taking flight; also sings 'ti-tuu-ui-tui-tui'. Pairs or small groups along fast-running rivers and streams. Hops and flits from boulder to boulder with much tail-wagging. 19-20 cm.

3 CAPE WAGTAIL *Motacilla capensis*. Common resident. Shorter-tailed than the previous two species and greyer than other wagtails. Northern races have breast-band absent or vestigial, see (b). Call a loud, cheerful 'tseep-eep' or 'tseeep'. Singly or in pairs near water, in suburban gardens, cities and sewage-farms. Walks about feeding on the ground, occasionally wagging its tail. If disturbed, will perch briefly on a tree, wall, fence or building. Tame and confiding. 18 cm.

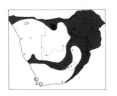

4 AFRICAN PIED WAGTAIL *Motacilla aguimp*. Common resident. Told from other wagtails by striking pied plumage, upperparts black (not grey), tail similar length to (3). Call a loud 'tu-weee' and 'twee-twee-twee'. Singly, in pairs and family groups near lakes, dams, large rivers, sewage-farms, lagoons and estuaries. Habits much as previous species, but enters suburbia only in the north of its range. 20 cm.

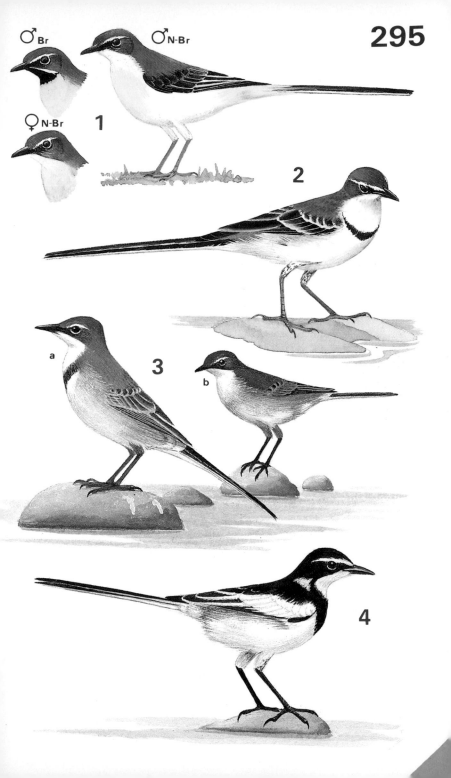

296

DRONGOS & SIMILAR BLACK BIRDS

Drongos. Family DICRURIDAE. Black insectivorous birds with prominent rictal bristles. They hawk insects from a perch in woodland and bushveld and are pugnacious, habitually mobbing larger birds, even pecking the heads of eagles. Numbers (2) and (3) are included on this plate for better comparison with drongos; the Black Flycatcher belongs to the family Muscicapidae (pages 360-4), the Black Cuckooshrike to the family Campephagidae (overleaf).

1 FORKTAILED DRONGO *Dicrurus adsimilis.* Common resident. Differs from all similar black birds in *prominent forked tail,* the outer feathers splayed outwards: cf. (4) which has only a shallow fork in its tail. Sexes alike, immature as illustrated. Has a variety of unmusical twanging notes interspersed with imitations of other bird calls, especially those of owls and other birds of prey. Found in almost any non-forest habitat with trees. Noisy and aggressive. 25 cm.

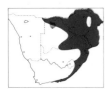

2 BLACK FLYCATCHER *Melaenornis pammelaina.* Common resident. The tail shows a *small indentation* at the tip (not a distinct fork), the outer tail-feathers being straight, not splayed. Sexes alike, immature as illustrated. Not very vocal, uttering various low sibilant sounds 'swee' or 'swee-ur'. Singly or in pairs in any woodland, thornveld or bushveld. Catches insects on the ground, flying down from a perch in typical flycatcher fashion. Often occurs alongside the previous species but, by contrast, is quiet. 19-22 cm.

3 BLACK CUCKOOSHRIKE *Campephaga flava* (see overleaf for full account). Males only are black, differing from similar black birds in having a *rounded tail* and prominent *orange-yellow gape;* sometimes has a yellow shoulder, see overleaf. A quiet, arboreal species.

4 SQUARETAILED DRONGO *Dicrurus ludwigii.* Common, localised resident. Has splayed outer tail-feathers as (1) but with only a *shallow indentation;* also has ruby-red eyes. Calls are a loud 'Cherit! Cherit!' or 'Cherit-wit-wit' plus other strident sounds and imitations of other bird calls. Singly or in pairs in evergreen forests, riparian forests and dense woodland where it frequents the mid-stratum, hawking from a perch. Active, noisy and aggressive. 19 cm.

Cuckooshrikes. Family CAMPEPHAGIDAE. Insectivorous, heavy-billed birds, some of cuckoo-like appearance, found in the larger trees of forest fringes, riparian forests and woodland.

1 WHITEBREASTED CUCKOOSHRIKE *Coracina pectoralis.* Uncommon resident. Adults as illustrated; immature like female but with white barring on upperparts, grey spotting below. The call is a softly whistled 'duid duid' by males, and a trilling 'che-e-e-e-e' by females. Usually singly in large trees in riparian forests and broadleafed woodland. A lethargic species, moving from branch to branch with long hops, peering closely at leaves in search of insects or making short aerial sallies. Sparsely distributed. 27 cm.

2 GREY CUCKOOSHRIKE *Coracina caesia.* Uncommon, localised resident. All-grey colouring diagnostic; females lack the black lores. Immatures have the feathers tipped white, giving a freckled appearance. The call is a quiet, high-pitched 'peeeeeooooo', usually while perched; also makes a variety of chittering and trilling sounds while feeding. Singly or in pairs in evergreen forests, riparian forests and forested valleys where it frequents the tree canopies. 27 cm.

3 BLACK CUCKOOSHRIKE *Campephaga flava.* Fairly common summer resident. See previous page for comparison of males with other similar black birds. About half of South African male birds show the yellow shoulder (a), whereas in Zimbabwe and Botswana most males lack this, as (b). Females strikingly different, cuckoo-like as illustrated; immatures like females, young males with increasing areas of black as shown. The call, not often heard, is a soft, high-pitched trill 'trrrrrrrr . . .'. Pairs occur in a variety of wooded habitats, thornveld, mixed bushveld, broadleafed woodland and coastal bush; sparse in drier regions. Unobtrusive unless calling, frequenting the mid-stratum. Often joins bird parties. 22 cm.

Crows. Family CORVIDAE. Large, mainly glossy black, omnivorous birds, largest members of the Passerines. Sexes are alike and young similar to adults. All have loud cawing calls.

1 PIED CROW *Corvus albus*. Common resident. Distinguished by white breast and collar. The call is a loud 'kwaak'. A widespread, bold species usually found in association with human settlement, where it gleans food scraps, especially haunting refuse dumps, school playing-fields, highways and farmlands. Usually in loose flocks or large communal roosts. 46-52 cm.

2 BLACK CROW (CAPE ROOK) *Corvus capensis*. Common localised resident. Entirely glossy black. The call is a high-pitched 'kraaa'. Singles, pairs and flocks frequent farmlands and open country. Generally less common than previous species. Habitually perches and nests on telephone poles. 48-53 cm.

3 WHITENECKED RAVEN *Corvus albicollis*. Common localised resident. Has a white nape only, otherwise black with a very heavy bill. The call is a falsetto 'kraak', although deeper notes are sometimes uttered. Normally occurs in montane regions but wanders far in search of food. A bold species and a great scavenger, often feeding on carrion. Individuals usually forage alone but many may gather at food sources. 50-4 cm.

4 HOUSE CROW *Corvus splendens*. Common localised resident. Lacks any white plumage. Smaller than the Black Crow (2) and with grey nape, mantle and breast. Voice a shrill 'kwaa, kwaa'. Strictly commensal with man, occurring in suburbs of Durban. 43 cm.

Orioles. Family ORIOLIDAE. Predominantly yellow, pink-billed, insectivorous and frugivorous birds with clear, liquid-sounding calls. They feed mostly in the canopies of large trees.

5 GREENHEADED ORIOLE *Oriolus chlorocephalus*. Rare, localised resident. Distinguished from other orioles by green upperparts including head and throat, plus yellow collar and underparts; females slightly duller than males, immatures undescribed. The call is very similar to the Blackheaded Oriole (overleaf). In the Southern African region occurs only in the montane forests of Mt Gorongosa in central Mozambique. 24 cm.

1 EUROPEAN GOLDEN ORIOLE *Oriolus oriolus*. Fairly common to uncommon summer visitor. Males differ from males of the next species in having black wings, females resemble the immature illustrated. The call is a ringing 'weela-weeoo', plus a churring alarm note common to all orioles. Singly in broadleafed woodland, mixed bushveld, riverine forests and various other wooded habitats including exotic trees. Infrequent over much of the interior. 24 cm.

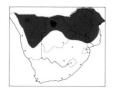

2 AFRICAN GOLDEN ORIOLE *Oriolus auratus*. Uncommon summer resident. Males are the yellowest of orioles with a distinct black line through the eyes to the ear-coverts, this also being present in immatures. Females are less bright than males, upperparts greener, underparts paler. The calls are liquid whistles 'wee-er-er-wul' or 'fee-yoo-fee-yoo-fee-yoo', longer than the calls of the next species. Occurs in any well-developed woodland or riverine forest. 24 cm.

3 BLACKHEADED ORIOLE *Oriolus iarvatus*. Common resident. Distinguished by black head; cf. Masked Weaver (page 412), which is smaller with a black bill. Immatures as illustrated; cf. Greenheaded Oriole (previous page). The usual call is a loud, liquid 'pheeoo' or 'pheea-pheeoo' but occasionally calls like the European Golden Oriole (1); also has a 'churr' alarm call. Singly or in pairs in well-developed woodland or mixed bushveld, riverine forests and exotic trees. A noisy, conspicuous species. 25 cm.

Bulbuls. Family PYCNONOTIDAE. Frugivorous and insectivorous birds with clear, whistling calls. They frequent evergreen bush and forests. Sexes are alike, immatures duller.

1 BUSH BLACKCAP *Lioptilus nigricapillus*. (Family TIMALIIDAE). Uncommon resident. Distinguished by black cap and pink or orange bill. The song is a lively jumble of notes similar to the Blackeyed Bulbul (overleaf) but more liquid and varied. Singly or in pairs in forest fringes and adjacent scrub, more particularly at higher altitudes. Keeps mainly within cover and is not easily seen. 17 cm.

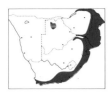

2 SOMBRE BULBUL *Andropadus importunus*. Common resident. Southern form (a) plain olive-green. Northern form (b), lower Zambezi Valley and beyond, much yellower, upperparts greener. Diagnostic creamy-white eyes in adults of both colour forms, greyish in immatures. Heard more often than seen. Usually calls a strident 'Willie!'; in the breeding season this is followed by a babbling trill likened to 'Willie! Come out and fight! Sca-a-ared', the final phrase barely audible. Usually singly in forest fringes and adjacent thickets, riverine forest and well-wooded valleys; especially common in coastal bush. Not particularly secretive but its cryptic colouring makes it difficult to see. 19-24 cm.

3 YELLOWSPOTTED NICATOR *Nicator gularis*. Uncommon to locally common resident. Identified by heavy bill and yellow-spotted wing-feathers, the spots smaller in immatures; cf. female Black Cuckooshrike (page 296) which has barred underparts. The call is a series of mellow trills and warbles. Singly in dense coastal, riverine and forest edge thickets or in the mid-stratum of riverine forests and mixed bushveld. Secretive and easily overlooked if not calling. Sparsely distributed. 23 cm.

4 YELLOWBELLIED BULBUL *Chlorocichla flaviventris*. Fairly common resident. Identified by olive-green upperparts and bright yellow underparts, including underwing, plus reddish eyes with conspicuous *white eyelids*. Immatures are similar but head-top same colour as back. Noisy at times, the call a loud 'pur, pur, pur, pur, peh, peh, peh, peh, peh...', often several birds calling at once. Singly or in pairs in well-developed riverine forests, coastal and lowland forests plus thickets on moist, rocky hillsides. Spends much time foraging on the ground or in the mid-stratum. 20-3 cm.

5 TERRESTRIAL BULBUL *Phyllastrephus terrestris*. Common resident. A very drab brown bird, apart from the white throat, the underparts barely paler than the upperparts; at close range a yellowish gape is discernible. Immatures have redder wing-feather edges. Feeding parties maintain a quiet chuckling or murmuring. Usually in parties of six or more in dense riverside and hillside thickets, plus dense undergrowth in forests and bushveld, scratching about in ground debris and seldom ascending above the lower stratum. Easily overlooked unless heard. 21-2 cm.

305

306

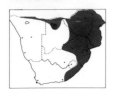

1 BLACKEYED BULBUL *Pycnonotus barbatus*. Very common resident. Dark, crested head, yellow vent and lack of conspicuous eye-ring identify this well-known species. Has several cheerful calls such as a short phrase sounding like 'Wake-up, Gregory' and a much repeated 'chit, chit, chit...'. Gregarious birds, inhabiting most regions with bush and trees, especially riverine forests and suburban gardens, but not evergreen forests. 20-2 cm.

2 REDEYED BULBUL *Pycnonotus nigricans*. Very common resident. Differs from previous species mainly in red eye-wattle. Has a variety of cheerful, chattering calls similar to that species and is very alike in most other ways. Frequents drier country than the Blackeyed Bulbul, usually associating with habitation and the bush of watercourses. 19-21 cm.

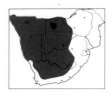

3 CAPE BULBUL *Pycnonotus capensis*. Common resident. Differs from both previous species in white eye-wattle and browner appearance of head. Has similar cheerful calls, including a liquid 'piet-piet-patata'. A lively, conspicuous species frequenting scrub, wooded watercourses and exotic coastal bush. 19-21 cm.

4 YELLOWSTREAKED BULBUL *Phyllastrephus flavostriatus*. Fairly common resident. Told from the next species by larger size, darker head, dark eye and prominent bill. Yellow streaks of underparts *not* a field feature. Has various strident call-notes 'chur, chur, chi-cheee, choo-choo-choo-choo-choo, chitchitchit-chit... chee-chwer-treee-treee...'. Small groups in the mid-stratum of evergreen forests and the adjacent bush. Clambers about moss-covered tree trunks, branches and creepers, often hanging head downwards. *Frequently flicks open one wing at a time*. Tame and conspicuous, often in mixed bird parties. 18-21 cm.

5 SLENDER BULBUL *Phyllastrephus debilis*. Fairly common resident. Much smaller than the previous species; head and eye paler, bill paler and shorter. Young birds have heads and faces greenish. Has a loud, warbling song of explosive quality plus a sibilant, ventriloquial call on a rising scale and a gurgling alarm note. Frequents evergreen forests and their fringing secondary growth. Warbler-like in behaviour, feeding in the upper and lower strata. 14 cm.

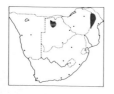

6 STRIPECHEEKED BULBUL *Andropadus milanjensis*. Fairly common resident. Distinctly green with dark grey cap and white streaks on ear-coverts. Underparts much greener than Yellowbellied Bulbul (previous page). Mostly silent but has various harsh calls 'chuck, churrr, chuck, churr-churr-trrrr...', made while sidling along a branch in small hops. Feeds at the edges of evergreen forests, dense lowland forest scrub, thickets and, sometimes, in broadleafed woodland. 19-21 cm.

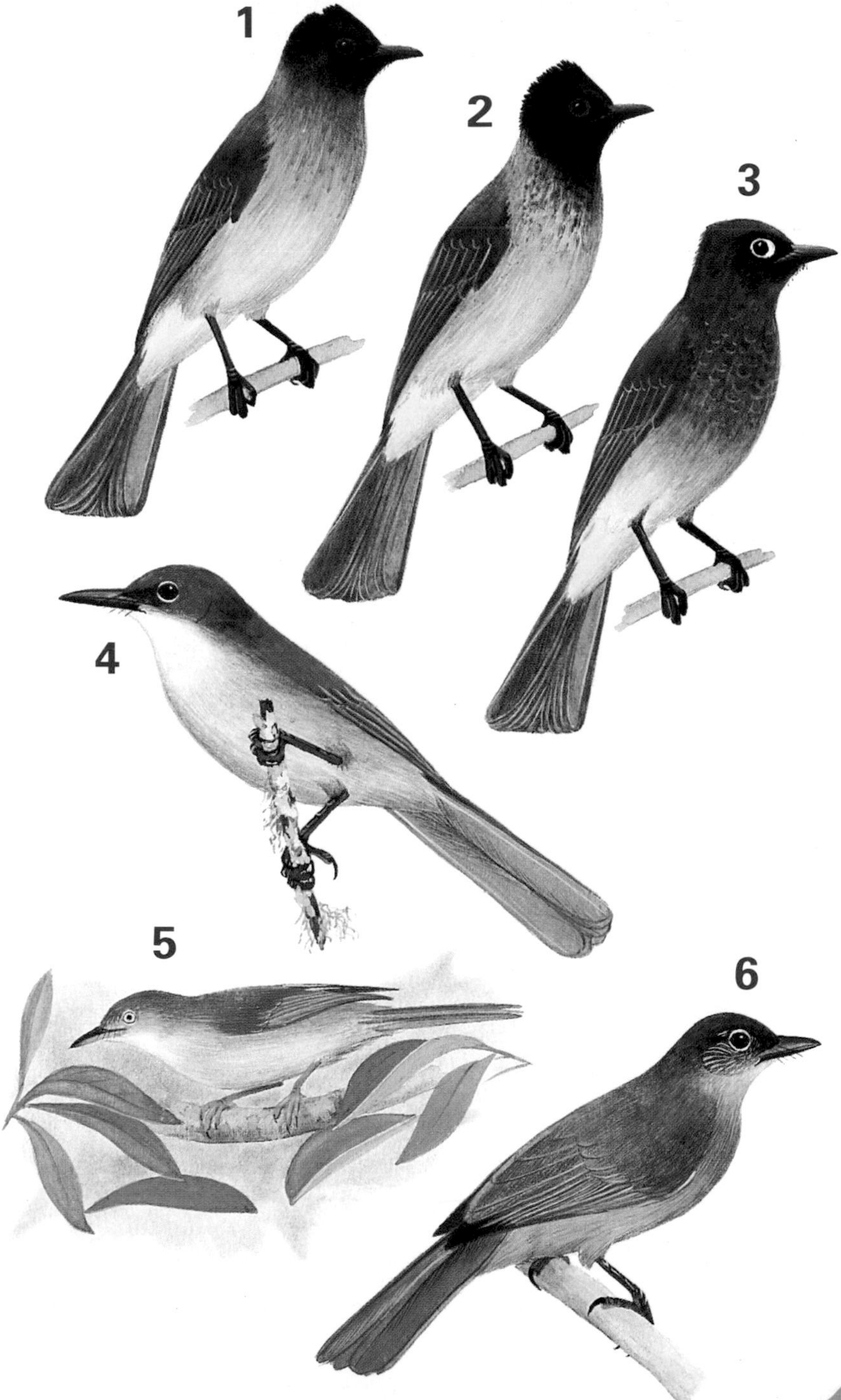
1
2
3
4
5
6

308

Tits. Family PARIDAE. Small insectivorous, arboreal birds with short, stout beaks, the nostrils obscured by bristles. Habitually forage in the tree canopies in bird parties; clambering about the branches in agile fashion frequently feeding in inverted positions or running up tree trunks like a woodpecker. They have rasping calls.

1 SOUTHERN BLACK TIT *Parus niger*. Common resident. Males distinguished from the next species by heavier bill and more white on the vent and undertail; northern races may show more or less white on the folded wing than illustrated. Females as illustrated or darker on underparts. Immatures resemble females. The calls are harsh and rasping, a rapid 'twiddy-zeet-zeet-zeet' or 'zeu-zeu-zeu-twit'. Pairs or groups occur in a wide variety of wooded habitats, including exotics. 16 cm.

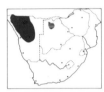

2 CARP'S BLACK TIT *Parus carpi*. Common, localised resident. Smaller than the previous species, the vent and undertail with either small traces of white or none, the bill smaller. Females and immatures are duller. Call as previous species. Habits as for the previous species. 14 cm.

3 SOUTHERN GREY TIT *Parus afer*. Common resident. Distinguished from the next two species by *grey-brown* (not blue-grey) mantle and back, more tawny appearance, shorter tail. Sexes are alike, immatures similar. The call can be likened to 'Piet-jou-jou'. Pairs in Karoo scrub, dry thornveld, rocky hills and gorges. A restless species, frequenting the smaller trees and bushes. 13 cm.

4 ASHY GREY TIT (ACACIA GREY TIT) *Parus cinerascens*. Common resident. Identified by *blue-grey* mantle, back and underparts; of generally greyer appearance than either (3) or (5). Sexes are alike, immatures duller. In pairs in thornveld and mixed bushveld, frequently in bird parties. 14 cm.

5 NORTHERN GREY TIT (MIOMBO GREY TIT) *Parus griseiventris*. Common resident. Distinguished from the previous species by *white underparts* (not grey) and broader white regions on sides of head. Pairs, often in bird parties, are found in the Miombo woodland of Zimbabwe. 14 cm.

6 RUFOUSBELLIED TIT *Parus rufiventris*. Uncommon, localised resident. Race (a) with black head, cream-coloured eyes and rufous underparts distinctive; the pale eastern race (b) occurs only in the Zimbabwe-Mozambique border regions. Immatures are duller, with brown eyes, the wing-feathers edged yellowish. Calls 'chik-wee' and a rasping 'chrrr'. Pairs and small groups frequent well-developed miombo woodland, feeding mostly in the upper stratum. 15 cm.

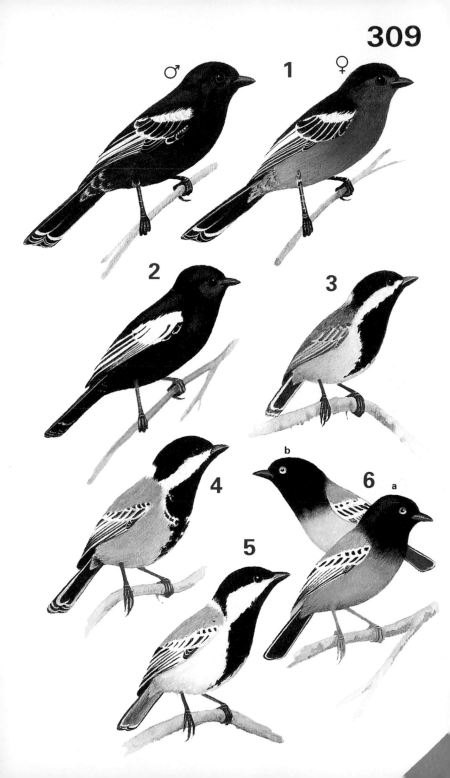

310

Babblers. Family TIMALIIDAE. Insectivorous, thrush-like terrestrial birds of gregarious habits and with distinctive babbling calls. Sexes are alike. (The aberrant Bush Blackcap appears on page 304.)

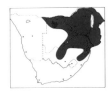

1 ARROWMARKED BABBLER *Turdoides jardineii*. Common resident. Identified by call and whitish, arrow-like streaks on the underparts; cf. Whiterumped Babbler (4), which has scale-like breast markings and white rump. Immatures lack the arrow marks but are usually seen with adults. The call is a noisy, excitable whirring started by one bird and taken up by all the others until it resembles hysterical giggling; the basic sound is 'scurr-scurr-scurr...', harsher and more mechanical-sounding than the similar call of the Redbilled Woodhoopoe (page 256). Occurs in parties of six to ten birds in any woodland, mixed bushveld, wooded hillsides and stands of exotic trees, plus suburbia in Zimbabwe. Usually in the lower stratum, calling frequently. 23-5 cm.

2 PIED BABBLER *Turdoides bicolor*. Common resident. Entirely white except for black wings and tail. Immatures are initially olive-brown, becoming white gradually. The call is a high-pitched babbling, one bird commencing 'skerr-skerr-skerr-kikikikikikerrkerrkerr...' and all others joining in; shriller than the previous species. Parties frequent dry thornveld and woodland. 26 cm.

3 BARECHEEKED BABBLER *Turdoides gymnogenys*. Fairly common, localised resident. Adults resemble juveniles of the previous species but differ from adult Pied Babblers in being less white, upperparts and sides of neck brown or cinnamon. Groups make a typical babbler cackling, a high-pitched 'kurrkurrkurrkurr-kurr...'. Found in arid thornveld and woodland in north-west Namibia, frequenting dry watercourses and hillsides with trees. 24 cm.

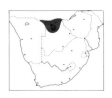

4 WHITERUMPED BABBLER *Turdoides leucopygius*. Common localised resident. Differs from the Arrowmarked Babbler (1) mainly in having a white rump, the head and breast with all feathers pale-edged, giving a scaly appearance; underbelly and vent also white. Immatures have paler throats. The call is a noisy, high-pitched babbling 'kwekwekwekwekwe-kwekwe...' or 'păpăpăpăpăpăpă...' similar to the next species. Parties occur in bushveld, reeds and papyrus-beds on floodplains of the Zambezi–Okavango–Cunene River system. 26 cm.

5 BLACKFACED BABBLER *Turdoides melanops*. Uncommon, localised resident. Black mask and distinctive yellow eyes diagnostic. The call is a high-pitched 'păpăpăpăpăpăpă...' by several birds. Small parties occur in woodland and grassland with tall grass. Shy and secretive, keeps to thick cover. 28 cm.

Thrushes, chats and robins. Family TURDIDAE. Largely terrestrial, insectivorous or frugivorous birds which sing from trees, some robins rating as among our finest songsters. The sexes are alike unless otherwise stated, while immatures usually have the feathers of the upperparts pale-edged, the underparts spotted.

1 GROUNDSCRAPER THRUSH *Turdus litsitsirupa.* Common resident. Differs from the next species in erect stance, absence of white wing-spots and habitat preference; in flight shows chestnut wings. Differs from the Dusky Lark (page 280) in grey-brown (not dark brown) upperparts. Calls 'lipsitsirupa' (hence its specific name) and sings a brisk, melodious song, the phrases continually varied. Singly in any woodland, mixed bushveld, cattle kraals and rural suburbia. 22 cm.

2 SPOTTED THRUSH *Turdus fischeri.* Fairly common, localised resident. Differs from the previous species in bold white wing-spots. Has a clear, flute-like song, the accent always on the first syllable '*tchee*ooo-che-chichoo, *tree*oo-tretrree . . .'. Found only in evergreen forests of the eastern seaboard; a winter visitor to Zululand forests. 23 cm.

3 ORANGE THRUSH *Turdus gurneyi.* Uncommon, localised resident. Told by dark bill, rich orange throat, breast and flanks plus bold *white wing-bars.* Immatures have the underparts mottled darker. Sings mostly at dawn and at last light, a variety of whistled phrases containing clear notes and complicated trills. Frequents mistbelt evergreen forests where it is sparse and secretive. 23 cm.

4 KURRICHANE THRUSH *Turdus libonyana.* Common resident. Differs from the previous and next species in distinct black and white throat-markings (see enlarged head illustration) and white eyebrows (no white wing-bars); immatures as illustrated. Calls a loud 'peet-peeoo' at dusk and has a mellow, complicated song with trills and warbles in short outbursts. Found in a variety of wooded habitats including rural suburbia. 22 cm.

5 OLIVE THRUSH *Turdus olivaceus.* Common resident. Duller than (4), differing in a speckled throat (see head illustration) and lack of white on the belly. Birds with extensive orange underparts and whitish vent (a) most widespread, those with dull orange on the belly only and brownish vents (b) mainly in highveld regions. On the ground or in flight calls a thin 'wheet'; from a tree sings 'trootee trootee trootee, treetrrroo'. Singly or in pairs, in the north mainly in evergreen forests, elsewhere also in riparian woodland, exotic plantations and suburbia, often numerous in parks and gardens. Males display with drooped wings, splayed tail dragging on the ground. 24 cm.

314

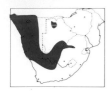

1 SHORT-TOED ROCK THRUSH *Monticola brevipes*. Fairly common resident. In western regions males distinguished by whitish crown, but in western Transvaal and south-eastern Botswana males *lack the pale crown* being of the race *M.b.pretoriae*, then difficult to distinguish from Cape Rock Thrush (4) except for greyer upperparts and whiter wing feather edges. Female told from female of (4) by paler upperparts and throat. Song unrecorded. Singly or in pairs in the more arid regions, frequenting bush-covered rocky hills. Often perches on roadside telephone wires in Namibia. 18 cm.

2 MIOMBO ROCK THRUSH (ANGOLA ROCK THRUSH) *Monticola angolensis*. Common, localised resident. Males distinguished by grey heads with *spotted crowns*, females by white throat plus moustachial-streaks. Immatures like females but throat more speckled, only the chin white. The song is 'pe-pe-per-pee-pew, per-per, pee-pew...' Pairs occur in broadleafed woodland (especially Miombo) and are not associated with rocky habitats. 18 cm.

3 SENTINEL ROCK THRUSH *Monticola explorator*. Common, localised resident. Males differ from other male rock thrushes in the grey of the head extending to the mantle and onto the breast. Has a lively, melodious song beginning 'chu-chu-chu-chee-chree, chee-chroo-chi-chi-chee-troo-tree...', followed by a sequence of warbles, trills and chattering phrases; females make a shorter, harsher version of the initial sequence. Alarm call a rapid, descending 'tre-e-e-e-e-e'. Pairs frequent rocky outcrops in summer, in winter move to lower levels and then favour burnt grasslands. Perches prominently with erect stance. 21 cm.

4 CAPE ROCK THRUSH *Monticola rupestris*. Common resident. Larger than other rock thrushes, both sexes more richly coloured; immatures more spotted than adults. The song is a soft 'checheroo' followed immediately by a loud 'cheewoo-chirri-cheewootiriri' often repeated. Pairs frequent montane slopes and rocky, bush-covered hillsides at all altitudes plus rocky gorges and, in some localities, suburbia. 21 cm.

1 CAPE ROCKJUMPER *Chaetops frenatus.* Common, localised endemic resident. Males more richly rufous than the next species; females with less black about the head and dull rufous underparts. The call is a rapid whistle 'pee-pee-pee-pee-pee . . .'. Pairs and small parties are found on rocky mountain slopes where they hop and run from rock to rock in a lively manner or fly from one outcrop to another, raising their tails after landing. The ranges of this and the next species are mutually exclusive. 25 cm.

2 ORANGEBREASTED ROCKJUMPER *Chaetops aurantius.* Common, localised endemic resident. Both sexes are paler than the previous species but are identical in all other ways. Occurs in the mountains of Lesotho, KwaZulu-Natal and the eastern Cape north of the previous species, mainly above 2 000 m. 21 cm.

3 MOCKING CHAT *Thamnolaea cinnamomeiventris.* Common resident. Sexes differ as illustrated. Differs from Cape Rockjumper (1) in plain upperparts; immatures like females. Has various mellow calls and an attractive song, mostly involving imitations of other bird-calls. Occurs in pairs in various rocky habitats with bushes, often becoming tame near country dwellings. Cheerful, lively birds which habitually raise the rear end of their bodies. 20-3 cm.

4 BOULDER CHAT *Pinarornis plumosus.* Fairly common, localised resident. Sooty-black except for white in the wings and tail; immatures similar. Makes a monotonous squeaking 'ink, ink, wink, wink' like an unoiled wheel, plus a clear whistle with the bill held vertically. Pairs frequent the well-wooded lower slopes of hills with granite boulders, occasionally in similar habitat at higher levels. Is most numerous in the Matopos Hills of southern Zimbabwe. Lively and agile, raising its tail when landing. Sparsely distributed in most regions. 23-7 cm.

1 EUROPEAN WHEATEAR *Oenanthe oenanthe*. Very rare summer visitor. Occurs in non-breeding plumage as shown. Has a characteristic wheatear bowing action with tail raised high, at which time the T-shaped tail-pattern can be seen; cf. immature Capped Wheatear (below) and others on page 448 from which it can only be distinguished with difficulty. The common call is 'chack-chack', similar to that of the Stonechat (page 324). Occurs singly in Kalahari grasslands and similar dry terrain with sparse grass cover. 16 cm.

2 MOUNTAIN CHAT *Oenanthe monticola*. Fairly common resident. Male variable as illustrated, usually as (a) or (b). Males in Namibia may have white underparts from lower breast to vent: see (c) on this page. Immature resembles female. Similar to the next species but occurs in totally different habitat: boulder-strewn slopes or grassland with rocks or anthills, and in farmyards. Sings early and late in the day, mainly September-January, the song a loud jumble of fluty notes. Singly or in small groups which perch conspicuously on rocks or anthills. May fly upwards a short distance, drop down and fly off low to another perch. 17-20 cm.

3 ARNOT'S CHAT *Thamnolaea arnoti*. Fairly common resident. Resembles the previous species but male has *white cap* (not grey), female has white throat. Has a song involving a musical 'feeee' ascending and descending the scale. Pairs or small parties beneath trees, hopping about on the trunks and on the ground. Only in broadleafed woodland with well-developed trees, especially Mopane woodland. 18 cm.

4 CAPPED WHEATEAR *Oenanthe pileata*. Common localised resident. Young birds lack the black breast-band, eyebrow barely discernible (see margin illustration); told from the rare female European wheatear (1) by paler tips to the feathers of the upperparts. Sings from some low prominence or while fluttering straight up into the air, the song variable with imitations of other birds, even mechanical sounds. Walks about with much wing-flicking and tail-jerking. Loose groups on bare ground and short grassland near dams, or airfields, well-grazed farmlands and burnt areas. 18 cm.

PIED WHEATEAR   see page 448.

ISABELLINE WHEATEAR   see page 448.

CHATS

The following four species are very alike in appearance and habits. All frequent open ground, perch conspicuously and flick their wings frequently. All have races showing plumage colour variations, darkest in eastern and palest in western forms with gradations between the extremes. No distinctive calls. Identity best confirmed by colours of tails and upper tail-coverts.

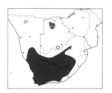

1 SICKLEWINGED CHAT *Cercomela sinuata*. Locally common resident. Most resembles the next species but dumpier, wing-feathers more distinctly edged rufous, legs longer and eye wattle more accentuated. Tail dark with buff outer edges; only upper tail-coverts rufous. Young birds spotted but tail pattern as adults. In open ground with short, sparse vegetation, including fallow croplands and road verges. 15 cm.

2 FAMILIAR CHAT *Cercomela familiaris*. Common resident. Very similar to previous species but of more elongated appearance, wing-feathers edged buffy, less obvious. Southern and eastern races (a) darkest and largest; Namib race (b) palest and smallest. Tail deep rufous with dark central feathers and subterminal band. Young birds told from Sicklewinged (1) only by tail-pattern. Tame, frequenting rocky ground, often in hilly terrain; also walls and outbuildings of farms. 15 cm.

3 TRACTRAC CHAT *Cercomela tractrac*. Common resident. Smaller, plumper than (1), (2) or (4). Dark southern race (a) has upper tail and coverts very pale buff, almost white; pale Namib race (b) has pure white on tail. Occurs in flat, arid grassland, spending much time on the ground where it runs swiftly. 14-15 cm.

4 KAROO CHAT *Cercomela schlegelii*. Common resident. Larger, more robust and elongated than previous three species. Southern and eastern races (a) darkest with grey rump and white on outer tail-feathers; smallest, palest Namib race (b) has white on outer tail-feathers and upper tail-coverts, beige rump. Has a rattling call 'tirr-tit-tat'. Frequents open ground but perches on bushes, fences and telephone wires. 15-18 cm.

322

1 WHINCHAT *Saxicola rubetra*. Very rare summer visitor. Non-breeding male resembles female; this plumage most likely in Southern Africa. Differs from Stonechat (overleaf) by slimmer build, bold white eyebrows, heavily streaked upperparts. Habits much like Stonechat, perching low down in open scrublands. 13-14 cm.

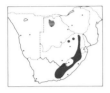

2 BUFFSTREAKED CHAT *Oenanthe bifasciata*. Common resident. Identified by striking plumage patterns and lively, demonstrative behaviour. Has a loud and pleasant song with snatches of mimicry, 'chit, chit, leleoo-chit, cherr-wee-oo, too-weelie, too-weeoo...'. Pairs inhabit rocky or stony hills and montane regions. Tame, flitting from rock to rock with much flirting of tail and wings. 15-17 cm.

3 HERERO CHAT *Namibornis herero*. Uncommon resident. Unlikely to be confused with any other within its restricted range. Silent except when breeding, then a subdued 'ji-ju-jiiu' contact call, a mellow warbling song uttered in jumbled, short phrases and a 'churrr' alarm note. Hunts from a low perch, occasionally flying down to seize insects on the ground. Found on hillsides, at the foot of hills and near dry watercourses in the arid fringes of the Namib Desert. Most plentiful at Groot Spitzkop, near Usakos. 17 cm.

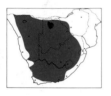

4 ANTEATING CHAT *Myrmecocichla formicivora*. Common resident. Entirely dull brown, the white shoulder patches of males frequently absent. Pale wing-feathers striking in flight. Call a sharp 'peek'. A terrestrial species. Often perches with erect stance on termite mounds, bushes and fences in grassland with short grass. Also makes brief fluttering flights. 18 cm.

5 WHITEBREASTED ALETHE *Alethe fuelleborni*. Status uncertain. Clear white underparts, lack of white eyebrows and robust appearance distinguish this from other robins. Sings a lively 'fweer-her-heee-her-hee-her'. Inhabits the lower stratum of montane forests in the Dondo and Gorongosa regions of Mozambique. A shy, retiring species. 18-20 cm.

324

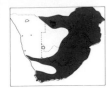

1 STONECHAT *Saxicola torquata.* Common resident. Females identified by white wing-patches; in flight both sexes identified by white rumps; cf. Whinchat, previous page. Immatures are like adults but more speckled. Makes a grating 'tsak, tsak'. Also has a short, shrill, warbling song. Usually in pairs in a wide variety of open habitats; near marshes, vleis, dams, streams, roadsides and in grassland, perching on some low bush or fence from where they watch the ground for insects. Is seasonal in some regions, moving to lower or higher altitudes. 14 cm.

(EURASIAN) REDSTART see page 448.

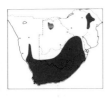

2 CAPE ROBIN *Cossypha caffra.* Common resident. Distinguished by white eyebrows, orange upper breast and greyish underparts; in flight showing orange tail-feathers and back. Immatures have pale orange breast spotted with black. Has a pleasant and continuing song, each passage starting on the same note and with the phrase 'Jan-Frederik' often repeated. Occurs on the edges of forests at all levels, in riverine bush, patches of bush and rock on heath-covered hillsides especially at the base of cliffs and, in many regions, is a common garden species. A winter visitor to the eastern coastal districts. Jerks its tail up when alert. 18 cm.

3 WHITETHROATED ROBIN *Cossypha humeralis.* Common resident. Distinguished by white breast and wing-bar. Immatures are well spotted like all young robins. In the early morning calls repeatedly 'swee-swer, swee-swer, . . .'; cf. Natal Robin (page 328). Alarm note a quiet 'tseep . . . tseep . . . tseep . . .'. Also has a beautiful subdued song. Singly or in pairs in thickets in dry mixed bushveld, in riverine forests and at the foot of rocky, bush-covered hills and termitaria. Frequents gardens in some regions. 16-18 cm.

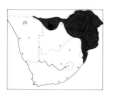

4 HEUGLIN'S ROBIN *Cossypha heuglini.* Common, localised resident. Identified by entirely deep orange underparts and black cap with prominent white eye-stripes. Immatures are similar but spotted. The song consists of various melodious phrases repeated, starting quietly then working up to a crescendo, 'pip-pip-uree, pip-pip-uree . . .' or 'don't-you-do-it, don't-you-do-it . . .' or 'tirrootirree, tirrootirree . . .' each phrase repeated up to about 16 times. Sings mostly at dawn and dusk, often two birds together from within a thicket. Inhabits dense thickets in riverine forests, at the base of densely wooded hills and termitaria. A garden bird in some Zimbabwe towns. 19-20 cm.

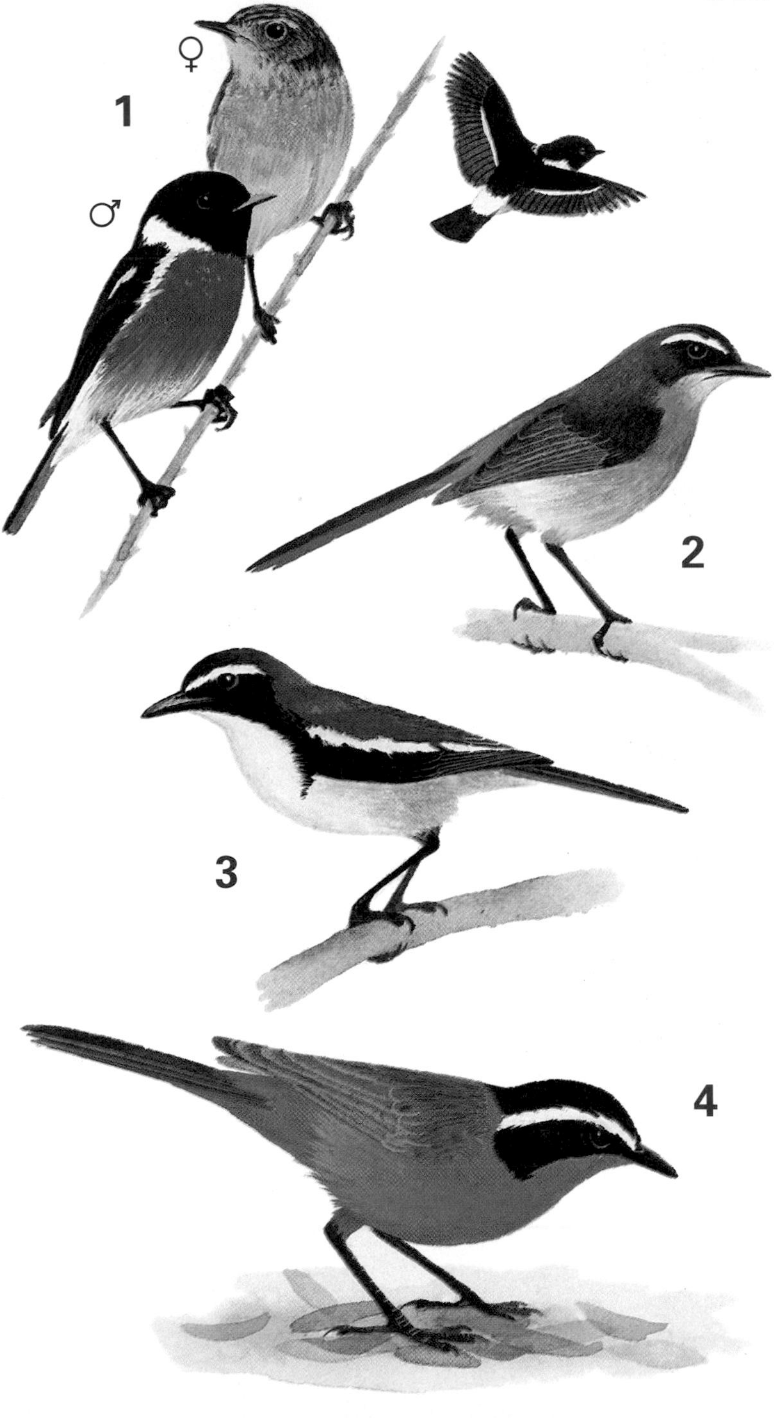
1
♀
♂
2
3
4

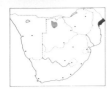

1 GUNNING'S ROBIN *Sheppardia gunningi*. Rare resident. Differs from other robins in entirely brown upperparts extending to below eye-level plus grey eyebrows with a small, barely visible white patch in front of the eyes. The song is loud, rapid and arresting, 'tirripeepoo-tirripeepoo-tirripeepoo, tirritee-tirritee-tirritee...' A small robin of Mozambique lowland forests in the Beira region and northwards. Keeps mostly to the lower stratum, feeding on the ground. Shy and little known. 14 cm.

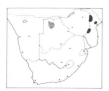

2 SWYNNERTON'S ROBIN *Swynnertonia swynnertoni*. Fairly common resident. Identified by white breast-band with black border. Frequently utters a quiet, sibilant 'si-see-see' and has a stuttering, drawn-out call-note 'trrr-e-e-e-e-e-e-e'. A small, tame robin of montane forests. Frequents the lower stratum, hopping about in lively manner with much wing- and tail-flicking. 14 cm.

3 STARRED ROBIN *Pogonocichla stellata*. Common resident. Told by entirely grey head, greenish upperparts and orange-yellow underparts; white 'stars' before eyes and on central breast evident only when the bird is excited or alarmed. Immatures fledge with typical spotted appearance of young robins; later attain lemon-yellow underparts as illustrated. The call in coastal areas is a piping 'too-twee' frequently repeated, in montane areas a repeated 'pee, du-du *wheee* . . .', the accent on the last syllable which has a whip-like quality; also has a subdued, piping song. Occurs in the lower stratum of coastal and montane evergreen forests. A quiet, lively species but not secretive. 15-17 cm.

4 CHORISTER ROBIN *Cossypha dichroa*. Common resident. A fairly large robin with blackish hood and clear orange underparts; immatures well-spotted as illustrated. Call-note a monotonous 'toy, toy, toy . . .' repeated for long periods; the song a variety of beautiful, mellow phrases incorporating imitations of other bird calls. Very vocal October-January. An evergreen forest species, inhabiting the mid-stratum. Often absent from montane forests April-September, but present in coastal forests at this time. 20 cm.

328

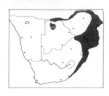

1 NATAL ROBIN *Cossypha natalensis*. Common resident. Entirely orange from *above the eyes* and sides of head to undertail, no white eyebrow. Immatures with pale spotting on the upperparts, dark spotting below. Has a monotonous double call-note 'trrree-trrirr, trrree-trrirr, trrree-trrirr...' continued for long periods; cf. Whitethroated Robin (page 324). The song is composed of various melodious phrases (remarkably similar to human whistling) and imitations of other bird-calls, often imitating the Chorister Robin (previous page). Singly or in pairs in thickets within coastal bush, forests, riverine forests and valley bush. Raises its tail frequently. Keeps mostly within dense cover in the lower and mid-strata but feeds in the open late in the day. 18-20 cm.

2 WHITEBROWED SCRUB ROBIN *Erythropygia leucophrys*. Common resident. A small brownish robin with white eyebrows and wing-markings plus a well-streaked breast; when flying the fanned tail shows white tips; see illustration. Immatures have mottled upperparts. Sings for long periods on warm days; various loud phrases repeated almost without pause 'pirit-pirit tertwee pirit-pirit tertwee-chee chee chu-it chu-it . . .'. Occurs in mixed bushveld, thornveld and woodland, especially within thickets formed by low bushes and long grass. Sings from an exposed bush-top perch, but is otherwise secretive in the lower stratum. 15 cm.

3 BEARDED ROBIN *Erythropygia quadrivirgata*. Fairly common resident. Identified by white eyebrows with a black line above and below, plus white throat with black moustachial-streaks and dull, pale orange breast. Immatures are more mottled. The song is loud and clear, a series of pleasant phrases each repeated three or four times with short pauses 'pee-pee-pee, terr-treee, chiroo-chiroo-chiroo, witcho̅o-witchoo-witchoo, pee-pee-pee-pee, chu-it, chu-it, chu-it...', some phrases rising in crescendo; also imitates. Usually singly in broadleafed and riverine woodland. Largely terrestrial unless singing. 16-18 cm.

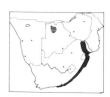

4 BROWN ROBIN *Erythropygia signata*. Uncommon endemic resident. A brown robin with white eyebrows and wing-markings plus whitish underparts. Immatures are spotted and scaled, otherwise similar. The song, rendered at dawn and last light, is a high-pitched series of melancholy phrases beginning always on a single or double high note 'treetroo-tretretre . . .'; the call is a sibilant 'zit-zeeeet'. Inhabits the interiors of evergreen forests and dense riparian bush within the lower and mid-strata. Difficult to see within its habitat. 18 cm.

1 KAROO ROBIN *Erythropygia coryphoeus*. Common resident. White eyebrows and throat with dark moustachial-stripes and white tail-tips identify this otherwise sombrely coloured robin. Immatures have buff-barred upperparts and dark mottled underparts. Has a song composed of short, choppy phrases 'pheeoo, tirrit-tirrit, chuck, chuck, sweeoo, chuck . . .'. Frequents Karoo veld, feeding on the ground and in the lower stratum of bushes. Conspicuous and noisy. 17 cm.

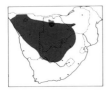

2 KALAHARI ROBIN *Erythropygia paena*. Common resident. Much paler, sandier-looking than the previous species with conspicuous rufous tail with black subterminal band and white tips; see illustration. Immatures with lightly spotted underparts. Often perches on a bush calling 'twee' intermittently for long periods. The song is a high-pitched sequence of repeated phrases, 'seeoo-seeoo' tweetoo-tweetoo-tweetoo, seetoo-seetoo, tritritri-tritri . . .'. Singly or in pairs in thornveld and in old cultivations, particularly in the arid western regions. Feeds on open ground and sings from a treetop, but enters thorn thickets when alarmed. 16-17 cm.

3 RUFOUSTAILED PALM THRUSH *Cichladusa ruficauda*. Uncommon, localised resident. Identified by rufous upperparts, plain buff underparts (rufous tail also shared by next species but ranges are mutually exclusive). Has a rich, melodious song heard mostly at dawn and dusk, pairs often singing in duet. Occurs in association with *Borassus* palms and oil palms on the Cunene River and northwards. Little known in the southern African region. 17 cm.

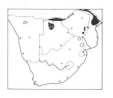

4 COLLARED PALM THRUSH *Cichladusa arquata*. Common, localised resident. Differs from the previous species mainly in black-bordered throat-patch (often broken or incomplete), grey nape, duller mantle and straw-coloured eyes, but has similar rufous tail to that species. Immatures are mottled below, black throat-border vestigial. Has a melodious, liquid song heard mostly mornings and evenings. Pairs and small parties in riverine forests with *Borassus* and *Hyphaene* palms, being especially numerous in the Victoria Falls region of the Zambezi River and the Gorongosa region of Mozambique. Lively and conspicuous, spends much time foraging on the ground. When perched on a branch droops its wings and raises and lowers its tail continuously. 19 cm.

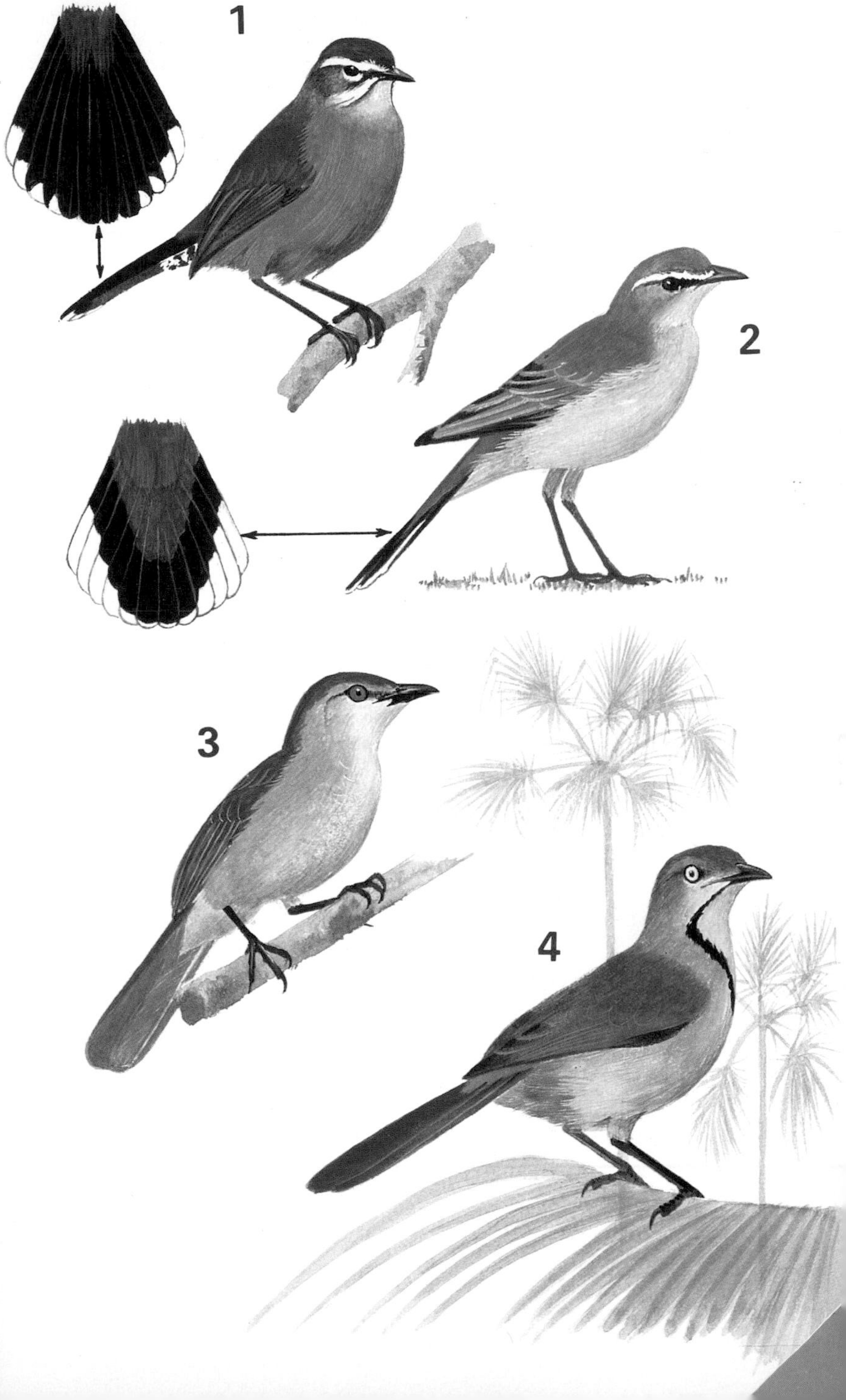
1
2
3
4

Warblers. Family SYLVIIDAE. Small, insectivorous birds of mostly sombre colouring. Many have attractive warbling songs which aid identification, several species visiting southern Africa from Europe during summer. Sexes are alike.

1 WILLOW WARBLER *Phylloscopus trochilus.* Common summer visitor. Also occurs in a much paler form than illustrated and in an entirely brown form with white underparts, but identified always by *distinct eyebrows and scalloped tail-tip;* cf. Garden Warbler (3). While feeding calls a querulous, quiet 'foo-wee'; sings, usually in the mornings, a descending jumble of notes 'tee-tee-tee-tee-tu-tu-tu-twee-twee-sweet-sweet-sweet-sweet . . .'. Occurs singly in almost any bush habitat, including suburbia. An active leaf-gleaner, which works its way busily through the canopy and mid-stratum, occasionally darting out to hawk a flying insect. 12 cm.

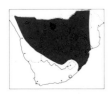

2 ICTERINE WARBLER *Hippolais icterina.* Fairly common summer visitor. Larger than the previous species, usually more yellow with clearly yellow-edged wing-coverts, sharply sloping forehead, orange lower mandible and *non-scalloped* tail-tip. Sings a repetitive, vehement jumble of warbled notes, some pleasant, others harsh. Singly, prefers *Acacia* thornveld and hops about actively while feeding in the tree canopies, often singing. Sparsely distributed. 14-15 cm.

3 GARDEN WARBLER *Sylvia borin.* Fairly common summer visitor. A plain-coloured warbler without distinctive markings. Usually located by song, a quiet warbling of rather monotonous quality uttered from the depth of a bush. Always singly in dense bush or thickets, especially along watercourses and in parks and gardens. In some regions is not present until February-March. 15 cm.

(EUROPEAN) BLACKCAP see page 448.

4 THRUSH NIGHTINGALE *Luscinia luscinia.* Rare to locally common summer visitor. Tail- and wing-feather margins rich rufous, underparts whitish with *mottled breast.* The song is a rich melody of variable notes, some sweet, some harsh. Occurs singly in dense thickets, often in riverine bush, but secretive. Returns to the same thicket each year. 16-18 cm.

5 OLIVETREE WARBLER *Hippolais olivetorum.* Uncommon, localised summer visitor. A large warbler with white eyebrows, sharply sloping forehead, large two-coloured bill and pale outer edges to wing-feathers and tail-tip. Song louder and deeper than most warblers, a grating jumble of notes with sharp 'tch-tch' sounds interspersed; similar to the song of the Great Reed Warbler (page 338). Singly in riverine bush and *Acacia* thornveld, feeding and singing from within the foliage of the mid- and upper strata. 16-18 cm.

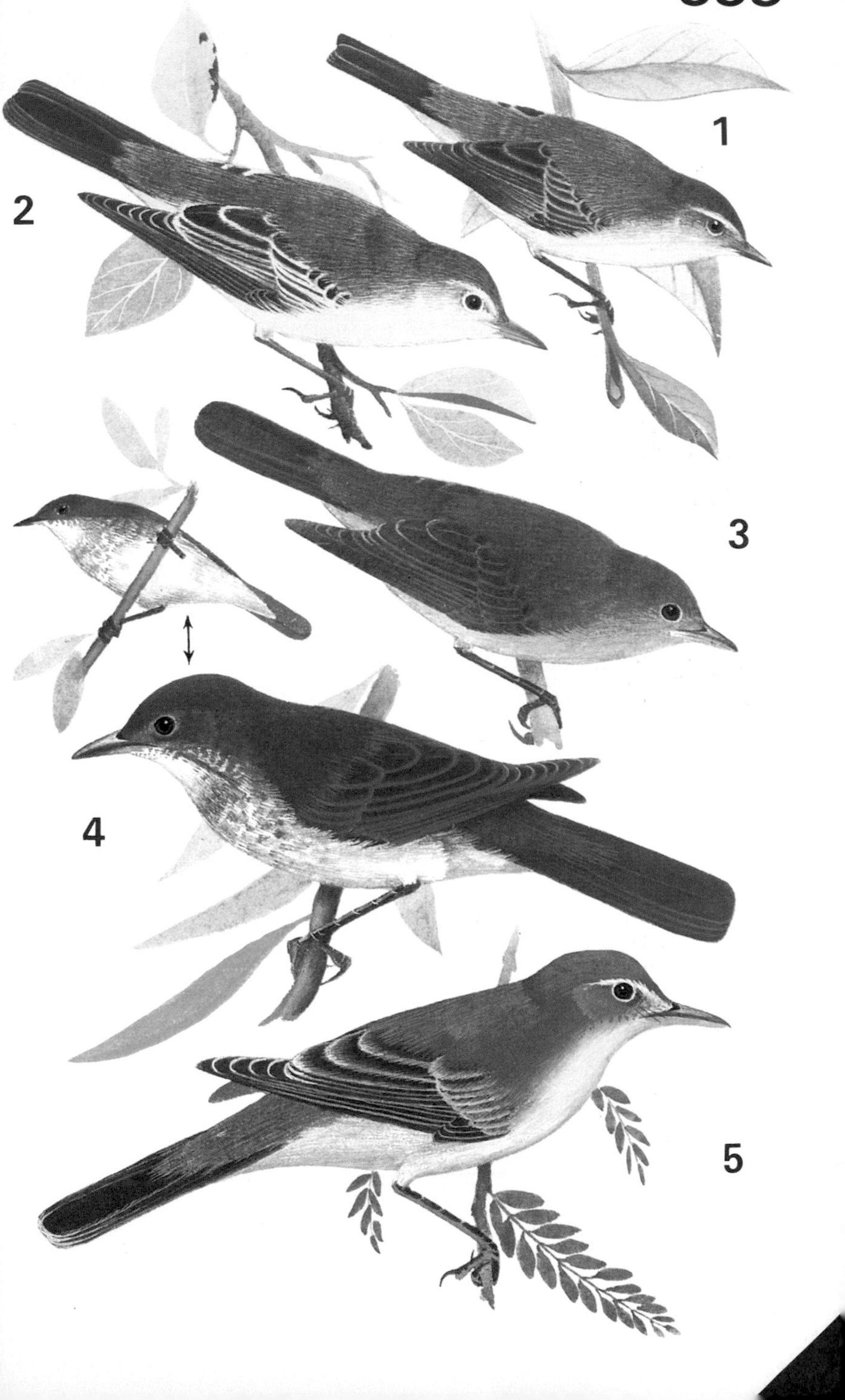
1
2
3
4
5

334

1 WHITETHROAT *Sylvia communis*. Uncommon summer visitor. Identified by white throat contrasting with pale buff breast, whitish eye-ring, *prominent rufous wing-feather edges* and white outer tail-feathers. The crown feathers are frequently raised which give a peaked appearance to the head. Has a sharp 'tacc-tacc' call, a conversational 'wheet, wheet, whit-whit-whit-whit' and a brisk, scratchy warble. A restless, lively species found in scrub thickets and in thornveld. 15 cm.

2 RIVER WARBLER *Locustella fluviatilis*. Rare mid-summer visitor. Similar to the next two species but broader breast-markings form distinct streaks radiating from the throat; *large undertail-coverts* pale-tipped, legs paler than either (3) or (4). Makes an intermittent, cricket-like 'zer - zer - zer - zer...'. Highly secretive in dense thickets, reed-beds and other herbage near streams, creeping about near to or on the ground. When alarmed drops to the ground and *runs away*. 13 cm.

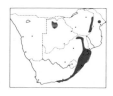

3 BARRATT'S WARBLER *Bradypterus barratti*. Fairly common resident. Very similar to the previous species except for narrower, more profuse breast-markings (extending onto flanks in southern races), large *rounded tail* and darker legs. Normal call a soft 'tuc' or 'trrr' as it creeps about or, in early summer, 'chree, chree, chooreereereereereeree.' Frequents patches of dense bush, tangled scrub and bracken in montane forest fringes. Highly secretive. 15-16 cm.

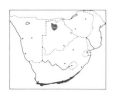

4 KNYSNA WARBLER *Bradypterus sylvaticus*. Fairly common, localised resident. Differs from the previous species in duskier underparts and lack of clear breast-markings. The normal call is a loud 'peeeit' or 'peeet' (cf. the 'Willie' call of the Sombre Bulbul, page 304), which is usually answered by another bird; this becomes 'peet-peet-peet...' when agitated. Also has a high-pitched, staccato song uttered with increasing speed and ending with a winding-down trill, 'tsip-tsip-tsip-tsip-tsiptsiptsiptsip-trrrrrrrrrrrrrrr'. Remains concealed in the dense foliage of forest fringes and wooded kloofs but lively and active, feeding in both the mid- and lower strata. 14-15 cm.

5 VICTORIN'S WARBLER *Bradypterus victorini*. Common localised resident. Best identified by *orange-yellow eyes*. In the brief song the notes go up and down with increasing rapidity 'mississippippippippippi'. Occurs in dense montane scrub on rain-exposed slopes, in rocky kloofs and alongside mountain streams. Emerges from cover to sing from a low bush. 16 cm.

6 BROADTAILED WARBLER *Schoenicola brevirostris*. Common resident. Recognised by the *voluminous black tail* with buff-tipped feathers. Males have a weak metallic 'trreep, trreep, trreep' call, females a harsh 'chick' and 'zink, zink, zink' repeated rapidly and regularly. Frequents tall grass, reeds and tangled vegetation near streams and vleis, mostly within the vegetation, but sometimes perching conspicuously in a *vertical position*. If flushed makes off with conspicuous bobbing flight, then drops down and runs off; seldom flushes a second time. 17 cm.

REED WARBLERS

1 EUROPEAN SEDGE WARBLER *Acrocephalus schoenobaenus*. Uncommon summer visitor. Recognised by boldy marked upperparts, especially eye-stripes, streaked crown and faintly blotched breast. Feeding call a quiet 'tick, tick, . . .', alarm call a harsh, rasping 'churrr'. Has a loud, hurried song with little repetition, chattering and sweet passages mixed with imitations of other birds. Singly in dense riverside vegetation, marsh fringes and thickets *away from water*. Creeps about at low level. 13 cm.

2 AFRICAN MARSH WARBLER *Acrocephalus baeticatus*. Common summer resident, occasionally winter. No distinctive eyebrow. Underparts predominantly white, legs purple-brown. Makes a sharp 'tik' while creeping about in thick cover, plus a harsh, racket-like 'churrr' when alarmed. Song is a slow, monotonous warbling 'chuck-chuck-weee-chirruc-churr-werr-weee-weee-chirruc . . .' for long periods when breeding; cf. European Marsh Warbler (6). In reeds or other dense herbage near swamps or away from water in tall grass, bushes and in suburbia. Remains well hidden but moves about constantly. 13 cm.

3 CAPE REED WARBLER *Acrocephalus gracilirostris*. Common resident. Has a distinct white eyebrow and dark brown legs. The rich, melodious song is 'chiroo-chrooo, tirirririririri', slowly at first, then fast. Always found *near fresh water* in reeds, bulrushes or other waterside herbage. Bold and inquisitive. 15 - 17 cm.

4 AFRICAN SEDGE WARBLER *Bradypterus baboecala*. Common resident. Upperparts dark, *tail broad and rounded,* definite eye-stripe plus faint markings on the upper breast. Call is a loud, distinctive 'cruk, cruk, cruk, crukcrukcrukcrukcrukcruk-cruyk' like a stick drawn across a railing, followed by wing-snapping. Singly or in pairs in dense vegetation *over water.* Secretive, mostly in the lower stratum. 17 cm.

5 CINNAMON REED WARBLER *Acrocephalus cinnamomeus*. Rare vagrant. A single specimen from Umvoti, Natal. Possibly regular in the Zambezi Valley. Similar to (6) and (7) but smaller, upperparts washed cinnamon. May be a race of the African Marsh Warbler (2). 10,5 cm.

6 EUROPEAN MARSH WARBLER *Acrocephalus palustris*. Common and widespread summer visitor. Eyebrows indistinct, underparts (except throat) lightly washed yellow-buff, upperparts including rump uniformly olivaceous-brown; cf. next species from which it cannot be distinguished in the field except by habitat. Makes a frequent 'tuc' while creeping about in cover, and has a pleasant, but varied, warbling song which includes mimicry. Is found *away from water* in dense bracken-briar patches, riparian thickets, parks and gardens from where it sings almost continuously December-March. Highly secretive. 12 cm.

7 EUROPEAN REED WARBLER *Acrocephalus scirpaceus*. Rare summer visitor. Very few records for the subregion. In the field indistinguishable from the previous species except by habitat. Found in waterside vegetation. 13 cm.

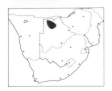

1 GREATER SWAMP WARBLER *Acrocephalus rufescens*
Fairly common, highly localised resident. A large, dark warbler
with prominent slender bill and dark legs; no eyebrow. Has a rich,
short song with guttural notes 'cheruckle, truptruptruptruptrup
weeweeweewee'. Heard more often than seen. Secretive in
permanent papyrus and reed-beds of the Okavango Delta in
northern Botswana. 18 cm.

2 BASRA REED WARBLER *Acrocephalus griseldis.* Rare
summer visitor. Sometimes regarded as a race of the next species
but is smaller, the legs grey-brown. Little known, the voice not
recorded in the subregion. A few records for eastern coastal
regions. 15 cm.

3 GREAT REED WARBLER *Acrocephalus arundinaceus*
Fairly common summer visitor. Best told by very large size (for a
warbler) and characteristic song: a slow, harsh warble 'gurk-gurk,
twee-twee, gurk-gurk, trrit-trrit, gackle, kurra-kurra . . .'. Occurs
singly in reed-beds, thickets or dense bush in suburbia. Less
secretive, more inquisitive than most reed warblers, occasionally
perching conspicuously, its movements heavy. 19 cm.

4 YELLOW WARBLER *Chloropeta natalensis.* Fairly common
resident. Differs from the yellow weavers in more slender bill.
Females are duller yellow. Immatures are orange-yellow, the
wing-edges, rump and tail more buff. The song is 'trrp-trrp
chirichirichirichiri', rendered quickly and frequently repeated.
Occurs singly or in pairs near water in reeds or other tall, rank
cover, or away from water in bracken-briar patches of highveld
valleys and forest fringes. Its habits are typical of the reed-warbler
group: secretive but ascends some vertical stem occasionally to
perch conspicuously. 14-15 cm.

339

340

1 BARTHROATED APALIS *Apalis thoracica*. Common resident. Highly variable; basic forms illustrated, all males. Most yellow form (a) northern Transvaal; brown-capped form (b) Zimbabwe; with grey upperparts'(c) south-western Cape. More subtle variations also occur. In females black throat-band usually narrower, sometimes entirely lacking. Told from next species by *pale yellow* eye, *white* outer tail-feathers, plus darker upperparts. Has a loud, distinctive call, 'pilly-pilly-pilly...'; pairs also sing in duet, the female's call being much faster than the male's. In pairs, frequently in bird parties, in heavily wooded kloofs, streams, hillsides and forests. 12-13 cm.

2 RUDD'S APALIS *Apalis ruddi*. Common resident. Differs from previous species in *dark* eye, *yellowish* undertail with white spots at the tips of the outer feathers, more yellow-green upperparts and buff wash to underparts, especially throat. The call is a fast, loud 'tritritritritritritritrit...' by one bird, the other calling at the same time (but out of phase) 'punk-punk-punk...'. Usually seen in pairs in coastal bush and dune forest, especially in dense thickets overgrown with creepers, though not secretive. 10.5-12 cm.

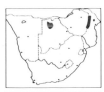

3 CHIRINDA APALIS *Apalis chirindensis*. Uncommon localised resident. More uniformly grey than the next species. The call is a rapid series of notes. Occurs in highland forests and dense woodland where it frequents open, sunny patches rather than the gloomy interior. Often joins mixed bird parties. 13.5 cm.

4 BLACKHEADED APALIS *Apalis melanocephala*. Common localised resident. Distinguished from the previous species by contrasting dark upperparts and whitish underparts. The call is a fast trilling 'pee-pee-pee-pee...' repeated 20-30 times, often answered by another. Occurs in lowland forest, dense woodland, thick riverine bush and coastal scrub, often in the tree canopies. 14 cm.

5 YELLOWBREASTED APALIS *Apalis flavida*. Common resident. Amount of grey on head varies; most extensive (a) northern Namibia, northern Botswana, least extensive (b) Mozambique, elsewhere variable between these extremes. Tail length also varies. In all races black central breast bar may be absent or vestigial. The normal call is 'skee-skee-skee-chiz*zick*-chiz*zick*', to which the mate replies 'krik-krik-krik'. Usually in pairs in a variety of bushveld habitats, riverine bush and forest fringes. 10-12.5 cm.

1 LONGBILLED CROMBEC *Sylvietta rufescens*. Common resident. Tailless appearance makes confusion possible only with the next two species. Most similar to (3) but has distinct eyebrow, dusky eye-stripe, paler colouring about face and ear-coverts and more prominent bill. Age differences negligible. The call is a loud, urgent-sounding 'tree-cheer, tree-cheer, tree-cheer...'. Usually in pairs in bushveld and woodland, often in bird parties. Feeds on branches and tree-trunks. 10-12 cm.

2 REDFACED CROMBEC *Sylvietta whytii*. Fairly common resident. Differs from the previous species in lacking any distinct eye-stripe, has more rufous face and ear-coverts and shorter bill. The call is a twittering 'si-si-si-see'; alarm call a sharp 'tip', uttered so frequently as to become a rattling trill. Occurs in broadleafed woodland feeding mainly among the small branches and outer twigs of trees. 10-11 cm.

3 REDCAPPED CROMBEC *Sylvietta ruficapilla*. Rare, exact status uncertain. Identified by chestnut ear-coverts and upper breast (crown may lack chestnut entirely); upperparts and underparts washed pale lemon. Young undescribed. The call is a loud 'richi-chichi-chichir' repeated about six times. Behaviour similar to that of other crombecs but feeds in the tree canopies. One record west of Victoria Falls. 11 cm.

4 LAYARD'S TITBABBLER *Parisoma layardi*. Uncommon resident. Told from the next species by *white undertail-coverts*; otherwise distinguished by pale yellow eye and spotted throat. Immatures have upperparts brownish, throat less clearly spotted. Has several clear song phrases, each interspersed with rattling notes, 'chiroo-chirroo-chirroo, trrrrr, chirree-chirree-chirree-trrrrr...'. Creeps about actively within dense cover, then darts to the next bush in quick, jerky flight. Occurs in Macchia, desert and mountain scrub. 15 cm.

5 TITBABBLER *Parisoma subcaeruleum*. Common resident. Told from the previous species by *chestnut* vent. Immatures resemble adults. Calls frequently, a variety of clear, ringing quickly rendered notes, typically 'cheriktiktik' or 'chuu-ti chuu-ti chuu-chuu'. Occurs in thickets in any woodland, mixed bushveld or thornveld, habits very similar to those of the previous species. 15 cm.

1 CAPE PENDULINE TIT *Anthoscopus minutus*. Common resident. Distinguished by very small size, black forehead and yellow underparts; young similar. Some western birds are greyer above than illustrated. Makes a sibilant 'swee-swee-swee-swee, tree-tree-tree'. Usually in groups of two to eight, in *Acacia* woodland. Feed in the outer canopies of trees, flittering one after the other from tree to tree, constantly on the move. Most common in the drier regions. 9-10 cm.

2 GREY PENDULINE TIT *Anthoscopus caroli*. Common resident. Underparts more buff than previous species, throat and breast pale grey; immatures similar. Western and some northern races are olive-green or yellow-green above, more yellowish on belly. The call is 'chikchikZEE, chikchikZEE, chikchikZEE . . .'. Occurs in small groups in broadleafed woodland where it feeds mainly in the tree-tops. 8-9 cm.

3 BURNTNECKED EREMOMELA *Eremomela usticollis*. Common resident. Distinguished by brown throat-bar when this is present, otherwise best distinguished from other small warblers by pale yellow-buff underparts and pale eye with brown surround. The call is a rapid, high-pitched 'teeup-ti-ti-ti-ti-ti-ti-ti . . .', followed by a short trill. In groups of two to five in *Acacia* woodland, feeding in the tree canopies. 12 cm.

4 YELLOWBELLIED EREMOMELA *Eremomela icteropygialis*. Common resident. Differs from White-eyes (page 402) in narrower white eye-ring and grey (not green) upperparts. Western birds generally paler, central Cape and Orange Free State birds with a fulvous wash to the breast. Has a lively song 'chirri-chee-chee-choo' or 'How are you two'. Occurs in pairs in mixed bushveld or, in arid regions, scrub, feeding in the outer and lower branches of bushes. 9-10 cm.

5 GREENCAPPED EREMOMELA *Eremomela scotops*. Uncommon resident. Identified by greyish lores and yellow eye surrounded by a red ring. North-western birds are whiter on lower abdomen and vent. Has various calls, a twittering 'nyum-nyum-nyum-' or a repeated, monotonous 'tip-tip-tip . . .', plus a liquid song. Found in the leafy canopies of woodland and riverine forest, often in small groups which chase about restlessly in the upper branches while feeding. In bird parties in winter. 12 cm.

6 YELLOWTHROATED WARBLER *Phylloscopus ruficapillus*. Common resident. Differs from other yellow warblers in brown cap and habitat preference. In southern birds yellow extends onto flanks and belly; in northern birds yellow confined mainly to throat. Immatures have a greenish wash to the breast. Has a plaintive 'tieuu' call repeated for long periods, a high-pitched 'zit-zit', a metallic 'tsit-sop-sop', and a duet 'tsee' replied to by 'tsik'. Also a song comprised mainly of a repeated 'chirreee-chirreee-chirreee . . .'; cf. Collared Sunbird (page 394). A bird of forests and forested kloofs. 11 cm.

346

1 BARRED WARBLER *Calamonastes fasciolata.* Common resident. Less white, less clearly barred on the underparts than (2), duller about the breast in non-breeding plumage. Normal call a mournful 'brreeet-brreeet-brreeet-brreeet . . .' uttered in bursts of three to five for long periods. Occurs in thornveld and broadleafed woodland, usually in pairs. Secretive, creeps about in thickets, gradually working its way to the top before flitting to the next thicket. Its tail is held raised when alarmed. 13 - 15 cm.

2 STIERLING'S BARRED WARBLER *Calamonastes stierlingi.* Common resident. Whiter, more boldly barred below than (1), tail shorter, bill blacker. Has a far-carrying, much-repeated call 'birribit-birribit- birribit-birribit'. Found in mixed bushveld and broadleafed woodland within thickets, but may ascend to the tree canopy if disturbed. Very secretive, often creeping about with tail raised. 11,5 - 13 cm.

3 CINNAMONBREASTED WARBLER *Euryptila subcinnamomea.* Fairly common, localised resident. Blackish tail, cinnamon forehead, breast and tail-coverts diagnostic. The call is a plaintive whistle 'eeeeeeee . . .', lasting about one and a half seconds. Found on rock and bush-strewn hills in the more arid regions. Hops about rocks with great agility, tail usually raised, and calls from the summit of the hill or cliff. 13 -14 cm.

BLEATING WARBLERS The two forms are treated by some as full species, by others as races of the same species. The Greenbacked occurs in moist, lowland habitats and has no distinct non-breeding plumage; the Greybacked frequents drier regions and has distinctly different breeding and non-breeding plumages. Sexes are alike.

4 GREENBACKED BLEATING WARBLER *Camaroptera brachyura.* Common resident. Upperparts entirely dark olive-green (has grey crown in central and southern Mozambique); closely similar to (5) but ranges are mutually exclusive. Makes a kid-like bleating 'bzeeeb' and, in the breeding season, a loud territorial call 'chirrup, chirrup, chirrup . . .' continued for long periods. Singly or in pairs in evergreen forest fringes, moist, well-wooded lowland valleys, riverine and coastal bush. Mostly secretive in the lower stratum except when males ascend to a higher level to call. 12 cm.

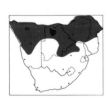

5 GREYBACKED BLEATING WARBLER *Camaroptera brevicaudata.* Common resident. Breeding and non-breeding plumages illustrated; in non-breeding plumage some races have white to deep cream-buff upper breasts, not grey. Differs from (4) in grey (not green) upperparts, except immature which *does* have green upperparts. Voice as previous species. Singly or in pairs in dry thickets in thornveld, woodland and especially bush-covered termitaria. 12 cm.

6 KAROO EREMOMELA *Eremomela gregalis.* Uncommon, localised resident. Distribution does not overlap with (5); differs in having pale yellow eyes, smaller bill and pale yellow undertail-coverts. Calls a wailing 'quee, quee-quee' and an ascending 'fwoee'. Feeding groups call continuously a quiet 'ti-ti-ti-ti . . .'. Small groups in Karoo scrub. 12 cm.

348

1 MOUSTACHED WARBLER *Melocichla mentalis*. Uncommon, localised resident. Identified from the next species by plain upperparts and underparts, rounded tail and rufous forehead, *not* crown. The song is 'tip-tiptwiddle-iddle-see', the first two sounds slow, the rest fast. Occurs in short rank grass, bracken and scattered bushes in marshy ground near streams. Very similar in behaviour to the next species, it remains mostly concealed within vegetation. 19 cm.

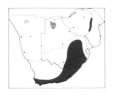

2 GRASSBIRD *Sphenoeacus afer*. Common resident. Differs from the previous species in heavily marked upperparts, streaked underparts (except race (b) of eastern Transvaal and Natal) and generally rusty colouring; from cisticolas by larger size, moustachial-streaks and tapering tail-feathers. Has a distinctive burst of song 'chirp-chirp-chirp-does it tickle yoooou', plus a cat-like mewing. Frequents the long grass and bracken of hillsides and unbushed streams away from hills. Occasionally perches prominently on some tall grass or weed-head, otherwise skulks within the vegetation. 19-23 cm.

3 ROCKRUNNER (DAMARA ROCKJUMPER) *Achaetops pycnopygius*. Common, localised resident. Differs from any other grass warbler within its limited range in heavy streaking of head and mantle, bold facial markings and habit of keeping its tail raised high. The song is a warbling 'tip-tip-tootle-titootle-tootle-too' heard early mornings and evenings. A shy but lively bird of grassy rock- and bush-strewn hillsides and dry watercourses in arid country. 17 cm.

Cisticolas. Small, closely similar, brown grass warblers. Breeding and non-breeding plumages often differ markedly as do tail-lengths and, frequently, the sexes. Best identified by song, habitat preference and behaviour. Territorial behaviour common to the very small 'cloud' cisticolas (this page and overleaf) is an aerial cruise by the males. They rise high into the air with rapidly whirring wings, often out of sight, and then cruise about singing, while some species make audible wing-snaps. The descent is a near-vertical plunge, but they check just above the grass and fly level briefly before dropping down. In some species the descent is accompanied by wing-snaps.

4 PALECROWNED CISTICOLA *Cisticola brunnescens*. Uncommon, localised resident. Males in summer identified by pale crown, both sexes otherwise indistinguishable from Cloud and Ayres' Cisticolas overleaf. Young have brightly sulphured underparts. The flight-song is a quiet, continually repeated 'siep-siep-siep...', sometimes varied every few seconds by scarcely audible notes '...twee-twee-twee-ti-ti-ti-ti-ti-ti-ti-tsee-tsee...'; this may be repeated rapidly during the descent which is *without* wing-snaps. Occurs in grassland in damp localities. 9-11 cm.

349

CISTICOLAS

The cisticolas on this plate are all so similar that accurate field identification based on plumage alone is almost impossible, but the main breeding and non-breeding differences are illustrated. They all indulge in aerial cruises combined with characteristic calls and behaviour during summer and this must be considered the most reliable guide.

1 FANTAILED CISTICOLA *Cisticola juncidis*. Common resident. Females resemble non-breeding males. Conspicuous only in summer when males cruise at a height of *c.* 50 m with dipping flight, calling 'zit zit zit zit . . .' at each dip at about half-second intervals. The call may also be made while perched on a grass stem. Does *not* snap its wings. Found in grassland, often near marshes or vleis, also fallow lands and waste ground. 10-12 cm.

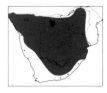

2 DESERT CISTICOLA *Cisticola aridulus*. Common resident. Sexes closely similar. In summer males make a repetitive, high-pitched 'zink zink zink zink . . .' while cruising *low* over grassland, climbing and dropping with *wing-snaps* and irregular dashes; also calls 'tuc tuc tuc tuc weee'. Occurs in more arid grassland than the previous species, especially old burnt areas and fallow lands; never in moist regions. 10-12 cm.

3 CLOUD CISTICOLA *Cisticola textrix*. Common resident. Females resemble males. In the southern Cape either sex may have clear or heavily spotted underparts. In summer males rise high into the air, usually being invisible to the naked eye, and cruise about, uttering a wispy 'see-see-seesee-chick-chick-chick' repeated at two- or three-second intervals. When descending makes an almost vertical plunge, calling a rapid 'chick-chick-chick-chick...'. Does *not* snap its wings when descending. Occurs in grassland at most levels but not montane grassland. 10 cm.

4 AYRES' CISTICOLA *Cisticola ayresii*. Common resident. In summer males cruise high in the sky, usually out of sight, calling a wispy, high-pitched 'soo-see-see-see . . .' at about three-second intervals while flying into wind. This is followed by ten or more volleys of wing-snaps while flying downwind before plummeting to earth while calling a rapid 'ticka-ticka-ticka . . .' with violent wing-snapping and terminal swooping and swerving. Occurs in short, dry grassland and near vleis; does not perch conspicuously. 9-11 cm.

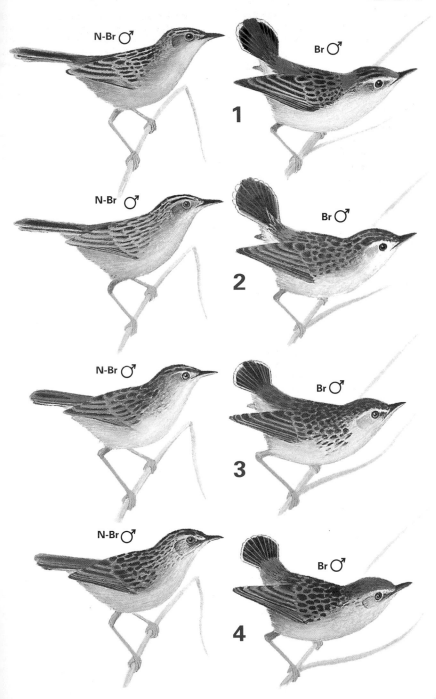

N-Br ♂   Br ♂   **1**

N-Br ♂   Br ♂   **2**

N-Br ♂   Br ♂   **3**

N-Br ♂   Br ♂   **4**

352

1 SHORTWINGED CISTICOLA *Cisticola brachypterus.* Uncommon, localised resident. *Dark brown cap* concolorous with rest of the *unmarked* upperparts; sexes alike. Immatures are more yellow-washed, eyes grey. In the breeding season males sing from the top of a dead tree, a wispy, descending series of notes 'seee see-see-see . . .'. Also has a high aerial display and plunge-dives like a Cloud Cisticola (previous page). Occurs in broad-leafed woodland where it forages below the canopy or in the grass. Occurs mostly in Mozambique, just entering eastern Zimbabwe. 10 - 11 cm.

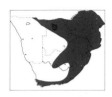

2 NEDDICKY *Cisticola fulvicapillus.* Common resident. Plain-backed like (1) but larger, longer-tailed, the *cap rufous.* Southern and eastern races (a) with blue-grey underparts, elsewhere as (b). Sexes are alike. Immatures are dull. In the rainy season sings for long periods 'chirri-chirri-chirri . . .'. The alarm call is a rapid tinkling by several birds 'ticki-ticki-ticki-ticki-ticki', while flitting from bush to bush. Pairs and family parties, (a) in montane regions, (b) in grassy woodlands and thornveld, frequenting the lower stratum. 10 - 11 cm.

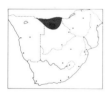

3 CHIRPING CISTICOLA *Cisticola pipiens.* Fairly common, localised resident. Non-breeding plumage illustrated; breeding plumage less rufous about the face, lores and underparts, the tail shorter; cf. Blackbacked Cisticola (overleaf). The song, in late summer, is four twanging notes repeated 'trrrit-trrrit-trree-trreeeeee . . .'. Occurs in the Okavango Delta, inhabiting reeds and papyrus in water, or shoreline bushes and grass. In flight the tail is fanned and flirted from side to side as though loose. 12.5-15 cm.

4 SINGING CISTICOLA *Cisticola cantans.* Uncommon, localised resident. The only plain-backed cisticola with *conspicuous reddish primary feathers,* these and the crown contrasting with grey-brown upperparts when breeding (summer). Brighter in winter, upperparts washed rufous with faint, darker blotches, eyebrow then distinct, tail longer. Immatures are duller, *sulphured on the breast and belly.* The call is a loud 'jhu-jee' or 'wheech-oo'; also 'cheer cheer cheer', reminiscent of a Rattling Cisticola (overleaf). Secretive in rank undergrowth and bracken-briar patches near forest fringes in eastern Zimbabwe. 12 - 14 cm.

5 GREYBACKED CISTICOLA *Cisticola subruficapillus.* Common resident. Southern race (a) has grey back with black streaking extending to forehead, ear-coverts and upper breast; north-western race (b) has upperparts less obviously grey, streaks finer, fainter, sub-loral spot absent. Immatures are rustier, ochreous about the face, eye grey, bill yellower, legs paler. The breeding song is a hurried, high-pitched jumble of descending notes 'weesisee-chizzarizzaree-chichioo . . .'; at other times calls 'prouee, tweep, tweep'. Alarm note a piping 'tee-tee-tee . . .'. A lively species found in coastal Macchia, scrub and grass of estuarine flats, montane foothills, the Karoo and semi-desert western regions. 12 - 13 cm.

353

1 BLACKBACKED CISTICOLA *Cisticola galactotes.* Common resident. Similar to the next species, the back even blacker when breeding, but the ranges of the two species overlap only slightly. Best identified by habitat, behaviour and call. Associated mostly with *large waterways,* marshes and swamps; also cane fields near water in KwaZulu-Natal. Frequents reed-beds, sedges and grasses. Usually secretive; conspicuous only when breeding, at which time males call from an exposed perch a loud, rasping 'zreeee' or 'rraaare' often interspersed with various 'chirps' or 'chit-chit-chit . . .' or 'trrrp-trrrp-trrrp . . .'. When alarmed calls a loud, deliberate 'prrrit-prrrit-prrrit'. 12-13 cm.

2 LEVAILLANT'S CISTICOLA *Cisticola tinniens.* Common resident. Superficially similar to the previous species in having a black back, but confusion is unlikely since there is *very little overlap* in the ranges of the two species. Best told by habitat, behaviour and call. Levaillant's is the common pond and stream-side cisticola frequenting waterside sedges and the edges of reed-beds (which it does not enter). It is not secretive, but perches conspicuously and sings 'chi-chi-chirrrueee', the first two notes almost inaudible, the final phrase loud; it also has a plaintive 'dzwee, dzwee, dzwee' alarm call. 12,5 cm.

3 RATTLING CISTICOLA *Cisticola chiniana.* Very common resident. A robust cisticola with few distinguishing features; seasonal differences slight. Best told by habitat, behaviour and song. The characteristic song of the male, with slight locality differences, is 'chi chi chi ch-r-r-r-r-r' the last syllable with a distinct rattle. When alarmed calls a continuing 'cheer, cheer, cheer . . .'. When singing the black interior of the mouth is visible. This is the common bushveld cisticola that can be heard, and seen, singing for much of the year from the top of a bush. Also occurs in thornveld and coastal bush. Forages low down in tangled grass and bush. 14-16 cm.

4 TINKLING CISTICOLA *Cisticola rufilatus.* Fairly common, localised resident. Has distinctly reddish head markings, white eyebrow and orange-brown tail. The male's song is a leisurely series of high, bell-like notes 'to-wee, to-wee, to-wee . . .' repeated six to eight times. The alarm call is a high-pitched series of 'dididididi' notes. Occurs in dry, small-tree bushveld or scrub. Shy and retiring. 13-14 cm.

5 WAILING CISTICOLA *Cisticola lais.* Common resident. The head is well-marked at all times, lores and ear-coverts dusky; plumage redder and tail longer when not breeding. Immatures have the underparts strongly sulphured. The characteristic call is a wailing 'hweeeeeet' or 'to-weee-yeh' increasing in volume. Occurs on grassy hillsides and mountain slopes, often in patches of scrub. Calls repeatedly when disturbed. 13-14 cm.

356

1 LAZY CISTICOLA *Cisticola aberrans*. Common, localised resident. Appears plain-backed; non-breeding plumage (April—October) generally warmer rufous on upperparts, underparts more strongly suffused with ochre, tail length constant. Immatures are more rusty coloured. The song is a series of fairly loud metallic notes 'tu-hwee-tu-hwee-tu-hwee...' reaching a crescendo; the alarm call a loud 'breeerp' or 'tu-hweeee', usually uttered with the longish tail cocked vertically. Frequents hillsides with bushes, rocks and long grass, often in the denser vegetation near the foot of the hill close to a stream, also forest edge scrub. Hops about on rocks and flirts its tail upwards like a prinia. 14-16 cm.

2 REDFACED CISTICOLA *Cisticola erythrops*. Common resident. A plain-backed cisticola, crown concolorous with rest of upperparts in all seasons, greyish when breeding (December—March), more rufous at other times; lores, eyebrow and ear-coverts washed reddish, most strongly when not breeding. The call, loud and arresting, is 'wink-*wink*-WINK' getting louder with successive notes or a series of eight to ten notes, 'weep, weep, weep...', in a crescendo. Inhabits waterside vegetation near rivers, dams, swamps or away from water in damp situations. Secretive but calls frequently. 12-13 cm.

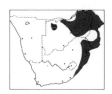

3 CROAKING CISTICOLA *Cisticola natalensis*. Common resident. A large, heavy-bodied, thick-billed cisticola with well-streaked upperparts and *without rufous crown*. Seasonal differences as illustrated; females smaller than males. Immatures are like non-breeding adults but bright sulphur below. When breeding males cruise about a few metres above the ground with a loose wing action, uttering a harsh 'cru-cru-cru-cru...'; also calls from a low bush, a harsh 'CHEE-FRO' or 'chip-MUNK'; alarm call a frog-like 'tee-YRRR'. Frequents rank grassland with scattered bushes, or grassy clearings in bushveld. Very active and conspicuous when breeding (November—March), unobtrusive at other times. Often feeds on the ground. 13-17 cm.

358

Prinias. Small warblers characterised by long tails frequently held in near vertical position. Sexes are alike. Calls consist of a single repetitive note and are often closely similar.

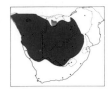

1 BLACKCHESTED PRINIA *Prinia flavicans.* Common resident. Distinctive in breeding plumage (summer); at other times the black breast-band is either absent or vestigial, the underparts more yellow. The call is a loud, much-repeated 'chip-chip-chip . . .': also an occasional 'zrrrrt-zrrrrt-zrrrrt'. Pairs and small family parties occur in thornveld and in suburbia. 13-15 cm.

2 TAWNYFLANKED PRINIA *Prinia subflava.* Common resident. Told by clear white underparts, rufous flanks and red-brown wing-edges. When disturbed makes a characteristic weeping sound 'sbeeeee-sbeeeee . . .'; the normal call is a loud, continuous 'przzt-ptzzt-przzt . . .' or 'trit-trit-trit . . .', the actual sound variable. Noisy and conspicuous, usually in parties of four to six in riverine vegetation and suburban gardens, preferring moister situations than the previous species. 10-15 cm.

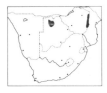

3 BRIAR WARBLER *Oriophilais robertsi.* Uncommon, localised endemic resident. A dusky, prinia-like bird lacking any distinctive markings. Makes occasional outbursts of noisy chattering 'cha cha cha cha . . .'. Usually in small groups in dense scrub and bracken-briar patches, or in bush among rocks and near forests in the eastern highlands of Zimbabwe. 14 cm.

4 KAROO PRINIA *Prinia maculosa* and **DRAKENSBERG PRINIA** *Prinia hypoxantha.* Common residents within their preferred habitats. Regarded as two distinct species by some, as races of a single species by others. The Karoo Prinia (4a), with the more southerly and westerly distribution, has the underparts suffused with pale yellow, the breast well spotted, while the Drakensberg Prinia (4b) with the easterly and northerly distribution, is more intensely yellow-buff on the underparts and has a lightly spotted breast. Both species have similar calls, a chirping 'tweet-tweet-tweet . . .' and a churring alarm note. Highly active little birds occurring in pairs and small family groups in dense, matted scrub, fynbos and rank grass along streams and forest fringes. Remain mostly concealed unless alarmed, when they move to a bush top and scold. 14 cm.

5 NAMAQUA WARBLER *Phragmacia substriata.* Fairly common, endemic resident. Differs from the previous species in white underparts with more rufous flanks and vent and more rufous upperparts. The call is an explosive 'chit-churrr'; also calls 'che-kee-kee', the song a rapid series of 'tik-tik-tik-tik . . .' notes. Often in small family groups; secretive and rapid in movements, occurring in *Acacia* scrub in dry Karoo river gullies and in reedbeds along watercourses and near dams. 14 cm.

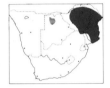

1 RUFOUSEARED WARBLER *Malcorus pectoralis*. Common resident. A prinia-like bird with black chest-band of varying thickness and rufous ear-patches, these being paler in the female. Has a loud, penetrating call 'tee, tee, tee, tee' plus a quiet 'chit'. Occurs in low, sparse vegetation where pairs or small parties spend much time on the ground, often preferring to run than fly. The long thin tail is characteristically held upright. 14-16 cm.

2 REDWINGED WARBLER *Heliolais erythroptera.* Uncommon resident. Seasonal plumage differences as illustrated. At all times the red-brown wings and yellowish-brown eyes are conspicuous and distinguish this species from other small warblers. Calls frequently, a squeaky 'pseep-pseep-pseep'; also makes a high-pitched 'chirr'. Active, restless birds which occur in well-grassed woodland, especially where long grass tangles with low branches. 13.5 cm.

3 MASHONA HYLIOTA *Hyliota australis*. Uncommon resident. Males differ from the next species in dull, purple-black upperparts and limited white wing-markings, these not extending onto the secondaries; underparts marginally paler; females by dark brownish upperparts, *not* grey. Immatures resemble females but are lighter brown. Has a two-syllabled chippering whistle and a trilling warble. Highly mobile, active leaf-gleaners, found mostly in the upper canopy of broadleafed woodland, often in bird parties. 14 cm

4 YELLOWBREASTED HYLIOTA *Hyliota flavigaster*. Rare resident. Males differ from the previous species in glossy-blue-black upperparts and white wing feather-edgings extending to the secondaries, the females being dark grey above (*not* brown). Immatures have finely barred upperparts, pale feather-edges. The calls and habits are very similar to those of (3). Occurs in Miombo woodland in Mozambique and northern Botswana. 14 cm.

Flycatchers. Family MUSCICAPIDAE. Small, insectivorous birds with prominent bristles protruding from the base of their bills. Many of the soberly coloured species catch insects on the ground or in flight while watching from a low perch, while others, especially the colourful and ornate species, are leaf-gleaners in addition to hawking insects in short aerial sallies.

5 COLLARED FLYCATCHER *Ficedula albicollis*. Very rare visitor. Males told from other pied flycatchers, especially the Fiscal Flycatcher (page 364) by smaller size, *white forehead* and *collar* and small bill (non-breeding males, normally seen in Southern Africa, resemble females and *lack a collar*); females by more extensive white on wings, duskier breast and small bill. The call is a sharp 'whit-whit'. Perches on some low branch from where it hunts insects; usually solitary. 13 cm.

FLYCATCHERS

1 SPOTTED FLYCATCHER *Muscicapa striata*. Common summer visitor. Distinguished from the next species by slimmer, less dumpy shape plus *streaked crown* and underparts. Sometimes makes a thin, sibilant, two-syllabled 'tze-ee' while flicking its wings. Singly in any woodland or mixed bushveld plus well-wooded suburbia. Perches on a low branch beneath a tree from where it hawks insects or catches them on the ground, frequently returning to the same perch. 14-15 cm.

2 DUSKY FLYCATCHER *Muscicapa adusta*. Common, localised resident. More dumpy than the previous species, the underparts duskier with faint smudges (not streaks). Immatures are like adults. Makes a thin, sibilant 'zeeet'. Singly or in pairs at forest edges, in riverine forests and broadleafed woodland in moister regions. Behaviour much the same as the previous species but frequents the more lush coastal and montane mistbelt regions. 12-13 cm.

3 MOUSECOLOURED FLYCATCHER (PALLID FLYCATCHER) *Melaenornis pallidus*. Uncommon resident. A dull, featureless bird, the underparts scarcely paler than the upperparts; cf. Marico and Chat Flycatchers (overleaf). Immatures have upperparts with buff-edged feathers. Mostly silent. Usually in pairs in broadleafed woodland or mixed bushveld (not thornveld). Perches on a low branch from where it watches the ground for insects. Sparsely distributed throughout its range. 15-17 cm.

4 FANTAILED FLYCATCHER (LEADCOLOURED FLY-CATCHER) *Myioparus plumbeus*. Uncommon resident. Differs from the next species mainly in behaviour and *white outer tail-feathers*. Immatures are similar to adults. The call is a loud, cheerful 'teee-reee' the second syllable lower than the first. Singly or in pairs in broadleafed woodland, mixed bushveld and riverine forests. Calls frequently and *fans its tail while raising and lowering it*, constantly moving through the mid-stratum; cf. habits of the next species. Often joins bird parties. 14 cm.

5 BLUEGREY FLYCATCHER *Muscicapa caerulescens*. Fairly common resident. Differs from the previous species in behaviour and lack of any white in the tail. Immatures have spotted upperparts, mottled underparts. Calls 'tsip-tsip-tsip-tsip-tse-tslipip' but is mostly silent. Usually singly in coastal bush, riverine forests, forest fringes and broadleafed woodland. Perches in the mid-stratum and watches the ground for insects or catches them in mid-air, often returning to the same perch. A quiet, inconspicuous species. 14-15 cm.

BLACK FLYCATCHER: See page 296.

363

FLYCATCHERS

1 CHAT FLYCATCHER *Melaenornis infuscatus*. Common resident. Very similar to the Mousecoloured Flycatcher (previous page) but larger, pale wing-edges more prominent. Immatures heavily speckled as illustrated. No distinctive calls recorded. Perches prominently on bush, post or wire from where it flies to the ground to seize insects. Common on roadside telephone wires in the dry west. (The ranges of this and the Mousecoloured Flycatcher are mutually exclusive.) 20 cm.

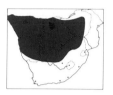

2 MARICO FLYCATCHER *Melaenornis mariquensis*. Common resident. Differs from similar flycatchers in white underparts contrasting strongly with brown upperparts. Immatures are spotted whitish above, streaked dark on white below as illustrated, this streaking more heavy than in young of previous species. Call a soft 'chew-week'. Frequents thornveld. Perches prominently on the outer branch of a bush from where it watches for insects on the ground, occasionally hawking them in the air. 18 cm.

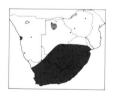

3 VANGA FLYCATCHER (BLACK-AND-WHITE FLY-CATCHER) *Bias musicus*. Rare; probably resident. Sexes markedly different as illustrated, both with crested heads, heavy bills, prominent rictal bristles, yellow eyes and short, yellow legs. Utters sharp whistling notes 'tchi-kik-you' or 'we-chip! we-chip!' and sings 'wit-tu-wit-tu-tu-tu', the notes first ascending then descending the scale. Pairs or parties occur in the tops of the taller trees of forest fringes and in bushveld in central Mozambique. Have the habit of circling round a tree in slow flight with rapid wing-beats. 16 cm.

4 FISCAL FLYCATCHER *Sigelus silens*. Common resident. Differs from Fiscal Shrike (page 372) in less robust bill and white 'windows' in the tail, while the white wing-bar extends only half-way along the folded wing, *not* to the shoulder. Has a sibilant, rather weak song 'swee-swee-ur', and other similar sounds often in prolonged sequence. Usually in pairs in bush country and in suburbia. Perch prominently on branch or post and fly to the ground to seize insects. 17-20 cm.

The **batis** group are small leaf-gleaning flycatchers of similar appearance, characterised by grey caps and upperparts, black masks, black or rufous breast-bands and varying amounts of rufous colouring elsewhere. Immatures are dull versions of adults. Often found in bird parties. When alarmed they fly about with whirring wings.

1 PRIRIT BATIS *Batis pririt*. Common resident. Most resembles the Chinspot Batis (5), the males difficult to tell apart; females with much paler buff throat and breast. (The ranges of the two species are mutually exclusive.) The call is a long, descending sequence of notes 'peep-peep-peep-peep . . . choo-choo-choo-choo . . .' up to 100 times or more. Pairs occur in the dry western thornveld, often along watercourses. 12 cm.

2 WOODWARDS' BATIS *Batis fratrum*. Fairly common resident. Males lack a black breast-band and resemble females; confusion with the previous species unlikely as their ranges are widely separated. The contact call by either sex is 'phoee-phoee-phoee', males also call 'chuririri, chuririri, chuririri...'. A species of coastal bush, forests and riverine forests, preferring dense undergrowth and usually remaining in the lower stratum. 11-12 cm.

3 MOZAMBIQUE BATIS *Batis soror*. Common resident. Like a very small version of the Chinspot Batis (5) (sometimes regarded as a race of that species), but in both sexes the markings of the underparts are less clearly defined, the male generally more speckled on back and flanks. The call is 'tiroo, tiroo, tiroo, whit, whit, whit, phep, phep...'. Habits as for the Chinspot Batis (5), but occurs only in the Mozambique coastal belt from Inhambane northwards. 10 cm.

4 CAPE BATIS *Batis capensis*. Common resident. The most heavily marked batis, males with a very broad black breast-band and rufous flanks, females with rich rufous breast-band, throat and flanks, both with rufous on wing-coverts; eyes yellow when not breeding. Has a grinding 'prrritt, prrritt, prrritt' alarm note, other calls variable, a monotonous 'keep, keep, keep ...', a grating '*wee*-warrawarra' and a soft 'foo-foo-foo-foo...'. In pairs and small parties in forests, forested kloofs and well-wooded suburban gardens; in the north is confined to montane forest. 12-13 cm.

5 CHINSPOT BATIS (WHITEFLANKED BATIS) *Batis molitor*. Very common resident. Males lack any rufous colouring; very similar to (1) and (2) but their ranges do not overlap. Females have clearly defined, rich rufous chin-spot and breast-band but *white* flanks. Has several calls, the most characteristic a descending series of three notes 'choi-choi-choi', sounding like 'Three blind mice'. Also calls 'chi-chirr' or 'chee-chir-chir'; one of the first species to be heard at dawn. Pairs are found in mixed bushveld and woodland, always in drier country than the previous species. Frequently joins bird parties, feeding in the mid- and lower strata. 12-13 cm.

368

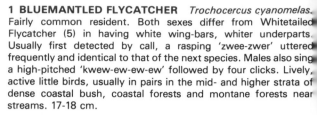

1 BLUEMANTLED FLYCATCHER *Trochocercus cyanomelas*. Fairly common resident. Both sexes differ from Whitetailed Flycatcher (5) in having white wing-bars, whiter underparts. Usually first detected by call, a rasping 'zwee-zwer' uttered frequently and identical to that of the next species. Males also sing a high-pitched 'kwew-ew-ew-ew' followed by four clicks. Lively, active little birds, usually in pairs in the mid- and higher strata of dense coastal bush, coastal forests and montane forests near streams. 17-18 cm.

2 PARADISE FLYCATCHER *Terpsiphone viridis*. Common summer resident, present all year in the east and north-east. The only small flycatcher with orange-brown upperparts and blue-grey underparts; some females have slightly elongated tails. The call, a sharp 'zwee-zwer', is identical to that of the previous species, the song a lively trill 'wee-te-tiddly, wit-wit'. Highly active and vociferous little birds found among large trees along rivers, forest fringes, well-wooded hills and suburbia. MM 41 cm. FF 23 cm.

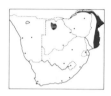

3 LIVINGSTONE'S FLYCATCHER *Erythrocercus livingstonei*. Uncommon resident. Colour combination distinctive. Young birds and adults of northern races have heads same colour as back. Has a sharp 'chip-chip' or 'zert' call, plus a sunbird-like 'tweet' in flight. Also gives an occasional outburst of warbling song and makes snapping sounds with its beak. Found in bird parties in thickets and the larger trees of riverine forests, also the edges of woodland clearings. Highly agile, restless little birds, constantly flitting from branch to branch or sidling down branches with fanned tail moving. 12 cm.

4 WATTLE-EYED FLYCATCHER (BLACKTHROATED WATTLE-EYE) *Platysteira peltata*. Uncommon resident. Female with all-black breast, male with narrow breast-band only, both with red eye-wattles. Immature males lack the breast-band. Has a guttural 'chak-chak' call, a weak, tinkling song 'er-er-fea-er-er-fea-fea' and a louder 'tree-tree-tree, che-chreet-che-chreet-che-chreet...'. Pairs live in the lower stratum of riverine and coastal thickets. 18 cm.

5 WHITETAILED FLYCATCHER *Trochocercus albonotatus*. Fairly common resident. Most resembles Bluemantled Flycatcher (1) but smaller, greyer, with duskier underparts and no white wing-bar or crest. The call is a rapid 'chrrit-tit-tit'. Highly active and agile in forest canopies and in trees bordering forests. Fans its tail frequently (thus revealing the white outer tail-feathers) while working its way up and down branches. 14-15 cm.

6 FAIRY FLYCATCHER *Stenostira scita*. Common resident. Very small grey and black bird with conspicuous white wing-bar and outer tail-feathers; the pink central belly is inconspicuous in the field. Young birds have brownish rather than grey plumage. The call is a short, sibilant trill 'kisskisskisskiss'. Flits about actively feeding within bushes or the outer canopy of trees, frequently bobbing and fanning its tail. In the south often occurs near rivers; moves north in winter when it frequents woodlands, montane scrub, thornveld, plantations and suburbia. 12 cm.

369

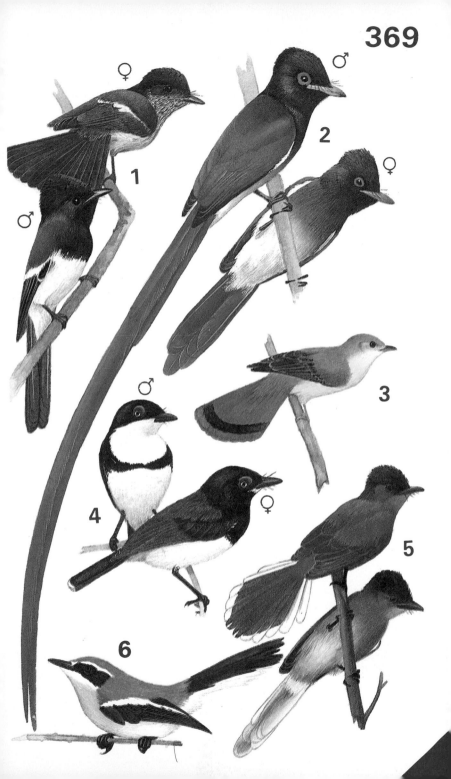

370

True shrikes (Family LANIIDAE) and allies. Insectivorous or partially carnivorous birds with stout, hooked or slightly hooked bills. Members of the various genera are illustrated according to plumage similarity.

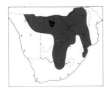

1 LONGTAILED SHRIKE *Corvinella melanoleuca*. Common resident. A distinctive, long-tailed, pied bird. Females may show white on their flanks and have shorter tails. Immatures are bronze-brown with grey rumps. The call is 'prooit-preeoo, prooit-preeoo-preeoo' the first sound descending, the second ascending. Small groups of three to ten birds occur in thornveld and mixed bushveld, preferring lightly wooded, well-grassed regions where they hunt while perched on a bush. 40-50 cm.

2 REDBACKED SHRIKE *Lanius collurio*. Common summer visitor. Sexes differ as illustrated, females differing from immature Fiscal Shrike (overleaf) in more rufous upperparts and lack of white wing-bars. Rarely, males occur with white wing-bars, then resemble Sousa's Shrike (page 374), but differ in more rufous *unbarred* mantle, clearer grey cap. Mostly silent, sometimes makes a harsh 'chak, chak'. Singly in a variety of wooded habitats, preferring mixed bushveld and thornveld. Perches conspicuously on a low branch and still-hunts. 18 cm.

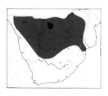

3 WHITECROWNED SHRIKE *Eurocephalus anguitimens*. Common resident. Distinguished by white crown and black mask. Sexes are alike. Makes a curious 'kwep, kwep' sound. Singly or in small, scattered groups in mixed bushveld, thornveld and broadleafed woodland. Perches conspicuously on a branch or roadside telephone wire from where it hunts. 23-5 cm.

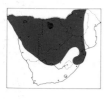

4 LESSER GREY SHRIKE *Lanius minor*. Fairly common summer visitor, a few all year. The full black mask (a) is often absent November to early January, then appears as (b). Sexes are alike. Normally silent. Singly in thornveld and mixed bushveld. Still-hunts from a branch. 20-2 cm.

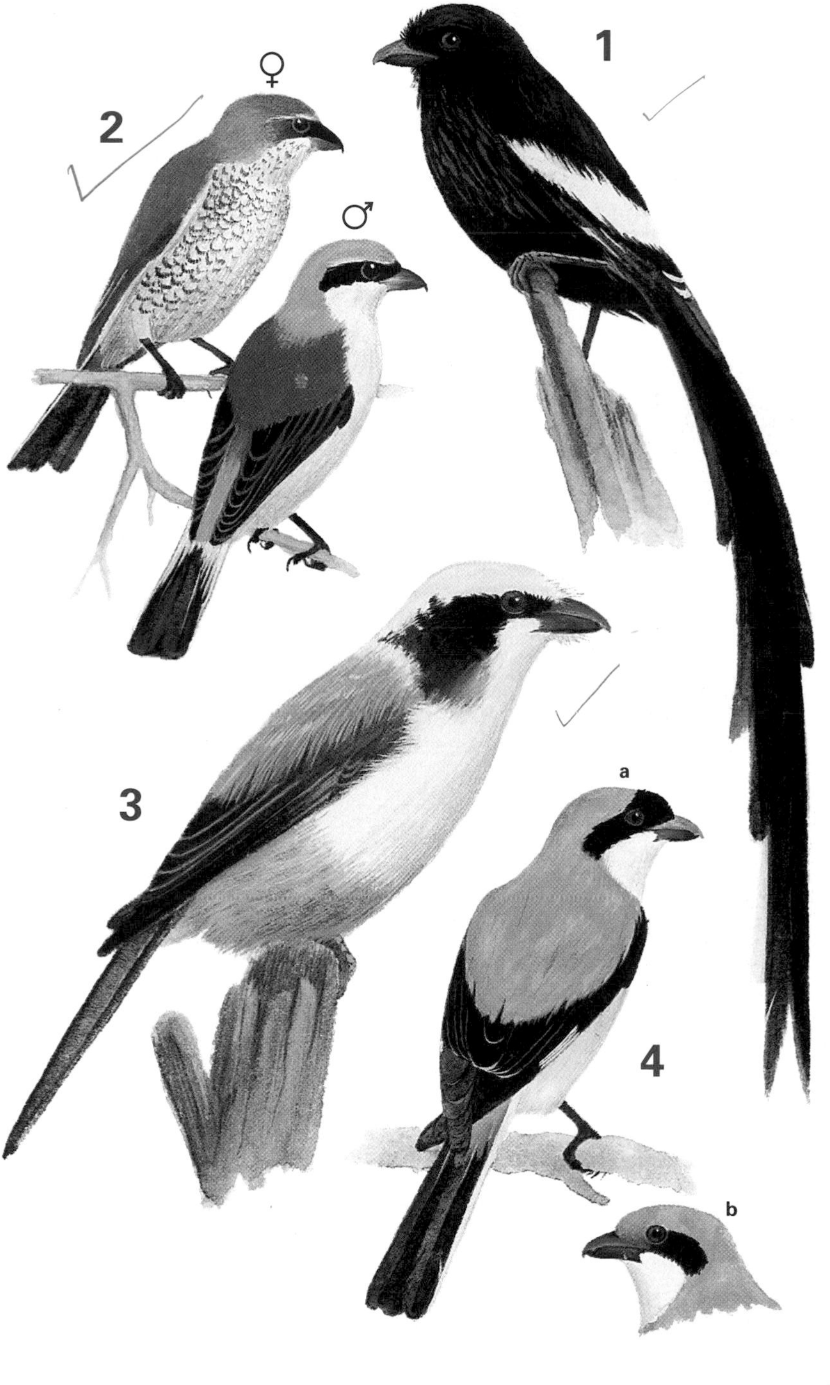
1
2
♀
♂
3
a
4
b

372

1 FISCAL SHRIKE *Lanius collaris*. Very common resident. Pied, heavybodied, heavy-billed bird with white wing-bar *extending to shoulder*. Female with rufous flanks. Compare with thinner-billed Fiscal Flycatcher (page 364) in which wing-bar does *not* reach shoulder. Western race (a) has white eyebrow. Young are ash-brown above, greyish-brown below with fine barring. Call a harsh 'gercha, gercha...' or 'skiza, skiza...'; also a rambling song incorporating sweet notes and the characteristic 'gercha' sound. Perches conspicuously on branch, post or wire, flying to ground occasionally to seize insects and other small prey. Singly or in pairs in lightly wooded country and suburbia. 23 cm.

2 BRUBRU *Nilaus afer*. Fairly common resident. Small pied bird with rich rufous flanks in both sexes. Females dark brown above. Young birds similar but with streaked breast. Males make a drawn-out, far-carrying whistle 'trrioooo' like a telephone, the female replying with a softer, wheezy 'wheee'. An active, restless species of open woodland. Usually in pairs, which call continuously while working their way through the mid-stratum. 15 cm.

3 PUFFBACK *Dryoscopus cubla*. Common resident. Small pied bird with crimson eyes. Female with white forehead and eyebrow, both with distinctive wing-barring. When excited male erects its back feathers to form a puff (see illustration); may fly from tree to tree like this while calling sharply 'chick-weeu, chick-weeu...'; also uttered less frequently while feeding. Flies in a heavy manner, the wings making a distinct purring sound. Pairs, often in bird parties, in woodland, riverine bush and evergreen forest, the canopies of the larger trees being favoured. 18 cm.

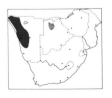

4 WHITETAILED SHRIKE *Lanioturdus torquatus*. Fairly common, localised resident. Small black, white and grey bird with a very short tail and long legs. Has a loud, clear 'huo-huo-huo' call similar to that of the Blackheaded Oriole (page 302) plus various querulous churrs, croaks and scolding notes. An active, restless species of striking appearance. In pairs or small groups (flocks of up to 20 in winter) in thornveld, and mixed woodland, spending much time hopping about on the ground with characteristic bouncing gait. 15 cm.

1 SOUSA'S SHRIKE *Lanius souzae*. Rare resident. Told from the Redbacked Shrike (page 370) by *dull* brown wings and tail, bold white wing-bar reaching to shoulder, and dusky underparts, only the throat being white. Tail-feathers very narrow. Female has tawny flanks and young are narrowly barred blackish on underparts. Has a low, scraping call-note. Perches on some low branch from where it flies down occasionally to seize insects on the ground. Singly or in pairs in broadleafed woodland and Kalahari sand. 17-18 cm.

2 SOUTHERN BOUBOU *Laniarius ferrugineus*. Common resident. Cinnamon colouring of belly sometimes extends in pale wash to throat, but is always richer towards belly and vent. White wing-bar appears narrow or wide depending on feather arrangement. South-eastern females of this species are dark brown above, not black. Calls in duet, first bird 'ko-ko' replied to by 'kweet', or 'boo-boo' replied to by 'whee-oo', or a liquid-sounding 'phooweeol' replied to by 'hueee' or 'churrr'. Many variations of these basic calls occur. Fairly secretive, pairs remaining concealed in dense bush, usually in the lower stratum. 23 cm.

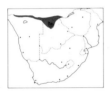

3 SWAMP BOUBOU *Laniarius bicolor*. Fairly common resident. Differs from (2) and (4) in underparts being white, no pinkish tinge even to feather-bases. Calls less musical than other boubous, a short-whistle replied to by a harsh 'kick-ick'. Also less secretive than other boubous, will perch openly while calling. Pairs occur in papyrus, riverine scrub and forest. 22-3 cm.

4 TROPICAL BOUBOU *Laniarius aethiopicus*. Fairly common resident. Differs from other boubous in entire underparts being lightly washed pinkish, less cinnamon on flanks and vent. Calls in a remarkable series of duets, the two calls uttered so instantaneously to appear as one; normally three liquid, bell-like notes answered by 'hueee', but variations occur. Pairs frequent dense vegetation in montane forests, and dense lowveld bushveld. 21 cm.

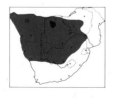

5 CRIMSON BOUBOU (CRIMSONBREASTED SHRIKE) *Laniarius atrococcineus*. Common resident. Distinctive, identical to other boubous but for entirely scarlet underparts; occasionally occurs with yellow underparts. Very young birds are ash-grey below, finely barred black. Calls in duet, both birds often calling almost simultaneously, a sharply delivered 'qui-quip-chiri'. Pairs occur in thornveld, frequenting the lower stratum. Most common in the drier western regions. 22-3 cm.

Tchagra Shrikes. Heavy-billed, similarly coloured shrikes which feed on or near the ground, creeping about in the lower stratum of their preferred habitat and moving from bush to bush in low, rather heavy flight. Often reveal their presence by distinctive calls.

1 MARSH TCHAGRA (BLACKCAP TCHAGRA) *Tchagra minuta*. Uncommon and localised resident. Told from the next three species by black cap extending to below eyes and very rufous body; females have a small white eyebrow forward of the eye. Immature birds have a brownish cap, horn-coloured bill. Call resembles the words 'today or tomorrow' uttered slowly. In courtship sings a shrill song while mounting steeply upwards on rapidly fluttering wings. Frequents tall grass and reeds in swamps or low bushes adjacent to damp regions. 18 cm.

2 SOUTHERN TCHAGRA *Tchagra tchagra*. Common to fairly common resident. Larger than the next species, differing from it and (4) in having a *reddish-brown* crown, this grading into olive-brown mantle, back and central tail-feathers. Immatures are duller with buffy wing-coverts and underparts fulvous-grey. The call is a loud rattling sound followed by a rapid 'chchchch..', ending with 'tew-a-tew'. Also has a loud whistle. Single birds or pairs in coastal bush and thornveld, less common in the north. A reluctant flier but performs an aerial display similar to the next species. 21 cm.

3 THREESTREAKED TCHAGRA *Tchagra australis*. Common resident. Smaller than (2) and (4), less rufous, more buff-brown. The flight pattern is very similar to that of the next species. Immatures are similar to but duller than adults. The alarm note is a guttural 'churr', but in the summer males display by flying steeply upwards to above tree height, then planing down with quivering wings while calling 'tui-tui-tui-tui-tui...' in a descending cadence. A thornveld species which spends much time on the ground under bushes. If disturbed, hops onto some low branch before hopping or flying into cover. Usually seen singly. 19 cm.

4 BLACKCROWNED TCHAGRA *Tchagra senegala*. Common resident. Told from the two previous species by *black* crown. Immatures have the crown blackish-brown, the bill horn-coloured. Has a 'krok-krok-krokrakror' alarm note and a loud, ponderous and rather flat-sounding call 'CHEER-tcharee, trichi CHEER-tcharoo, cheeroo, cheeroo'. Pairs also duet with a variety of grating, churring and whistling calls. Singly or in pairs in thornveld, woodland, coastal bush and plantations, frequenting the lower stratum. 21-3 cm.

377

378

Bush Shrikes. Colourful shrikes with olive-green and grey upperparts and yellow or orange-yellow underparts. Most frequent dense bush and all have distinctive calls.

1 OLIVE BUSH SHRIKE *Telophorus olivaceus*. Common resident. Two forms: (a) with cinnamon breast (intensity variable), males with an additional white eyebrow; (b) with entirely green upperparts, yellow underparts, both sexes; of. (3) and (4). Immatures as illustrated. The calls are about six notes of varying pitch, sometimes preceded by a single higher note, 'phwee-phwee-phwee-phwee-phwee-phwee' or 'tew-tew-tew-tew-tew' or 'tee-toy-toy-toy-toy'; also a descending cadence 'CHE-*che*-che-che-che-che' and a warbling trill. Pairs in coastal and montane forests, montane scrub, dense bush and plantations. In bush habitats feeds in the lower stratum, in forests in the mid- and lower strata. Secretive at all times. 17 cm.

2 GORGEOUS BUSH SHRIKE *Telophorus quadricolor*. Fairly common resident. Males distinguished by scarlet throat and black gorget, females similar but black gorget much reduced. Immature shown in first plumage. The call is a liquid, ventriloquial and rapidly delivered 'kong-kong-koit'. Pairs in dense coastal and valley bush, lowland forests, riverine forests and mixed bushveld. Secretive, frequenting the lower stratum. 20 cm.

3 ORANGEBREASTED BUSH SHRIKE *Telophorus sulfureopectus*. Common resident. Males distinguished by yellow forehead and eyebrow plus yellow underparts with only the *breast* orange, this much reduced in females. Immature shown in first plumage. Calls a musical, much-repeated 'poo-poo-poo-pooooo' or 'pipit-eeez, pipit-eeez...'. In pairs in mixed bushveld, thornveld and valley bush, plus riverine and coastal thickets, usually in the mid-stratum. Not secretive. 18-19 cm.

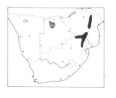

4 BLACKFRONTED BUSH SHRIKE *Telophorus nigrifrons*. Uncommon, localised resident. Males identified by black forehead and facial mask (no eyebrow) plus extensive orange wash from throat to belly, female's underparts less orange than male's, distinguished from female of (1b) by *grey head and mantle*. Normal call a repetitive 'oo-poo', sounding like 'doh-me' in the tonic sol-fa scale. Pairs mainly in montane forests, also lowland forests in Mozambique. Feed in the upper and mid-strata and join bird parties in winter. 19 cm.

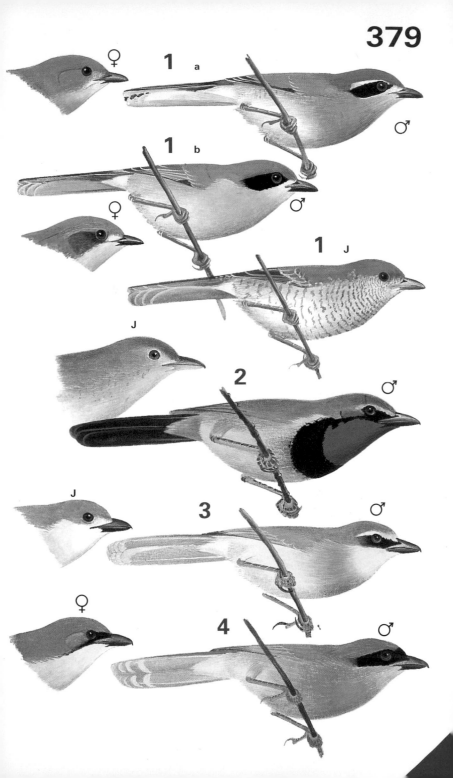

379

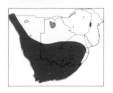

1 BOKMAKIERIE *Telophorus zeylonus*. Common resident. Distinguished from Yellowthroated Longclaw (page 292) by grey and green upperparts. Immatures lack the black gorget. The calls are duets between both sexes and are variable, eg. 'bok-makiri', 'kok-o-vik', 'bok-bok-chit', 'wit, wit-wit' or 'pirrapee-pirrapoo', each sequence repeated at about three-second intervals. Pairs occur in a wide range of habitats from montane foothills to the coast, usually in bush patches in grassland or on rocky hillsides, in semi-arid regions in the west and common in suburbia in most regions. Spends much time on the ground. 23 cm.

2 GREYHEADED BUSH SHRIKE *Malaconotus blanchoti*. Fairly common resident. Identified by large size, *very heavy bill* and white patch before a yellow eye. Immatures have a horn-coloured bill. The most characteristic call is a haunting, drawn-out 'hoooooooooop', but also makes a 'clip-clip . . . .' sound. Singly or in pairs in coastal and lowland forests, riverine forests, mixed bushveld and thornveld. Usually feeds in the mid- and lower strata. 25-7 cm.

Helmetshrikes are characterised by intense sociability, usually groups of six to twelve birds of all ages which feed and roost together, share nest-building and chick-feeding. Nomadic unless breeding, they move from tree to tree continuously and maintain a noisy chattering, comprised of harsh whirring and grating sounds plus bill-snapping. Sexes are alike.

3 CHESTNUTFRONTED HELMETSHRIKE *Prionops scopifrons*. Rare resident in the north, rare vagrant in the south. Distinguished by grey underparts and chestnut forehead plus white lores and chin. In young birds the forehead is dusky. Occurs in the lowland forests and adjacent woodland of the Lusitu-Haroni region of Zimbabwe, where it frequents the tree canopies. 19 cm.

4 REDBILLED HELMETSHRIKE *Prionops retzii*. Fairly common resident. Entirely black except for white vent and tail-tips. Immatures are browner. Parties in broadleafed woodland or well-developed riverine forests where they frequent the tree canopies, sometimes in company with the next species. 22 cm.

5 WHITE HELMETSHRIKE *Prionops plumatus*. Common resident. Identified by pied plumage and butterfly-like flight. Young birds have browner crowns. Parties in broadleafed woodland and mixed bushveld, frequenting the mid- and lower strata. 20 cm.

381

382

STARLINGS

Starlings. Family STURNIDAE. A well-known family of frugivorous and insectivorous birds with strong, slightly arched bills and strong legs. Many species form flocks, especially when roosting. Their calls mainly various unmusical squeaks and squawks. Several species have adapted to town life and two have been introduced from other countries. Unless stated the young resemble adults.

1 WATTLED STARLING *Creatophora cinerea*. Common resident. A pale starling, males particularly so when breeding, at which time the head may be ornamented with yellow and black skin plus wattles as illustrated (b), or have only the wattles as (c). Females and non-breeding males (a) appear drab, but can be told by diagnostic white rump in flight. The call is a rasping, squeaky sound. Highly gregarious in grassland or open bushveld, often associating with cattle. When breeding build hundreds of nests colonially in bushes; highly nomadic when not breeding. 21 cm.

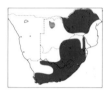

2 REDWINGED STARLING *Onychognathus morio*. Common resident. Told from the next species by larger size, entirely red-brown flight feathers and sexual plumage differences as illustrated. The eye is dark. Has a variety of pleasant, loud whistles, the most frequent being a drawn-out 'spreeooo'. Pairs and flocks (large at communal roosts) frequent cliffs, caves or buildings where they roost and breed, dispersing daily to seek fruits and berries. 27-8 cm.

3 PALEWINGED STARLING *Onychognathus nabouroup*. Common resident. Told from the previous species by orange eyes and whitish wing-feathers tinged orange only on the leading-edge; the outer half of the wings appears entirely pale in flight; cf. Redbilled Buffalo Weaver (page 404). Has similar melodious whistles to (2). Flocks occur in rocky localities in the drier regions, especially in the west. 26 cm.

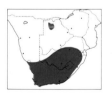

4 PIED STARLING *Spreo bicolor*. Common resident. A long-legged, dark brown starling with purple-green iridescence to the plumage and white vent and belly; the pale yellow eye and prominent orange gape are good field features. Call is a soft 'squeer' and similar melancholy whistles. Occurs in flocks in grassveld, dry dongas and river-beds; a common roadside bird in many regions. 25-7 cm.

383

384

1 EUROPEAN STARLING *Sturnus vulgaris*. Common resident. At a distance looks blackish; longer-billed, shorter-tailed and stockier than Blackbellied Glossy Starling (overleaf). Sexes are very similar when not breeding (winter). Immatures are an almost uniform mouse-brown with whitish throat, as illustrated. Usual call-note a grating 'tcheerr'; also a rambling song of throaty warbles, 'chirrup' notes and whistles with a creaking quality. Walks with a quick, jerky action, occasionally runs or hops, and feeds mostly on the ground. Often in flocks, especially when roosting. Occurs in various man-made coastal habitats: suburbia, playing fields, farms, etc. 20-2 cm.

2 INDIAN MYNA *Acridotheres tristis*. Very common or abundant resident. In flight large white wing-patches conspicuous. Immatures have duller facial skin. Has a variety of chattering calls, clucking sounds, squeaks and some melodious phrases. Struts about with a swaggering gait, in pairs or small flocks, gathering in large flocks to roost. Commensal with man, frequenting urban habitats. 25 cm.

3 PLUMCOLOURED STARLING *Cinnyricinclus leucogaster*. Fairly common summer resident. Females differ from spotted thrushes (page 312) in stockier build, shorter bill with yellow gape, yellow eyes and lack of black markings on ear-coverts. Immatures are like females, eyes darker. The call is a short series of pleasant, slurred notes. An arboreal, frugivorous species of woodland and riverine forests. In pairs when breeding, otherwise in nomadic flocks of mostly one sex. Resident in the extreme north-west, a few remain all year elsewhere. 18-19 cm.

4 LONGTAILED GLOSSY STARLING *Lamprotornis mevesii*. Common resident. Differs from other glossy starlings in combination of *dark eyes* and long graduated tail; legs shorter than the next species. Immatures are similar, duller. Groups make a chattering 'trrreer-eeear...'. Usually in small flocks in well-developed woodland (especially Mopane woodland) and river valleys. 30-4 cm.

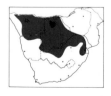

5 BURCHELL'S GLOSSY STARLING *Lamprotornis australis*. Common resident. The largest glossy starling, differing from most others in dark eyes, from the previous species in dark ear-patch, lanky appearance and shorter, ungraduated tail. Immatures are duller, brownish below. The call is a squeaky 'churrik-urr, churrick-urrik-kerr...'. In pairs, small parties or large flocks in well-developed woodland. Feeds on the ground, preferring heavily grazed areas. 30-4 cm.

♂ Br J 1 N-Br

2

♂ 3 ♀

4 ✓

5

1 BLACKBELLIED GLOSSY STARLING *Lamprotornis corruscus*. Common resident. Dullest of the glossy starlings, appearing black at a distance; females and immatures dullest. Eye colour orange-yellow to red in adults, dark grey in immatures. Flocks utter various pleasant warbling notes while feeding. Breeding pairs make a garbled series of mellow trills interspersed with harsher notes. Nomadic when not breeding. Occurs in coastal towns, forests and bush, extending inland to riparian and lowland woodland in the north. In Zimbabwe occurs in summer only in the Rusitu-Haroni region. 20-21 cm.

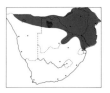

2 GREATER BLUE-EARED GLOSSY STARLING *Lamprotornis chalybaeus*. Common resident. One of three short-tailed and closely similar glossy starlings; cf. (3) and (5). Differs from (5) in having a blackish ear-patch and royal-blue belly and flanks, from (3) by larger size, blue (not magenta) flanks and two distinct rows of black spots on the wing-coverts. Immatures are duller, underparts sooty, eye grey. The call is 'sque-eear, sque-eeareeear'. Pairs when breeding, otherwise in large flocks in woodland and bushveld; in the Kruger National Park lives commensally with man at rest camps during winter. 21-3 cm.

3 LESSER BLUE-EARED GLOSSY STARLING *Lamprotornis chloropterus*. Common resident. Smaller than the previous species, flanks more magenta, the upper row of wing-covert spots usually obscured, otherwise closely similar to (2). Immatures as illustrated, frequently flocking with adults. The song is a variety of pleasant notes 'chirp-chirrup-treerroo-chirp-trooo'; on take-off and in flight calls 'wirri-girri'. Occurs in broadleafed woodland and bushveld, usually in flocks when not breeding. 20 cm.

4 SHARPTAILED GLOSSY STARLING *Lamprotornis acuticaudus*. Fairly common, localised resident. Identified by wedge-shaped tail. General colouring like next species but black ear-patch present, flanks blue, eyes red in males, orange in females. Immatures are grey on underparts, the feathers tipped buff. Voice not known. Occurs in woodland of northern and north-eastern Namibia. 26 cm.

5 CAPE GLOSSY STARLING *Lamprotornis nitens*. Common resident. Differs from (2) and (3) by *lack of black ear-patch*, underparts uniformly coloured blue-green. In poor light appears blue overall, even blackish, in good light is peacock-blue or green. Immatures are drabber with much dull, blackish feathering. Song a pleasant 'trrr-treer-treer-cheer...'. Pairs or flocks in thornveld, mixed woodland and suburbia. Particularly common at camps in the southern Kruger National Park in winter. Also in arid western regions, extending into the Namib desert within riverine bush. 23-5 cm.

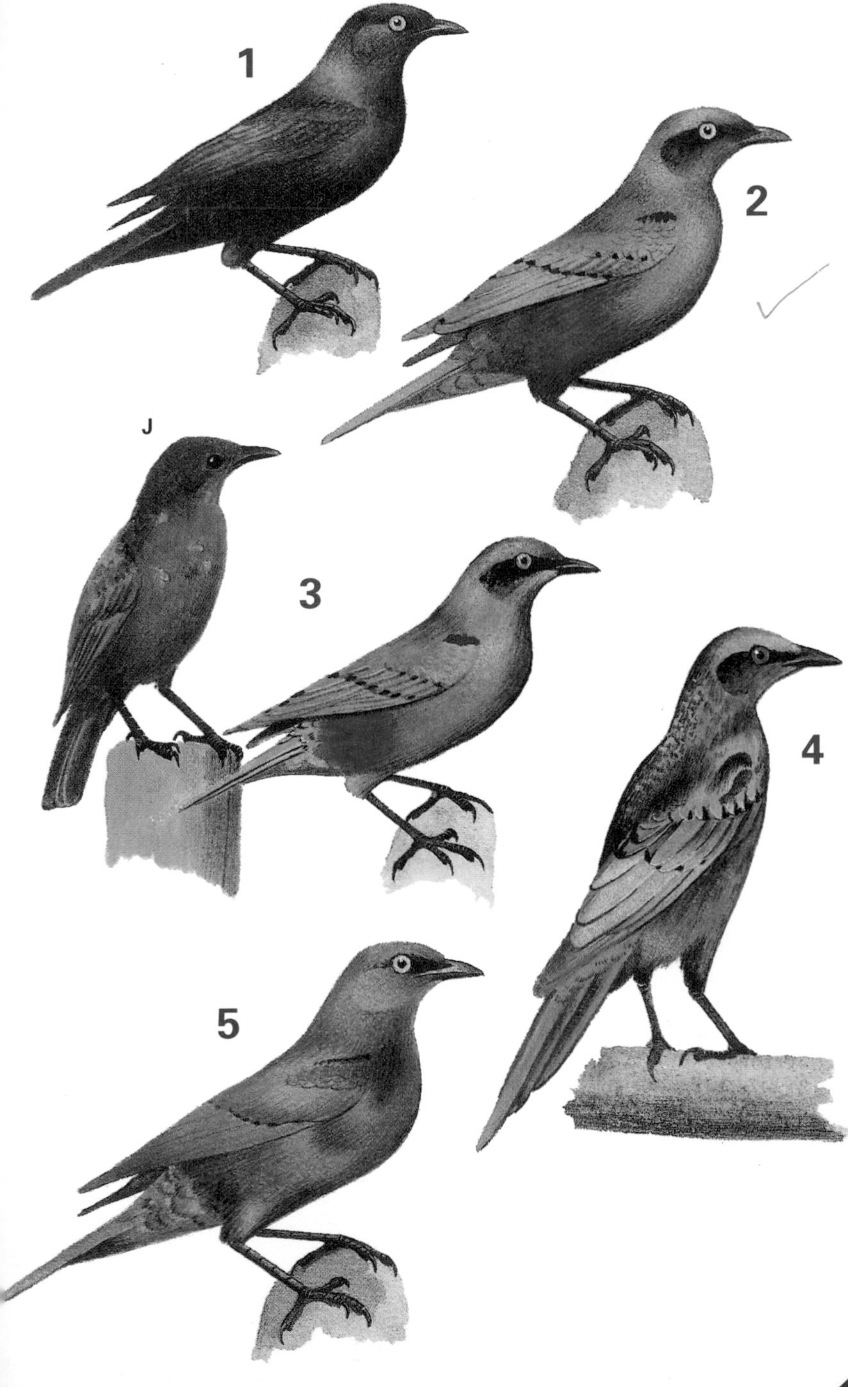
1
2
J
3
4
5

Sugarbirds. Family PROMEROPIDAE. Related to starlings and characterised by long, graduated tails, curved bills and brown plumage with yellow vents. They feed on insects and nectar.

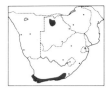

1 CAPE SUGARBIRD *Promerops cafer*. Very common resident. Females identified from next species by shorter tail, pronounced moustachial-streak, less rufous breast and lack of rufous cap. The song is a series of jumbled metallic, grating and churring notes. When breeding (winter) males call conspicuously from a perch or fly about in undulating flight wing-clapping with tail held high. Pairs occur where proteas are flowering on coastal mountain slopes and flats, moving about between seasons. MM 37-44 cm FF 24-9 cm.

2 GURNEY'S SUGARBIRD *Promerops gurneyi*. Common resident. Known from previous species by more rufous breast and rufous cap. The call is three or four ascending notes, the last one repeated several times. Occurs on eastern mountain slopes where proteas or aloes are flowering; unless breeding (summer) somewhat nomadic. 25-9 cm.

Oxpeckers. Family BUPHAGIDAE. Related to starlings, but with very sharp claws for clinging to large mammals. Their bills are used to comb the animals for ticks and bloodsucking flies, the tails used as props in woodpecker fashion as they clamber all over their hosts.

3 YELLOWBILLED OXPECKER *Buphagus africanus*. Uncommon, localised resident. Differs from the next species in heavy yellow bill with red tip, *pale rump and upper tail-coverts* and longer tail. Young birds have a dusky brown bill, are generally duller. Makes a hissing 'kuss, kuss' sound. Flocks are normally seen in association with buffalo, rhinoceros and domestic cattle. 22 cm.

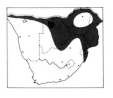

4 REDBILLED OXPECKER *Buphagus erythrorhynchus*. Common resident. Differs from the previous species in entirely red bill and *larger* yellow eye-wattle; does *not* have a pale rump. In young birds the bill is blackish, the gape yellow, general appearance duller. Makes a hissing 'churr', and a 'tzik, tzik' sound; most noisy when flying. Normally seen in association with giraffe or antelope in game reserves; in the remoter rural areas on domestic cattle. In the evenings flocks gather to roost on dead trees standing in water. 20-2 cm.

Sunbirds. Family NECTARINIIDAE. Small, insect and nectar-eating birds with down-curved bills adapted to flower-probing. Males with iridescent plumage and yellow, orange or red tufts (pectoral tufts) on the sides of the breast which are displayed in excitement. Some males undergo an annual 'eclipse' when they adopt a drab, non-breeding plumage resembling the normal plumage of the female. Young birds are as females, often with a dark throat. Their flight is swift and erratic, males spending much time chasing females and other males. Often gather in numbers when favoured nectar-rich plants are in blossom.

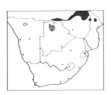

1 MALACHITE SUNBIRD *Nectarinia famosa*. Common resident. Breeding males entirely iridescent green except for blue-black wings and tail; non-breeding males yellow below, variably speckled overall with green feathers as illustrated; females told by large size and long bill. Call is 'chew-chew-chew, chi-chi-chi-chiew...chit-chit-chit...' with variations in speed and sequence; also a rapid warbling song. Usually found in groups on Macchia-covered hillsides (including suburbia in coastal regions), Karoo hills and montane foothills. Males frequently call from a high vantage-point and are highly aggressive towards other males. MM 25 cm. FF 15 cm.

2 COPPERY SUNBIRD *Nectarinia cuprea*. Uncommon, localised resident. Males differ from the next species in absence of long tail; females in clear, pale yellow underparts except for some speckling on the throat and upper breast. Has a harsh 'chit-chat' call and a high-pitched 'cher, cher, cher...' alarm note, plus a soft warbling song. Pairs occur in a variety of habitats including woodland, riverine forest, montane forest fringes, the edges of marshlands and suburbia. Sometimes roost in large groups. 12 cm.

3 BRONZE SUNBIRD *Nectarinia kilimensis*. Common localised resident. Males differ from males of the previous species in having long tail-shafts, females in having streaked underparts. Call is a shrill 'chee-oo, chee-oo' or 'pee-view, pee-view'. Pairs occur in montane grassland fringing forest and in woodland. MM 21 cm. FF 14 cm.

392

1 NEERGAARD'S SUNBIRD *Nectarinia neergaardi*. Uncommon, localised resident. Males distinguished from males of the next species by short bill, *blue* rump and narrower breast-band, from (3), (4) and (5) by *blackish* belly; females by short bill and *plain* yellow underparts. The ranges of this and the next species are mutually exclusive. Call unknown. Pairs, mostly in dry, mixed coastal woodland. 10 cm.

2 SHELLEY'S SUNBIRD *Nectarinia shelleyi*. Fairly common, localised resident. Males distinguished from males of the previous species by longer bill, green rump and wider breast-band, from (3), (4) and (5) by *blackish* belly; females by pale yellow underparts and streaked breast. The ranges of this and the previous species are mutually exclusive. The call is a rapidly repeated 'didi-didi', the song a nasal 'chibbee-cheeu-cheeu'. Pairs in broadleafed woodland, usually frequenting the tree canopies. 12.5 cm.

3 LESSER DOUBLECOLLARED SUNBIRD *Nectarinia chalybea*. Common resident. Males distinguished from the previous two species by longer bill and greyish (not black) belly, from the next species by *blue* rump and from (5) by shorter bill and narrower breast-band; females differ from females of the previous two species in having greyer, less yellow underparts, but distinguishable from the next species and from (5) by bill length only. Calls a harsh 'zzik-zzik' and a soft, abrupt 'swik, swik'; also has a high-pitched, swizzling song. Pairs in a variety of habitats from forest fringes to Karoo; a common garden species in many regions. 12.5 cm.

4 MIOMBO DOUBLECOLLARED SUNBIRD *Nectarinia manoensis*. Common resident. Males differ from the previous species only in grey rump and paler belly; females indistinguishable. Voice and behaviour as previous species. Pairs in Miombo and other broadleafed woodlands, montane forest fringes and suburbia. 13 cm.

5 GREATER DOUBLECOLLARED SUNBIRD *Nectarinia afra*. Common resident. Distinguished from the previous two species by larger size, longer bill; males by *broad* red breast-band. Song a loud, scratchy jumble of rapidly warbled notes frequently repeated. Pairs and small groups near coastal and montane forests plus coastal and valley bush, frequenting the fringes and canopies. 14 cm.

SUNBIRDS

1 WHITEBELLIED SUNBIRD *Nectarinia talatala*. Common resident. Males unique in having bright iridescent *blue-green* head, mantle, throat and breast and white underparts; cf. Dusky Sunbird (page 400). Female very similar to female Dusky Sunbird but underparts less clear white. Note that the immature male may have pale yellow underparts and blue throat-patch (see illustration on this page), then can be mistaken for the smaller Blue-throated Sunbird (page 400) in eastern regions where ranges of both species overlap. Has a loud, distinctive song, 'chu-ee, chu-ee, chuee-trrrrrr' repeated frequently. Pairs occur in mixed bush-veld, any woodland and in suburbia. Males are conspicuous from their habit of singing for long periods from a prominent perch. 11.5 cm.

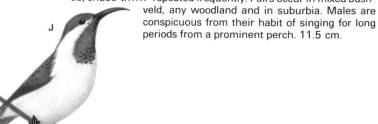

2 COLLARED SUNBIRD *Anthreptes collaris*. Common resident. Both sexes differ from the Bluethroated Sunbird (page 400) in *bright iridescent* green upperparts and rich yellow underparts, males in all-green heads and throats with blue and purple collar; from the next species by short bill and narrow collar. Song is a weak, cricket-like 'chirrreee, chirreee, chirreee', or a brisk 'tseep, t-t-t-t-t'. Pairs frequent the fringes of forests, riverine forests, coastal bush and valley bush, especially where flowering creepers are present. Often joins bird parties. 10 cm.

3 YELLOWBELLIED SUNBIRD *Nectarinia venusta*. Fairly common resident. Larger and longer-billed than the previous species, males more blue-green on the upperparts and with a *broad* purple breast-band; females differ from doublecollared sunbird females (previous page) in whiter breast and throat. Calls are 'tsiu-tse-tse' and an occasional trill, the song a rippling burst of twittering notes. Occurs on the fringes of forests, in riverine forests and patches of hillside bush, always preferring the lower scrubby vegetation and briar-bracken patches. 11 cm.

395

1 SCARLETCHESTED SUNBIRD *Nectarinia senegalensis*. Common resident. Males resemble only the next species but the large red breast-patch is diagnostic, as are the heavy dark markings of the females' underparts. Makes a high-pitched chattering sound and a much-repeated 'cheep, chip, chop' from a prominent perch. Pairs occur in a variety of habitats including bushveld, woodland, riverine forest and in suburbia where they are attracted to flowering creepers. A noisy, conspicuous species. 13-15 cm.

2 BLACK SUNBIRD *Nectarinia amethystina*. Common resident. Males lack the scarlet breast of the previous species, appearing all-black; females identified by creamy underparts and dusky throat with *pale yellow moustachial-streak*. Call, often given in flight, is 'tschiek' or 'zit'; also makes a stuttering 'chichichichi' and a pleasant, subdued warbling song uttered for long periods while concealed in foliage. Pairs and single birds occur in woodland, forest and riverine forest fringes, less often in bushveld, frequently in suburbia. Lively and conspicuous. 15 cm.

397

398

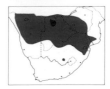

1 MARICO SUNBIRD *Nectarinia mariquensis*. Common resident. Males distinguished from males of the next species by larger size and longer, more curved bill; from Neergaard's Sunbird (page 392) also by these features plus *deep claret-red* (not bright red) breast-band; from the doublecollared sunbirds (page 392) by black belly. Female told by long bill, dusky throat and orange-yellow breast. Immature starts with yellow underparts and black bib (see illustration); as the yellow fades with ageing the plumage can resemble female Black Sunbird (page 396). The call is a brisk 'chip-chip' or a husky 'schitz-schitz' often given as a stuttering series. The song is a rapid warbling. Usually in pairs in mixed bushveld and dry thornveld. 13-14 cm.

2 PURPLEBANDED SUNBIRD *Nectarinia bifasciata*. Fairly common resident. Similar colouring to the previous species but much smaller, the bill short and only slightly curved; males differ from Neergaard's Sunbird (page 392) in having *deep claret-red* (not bright red) breast-bands. Call is a distinctive 'tsikit-y-dik' plus a trill, often by two birds in unison; the song is a high-pitched, descending trill. Pairs occur in riverine forest, the fringes of coastal evergreen forests, woodland, coastal bush and occasionally mangroves, preferring the denser thickets in all habitats. A restless, nomadic species. 10-11.5 cm.

3 VIOLETBACKED SUNBIRD *Anthreptes longuemarei*. Fairly common resident. The violet upperparts and white underparts of males and violet tail of females unmistakable. The call is a sharp 'chit' or 'skee'; the song undescribed. Pairs occur in broadleafed woodland where they frequent the tree canopies, feeding in the foliage and probing beneath loose bark; sometimes in groups on flowering trees. 12.5-14 cm.

1

♀

♂

♂ J

2

♀

♂

3

♂

♀

400

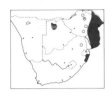

1 BLUETHROATED SUNBIRD *Anthreptes reichenowi.* Uncommon localised resident. Males identified by dark blue throat and forehead. Females resemble a white-eye (overleaf), but have slightly longer, slightly curved bills and no white eye-rings; both sexes have *dull olive-green* upperparts, not iridescent green as in the Collared Sunbird (page 394). Call is 'tik-tik'. Pairs occur in coastal, montane and riverine forests, feeding unobtrusively both in the upper and lower strata. 10 cm.

2 DUSKY SUNBIRD *Nectarinia fusca.* Common resident. Breeding male blackish with white belly, the breast with a coppery iridescence, pectoral tufts bright orange. Non-breeding male has dull brown upperparts, the underparts with an irregular blackish patch from chin to breast (see small illustration). Female smaller, underparts white; cf. female Whitebellied Sunbird (page 394). Has a loud warbling song reminiscent of a Whitebellied Sunbird 'chuee-chuee-trrrrr' and 'tiroo tiroo tiroo sweet sweet sweet' with variations. Occurs in pairs in Karoo and Kalahari scrub, the riverine growth of dry river courses and even on rocky outcrops almost devoid of vegetation. 10-12 cm.

3 ORANGEBREASTED SUNBIRD *Nectarinia violacea.* Common resident. Females differ from female Lesser Doublecollared Sunbird (page 392) in yellower underparts. Call is 'sshraynk' uttered one or more times; the song a subdued, high-pitched warbling. Pairs or loose parties occur on Macchia-covered coastal hillsides. Males indulge in much chasing with conspicuous aerial manoeuvres. MM 15 cm. FF 12 cm.

4 GREY SUNBIRD *Nectarinia veroxii.* Common resident. Sexes are alike. Southern race (a) with pink-grey underparts, northern race (b) with pale green-grey underparts. Calls are a husky 'zzip', or 'tsit-tswaysit' and similar brisk notes; the song is loud, starting with single slow syllables and speeding up to a stuttering finish, 'styeep-styip-styip-styip, yip, yip, yip, yip, yipyipyip . . .'. Pairs occur in coastal forests, riverine forests and valley bush, feeding in both upper and lower strata. When singing often flicks its wings and displays its pectoral tufts. 14 cm.

5 OLIVE SUNBIRD *Nectarinia olivacea.* Common resident. A large, dull sunbird. Sexes are alike. Southern race (a) with orange on throat and upper breast, northern races (b) smaller, much paler on underparts, no orange on throat. Calls a sharp 'tuk, tuk, tuk', sings a reedy 'tsee-tsee-tsee-tsee, tseedlee, eedlee-id-id-id-seedle . . .'. Singly or pairs in coastal and montane forests, mixed woodland, valley bush, riverine forests and suburban gardens. 13-15 cm,

White-eyes. Family ZOSTEROPIDAE. Very small, yellow-green birds, which glean insects from leaves and probe flowers for nectar. Unless breeding, occur in flocks which go from tree to tree where they search the foliage closely, frequently in the inverted position. Young birds are duller and lack white eye-wattles initially.

1 CAPE WHITE-EYE *Zosterops pallidus.* Very common, endemic resident. Three basic colour forms occur as illustrated, with intergrading between each: (a) in southern and western Cape with grey underparts; (b) in eastern regions and highveld with greener underparts; (c) in Orange River to western regions with paler underparts and flanks washed cinnamon. Normal call is a continual melancholy 'phe' by several in a party; also sings a loud rambling song from tree-tops in summer, plus a subdued warbling song from the depths of bushes. Gregarious, flocks occurring in almost any well-wooded habitat, including gardens. 12 cm.

2 YELLOW WHITE-EYE *Zosterops senegalensis*. Common resident. Distinguished from all forms of the previous species by clear yellow underparts and more yellow-green upperparts. The calls resemble those of the Cape White-eye. Occurs in riverine forest, forests, broadleafed woodland (Miombo), exotic plantations and suburbia. Behaviour and habits as for the previous species. 10.5 cm.

Weavers, sparrows and allies. Family PLOCEIDAE. A very large group of conical-billed, mainly seedeating birds. Many breed colonially and weave complicated nests which help in identification. See nest drawings on pages 414-15.

3 REDHEADED QUELEA *Quelea erythrops*. Uncommon to locally common resident. Differs from the Redbilled Quelea (overleaf) in brownish-horn bill of both sexes, entirely red head of males and more ochreous colouring of females; males distinguished from male Redheaded Finches (page 428) by very small size and lack of 'scaly' appearance on underparts. Young resemble females. No distinctive call, flocks make a twittering sound. In flocks, often with other small seedeaters, in damp grasslands, marshes and woodland where they feed on grass seeds. Irregular and nomadic. 11.5 cm.

CARDINAL QUELEA *Quelea cardinalis*. Status uncertain. Similar to the previous species, but red of head extends onto the breast. May possibly occur in the middle Zambezi Valley. 13 cm.

1 YELLOWTHROATED SPARROW *Petronia superciliaris*. Fairly common resident. Yellow breast-spot *not* a field character. Best identified by *broad white eyebrows*; cf. Streakyheaded Canary (page 438) which also has broad white eyebrows, but lacks the white wing-bars of this sparrow. Usual call a rapid 'chree-chree-chree-chree'. Usually in pairs, frequenting tall woodland, thornveld and mixed bushveld. Frequently common around villages and camps. On the ground it walks, rather than hops like other sparrows. 15-16 cm.

2 GREYHEADED SPARROW *Passer griseus*. Common resident. Identified by entirely grey head and single white wing-bar; bill black when breeding, otherwise horn-coloured. Sexes are alike. Immatures are more streaked on mantle. Makes a repetitive 'cheep-chirp', the first note descending, the second ascending, plus an occasional trill. Pairs occur in summer, small flocks in winter, in various wooded habitats including thornveld and mixed bushveld but not forests. Common in many towns and generally frequents the larger trees, feeding on the ground. 15-16 cm.

3 HOUSE SPARROW *Passer domesticus*. Very common resident. Males distinguished by grey cap and black bib; cf. larger, brighter Great Sparrow (overleaf). Females and immatures differ from the previous species in having white eyebrows and much paler colouring. The call is 'chissip' or 'chee-ip'. Pairs and small parties occur in association with human habitation, breeding under the eaves of houses. An introduced species now found in most towns and small settlements, even isolated permanent camps. Distribution patchy but widespread. 14-15 cm.

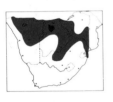

4 REDBILLED BUFFALO WEAVER *Bubalornis niger*. Fairly common resident. Distinctive blackish birds with red bills, plus white feathers on the flanks and shoulders. Immatures are greyish with much mottling on sides of head and underparts, the bill initially horn-coloured, then dull yellow, then orange. Makes chattering sounds at the nest plus a mellow trill, 'triddlyoo-triddlyoo-triddlyoo-triddlyoo'. Pairs and small flocks in thornveld and mixed bushveld, especially in the drier regions, in association with baobab trees and large *Acacia* trees in which they build their communal nests (see illustration on page 414). Patchily distributed and nomadic when not breeding. 24 cm.

5 REDBILLED QUELEA *Quelea quelea*. Common to locally abundant resident. Breeding male variable as illustrated; breeding female has yellow bill. Non-breeding birds all have red bills. Occurs in flocks and is nomadic when not breeding, mainly in dry thornveld and mixed bushveld. Flocks make a twittering when flying and nesting. Breeding colonies usually large, involving tens of thousands, and cover many hectares of bush. Flying flocks resemble columns of smoke. 13 cm.

406

1 SCALYFEATHERED FINCH (SCALY WEAVER) *Sporopipes squamifrons*. Common resident. Identified by very small size, pink bill, 'bearded' appearance and black wing-feathers boldly edged with white. Sexes are alike. Immatures are much duller, bill horn-coloured. When disturbed, fly off making a chattering sound. Small parties are found in the drier thornveld regions, often around human settlements, frequenting fowl-runs, gardens and camps. 10 cm.

2 SOCIABLE WEAVER *Philetairus socius*. Common resident. Pale beak offset by black face and throat diagnostic; a small, pallid, highly gregarious weaver. Sexes are alike. Immatures are similar. Groups make an excitable twittering at the nest. Flocks occur in the vicinity of their communal nests in the dry western regions. The huge nests are placed in a large tree, frequently a thorn, and accommodate many pairs of birds for both breeding and roosting. 14 cm.

3 CAPE SPARROW *Passer melanurus*. Very common resident. Black-and-white head and breast pattern of males distinctive, females distinguished from female House Sparrow (previous page) by richer colouring, greyer head and *black bill*. Immatures resemble females. Normal call 'chirrup' or 'chissik'. Usually seen near human habitation. When not breeding, flocks occur in farmlands and cattle kraals. Tame and confiding. 15 cm.

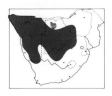

4 GREAT SPARROW *Passer motitensis*. Uncommon resident. Most resembles House Sparrow (previous page) but larger, more brightly coloured. The call is a typical sparrow 'chirrup, chirroo, t-t-t-t-t'. Pairs occur in dry thornveld regions, *seldom near human settlements*, differing in this respect from the House and Cape Sparrows. 15-16 cm.

5 WHITEBROWED SPARROW-WEAVER *Plocepasser mahali*. Common resident. Distinguished by bold white eyebrow and, in flight, by white rump and uppertail-coverts; also occurs with pure white underparts. Sexes are alike. Immatures have horn-coloured bills. Call is a harsh 'chick-chick' and also a loud, rambling song of liquid notes, 'cheeoo-preeoo-chop-chop-, cheeoo-trroo-cheeoo-preeoo-chop-chip...'. Pairs and loose flocks are found in dry thornveld, usually near the trees containing their nests. Conspicuous and active, nest-building at all times of year. 18 cm.

Weaver nest illustrations will be found on pages 414-15.

1 CHESTNUT WEAVER *Ploceus rubiginosus*. Uncommon, localised summer resident. Females and non-breeding males best identified by *grey bill* and brownish (not greenish) colouring. Call is a swizzling sound like the Cape Weaver (3). Usually in flocks, females outnumbering males while breeding, frequenting thornveld in the arid north-western regions of Namibia. 14-15 cm.

2 FOREST WEAVER *Ploceus bicolor*. Common, localised resident. Adults maintain same plumage all year. Immatures are very similar. Call is a very high-pitched series of pleasant notes, 'fee, fee-fee-fo-feee, fo-fo-fo-fwee...' with variations. Singly or in pairs in coastal and inland forests, riverine forests and valley bush. A quiet species which creeps about branches and probes beneath bark in search of insects. 16 cm.

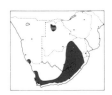

3 CAPE WEAVER *Ploceus capensis*. Common resident. Breeding males distinguished from female Spectacled Weaver (overleaf) by large size and black eye-line not extending behind the eye; non-breeding males like females but yellower on underparts and with pale eye. Females distinguished from female Masked or Lesser Masked Weavers (page 412) by larger size and heavier, more sharply pointed bill. The normal sound in the vicinity of nests when breeding is a rapidly repeated swizzling, 'a-zwit, a-zwit, zweeeeee-zt-zt-zt-zt...', similar to that of Masked and Spottedbacked Weavers but harsher. Singly, in pairs or flocks almost anywhere where there are trees, especially near water and in suburbia where exotic trees are used for nesting. 16-18 cm.

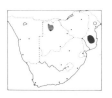

4 OLIVEHEADED WEAVER *Ploceus olivaceiceps*. Uncommon, localised resident. Unmistakable within its restricted range and preferred habitat; females have the entire head olive. The song is 'tzee-twa-twa-twa-twa'. Usually in pairs in broadleafed (Miombo) woodland where it feeds on insects in the tree canopies, often in bird parties. 14.5 cm.

WEAVERS

Weaver nest illustrations will be found on pages 414-15.

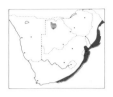

1 YELLOW WEAVER *Ploceus subaureus*. Common resident. Palest yellow of the yellow weavers, upperparts slightly greener when not breeding. Immatures resemble females. Makes a harsh 'zik' and a soft swizzling sound. Pairs and flocks are found on the eastern coastal and littoral zones, moving inland along rivers to the eastern Transvaal, breeding in reed-beds and trees on rivers and lagoons, when not breeding in riverine bush and adjacent woodland. 16 cm.

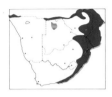

2 SPECTACLED WEAVER *Ploceus ocularis*. Common resident. Distinguished by pale eyes and black streak through eyes to ear-coverts, males with additional black bib; cf. Cape Weaver (previous page). Immatures have horn-coloured bills. Call is a good identification character, a descending 'tee-tee-tee-tee-tee-tee-tee'. Pairs occur in riverine forests, fringes of lowland and coastal forests, in thornveld around pans and vleis, around farmsteads and in suburbia. Not a social weaver. 15-16 cm.

3 BROWNTHROATED WEAVER (BROWNTHROATED GOLDEN WEAVER) *Ploceus xanthopterus*. Uncommon or locally common resident. A small, short-tailed weaver, males with brown patch on throat and lores, females with pale bills; cf. Yellow Weaver (1) and Cape Weaver (previous page). Pairs and flocks occur in large reed-beds over water when breeding, in adjacent riverine forests and thickets when not breeding. Mostly on the east coast and littoral, the Zambezi River and Okavango Delta. Seldom far from water or swamps. 15 cm.

4 GOLDEN WEAVER *Ploceus xanthops*. Uncommon to locally common resident. A large yellow weaver with heavy bill and pale eyes, males even yellower when not breeding; cf. smaller Yellow Weaver (1). Immatures are like females but greener above, more streaked. Makes a harsh chirp and a prolonged swizzling. In pairs or small flocks in reeds and thickets on rivers and marshes at all altitudes, less gregarious when breeding. Sparse in the south. 18 cm.

5 THICKBILLED WEAVER *Amblyospiza albifrons*. Common resident. Heavy bill diagnostic. Immatures are like females, bill yellower. Nesting birds make a monotonous chattering, males occasionally sing an almost musical song. Pairs and small parties occur in reed-beds and the bush adjacent to rivers, pans and swamps when breeding; at other times coastal bush, forest fringes, riverine forests and wooded valleys. 18 cm.

Weaver nest illustrations will be found on pages 414-15.

1 MASKED WEAVER *Ploceus velatus*. Common resident. Breeding males distinguished from the next species by *red eyes* and more yellow crown (black mask extends across forehead only), from (3) by plain back and black forehead. Non-breeding males resemble females. Breeding females with slightly more yellow underparts and redder eyes. Immatures are duller, greyer on underparts. Makes prolonged swizzling sounds when breeding plus a sharp 'zik'. Gregarious at all times, small parties and flocks in thornveld, riverine bush, exotic trees around homesteads and farms. Breeds in small colonies in trees away from water, commonly in suburbia, or in large colonies in waterside bushes and reeds. Nomadic when not breeding, often in farmlands. 15 cm.

2 LESSER MASKED WEAVER *Ploceus intermedius*. Fairly common, localised resident. Breeding males differ from males of the previous species and next species in having *pale yellow* eyes and black mask extending over the top of the head; females more yellow at all times. Immatures are like females but whitish on belly. Makes swizzling sounds typical of most weavers, especially when nesting. Occurs in thornveld, mixed bushveld and riverine forests, being attracted to *Acacia* trees or reeds when breeding; colonies often large and sometimes with the previous or next species. 15 cm.

3 SPOTTEDBACKED WEAVER *Ploceus cucullatus*. Common resident. Breeding males identified by spotted back and, in the northern race (a), by entirely black head; in the southern race (b) by the *clear yellow crown* with black only on face and throat; eyes red. Females have yellow breasts and white underparts plus brown eyes. Non-breeding males like females but retain the red eyes. Breeds in colonies, often large, in thorn trees overhanging water, sometimes in reeds or away from water in exotic trees at farms and in suburbia. Males display by hanging beneath the nests, swinging from side to side with quivering wings while making husky swizzling sounds. Nomadic in flocks when not breeding. 17 cm.

4 REDHEADED WEAVER *Anaplectes rubriceps*. Fairly common resident. Breeding males with red heads and mantles, non-breeding males and immatures like females. Normally silent but make a squeaky chattering at the nest. Pairs or males with several females occur in broadleafed woodland and thornveld, breeding in isolation. Nomadic when not breeding. 15 cm.

413

♂ Br   ♀ N-Br   1

♂ Br   ♀   2

a   b   ♀ N-Br
♂ Br   3

♂ Br   ♀   4

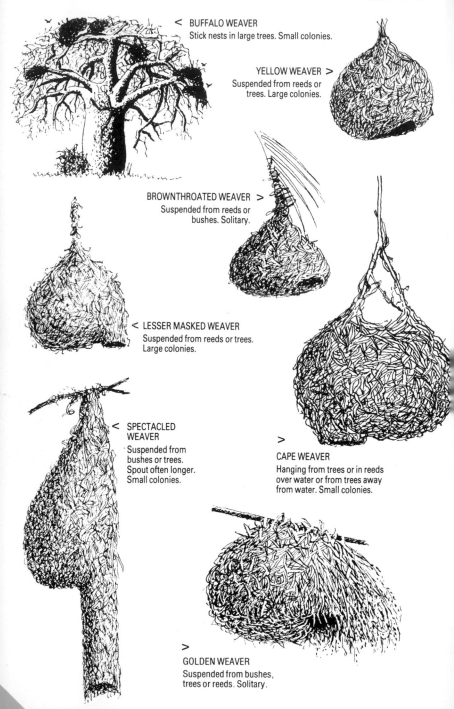

< BUFFALO WEAVER
Stick nests in large trees. Small colonies.

YELLOW WEAVER >
Suspended from reeds or trees. Large colonies.

BROWNTHROATED WEAVER >
Suspended from reeds or bushes. Solitary.

< LESSER MASKED WEAVER
Suspended from reeds or trees. Large colonies.

< SPECTACLED WEAVER
Suspended from bushes or trees. Spout often longer. Small colonies.

>
CAPE WEAVER
Hanging from trees or in reeds over water or from trees away from water. Small colonies.

>
GOLDEN WEAVER
Suspended from bushes, trees or reeds. Solitary.

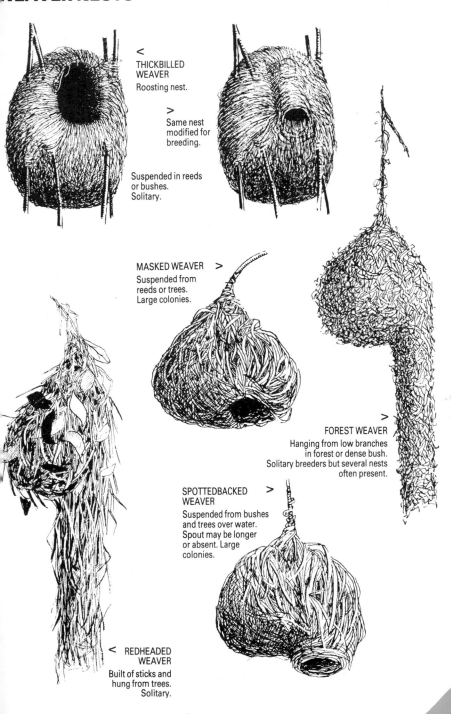

< THICKBILLED
WEAVER
Roosting nest.

> Same nest
modified for
breeding.

Suspended in reeds
or bushes.
Solitary.

MASKED WEAVER >
Suspended from
reeds or trees.
Large colonies.

> FOREST WEAVER
Hanging from low branches
in forest or dense bush.
Solitary breeders but several nests
often present.

SPOTTEDBACKED >
WEAVER
Suspended from bushes
and trees over water.
Spout may be longer
or absent. Large
colonies.

< REDHEADED
WEAVER
Built of sticks and
hung from trees.
Solitary.

416

Widowbirds and bishopbirds. Reed- and grass-loving weavers, differing from other Ploceidae in that males are predominantly black when breeding, some with long tails, and habitually puff out their plumage in display. Non-breeding males resemble females, as do immatures. Thin, ball-type nests are placed in grass or reeds.

1 REDSHOULDERED WIDOW *Euplectes axillaris*. Common resident. Breeding males identified by short tail and red shoulders. Males make a husky 'tseek, wirra, wirra, wirra, wirra' when displaying. Occurs in grass and coarse vegetation fringing marshes, riverine reed-beds and papyrus, cultivated fields and fallow lands and, in Natal, canefields. In summer males fly about conspicuously over their territories, otherwise inconspicuous and in flocks. 19 cm.

2 REDCOLLARED WIDOW *Euplectes ardens*. Common, localised resident. Breeding males have red collar only, much smaller than the Longtailed Widow (overleaf), tail thinner. When displaying, males make a weak 'kizz-zizz-zizz-zizz'. In well-grassed bushveld, vleis, streams, rank grass in old cultivations and on hillsides. In summer males fly about with spread tail or perch conspicuously on bushes. 15-40 cm.

3 WHITEWINGED WIDOW *Euplectes albonotatus*. Common resident. Breeding males are recognised by yellow and white wings, bluish bill and broad tail frequently fanned. Makes a twittering sound when displaying. Frequents marshes or damp vleis in otherwise dry thornveld and mixed bushveld, also rank vegetation bordering cultivations. Males display and perch conspicuously during summer. 15-19 cm.

4 RED BISHOP *Euplectes orix*. Common resident. Breeding males could be mistaken in north-eastern regions for next species which has an entirely red crown. In summer males call a wheezy, spluttering 'zik-zik-zik...zayzayzayzazay'. Occurs in flocks in association with reeds, rank grassland and cultivations; common in vleis. In summer males display by puffing out their plumage while perched or flying over their territory, usually several visible at a time (see illustration). In winter form flocks and are nomadic. 14 cm.

FIRECROWNED BISHOP (BLACK-WINGED BISHOP) *Euplectes hordeaceus*. Fairly common, localised resident. Breeding males differ from the previous species in entirely red crown plus longer, blacker wings (illustration, left); non-breeding males and females also distinguished by blacker wings. Behaviour and habitat very similar to the Red Bishop but usually occurs in pairs. Found in eastern Zimbabwe and Mozambique. 13-15 cm.

5 GOLDEN BISHOP *Euplectes afer*. Common resident. Breeding males conspicuous, displaying by flying about puffed up with rapidly whirring wings while making various buzzing sounds. Found in vleis, near dams, in grassland and cultivations when breeding, otherwise in nomadic flocks which wander widely, often with other weavers. 12 cm.

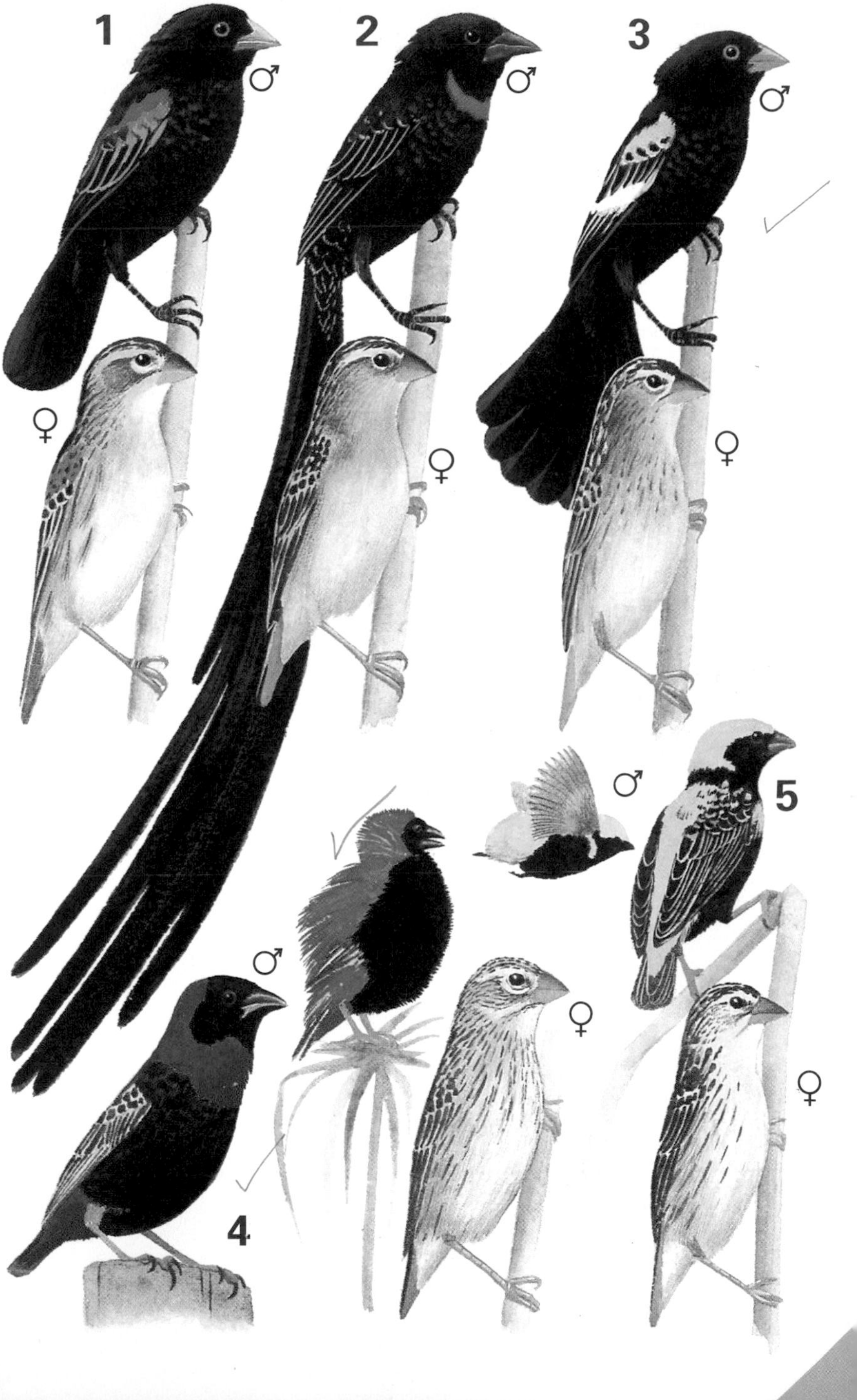
1
♂
♀
2
♂
♀
3
♂
♀
4
♂
♀
5
♂
♀

1 LONGTAILED WIDOW *Euplectes progne*. Common resident. Breeding males have the tail longer and fuller than Red-collared Widow (previous page), red shoulder-patch and pale bill good field features. Non-breeding males have same wing-pattern, are much larger than females and all others in this group. Females and immatures normally seen in flocks with males. Normal call is a repeated 'chip...chip...chip...'; while breeding the males have a subdued, swizzling song. A grassland species, especially in vleis and valleys with richer growth. When breeding (summer) females are inconspicuous but males perch prominently on a tall weed near the nest, or patrol their territory in low flight, wings flapping slowly and deliberately. When not breeding, form flocks, often mixing with other grassland seedeaters. MM 19-60 cm. FF 15 cm.

2 YELLOWRUMPED WIDOW (CAPE BISHOP) *Euplectes capensis*. Common resident. Non-breeding males resemble females but *retain the yellow rump and shoulders*. Females and immatures have dull yellow rumps. Breeding males call 'skeet' from the top of a tree. Family groups or flocks (when not breeding) in vleis and marshy regions near streams in foothills and bracken slopes near montane forests and plantations. Displaying males make audible wing-flutters both at rest and in flight. At these times the plumage is puffed out, the yellow rump conspicuous. 15 cm.

3 YELLOWBACKED WIDOW *Euplectes macrourus*. Locally common resident. Breeding males with *yellow shoulders and back*, cf. previous species from which it is also identified by longer tail. Non-breeding males resemble females but retain *yellow shoulders*, distinguished from Whitewinged Widow (previous page) by lack of white in wings. Immatures resemble females. Call is a thin buzzing sound. Occurs in grassland near water. Breeding males display with a jerky flight, the tail jerking up and down. When not breeding form flocks, often with other grassland species. 14-22 cm.

Finches, waxbills, twinspots, mannikins, etc. Family ESTRILDIDAE. Small, conical-billed, ground- or grass-feeding seed-eaters. Mostly colourful; gregarious when not breeding.

1 MELBA FINCH *Pytilia melba.* Common resident. Both sexes differ from the next species in having black-and-white barred underparts, all-green wings and longer, predominantly red bills. Usual call a single, low 'wick'; also makes a plaintive whistle and has an attractive short song. Pairs frequent thorny thickets, often near water, and associate with other waxbills and firefinches, feeding on open ground. 12-13 cm.

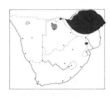

2 GOLDENBACKED PYTILIA *Pytilia afra.* Locally common resident. Differs from the previous species mainly in the underparts being barred green (not black) and in having orange-edged wing-feathers, which appear as an *orange patch on the folded wing;* the bill is shorter and mostly brown on the upper mandible. Call is a single, flat 'seee' and a two-note, piping whistle. Behaviour and habitat preferences very similar to the last species. 11 cm.

3 REDFACED CRIMSONWING *Cryptospiza reichenowii.* Rare, localised resident. Distinctive dark green birds with deep crimson wings and back, thus differing from the next species which is predominantly brown; males only have a red mask. The call is a high-pitched 'zeet'; also has a descending song of four notes followed by a chirp. A very shy, mostly silent species of forests. Small parties feed on the ground in dense shade by forest streams and at forest edges, seldom flying more than a few metres when disturbed. 12 cm.

4 NYASA SEEDCRACKER *Pyrenestes minor.* Uncommon, localised resident. Males have a larger area of red which extends to the breast. Differs from the previous species in being generally earth-brown (not green) and lacking red wings. Call is 'tzeet', plus a sharp clicking when alarmed. Pairs frequent thick woodland along streams or forest edges, preferring hilly regions with a high rainfall. Stays low down in the vegetation but not in dense cover. 13 cm.

1 BROWN FIREFINCH *Lagonosticta nitidula.* Fairly common, localised resident. Might be confused with the next species, but the red is confined to the face, throat and upper breast; *the rump has no red.* Sexes are similar. Call is a flat, unmusical 'tsiep, tsiep' or 'chick, chick'. Occurs in thickets and reeds near water in the extreme north of our region. Is host to the Violet Widowfinch (page 434). 10 cm.

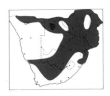

2 REDBILLED FIREFINCH *Lagonosticta senegala.* Common resident. Both sexes have red rumps (cf. previous species), males with more extensive red on head and underparts. Distinguished from other firefinches by reddish bill or, in mixed parties, by the grey-brown females. The call is a nasal 'fweet, fweet'. Occurs in pairs or small parties in mixed bushveld, especially near watercourses and, in the north, in suburbia. Is host to the Steelblue Widowfinch (page 434). 10 cm.

3 BLUEBILLED FIREFINCH *Lagonosticta rubricata.* Common resident. The bill appears black in the field. Identified by *grey crown and nape* plus blackish belly in the male; Zimbabwe birds have crown and nape grey *washed with pink*, but differ from the next species in distinctly browner wings and mantle. Has a trilling, bell-like call involving 'chit-chit-chit' sounds and ending with 'wink-wink-wink'; also a stuttering alarm call. Pairs and small parties found in dense bushveld, forest edges and in thorn and grass tangles. Is host to the Black Widowfinch (page 434). 11 cm.

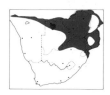

4 JAMESON'S FIREFINCH *Lagonosticta rhodopareia.* Common resident. The reddest firefinch; bill blackish in both sexes. Male has the crown, nape and mantle washed pink, rest of upperparts less dark than (3), underparts rose-pink. Female more orange-pink on underparts. Immature male (see below) more uniformly brown above, below rose-pink with a brownish wash on lateral breast. Has a tinkling 'trrr-trrr' alarm note plus various musical calls 'tewee-tewee . . .' or 'fweeee' or 'zik, zik'. Frequents thickets and rank grass in thornveld, and riparian and secondary growth around cultivated lands. Is host to the Purple Widowfinch (page 434). 11 cm.

J ♂

4

424

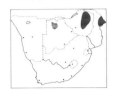

1 LOCUST FINCH *Ortygospiza locustella*. Common, localised resident and visitor. Very small, ground-feeding birds, females have much darker upperparts than the next species, and orange edges to wing-feathers. Call is a querulous 'pink-pink'. Frequents wet grasslands in dense flocks except when breeding (late summer). Flocks usually fly only a short distance before resettling, but flight fast and dipping. 9 cm.

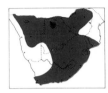

2 QUAIL FINCH *Ortygospiza atricollis*. Common resident. Differs from the previous species in paler, less striking colouring, well-banded breast and flanks, plus white facial markings. Call is a querulous, metallic 'tirrilink', given in flight and often the only clue to the species' presence. Pairs or small parties frequent grasslands, especially over-grazed regions, pan-fringes and other damp localities. Occasionally take off in brief flight, suddenly descending again. In courtship individual males tower to a great height and then descend like a falling object while making a clicking sound; cf. cloud cisticolas (page 350). 9.5 cm.

3 GREEN TWINSPOT *Mandingoa nitidula*. Uncommon resident. Mature adults differ from other small green birds in having white-spotted underparts, but in immature plumage are plain green. Call is a chirping 'tzeet', and also has a subdued song. An elusive, shy species which frequents the edges of forests and coastal bush, feeding in areas of open ground, but darting into thick cover if disturbed. 10 cm.

4 PINKTHROATED TWINSPOT *Hypargos margaritatus*. Common localised resident. Most resembles the next species, but red colouring of males *dull rose pink*, not deep crimson; females have only rump and tail pink. Call is a trilling 'tit-it-it-it-it-it-it' or 'trrr-it'. Pairs or small groups frequent dense, tangled scrub in patches of open ground and forest fringes, darting into cover when alarmed. 12 cm.

5 REDTHROATED TWINSPOT *Hypargos niveoguttatus*. Common localised resident. Males differ from the previous species in *deep crimson* colouring; females by more rusty breast. Call is a stuttering, grasshopper-like trill 'trree-rree'. Pairs and small parties in open ground near forests, dense bush, streams or in dry, open country. 12.5 cm.

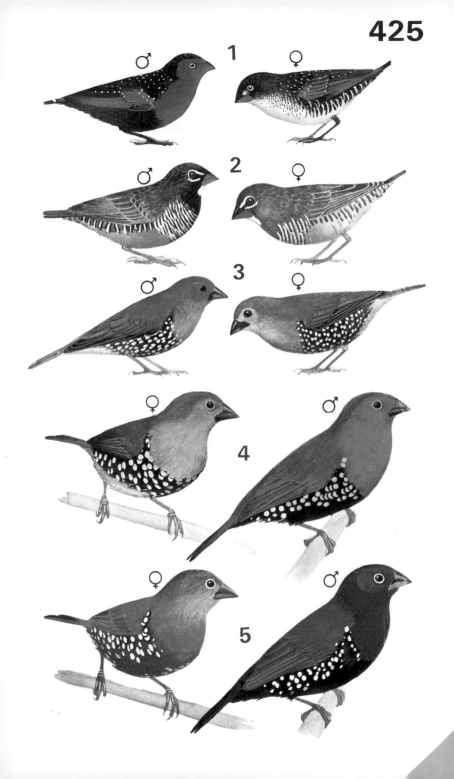

426

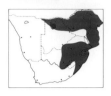

1 ORANGEBREASTED WAXBILL *Sporaeginthus subflavus*. Common resident. The male's orange breast variable in extent, sometimes absent. Immatures are like females but bill black. Call is a quiet, metallic tinkling often made in flight. Pairs and small flocks occur in waterside grass and reeds, especially in vleis and other marshy regions plus cultivated fields. Very active, mobile little birds, which make off in straggling sequence at low height, then suddenly drop down again. 8.5-9 cm.

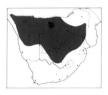

2 BLACKCHEEKED WAXBILL *Estrilda erythronotos*. Fairly common resident. Females are slightly duller, less red. Immatures are like females. Call is an ascending 'fwooee'. Pairs or flocks occur when not breeding. In dry thornveld and, in the Transvaal, also on the slopes of the eastern escarpment in mistbelt conditions. Feeds mainly on the ground but flies into trees if disturbed. Seldom plentiful and probably nomadic much of the year. 12-13 cm.

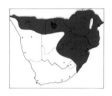

3 BLUE WAXBILL *Uraeginthus angolensis*. Very common resident. Immatures paler than females, bills black. Calls frequently on the ground and in flight, a high-pitched 'weet-weet'. Pairs and small parties, frequently with other small seedeaters, in dry thornveld, often in dry watercourses, bare patches of ground under bushes and in kraals, flying into bushes when disturbed. 12-14 cm.

4 COMMON WAXBILL *Estrilda astrild.* Very common resident. Red bill, facial skin and under-belly distinctive; immatures have blackish bills. The call is 'chik-chik-ZEEE, chik-chik-ZEEE', descending on the third syllable. Small or large flocks in grassy riverbanks, reed-beds, vleis and rank vegetation bordering cultivated lands. Very active birds, flocks always flying off in straggling procession from place to place. Feeds on the ground and on seeding grasses. 13 cm.

5 VIOLETEARED WAXBILL *Uraeginthus granatinus*. Common resident. A long-tailed species. In flight the tail appears broad. Immatures are duller than females. The often-repeated call is 'tiu-woowee'. Pairs, often in company with Blue Waxbills (3), in dry thornveld, especially sandveld. Feeds on the ground, flying into bushes when disturbed. 13-15 cm.

1 SWEE WAXBILL *Estrilda melanotis*. Common resident. The ranges of this and the next species are mutually exclusive. The crimson rump and upper tail-coverts, and the yellow belly are distinctive in the field. Usual call is a soft 'swee-swee'. Inconspicuous little birds which occur in flocks, feeding in tall grass near forest fringes and thick bush, in montane regions usually near wooded streams. When flushed the flock makes off, calling, and settles briefly in a bush before again flying to feed in the grass. 9-10 cm.

2 EAST AFRICAN SWEE *Estrilda quartinia*. Uncommon, localised resident. Both sexes are identical to the female of the previous species; often regarded as a race of that species. Habits, habitat and voice identical. 10 cm.

3 GREY WAXBILL *Estrilda perreini*. Uncommon resident. Similar to the next species but darker grey with a black bill, no red on the flanks. The only grey waxbill likely to be seen in Southern Africa becoming darker grey in northern races. Call is a thin 'pseeu, pseeu'. An inconspicuous species of woodland and open forest where thick bush tangles with tall grass. Usually in pairs, which seldom venture far from dense cover. 11 cm.

4 CINDERELLA WAXBILL *Estrilda thomensis*. Fairly common, localised resident. Superficially resembles the previous species, but the grey is paler with a rosy flush on the upperparts and belly; the bill is red with a black tip, the flanks red and black. Small parties occur along the Cunene River in northern Namibia. Behaviour and voice not recorded. 11 cm.

5 CUTTHROAT FINCH *Amadina fasciata*. Common resident. Females have a generally scaly appearance with a pale bill, smaller and darker than females of the next species. A thin 'eee-eee-eee' call is made in flight. In pairs when nesting, otherwise in flocks in dry thornveld, often near villages and cultivations. 12 cm.

6 REDHEADED FINCH *Amadina erythrocephala*. Common resident. Larger than the previous species, males with an entirely red head, females paler, plainer on the upperparts, lightly barred below, bill dark horn. Call a distinctive double-note, 'chuck-chuck'. Mostly seen in small flocks in dry thornveld or grasslands, feeding on the ground, often with other species. A frequent visitor to waterholes. 12-13 cm.

430

1 BRONZE MANNIKIN *Spermestes cucullatus*. Very common resident. Adults differ from the next species in earth-brown upperparts grading to blackish over the head, face, throat and upper breast, all blackish areas washed with bottle-green or bronze, some bottle-green feathers present on the mantle, the bill with dark upper mandible. Immatures are as illustrated, upperparts less rufous than immatures of (2), bill all-dark. Call is a wheezy 'chik, chik, chikka'. Found in a wide variety of mixed grass and bushveld, forest fringes, coastal scrub and old cultivated lands. Very small, highly gregarious birds. Feed in flocks, clambering about grass stems to obtain the seeds; when flushed all fly into a bush, eventually returning to feed in one's and two's. 9 cm.

2 REDBACKED MANNIKIN *Spermestes bicolor*. Fairly common resident. Differs from the previous species in having red-brown upperparts and more extensive area of black over the sides of head and breast; bill uniform blue-grey. Immatures are duller. Makes a clear whistling note in flight. Small flocks occur in open bushveld and coastal dune forests, feeding on the seeds of grasses. 9.5-10 cm.

3 PIED MANNIKIN *Spermestes fringilloides*. Uncommon resident. Much larger than the previous two species, with distinctly pied appearance and heavy black bill. Immatures also told by robust build and black bill. Makes a chirruping 'pee-oo-pee-oo'. Small flocks in clearings in coastal bush and riverine woodland, usually near bamboo thickets. Behaviour much as for (1) and (2). 12-13 cm.

Cuckoo finch. Family PLOCEIDAE (pages 402-12).

4 CUCKOO FINCH *Anomalospiza imberbis*. Fairly common resident. Adults most resemble one of the yellow weavers (pages 408-12), but the black bill is shorter and stouter. Juveniles (a) and immatures (b) have a two-coloured bill and more orange-brown appearance. Males call 'tsileu, tsileu, tsileu' or, in display, make a weaver-like swizzling. Usually in small flocks in grassland, or grassland with scattered bushes. Unlike other weavers, is a brood-parasite parasitising small warblers; see pages 432-4. 12-13 cm.

Whydahs and widowfinches. Family VIDUIDAE. Small, ground-feeding, seedeating finches, which are brood parasites, laying their eggs in the nests of waxbills. Male whydahs in breeding plumage have very long tails, different in all species, and when not breeding they resemble the confusingly similar females. At times males may be seen in transient plumage with traces of the breeding colours visible. Immatures are very plainly coloured and are probably indistinguishable. See overleaf for description of widowfinches.

1 PINTAILED WHYDAH *Vidua macroura*. Common resident. Breeding males distinctive; the red bill is retained in non-breeding plumage. Courting males hover over the females, describing a circle in the vertical plane, while calling a continuous wispy 'peetzy-peetzy-peetzy . . .'. In normal flight calls 'tseet-tseet-tseet'. Males are pugnacious, chasing other small birds and dominating food sources. Usually in parties, one male and several females, which frequent a wide variety of habitats including suburbia. Parasitises the Common Waxbill (page 426). 12-34 cm.

2 PARADISE WHYDAH *Vidua paradisea*. Common resident. Distinctive plumage of breeding males (a) similar only to the Broadtailed Paradise Whydah (overleaf), but differs in *tapering* tail-feathers; transitional plumage (b) frequently seen. Females and non-breeding males have whiter head-stripes than previous species. Has a short sparrow-like song and utters an occasional 'chit'. Small flocks mainly in thornveld. Breeding males have a display flight in which the two short tail-feathers are held erect; see illustration overleaf. Also hover over females in slow, bobbing flight causing the tail to undulate. Parasitises the Melba Finch (page 420). 12-38 cm.

3 SHAFTTAILED WHYDAH *Vidua regia*. Common resident. Breeding males distinguished by colour of underparts plus tail-shafts with *bulbous ends*. Females and non-breeding males have less distinctive head-markings than other whydahs. The voice is 'chit-chit-chit . . .'. Singly or in small flocks, females predominating, in dry thornveld, sandveld with sparse vegetation and grassland with scattered thornbush. Males chase other small birds at feeding assemblies. Parasitises the Violeteared Waxbill (page 426). 12-34 cm.

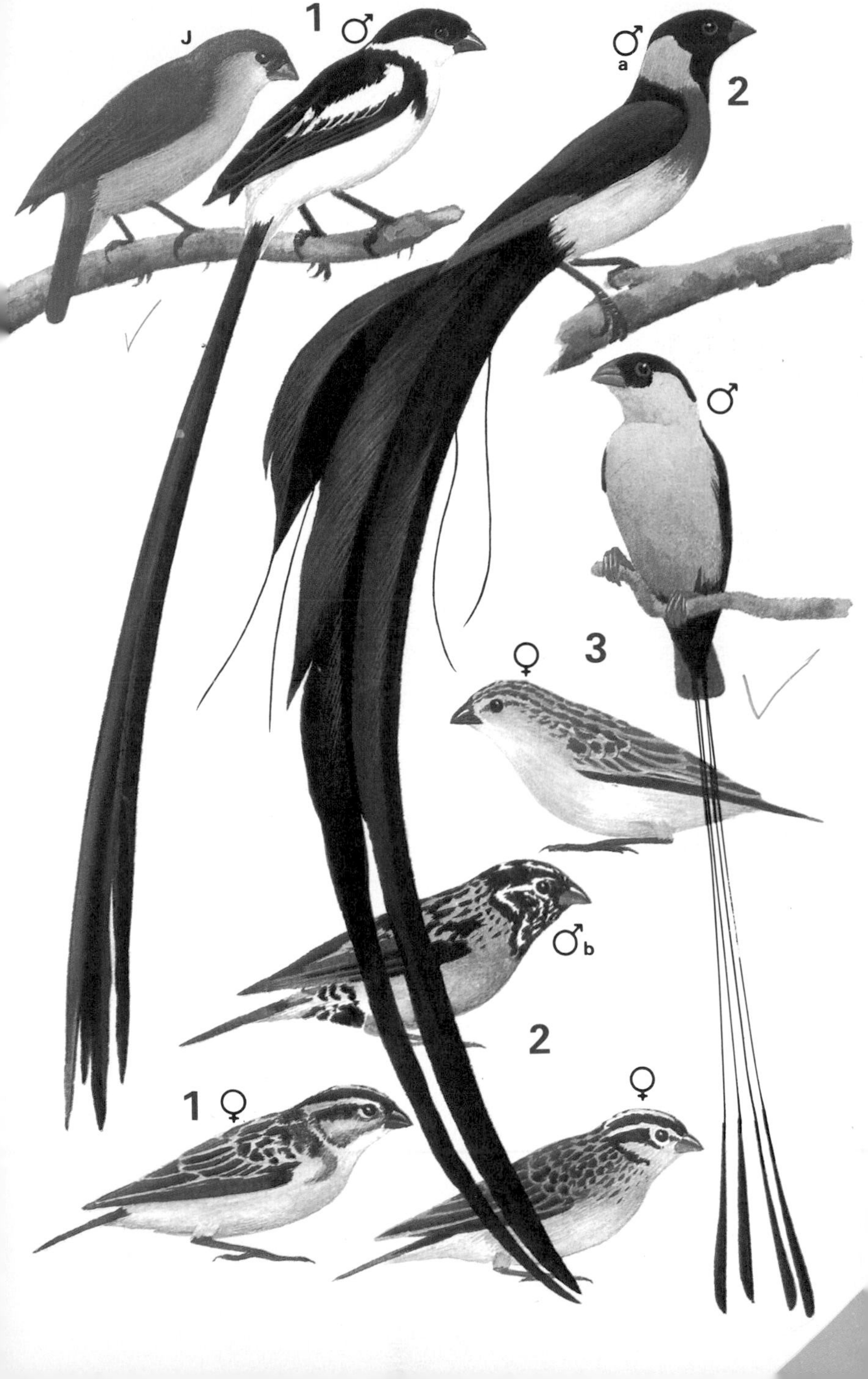
J
1 ♂
♂ a
2
♂
♀ 3
♂ b
2
1 ♀
♀

434

1 BROADTAILED PARADISE WHYDAH *Vidua obtusa*. Common resident. Male differs from the Paradise Whydah (previous page) only in the *wide tail-feathers*, not tapering as in that species. Females and young of the two species are indistinguishable. Males have a display flight as in (b); identical in all other respects to Paradise Whydah, its distribution linked to that of its hosts, the *Pytilia* group (page 420). 12-38 cm.

Widowfinches. Brood-parasites of the firefinches (page 422). They appear to be so strictly host-specific that their presence in a region is an indication of the presence of the firefinch they parasitise. Breeding males are black with a blue or mauve iridescence. Non-breeding males resemble females, illustration (2). Immatures are more russet-brown, especially on underparts, crowns unstreaked. Males are identified by bill and leg colouring plus song, which mimics that of the host.

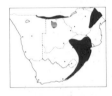

2 BLACK WIDOWFINCH *Vidua funerea*. Common resident. Has *whitish* bill and *reddish* legs. Males have a grating song interspersed with the notes of the Bluebilled Firefinch, which the female parasitises; may bob up and down in front of the female calling a harsh 'cha, cha'. Occurs in thornveld and forest fringes. 11 cm.

3 PURPLE WIDOWFINCH *Vidua purpurascens*. Fairly common resident. *Whitish bill and legs* in both sexes. Parasitises Jameson's Firefinch; the song has the same bell-like trilling and 'tink-tink' notes of the host. Inhabits dry thornveld thickets. Habits much as for the previous species. 11 cm.

4 STEELBLUE WIDOWFINCH *Vidua chalybeata*. Common resident. Told by *red bill and legs*. Parasitises the Redbilled Firefinch. Habits and habitat as for the previous two species. 11 cm.

VIOLET WIDOWFINCH *Vidua incognita*. Status uncertain. A recently (1972) named species known to parasitise the Brown Firefinch. Very similar to the previous three species in all respects; bill and leg colours unknown. Not illustrated.

CANARIES

Canaries, siskins and buntings. Family FRINGILLIDAE. Sparrow-sized songbirds, canaries and siskins with strong conical bills, usually notched tails and undulating flight, buntings strongly terrestrial and with weaker, narrower bills. Many species are nomadic.

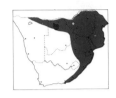

1 YELLOWEYED CANARY *Serinus mozambicus*. Common resident. A small canary with bold facial markings, greyish crown and nape, plus yellow rump. Sexes are alike. Immatures are duller. Has a lively song delivered in short bursts. Occurs in small parties and flocks in all types of woodland, bushveld, forest and plantation fringes and suburbia. Feeds both in the grass and in trees. 12 cm.

2 FOREST CANARY *Serinus scotops*. Common resident. Heavily streaked appearance diagnostic, boldest in northern birds. Immatures resemble adults. Normal call a thin, plaintive 'tweetoo, twee-ee' given frequently and often the first clue to the species' presence; also has a brisk warbling song of sibilant quality. Pairs and small parties frequent the tree canopies in forests at all altitudes, as well as adjacent forested kloofs and plantation fringes. 13 cm.

3 YELLOW CANARY *Serinus flaviventris*. Common resident. Palest, yellowest males with bright yellow rumps (a) occur in the north-west (cf. Bully Canary (5b)); darkest males with greenish rumps (b) in the south-east, with degrees of intergrading elsewhere. Females of (b) duskier about the breast, streaking less obvious than in females of (a). Immatures are like females, upperparts greener. Males sing well and vigorously from treetops. Small parties and flocks in semi-arid regions, frequenting low-growing bushes of mountain sides, Karoo and coastal scrub, especially along watercourses; also enter small towns. Nomadic in some regions. 13-14 cm.

4 CAPE CANARY *Serinus canicollis*. Common resident. Identified by grey nape, ear-coverts and sides of neck. Females and immatures are duller than males. Song a series of loud, rolling warbles and trills. Singly or in flocks in a wide variety of habitats from coastal scrub to montane grassland and *Protea*-covered slopes, plantations and farmlands. Feeds mostly on the ground. 13-14 cm.

5 BULLY CANARY *Serinus sulphuratus*. Common resident. A thick-set, heavy-billed species. Southerly birds (a) mainly dull olive-green with dark-streaked upperparts; northern birds (b) much paler, more yellow and smaller; other races between these extremes. Race (b) differs from Yellow Canary (3a) by lack of white edges to wing-coverts, plus dark crown extending to base of beak. Immatures are duller than adults. Song slower, huskier, less tuneful than other canaries. Singly, in pairs or small flocks in various bushy habitats: hillsides, kloofs, forest fringes, bracken–briar patches and riverside thickets. 14-15 cm.

1

2

♂a

3

♂b

♀

4

5

a

b

1 BLACKHEADED CANARY *Serinus alario*. Common resident. Males distinctive: (a) southern and eastern races, (b) northwestern race, plus variations between these. Females sparrow-like. Immatures are duller, more streaky above. Calls 'sweea' and has a subdued song. Pairs and flocks in the drier regions, frequenting scrubby vegetation, rocky koppies, cultivated lands and suburbia, usually near water. 12-15 cm.

2 BLACKEARED CANARY *Serinus mennelli*. Common resident. Distinguished from next species by darker upperparts plus breast-streaking, males with bold black mask, browner in females and immatures. In summer males sing for long periods, 'teeu-twee-teu, twiddy-twee-twee'. Pairs and small parties occur in broadleafed woodland, often in bird parties, feeding in trees or on the ground. 13-14 cm.

3 STREAKYHEADED CANARY *Serinus gularis*. Common resident. Identified by *very bold white eyebrows* and streaked crown; from the previous species by lack of a distinct mask or any breast-streaking; cf. Yellowthroated Sparrow (page 404) which has similar bold eyebrows. Has a pleasant song, rendered in short bursts 'wit-chee-chee-chee-cha, cha, cha, cha, cha, chip', rising to a crescendo; when nest-building a repetitive 'tweu, tweu, tirrirrit-tirik'. Singly, in pairs or small parties in woodland, fallow farmlands and suburbia. Inconspicuous and seldom numerous. 16 cm.

4 WHITETHROATED CANARY *Serinus albogularis*. Common resident. Distinguished from all other brown canaries (except (6)) by yellow rump; palest birds with brightest rump in Namibia (b), darkest with greenish-yellow rump in south (a), with intergrades elsewhere. Distinguished from (6) by white throat. Has a strong, tuneful song, 'weetle, weetle, frrra, weetle, frree, tee, chipchipchipchip...'. Singly or in small flocks in dry thornveld, Karoo, desert and coastal dunes, generally not far from water. 14-15 cm.

5 PROTEA CANARY *Serinus leucopterus*. Fairly common, localised resident. A large, drab canary with a pale bill and two distinct light wing-bars on the folded wing; cf. (3). Distinctive call is 'tree-lee-loo', the song soft, sweet and varied; an excellent mimic. Small, scattered parties occur in *Protea* bush on the Cape mountains, occasionally in wooded kloofs and forest fringes. Shy and retiring, the flight swift and direct. 16 cm.

6 BLACKTHROATED CANARY *Serinus atrogularis*. Common resident. A small canary with yellow rump; black throat diagnostic when present but *may be absent* or vestigial. Gives a strong and sustained, rambling song from a treetop. Small flocks feed on grass and weed seeds in woodland, fallow farmlands, waste ground and on roadside verges. 11-12 cm.

439

1 CAPE SISKIN *Pseudochloroptila totta.* Common, localised resident. Males identified from males of the next species mainly by white tips to primary feathers. Immatures are like adult females. The call is a high-pitched, metallic 'tchwing, tchwing, tchwing, tchwing'; also calls 'pitchee' during each dip of its pronouncedly undulating flight. Pairs and small parties occur on Macchia-covered mountain slopes, or in valleys and forest clearings. Feeds on the ground and in bushes, but is shy. 13 cm.

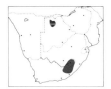

2 DRAKENSBERG SISKIN *Pseudochloroptila symonsi.* Common, localised resident. Males lack any white in the wings. Females are much browner than females of the previous species. Sings well. Pairs and small parties occur on high grassy slopes of the Drakensberg, moving to lower levels in winter. Habits much as for the previous species. 13 cm.

3 LEMONBREASTED CANARY *Serinus citrinipectus.* Fairly common, localised resident. Told by very small size, males with buffy flanks and belly; cf. Yelloweyed Canary (page 436). Females with buffy underparts, yellow rumps. Has a pretty song with a sparrow-like quality. Flocks, often with Yelloweyed Canaries, occur in dry woodland, also cultivated lands and coastal grassland. Like the Yelloweyed Canary, is attracted to seeding grasses. Somewhat nomadic when not breeding. 9.5-10 cm.

4 CHAFFINCH *Fringilla coelebs.* Uncommon, localised resident. An introduced species. Calls 'chink, chink' and has a distinctive, frequently repeated song, 'chip-chip-chip-tell-tell-tell-cherry-erry-erry-tissi-cheweeoo'. Singly or in pairs in suburban gardens, parks and pine plantations of the Cape Town region. Has declined in recent years. 15 cm.

442

1 LARKLIKE BUNTING *Emberiza impetuani*. Common resident. A small, pale, cinnamon-washed bunting, mostly lacking in diagnostic features. Sexes are alike. Immatures are closely similar to adults. Call, uttered at take-off, is a nasal 'chut'; the song a rapidly delivered 'trrrooo-cheeoo-cheepp-trree' repeated frequently with variations. Usually in small flocks in grassland, Karoo and semi-arid woodland, often in rocky regions with sparse bushes and in exotic plantations. Nomadic, in very cold periods sometimes 'erupting' into new areas in large numbers. 13-14 cm.

2 CABANIS'S BUNTING *Emberiza cabanisi*. Uncommon, localised resident. Distinguished from Goldenbreasted Bunting (4) by black face and ear-coverts, no white line below eyes, plus greyer mantle. Females are like males but head-markings more brown than black. Immatures have head-streaks brownish (not white), flanks browner. Has a soft 'tureee' call and a sweet but variable song 'wee-chidderchidder, chidder-wee' or 'her-ip-ip-ip . . . her-hee'. Usually singly or in pairs in Miombo woodland. 15 cm.

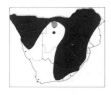

3 ROCK BUNTING *Emberiza tahapisi*. Common resident. Distinguished by cinnamon colouring of body with black, white-streaked head. Immatures resemble females. The short, distinctive song is repeated at frequent intervals, 'tee-trrr, chirri-chee' or 'swiddle-swiddle-saaa'. In pairs, occasionally flocks, on rocky or stony ground with or without bushes, often on soil-eroded ground or in broadleafed woodland and mixed bushveld. 13-14 cm.

4 GOLDENBREASTED BUNTING *Emberiza flaviventris*. Common resident. Distinguished from Cabanis's Bunting (2) by white stripe *below* eyes plus browner mantle and more orange breast. Females have the head-streaks yellowish, immatures have them brown. The normal call is 'pret-ty-boyeee', sometimes answered by the mate 'sitee'; the song is a frequently repeated 'chipchipchipchipchip-teee, teeu-teeu-teeu-teeu'. Pairs occur in mixed bushveld, thornveld, broadleafed woodland and exotic plantations. 16 cm.

5 CAPE BUNTING *Emberiza capensis*. Common resident. Sexes are alike. Immatures are duller. Call is 'cheriowee', the song, uttered from a rock or bush-top, is 'cheep, cheep, tip, cheeucheeu, tip-cheeu-tip-cheeu'. Singly, in pairs or flocks in a variety of semi-arid, coastal montane regions, coastal sand dunes with sparse scrub, rocky hillsides both in the Karoo or, in Zimbabwe, in broadleafed woodland plus suburbia in many regions. 16 cm.

1

2 ♂

3 ♀ ♂

4 ♂

5

RECENT VAGRANTS TO SOUTHERN AFRICA

(Recorded after the original publication of this fieldguide)
Illustrations not to scale

1 AMERICAN SHEATHBILL (SNOWY SHEATHBILL) *Chionis alba*. Differs from Lesser Sheathbill (p. 24) in pink cere, yellow bill with black tip and grey legs. A conspicuous terrestrial scavenger from the Antarctic from where it migrates northwards to the southern tip of South America; unafraid of humans. Birds recorded in our region may have been ship-assisted. 40 cm.

2 LAYSAN ALBATROSS *Diomedea immutabilis*. Cf. similar dark-backed albatrosses on pp. 30 and 32. Underwing pattern not unlike that of Greyheaded, Blackbrowed and Yellownosed Albatrosses but blackish marks on underwing coverts usually present, though variable; dark eye-patch visible only at close range. Bill dull yellow with dark tip, pinkish feet protrude beyond tail. A wanderer from the Pacific Ocean. 80 cm.

3 REDBILLED TROPICBIRD *Phaethon aethereus*. Adults have red bills and white tail-streamers; barred upperwings resemble those of immatures of other tropicbirds (p. 48). Immature of this species has dull yellow bill and no tail-streamers, differing from other immatures only in blackish eye-stripe which extends to the nape. A wanderer from the Atlantic and northern Indian Oceans. 50 cm (excluding tail-streamers).

4 MATSUDAIRA'S STORM PETREL *Oceanodroma matsudairae*. Dark brown storm petrel, slightly larger than others in our waters (cf. p. 46). Upperwings show small but clear white patch at base of primaries and distinct crescent shape formed by pale wing covert edges. Flight mostly leisurely with frequent gliding action. A wanderer from islands near Japan. 25 cm.

5 HERRING GULL *Larus argentatus*. Adults differ from gulls on p. 54 in having pale grey upperwings with black tips (not black upperwings as in Kelp Gull or dark grey as in Lesser Blackbacked). Underparts white, legs and feet either pink or grey. A wanderer from the northern hemisphere. 56 - 65 cm.

Illustrations not to scale.

445

1 GREATER YELLOWLEGS *Tringa melanoleuca.* Occurs in non-breeding plumage. Larger than Lesser Yellowlegs (p. 116) with longer, Greenshank-like bill, and orange-yellow (not lemon-yellow) legs. Compared to Greenshank (p.108) the bill is straighter with greenish or yellowish base, while the breast has greyish streaking. In flight very long wings and square, white tail-patch diagnostic. Breeds in North America. 29-33 cm.

2 HUDSONIAN GODWIT *Limosa haemastica.* Occurs in non-breeding plumage, when similar to Blacktailed and Bartailed Godwits (p. 118). Most diagnostic features are seen in flight when black underwing coverts are apparent; rest of underwing grey except for narrow white region at base of secondaries and inner primaries (the other godwits have mostly white underwings, dark edged in the Blacktailed). May mix with other godwits. Breeds in northern Canada. 37-42 cm.

3 KENTISH PLOVER *Charadrius alexandrinus.* In non-breeding plumage easily confused with Whitefronted Plover (p. 108) or immature Chestnutbanded Plover (p. 106) but best told by clear white hind collar and lateral breast patches which, however, never form a complete breast-band. In breeding plumage upperparts are darker, the male with forecrown, eyestripe and breast patches black. Frequents sandy beaches or shorelines of brackish pans. Breeds throughout the tropics. 15-17,5 cm.

4 (EUROPEAN) TURTLE DOVE *Streptopelia turtur.* About the size of a Cape Turtle Dove (p. 196). Folded wings dark chestnut mottled black, crown and nape grey; no black collar but black and white patches on either side of neck, breast pinkish, underbelly white. From below shows dark underwings and black tail fringed white. Breeds in Europe and North Africa, winters in sahelian zone. 27 cm.

5 REDTHROATED PIPIT *Anthus cervinus.* In breeding plumage has variable amount of brick-red on its throat, even on the breast and eyebrow, traces of which may be visible in non-breeding plumage. Otherwise differs from similar Tree Pipit (p. 290) in smaller size, heavier breast-streaking and a *streaked rump;* outer tail feathers appear very white in flight. Frequents marshes, estuaries, vleis, wet fields. Breeds in the Arctic, winters in East Africa. 14,5 cm.

Illustrations not to scale.

1 PIED WHEATEAR *Oenanthe pleschanka*. Whereas the male in breeding plumage is distinctive, it is most likely to be seen in our region in non-breeding plumage, which often retains some vestige of the dark head pattern. Female (larger illustration) can be confused with a chat (p. 320) or female European Wheatear (p. 318) and is probably indistinguishable except for the upper tail pattern. Has a 'zack' call note. Prefers stony scrublands, cultivated and fallow lands. 15 cm.

2 ISABELLINE WHEATEAR *Oenanthe isabellina*. Another rare, non-breeding wheatear from the north, told from a non-breeding European Wheatear (p. 318) and female Pied Wheatear (1) only with difficulty unless the diagnostic upper tail pattern can be seen. Isabelline has the terminal half of the tail black, and less extensive white on the rump; other pointers are longish legs, the black alula and an erect posture. Only one record from Botswana, but may prove to be more widespread. 16,5 cm.

3 (EURASIAN) REDSTART *Phoenicurus phoenicurus*. A robin-like bird with rufous tail in both sexes. Male in breeding plumage (recorded in s.Africa) is distinctive with grey upperparts, white eyebrow, black mask and throat and rufous breast; female much duller; except for rufous tail has pale sandy-grey upperparts and whitish underparts. Calls 'hwee-tuc-tuc' and frequents a range of lightly wooded habitats. Breeds in Europe, winters in Africa. 14 cm.

4 (EUROPEAN) BLACKCAP *Sylvia atricapilla*. A small warbler easily identified by the black cap of the male and rusty cap of the female. Calls 'tuc-tuc' or 'churr' and has a subdued warbling song. Frequents mixed woodland and gardens. Breeds in Europe, winters in Africa. 14 cm.

Illustrations not to scale.

449

♂
N-Br
Br

♂
N-Br

1

2

♀
♂
3

♂   4   ♀

1 WHITETHROATED BEE-EATER *Merops albicollis*. A greenish bee-eater told by its prominent black and white head pattern; the tail-streamers are longer than in any local bee-eater. Flocks behave much as other colonial bee-eaters. Normally occurs in Central and West Africa, extending southwards occasionally to northern Angola and eastern Tanzania. See also pp. 244-6. 20-32 cm.

2 REDRUMPED SWALLOW *Hirundo daurica*. Told from other red-rumped swallows by tawny underparts and chestnut band across the nape. Utters a hoarse 'chirp' and a subdued twittering. Frequents hilly districts and mixes with other swallows when feeding. A wanderer from Zambia and further north. 18 cm.

3 WHITEHEADED SAW-WING SWALLOW *Psalidoprocne albiceps*. A blackish swallow, the male distinctive with its white head and black eye-stripe, the female with white throat only. Frequents broadleaved woodland. Its home range is Angola and East Africa. 15 cm.

4 SPURWINGED PLOVER *Vanellus spinosus*. Differs from superficially similar Blacksmith Plover (p. 122) in lacking any grey plumage; having entire cap black; upper breast to neck white with an expanding black stripe from chin to black lower breast and upperparts dull brown. When alarmed calls a sharp, metallic 'pick' repeated. Could occur on any wetland, especially shorelines of large rivers. 25-8 cm.

5 LITTLE BLUE HERON *Ardea caerulea*. A slate-blue heron, head and neck washed maroon-red, the bill grey with a black tip, legs and feet greenish-grey. Frequents rivers, lagoons and marshlands where it stalks its aquatic prey while walking slowly. A wanderer from the Americas. 64-74 cm.

Illustrations not to scale.

1 GREATER FRIGATEBIRD *Fregata minor.* Males told by large, angled wings and all-dark appearance; females similar but for white throat and breast. Immatures have head and neck buffy. A straggler to eastern shorelines, especially Mozambique, where occasionally in small numbers after cyclones. Soars effortlessly and pursues other seabirds for food, causing them to disgorge, or snatches fishing bait. Roosts in trees at night. 100 cm.

2 LESSER FRIGATEBIRD *Fregata ariel.* Smaller than the Greater Frigatebird (1), males told by white 'armpits', females by less extensive white on the breast. Like the previous species a straggler to the Mozambique coast; behaviour identical. 76 cm.

3 ELEONORA'S FALCON *Falco eleonorae.* In size between Peregrine and Hobby Falcons (p. 188). Colouring highly variable between pale morph (illustrated) and dark morph, which has blackish underparts. In flight both morphs have sooty-brown underwings and appear *much darker* (almost black) than the Hobby Falcon; light morph only with chin and throat-patch paler. Has a unique flight action with soft, slow wing-beats, but capable of fast, dashing flight when hunting. Occurs in eastern coastal districts, especially Mozambique. 38 cm.

Illustrations not to scale.

Glossary of terms

Acacia: deciduous trees of the genus *Acacia*. In Africa these are thorny, with bipinnately compound leaves (each leaf is again divided into small leaflets) and small, powderpuff-like or elongated flowers.

Accipiter: sparrowhawks and goshawks. Long-tailed, short-winged raptors with long, unfeathered legs and long toes. They specialise in catching small birds (or small mammals in the larger species) in swift pursuit from a standing start.

Afrotropical Region: Africa south of the Palaearctic Region, the Tropic of Cancer roughly forming its northern limit. Formerly called Ethiopian Region.

Aggregation: a gathering (of birds) brought about by some common interest such as a temporary food availability, after which individuals disperse separately.

Albinistic: white or partially white plumage resulting from a lack of normal colour pigmentation.

Altitudinal migrant: birds which move seasonally from one altitude to another.

Brood parasite: birds which deposit their eggs in the nest of another species, e.g. cuckoos, honeyguides, whydahs, etc.

Broadleafed woodland: woodland comprised of trees with broad leaves as opposed to thornveld where trees of the genus *Acacia* are dominant.

Bush: refers to any terrain with trees of moderate height as opposed to the taller, more luxuriant growth of forests; see Bushveld.

Bushveld: a terrain with mixed tree species of moderate height (5-10 m) where the trees frequently touch each other below canopy height; sometimes in dense thickets and usually with a grassy groundcover.

Coastal bush: dense, humid, evergreen bush found on coastal dunes; mainly east coast.

Coastal forest: larger trees than in coastal bush and frequently extending inland in dense patches with grassland in between.

Conspecific: being of the same species.

Crepuscular: active at dusk. When applied to birds, it usually infers that they are active in the half-light hours, *dawn* and dusk.

Dam: a man-made water impoundment, usually with a retaining wall at the opposite end to the in-flow.

Damaraland Plateau: the inland plateau region of north-central Namibia, the home of many endemic bird species. The biotope varies from semi-desert or Karoo transition in the south to thornveld in the north-east and Mopane and teak woodland in the north.

Delta: a river mouth with several diverging branches which form a triangle. In the context of this fieldguide, usually refers to the inland delta of the Okavango River drainage system (also known as the Okavango Swamps) in northern Botswana.

Desert: a region of extremely low annual rainfall, usually less than 25 mm. In Southern Africa the driest desert is the Namib, comprised of sand dunes in the southern and coastal regions and stony plains elsewhere, with isolated patches of thornbush in some lower-lying areas or on hillsides. The Kalahari Desert in central Botswana consists of dunes in the south and sandy or stony plains, with sparse scrub-thorn elsewhere, merging into Kalahari thornveld further north.

Dispersal: a more or less random centrifugal movement away from a locality.

Display:	a term used to denote actions that have become specialised in the course of evolution: threat display, courtship display, social displays, etc.
Donga:	a gulley caused by erosion.
Egg-dumping:	the habit among secondary females in such social species as the Ostrich, guineafowls and others, of laying their eggs in the nest of another female of the same species, usually the dominant female in a flock. Also refers to random egg-laying in places other than nests by immature or unmated hens of any species.
Endemic:	refers to species found only in a specific region or country.
Estuary:	the tidal mouth of a large river, an important feeding area for many water-associated birds because of its food-rich mud-flats and floodplains.
Escarpment:	the long steep face of a plateau. In Southern Africa usually refers to the eastern escarpment which forms the edge of the inland plateau or highveld.
Ethiopian Region:	old name for Africa south of the Palaearctic Region, now replaced by the term Afrotropical Region.
Falcon:	small, swift-flying raptors with pointed wings; they specialise in catching flying birds by means of a rapid descent from above, known as a 'stoop'.
FF:	females.
Flats:	level grassland.
Fledgling:	a young bird that has recently acquired its first feathers.
Flock:	a group of birds that moves as a more or less cohesive unit.
Floodplain:	grassland, especially that adjacent to estuaries, which becomes inundated from river spillage.
Forest:	a tract of land covered with tall evergreen trees with interlocking canopies.
Gamebird:	an outdated term used by hunters. Refers to ducks, geese, pheasants, partridges, guineafowls and others. In the past bustards were included in this category.
Graduated tail:	a tail in which the central feathers are the longest and all others progressively shorter, the outermost being shortest.
Grassland:	any region with extensive grass coverage, especially the plateau or highveld regions of Southern Africa, but can also refer to grass-covered foothills or montane grassland.
Gregarious:	living in flocks or communities.
Highveld:	the plateau region of inland Southern Africa; consists mainly of grassland above *c.* 1,500 m.
Immature:	in the context of this fieldguide, refers to any young bird beyond the nestling stage.
Intra-Africa migrant:	birds that migrate regularly within the African continent.
Irruptive:	an irregular migration into a new area, often brought about by unfavourable conditions in the normal range of a species, and usually of a temporary nature.
Juvenile:	a young bird below sub-adult stage.
Kalahari thornveld:	thornveld with stunted, scattered or more or less continuous *Acacia* or *Dichrostachys* species on Kalahari sand and calcareous soil with tufty grasses.

Karoo veld:	stony plains with little soil, dotted with dwarf trees and succulent plants, or undulating stony plains with numerous grasses and shrubs but succulents and trees scarce, or rocky hills with scrub. Annual rainfall 150-300 mm. The driest region is known as Arid Karoo where desert grasses predominate. Annual rainfall 50-200 mm.
Kloof:	a cleft or valley, usually with steeply inclined or rocky sides, often well-wooded.
Koppie:	a small hill, often with a rocky summit.
Lagoon:	a stretch of salt water separated from the sea by a low sandbank.
Leaf-gleaner:	a bird that seeks insects from the leaves in a tree canopy.
Littoral:	the region of land lying along the sea shore.
Local movement:	a mass movement, not necessarily regular, within a comparatively small area.
Lowland:	those regions lying below *c.* 900 m. Mixed bush and grassland.
Lowveld:	term applied to the eastern part of Southern Africa which lies between *c.* 100 and 900 m and is bushveld.
Macchia:	a natural habitat occurring in the south-eastern and south-western coastal regions of the Cape Province: a Mediterranean-type scrub composed of Proteas, Ericas and legumes among other plants.
Mangrove:	a forest of mainly trees of the family Rhizophoraceae which grows in tidal estuaries. The trees produce air roots, which protrude upwards from the mud.
Melanistic:	darkness of plumage colour resulting from abnormal development of black pigmentation.
Migration:	a regular movement of birds (or other animals) between two alternative regions inhabited by them at different times of the year, one region in which they breed and the other region used by them when not breeding.
Miombo:	broadleafed woodland in which trees of the genus *Brachystegia* dominate; common in Zimbabwe.
Mistbelt:	the eastern region of southern Africa at 900-1350 m above sea level (otherwise known as the escarpment) where the rainfall is between 900 and 1150 mm per annum and the conditions are frequently misty during easterly maritime winds; of mostly hilly or montane grassland with isolated forest patches and, these days, with extensive exotic plantations.
Mixed bushveld:	a region of mixed tree types, including both broadleafed and thorny species, growing more or less continually or in clumps, to an average height of *c.* 7-10 m. This form of bush covers much of the eastern lowveld of the Transvaal and Mozambique plus the northern lowlands regions of Mozambique where various palms become dominant. Soils may be sandy or stony, with good grass cover.
MM:	males.
Monoculture:	regions extensively planted with one crop, e.g. sugarcane.
Montané:	mountainous country.
Mopane:	a broadleafed, deciduous tree, *Colophospermum mopane*. In some regions remains as a smallish bush, in other regions grows to a height of *c.* 12 m. Leaves are rounded, heart-shaped and reddish when young.
Morph:	an alternative but permanent plumage colour.
Nomad:	a species with no fixed territory when not breeding.

Palaearctic Region:	the northern hemisphere, incorporating North Africa, Europe, Scandinavia and Asia.
Pan (or flood-pan):	a natural depression which fills with water as the result of rainfall or river spillage.
Parkland:	regions of woodland with well-spaced trees, little secondary growth and a grassy groundcover.
Passerine:	birds that habitually sing or call and that have 'normal' feet, with three toes facing forward and one facing backward; excludes birds with webbled, lobed, or zygodactylous feet.
Pectoral:	the breast region; in birds especially the lateral breast regions.
Pelagic seabird:	a bird of the open seas as opposed to one which roosts or breeds on mainland shores.
Plantation:	trees, usually exotic species (gums, wattles or pines) planted for timber; usually closely planted and devoid of groundcover, their interiors unattractive to most birds.
Range expansion:	the process in which a species increases its breeding range; a spread into regions not previously occupied.
Raptor:	a bird of prey; one which hunts and kills other animals for food.
Rectrices:	the main tail feathers of a bird (Rectrix in the singular).
Recurved bill:	a bill that bends upwards, e.g. Avocet.
Remiges:	the primary and secondary wing feathers of a bird (Remex in the singular).
Riparian:	of or on riverbanks.
Riverine forest:	the trees fringing a river, usually evergreen and more luxuriant than trees of the surrounding country and often with an understorey of dense thickets and secondary growth. In the more arid regions growth is less well developed, then often referred to as Riverine Bush.
Sexual dimorphism:	differences in appearance between male and female of a species.
Soft parts:	a bird's bill, legs and feet, eye-surround and bare facial skin if present.
Speculum:	a patch of iridescent colour on the wings of some birds, notably ducks.
Still-hunt:	watching for prey (usually on the ground) while perched.
Subantarctic:	the southern oceans between 45°S and the Antarctic Circle.
Sub-song:	a bird song of lower than normal pitch, sometimes of longer than normal duration.
Scrub:	brushwood or stunted bushes.
Tail-streamer:	elongated tail-feathers, often the central or outer feathers.
Teak:	the tree *Baikiaea plurijuga* (Rhodesian Teak), which grows extensively in the northern parts of Southern Africa.
Thicket:	a number of shrubs or trees growing very close together.
Thornveld:	a bush habitat or woodland comprised of *Acacia, Albizia* or *Dichrostachys* trees, all of which are thorny.
Understorey:	refers to the lowest stratum in (usually) forest or woodland: secondary growth consisting of young trees, small bushes and annual plants.
Upland:	refers to high altitude regions below that of montane.
Valley bush:	narrow belts of dense bush, often thorny and with succulent plants species, found in hot river valleys which drain into the Indian Ocean. Rainfall 500-900 mm per annum.

Veld:	a term used loosely in reference to various types of terrain, thus grassveld, bushveld, etc.
Vlei:	a marshy area, usually in grassland.
Watercourse:	the dry course of a river that flows only during good rains.
Waterhole:	any natural or man-made waterpoint used by animals for drinking.
Woodland:	regions with trees of moderate height and well-developed canopies which are so spaced as not to interlock; may cover flat ground or hillsides, with or without well-developed secondary growth or groundcover.
Zygodactyl:	feet which, in certain non-passerine birds, have two toes directed forward and two backward: cuckoos, barbets, woodpeckers, honeyguides and others.

References used

A Check List of the Birds of the Bechuanaland Protectorate and the Caprivi Strip. Reay H.N. Smithers (1964). Trustees of the National Museums, S. Rhodesia.

A field guide to the Seabirds of Southern Africa and the World. G. Tuck & H. Heinzel (1979). Collins, London.

A Handlist of the Birds of Southern Mozambique. P.A. Clancey (1971). Instituto de Investigação Cientifica de Moçambique, Lourenço Marques.

Bird Atlas of Natal. Digby Cyrus & Nigel Robson (1980). University of Natal Press, Pmb.

Birdlife in Southern Africa. K. Newman (ed) (1980). Macmillan South Africa, Johannesburg.

Birds of Africa. Vol 1. L.H. Brown, E.K. Urban, K. Newman (1982). Academic Press Inc., London.

Birds of Prey of Southern Africa. Peter Steyn (1982). David Philip, Cape Town.

Birds of the Antarctic and Sub-Antarctic. George W. Watson (1975). American Geophysical Union, Washington, D.C.

Birds of the Dan Viljoen Game Park. C.F. Clinning & R.A.C. Jensen (1973). Division of Nature Conservation & Tourism, S.W.A. Administration, Windhoek.

Birds of the Etosha National Park. R.A.C. Jensen & C.F. Clinning (1976). Division of Nature Conservation & Tourism, S.W.A. Administration, Windhoek.

Birds of the Kruger National Park. K. Newman (1980). Macmillan South Africa, Johannesburg.

Birds of the Southern Third of Africa. Vols. 1 & 2. C.W. Mackworth-Praed & C.H.B. Grant (1962-3). Longmans, Green, London.

Check List of Birds of the Southern Central Transvaal. W.R. Tarboton (1968). Witwatersrand Bird Club, Johannesburg.

Ecology of Birds in the Eastern Cape Province. C.J. Skead (1967). *Ostrich*, Suppl. 7.

Roberts' Birds of South Africa. G.R. McLachlan & R. Liversidge (Eds). (1978). Trustees of the John Voelcker Bird Book Fund, Cape Town.

Roberts' Birds of Southern Africa. Gordon Lindsay Maclean (Ed.) 1985. Trustees of the John Voelcker Bird Book Fund, Cape Town.

SAOS Check List of Southern African Birds. P.A. Clancey (Ed). (1980). Southern African Ornithological Society, Johannesburg.

The Birds of Zimbabwe. M.P.S. Irwin (1981). Quest Publishing, Harare.

The Plovers, Sandpipers, and Snipes of the World. Paul A. Johnsgard (1981). University of Nebraska Press, Lincoln & London.

Index to scientific names

Index to Afrikaans names

465

467

471

Index to German names

The German bird names and spellings are those recommended by the Ornithology Working Group of the Namibian Scientific Society. Kindly prepared by Hermann Kolberg.

475

480

Index to English names and life list

484

485

487

488

489

490

491

492

493

495

496

	Place	Date

Popular bird names in general use

African Sand Martin	Brownthroated Martin
Amethyst Starling	Plumcoloured Starling
Amethyst Sunbird	Black Sunbird
Anhinga	Darter
Banded Harrier Hawk	Gymnogene
Bellbird	Tropical Boubou Shrike
Blue Jay	Erroneous name for Lilacbreasted Roller
Bosunbird	Any tropicbird
Bottlebird	Burchell's Coucal
Butcherbird	Fiscal Shrike
Cape Dikkop	Spotted Dikkop
Cape Hen	Whitechinned Petrel
Cape Pigeon	Pintado Petrel
Cape Rook	Black Crow
Cape Thrush	Olive Thrush
Cloud Scraper	Fantailed, Desert, Cloud, Ayres' or Palewinged Cisticola (any small cisticola with high territorial display flight)
Collared Pratincole	Redwinged Pratincole
Coly	Any mousebird
Comic tern	Either a Common or Arctic Tern in non-breeding plumage
Crimsonbreasted Shrike	Crimson Boubou
Duiker	Any cormorant
Fasciated Snake Eagle	Southern Banded Snake Eagle
Fleck's Coucal	Senegal Coucal
Flop	Longtailed Widow
Fret	Bronze Mannikin
Fruit Pigeon	Green Pigeon
Gadfly Petrel	Any petrel of the genus *Pterodroma* or *Bulweria*
Glasseye	Bleating Bush Warbler
Glossy Starling	Cape Glossy Starling
Go-away Bird	Grey Lourie
Great Sand Plover	Sand Plover
Green Eremomela	Karoo Eremomela
Greenspotted Dove	Emeraldspotted Dove
Griffon	Any vulture of the genus *Gyps*
Gurney's Thrush	Orange Thrush
Harrier Eagle	Any snake eagle
Honeysucker	Any sunbird
Indigobird	Any widowfinch
Jacky Hangman or Hanger	Fiscal Shrike
Jeager	Any skua
Kaffervink	Any widowbird
Kakelaar	Redbilled Woodhoopoe
Kiewietjie	Crowned Plover
King of Six	Pintailed Whydah
Konkoit	Gorgeous Bush Shrike
Lady Ross's Tauraco	Ross's Lourie
LBJ	A general name for any small, brownish bird
Lesser Sand Plover	Mongolian Plover
Lesser Swamp Warbler	Cape Reed Warbler
Lily-trotter	African Jacana
Little Rush Warbler	African Sedge Warbler
Magpie Shrike	Longtailed Shrike

Malgas	Any gannet
Man-o'-War Bird	Any frigatebird
Mollymawk	Any albatross with black upperwings and mantle
Morning Warbler	Collared Palm Thrush
Mossie	Any sparrow
Mother Cary's Chicken	Any storm petrel
Mottonbird	Any shearwater
Mountain Buzzard	Forest Buzzard
Namaqua Prinia	Namaqua Warbler
Natal Thrush	Spotted Thrush
Nellie	Giant Petrel
Nyasa Lovebird	Lilian's Lovebird
Openbill	Openbilled Stork
Peach Canary	Blackthroated Canary
Pediunker	Grey Shearwater
Piet-my-vrou	Redchested Cuckoo
Rainbird	Burchell's, Whitebrowed or Senegal Coucal
Reeve	Female Ruff
Richard's Pipit	Grassveld Pipit
Ring Dove	Cape or Redeyed Turtle Dove
Roberts's Prinia	Briar Warbler
Roughwing Swallow	Saw-wing Swallow
Rufous Reed Warbler	Greater Swamp Warbler
Rufoustailed Morning Warbler	Rufoustailed Palm Thrush
Sakabula	Any longtailed widow
Sea Swallow	Any tern
Shoemaker	Whitechinned Petrel
Short-toed Lark	Redcapped Lark
Singing Bush Lark	Melodious Lark
Snakebird	Darter
Spreeu	Any starling
Sprosser	Thrush Nightingale
Stinker	Any giant petrel
Sugarbird	Erroneous name for any sunbird; correctly refers to the family Promeropidae
Thick Knees	Spotted Dikkop
Tickbird	Erroneous name for Cattle Egret
Tinkerbird	Any tinker barbet
Tinktinkie	A general name for a small, brownish bird, especially a cisticola
Toppie	Blackeyed or Cape Bulbul
Turkey Buzzard	Erroneous name for Ground Hornbill
Violetbacked Starling	Plumcoloured Starling
Vlei Lourie	Burchell's Coucal
Waterhen	Moorhen
Whale Bird	Mediumbilled Prion
Whitecollared Pratincole	Rock Pratincole
Wigeon (Cape)	Cape Teal
Willie	Sombre Bulbul
Willie Wagtail	Cape Wagtail
Willow Wren	Willow Warbler
Wood Ibis	Yellowbilled Stork
Wren Warbler	Any prinia
Yellow Finch	Any yellow weaver
Yellow Weaver	Masked or Lesser Masked Weaver